Bound to become the go-to-guide when it comes to new venture creation. For students and practitioners alike, this is a must read.

Philip Kappen,
Copenhagen Business School

David Storey, University of Sussex

Paul Burns has a distinguished track record in producing well-informed, practical and engaging texts on new ventures. His success stems from an ability to capture the true essence of entrepreneurship.

Ivo Zander, Uppsala University

Spiced with an abundant number of case insights and analytical techniques, this is an invaluable book for anyone seriously interested in launching and growing entrepreneurial ventures.

'Paul Burns clearly knows what he's talking about and brings a wealth of knowledge and insight to the subjects of new venture creation and business planning. This text bridges theory and practice well and will be a useful guide to enterprising students and start-up founders.'

Gregg Vanourek,
Royal Institute of Technology

'This comprehensive text brings together theory and practice in an accessible manner, meeting the needs of lecturers, students and practitioners who want authoritative insight into new venture creation. Students and practitioners will appreciate the layout, up-to-date examples, practical tips all bound together in a clear process. Academics will value the tools, case studies and academic insights, which include a synthesis of the latest thinking in the field.'

Shahid Rasul,
Bradford University School of Management

Jens Holmgren, Aarhus University

The combination of theory and empirical case studies is excellent and gives the right balance between the academic and the practical sides of entrepreneurship.

Amanda Jones, University of South Wales

New Venture Creation provides a comprehensive and detailed overview of all areas of the business planning process Friendly and accessible, with just the right balance of theory throughout, this is a book that students can both learn from and enjoy.

'This is a very comprehensive book covering interesting topics in venture creation. The Academic Insights throughout the book will help potential entrepreneurs to understand themselves better before starting their ventures. I recommend this book to students and young people who want to be their own boss.'

Wilton Chau,
Centre for Entrepreneurship,
the Chinese University of Hong Kong

Parents

We owe them our existence

They share the credit and the blame for who we are

But did we ever thank them?

———————————————

In memory of my parents,
Jeanne and Jim

∞

NEW VENTURE CREATION

A framework for entrepreneurial start-ups

PAUL BURNS

Professor of Entrepreneurship
University of Bedfordshire
Business School, UK

First published 2014 by
PALGRAVE MACMILLAN

Palgrave Macmillan in the UK is an imprint of Macmillan Publishers Limited,
registered in England, company number 785998, of Houndmills, Basingstoke,
Hampshire RG21 6XS.

Palgrave Macmillan in the US is a division of St Martin's Press LLC,
175 Fifth Avenue, New York, NY 10010.

Palgrave Macmillan is the global academic imprint of the above companies
and has companies and representatives throughout the world.

Palgrave® and Macmillan® are registered trademarks in the United States,
the United Kingdom, Europe and other countries

ISBN: 978-1-137-33289-9   paperback

This book is printed on paper suitable for recycling and made from fully
managed and sustained forest sources. Logging, pulping and manufacturing
processes are expected to conform to the environmental regulations of the
country of origin.

A catalogue record for this book is available from the British Library.

A catalog record for this book is available from the Library of Congress.

Printed in China

Typeset by EMC Design Ltd.

NEW VENTURE CREATION: A FRAMEWORK FOR ENTREPRENEURIAL START-UPS

CONTENTS OVERVIEW

CONTENTS

① The New Venture Creation Framework 1

- The attraction of entrepreneurship
- Barriers and triggers to entrepreneurship
- New venture creation
- Business planning
- The New Venture Creation Framework
- The business plan
- Summary

Academic insights 📖

- Gazelles and economic growth
- Myths about entrepreneurs
- The Business Model Canvas

Case insights 💼

- Kiran Mazumdar-Shaw and Biocon
- Julie Spurgeon and Material Pleasures
- John Bird and The Big Issue
- Tony Fernandes and AirAsia (1)
- Marc Demarquette
- eBay

Part 1: You and your business idea

② What you bring to entrepreneurship 19

- Your personal drivers
- Your resources
- Character traits of entrepreneurs
- Factors that influence the entrepreneurial character
- Measuring your personal character traits
- Measuring your creativity
- How entrepreneurs manage
- Summary
- New Venture Creation Framework exercises

Academic insights 📖

- Cognitive development theory
- National culture
- General Enterprise Tendency test
- Effectuation

Case insights 💼

- Golden Krust (1)
- Steve Jobs and Apple (1)

③ Finding your business idea 40

- New venture typologies
- The 'eureka moment'
- Creating opportunity
- Spotting opportunity
- Generating a business idea
- Connectivity and networking
- Techniques for generating ideas
- Is the business idea viable?
- Characteristics of a good business idea
- Summary
- New Venture Creation Framework exercises

Academic insights 📖

- How to challenge market conventions
- Sources of entrepreneurial opportunity
- Discovery skills
- Connecting good ideas
- Inside the box thinking
- Lean start-up

Case insights 💼

- Bizarre start-up ideas from the USA
- Summly App
- Streetcar (now Zipcar)
- TutorVista
- OnMobile
- MOMA!
- Nuffnang
- Swarfega
- Great Ormond Street Hospital
- The Million Dollar Homepage

Part 2: Market segments and the value proposition

④ Understanding your market/industry 71

- Defining your market/industry
- Describing your market/industry
- Researching your market/industry
- Identifying your competitors
- Industry futures
- Summary
- New Venture Creation Framework exercises

Academic insights 📖

- Porter's Five Forces – assessing industry competitiveness

Case insights 💼

- Novo Nordisk
- Bill Gates and Microsoft
- Amazon, Apple, Facebook, Google and Microsoft

Contents

vii

Part 4: Operations plan

Part 5: Risk and strategic options

Part 6: Resources

Contents

ix

Figures

Tables

Paul Burns is Professor of Entrepreneurship at the University of Bedfordshire Business School, UK. He has been Pro-Vice Chancellor and for 10 years was Dean of the Business School. Over his 40-year career he has been an academic, an accountant and an entrepreneur – giving him unrivalled academic and practical insight into the entrepreneurial process. As well as launching and running his own business, he has helped develop hundreds of business plans and has worked with entrepreneurs, small firms and their advisors in helping launch successful businesses.

For ten years Paul was Professor of Small Business Development at Cranfield School of Management, UK, where, in 1983, he launched the Graduate Enterprise Programme in England, which was offered at dozens of universities. He started his academic career at Warwick University Business School, UK, where he set up their first Small Business Unit. For eight years he was Director of 3i European Enterprise Research Centre researching small firms and entrepreneurs across Europe.

He has been a Visiting Fellow at Harvard Business School, USA and for three years was Visiting Professor at the Open University Business School, UK, where he developed the multi-media Small Business Programme which was screened on BBC2. He is Fellow and a former President of the Institute for Small Business and Entrepreneurship (ISBE).

Paul qualified as a Chartered Accountant with Arthur Andersen & Co., where he worked with many growing businesses. He launched and ran his own business, Design for Learning Ltd., advising and training on entrepreneurship and growing firms. Here he worked with organizations such as the accounting firms Grant Thornton and BDO Stoy Hayward, venture capitalists 3i, and banks such as the Royal Bank of Scotland, Barclays and Lloyds. He has advised and consulted at various levels of government in the UK and overseas, and Margaret Thatcher wrote the foreword to one of his books, *Entrepreneur: Eight British Success Stories of the Eighties* (Macmillan, 1988).

Paul has authored dozens of books and hundreds of journal articles and research reports. *Entrepreneurship and Small Business: Start-up, Growth and Maturity* (Palgrave Macmillan) was first published in 2001. The third edition, published in 2011, is the market-leading entrepreneurship text book in the UK, praised for its authoritative blend of theory and practice and described as a 'joy to read' and 'indispensable for any student of entrepreneurship'. *Corporate Entrepreneurship: Innovation and Strategy in Large Organizations* (Palgrave Macmillan) was first published in 2005. It shows how strategies for encouraging entrepreneurship and innovation might be embedded in larger organizations through the concept of 'architecture' – leadership, culture and structure. The third edition, published in 2013, was praised as a 'definitive guide' that 'combines a profound understanding of theory with practical guidance'.

Creating a new venture is essentially a practical activity. Many believe it cannot be taught. Based upon over forty years' experience, I disagree, and this book dispels the myth by breaking the process down into a eight-stage New Venture Creation Framework.

The New Venture Creation Framework

The New Venture Creation Framework provides a comprehensive, practical guide to help you find a business idea, develop a 'value proposition' for customers and refine a business model that delivers your proposition to those customers. It takes you through the whole process of planning for a new venture in a way that gives you the best chance of success. The book explains each stage in the Framework and the exercises at the end of each chapter help you to assemble and evaluate the information you need and present it in the best possible way.

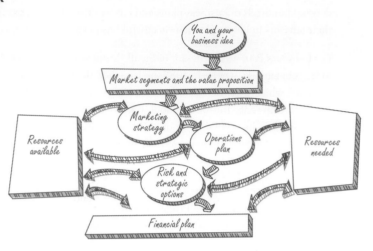

The New Venture Creation Framework can be used as an informal canvas onto which to plot your business idea and develop and improve it. However, the exercises also build into a comprehensive business plan that can then be used to obtain finance. This step-by-step, chapter-by-chapter approach to planning aims to better integrate learning from each chapter with the final business plan you produce. If entrepreneurs learn by doing, then this is the way entrepreneurship should be taught.

Learn from theory and practice

Creating a new venture is a risky activity and anything you can do to reduce the risk of failure must be good. So, you can learn from the successes and mistakes of other entrepreneurs. You can learn from their tips and practical advice. However, you can also learn from academic research and theory. Research can tell you which tips have the best chance of working (and which do not) and theory tells you why they might work. Of course, luck places an important part in life and creating a new venture – but it always pays to 'play the odds'. All these things improve your chances of success.

Concepts and theories do not have to be complicated. This book makes them easy to understand. It blends the practice and the theory of creating a new venture in an informal, accessible style. It includes:

- Quotes from entrepreneurs – practical tips and advice on how to do it.

- Case insights – over 70 cases from around the globe giving practical examples of how organizations have tackled issues in the real world.

- Academic insights – these provide the research and theoretical underpinning in a digestible form so that the main body of the book can have a more informal and understandable style.

The examples use GBP (£) but the calculations are equally applicable to US dollars ($) or any other currency.

Creating a new business venture is an ideal focus for teaching business and management. It is exciting and motivating. At its core is creativity and innovation – invaluable skills in today's competitive markets. Its holistic nature crosses artificial subject boundaries and integrates traditional disciplines. Its practical focus means that skills have to be applied. This book does all these things. It can be used to help teach the basics of business or to get business students to apply their already developed skills. It is particularly suitable for MBA students.

The book will help you:

- Assess whether you have the character traits of an entrepreneur
- Find a business idea
- Develop an innovative business model – how you go about delivering your business idea to customers
- Develop a strategic framework for how the business can grow to achieve its full potential
- Critically analyze what is needed to become an entrepreneurial leader and how to structure an organization so as to maintain its entrepreneurial character
- Write a professional business plan

It will help you develop a holistic range of applied business and management skills to enable you to start up a new venture. It will help you develop cognitive skills in the following areas:

- Data and information interpretation, critical analysis and evaluation
- Problem identification and solving
- ICT, in particular the use of computers and the internet
- Ability to use research and link theory with practice
- Writing and presentation

Learning outcomes

Identify the key concepts to be covered in the chapter and the key knowledge and skills that students will acquire by reading it and undertaking the related exercises

Case insights

Some with questions, give practical examples of how organizations have tackled issues in the real world

---

Contents

- Growth options
- Market development
- Entering foreign markets
- Product development
- Developing a product portfolio
- Marketing strategy and product portfolios
- Financing implications of product portfolios
- Diversification
- Using acquisition for market and product development
- Summary

Academic insights 📖
- Strategies that build potential: playing the odds
- Sticking to the knitting

Case insights 📖
- Web 2.0
- Fat Face
- B&Q China
- American Giant
- Crocs
- Reliance Industries

Learning outcomes

When you have read this chapter and undertaken the related exercises you will be able to:
- Understand which broad strategies are most likely to lead to successful growth
- Critically evaluate the strategic options for growth and understand the implications for a start-up
- Critically evaluate the effects of product life cycles on marketing strategy and how the life cycle can be lengthened through product expansion and extension
- Use the Growth Share Matrix to communicate marketing strategies for a portfolio of products
- Show advanced knowledge of the effects of the product portfolio on cash flow and how the product portfolio can be managed
- Critically evaluate the use of acquisition as part of a growth strategy and the advantages and disadvantages of diversification

Growth options

The previous chapter looked at ways in which you could increase sales by penetrating the market you have identified for your product or service. You will probably already have started to move from a selective distribution network to a more intensive network. At the same time you may already be adopting a more aggressive promotion and pricing strategy that encourages further market penetration ahead of the rapidly emerging competition. Alongside this, you will be building the brand as a vital part of the promotional message. This chapter will look at how you can build potential by considering new or different markets and think through how the product or service might be developed as you move into selling to the middle and late majority of customers and the product or service itself starts to age and move through its life cycle.

However, before doing this it is always worth having a moment of reflection, looking back on what has worked and what has not, understanding how you have modified your original value proposition to better meet the needs of customers. It is also important to understand

> After you've launched your business, while you are still privately-owned ... what you have to do is **grow very fast**, so that some day when you have to really drop a lot of dollars to the bottom line, you've laid in a base that can still **grow** at maybe 10% or 20% a year ... Five years into being a public company, you can never do that again.
>
> *Kevin Ryan, founder Serious Materials BBC News Business 29 June 2010*

Quotes from entrepreneurs

Give the inside view on the new venture process

Academic insights

Give the research background and theoretical underpinning for the concepts outlined

---

🇬🇧 UK **Summly App**

Creating opportunity

Born in London to well-off parents but brought up in Australia for his first seven years, Nick D'Aloisio became adept at using the computer at an early age. It was his hobby. He used it to make animations and films and even apps. Aged 15, he created an algorithm that formed the basis for an app called Trimit that summarized long articles down to tweet-lengths.

> I was using **Twitter** a lot on my phone, and was realizing there was a **massive gap** between the link on the tweet and the full story. If you could come up with a summary layer to show in Twitter, that would be awesome.
>
> *The Guardian 29 March 2013*

Trimit enjoyed mixed commercial success but attracted good reviews, wide publicity and thousands of downloads. It was this that attracted the attention of Horizon Ventures, a venture company led by Li Ka-shing, a Hong Kong billionaire and Asia's richest man. Horizon Ventures decided to invest $300,000 in the venture. This allowed D'Aloisio to recruit a small team in London to develop a completely redesigned version of the app, which was launched as Summly beta in December 2011.

Summly summarizes news articles for mobile phone users. If they are sufficiently interested, they can then read the full article on the original website. The app generates traffic for these websites from users of mobile phones and creates a market for this content with a wider, younger demographic.

Nick D'Aloisio

> There is a **generation of skimmers**. It's not that they don't want to read in-depth content, but they want to **evaluate** what the **content** is before they **commit** time. Especially on a **mobile** phone – you don't have the phone, or cellular data, or screen size to be reading full-length content.
>
> *The Guardian 9 March 2013*

In 2012, D'Aloisio secured funding of £1 million to further develop the app. Working with partners such as Stanford Research Institute, D'Aloisio also managed to obtain the help and support of a network of technology experts and celebrities such as Ashton Kutcher, Wendi Deng, Mark Pincus, Brian Chesky, Stephen Fry and Yoko Ono. The full Summly app was launched in November 2012. It reached number nine in the free iPhone app chart in the same month and within one year attracted more than one million downloads and more than 250 publishers, including News Corp.

In 2013, still aged only 17, D'Aloisio sold Summly to Yahoo, reportedly for $30 million (£19 million). Yahoo intends to integrate the app into its own mobile services and therefore withdrew it from the App Store. They plan to apply the summarization algorithm to a wider range of web services, and Nick and his team have joined Yahoo to help with this development.

Market paradigm shift – Just like disruptive innovation, this happens when entrepreneurs challenge the conventional ways of marketing a product/service. In most sectors there are factors that managers believe are critical to the success of their business. These paradigms become part of the dominant logic of an industry. But circumstances and the environment can change and the managers running the industry may not adapt their way of thinking. To see an opportunity for market paradigm shift you need to be constantly questioning the status quo. You need to ask the question *'why* are things done this way?' followed by the question *'why not* do them a different way?' This willingness to continually question the status quo is one of the five fundamental 'discovery skills'

> We learned the importance of ignoring conventional wisdom ... It's fun to do things that people don't think are possible or likely. It's also exciting to achieve the unexpected
>
> *Michael Dell Direct from Dell: Strategies that Revolutionized an Industry (1999, New York, Harper Business)*

---

exhibited by successful entrepreneurs that we shall discuss later in this chapter. Sometimes doing things differently can add value for the customer without involving extra costs – indeed sometimes doing things differently can reduce costs – whilst still giving you the opportunity to charge a high price. You can approach the task of challenging market paradigms by systematically looking at sectoral, customer and performance conventions and continually asking the questions 'why?' and 'why not?' (see Academic insight).

To find disruptive innovation or ways of changing market paradigms you need to be able to think creatively 'outside the box'. You need to be able to generate new ideas and knowledge, a vision of the future that links market opportunities to your key capabilities. You need to be able to challenge conventions and be open to new ideas. You need to be able to deal with rapidly changing and disparate information in a wide range of new technologies and in diverse, fragmented and often geographically widespread markets. You need to be able to chart a way through often uncertain political and unstable regulatory environments. And in these circumstances knowledge and information are powerful sources of opportunity and innovation. But remember, creating opportunity can be risky because there is no guarantee that the market will agree with your vision of the future.

How to challenge market conventions

Based on a sample of 108 companies, Kim and Mauborgne (2005) estimated that, whereas only 14% of innovations created new markets, these innovations delivered 38% of new revenues and 61% of increased profits. So how might you go about creating completely new markets? Ian Chaston (2000) argues that you have to systematically challenge established market conventions and develop new solutions. Kim and Mauborgne call this 'blue ocean strategy'. Companies creating blue ocean strategies never benchmark against competitors, instead they make this irrelevant by 'creating a leap in value for both the buyers and the company itself'. Chaston's approach is simple: understand how conventional competitors operate and then challenge their approach by asking whether a different one would add customer value or create new customers – our 'why?' and 'why not?' questions. There are many conventions that can be challenged. Chaston suggests three categories:

1. **Sectoral conventions:** These are the strategic rules that guide the marketing operations of the majority of firms in a sector, such as efficiency of plants, economies of scale, methods of distribution and so on. Kim and Mauborgne talk about re-orientating analysis from *competitors* to *alternatives*. So, for example, in the UK insurance used to be sold

Academic insight 📖

through high street insurance brokers until Direct Line challenged the conventional wisdom and began to sell direct over the telephone, then on the internet. Now this is the norm.

2. **Performance conventions:** These are set by other firms in the sector and include profit, cost of production, quality and so on. Kim and Mauborgne argue that both value enhancement and cost reduction can be achieved by redefining industry problems and looking outside industry boundaries, rather than simply trying to offer better solutions to existing problems as defined by the industry. In the 1960s, Japanese firms ignored Western performance conventions en masse and managed to enter and succeed in these markets.

3. **Customer conventions:** These conventions make certain assumptions about what customers want from their purchases, for example price, size, design and so on. Kim and Mauborgne talk about re-orientating analysis from *customers* to *noncustomers*. The Body Shop redefined the cosmetic industry's 'feel-good factor' to include environmental issues. Companies like Southwest Airlines, Ryanair and easyJet pioneered low-price air travel and redefined the airline industry.

Summaries

Provide an overview of the main points covered in the chapter

Summary

- You need to identify and be able to describe the characteristics of the market or industry within which you will operate. However, drawing the boundaries of your industry can be difficult and is a question of judgement.

- Desk research is cheap and quick. It should help you to estimate the size of your market.

- Your total available market (TAM) is the size of your potential market – those who might be interested in buying your particular product. This reflects the total sales of competing products. Your served available market (SAM) is the size of the target market segment you wish to serve within the TAM. Your penetrated market is the size of the SAM you actually capture. Your market share is your penetrated market divided by SAM.

- Porter's Five Forces will help you assess the degree of competition within established industries.

- The profitability of individual companies within an industry can vary widely, implying that your choice and, just as important, execution of strategy is probably more significant than your choice of industry.

- Your interest in industry analysis is about trying to predict the future – the threats and opportunities you might face. You can use techniques such as SLEPT analysis, brainstorming, futures thinking and scenario planning to help you do this.

- Your analysis should generate a series of risks and opportunities, as well as strategic options that you might undertake if they actually materialize. The more strategic options that you can identify, the more flexibility you have. They are sources of real value to you and potential investors.

- Your analysis should also generate a series of critical success factors – things you need to get right in order to ensure survival and success. These will be amplified and developed as you develop your business model.

Exercise 4.1
Describing your market/industry

1. Research your general market/industry and your TAM at a macro level. Find out as much as you can about the size, growth and structure of the market, market trends, customer demographics, buying patterns, established channels of distribution etc. Which market/industry typologies characterize it? Note the implications of this.

2. How is the particular market you are targeting – your SAM – different (e.g. local vs national, other characteristics)? Repeat 1 for your SAM.

3. List your direct and indirect competitors. Against each, list their strengths and weaknesses as companies.

4. List the strengths and weaknesses of the products or services they produce that compete with yours. Combine the two lists.

Exercise 4.2
Assessing the degree of competition

The Five Forces model can be used to assess the degree of competition you face in an existing market/industry and, hence, the threat to your profitability. However, there may be things you can do to mitigate this threat.

Using the format opposite, for each of the forces:

1. Assess the threat to industry profitability.

2. Note the implications of this for you.

3. List the actions you need to take to ensure that you can avoid or lessen the effect of high threats to profitability.

4. List the actions you need to take to create a sustainable position that means others cannot copy these actions.

If there are no actions you can take in an industry with a high degree of competition, you may want to reconsider whether you want to enter it and return to the exercises in the previous chapter to find another business idea. However, if there is a low degree of competition you may equally need to consider why this is the case and whether it will stay the same after your entry. How will existing companies react to your entry? If the threat of new entrants and/or substitutes is low, how will you be able to enter the market?

Competitive Force:	Threat to industry profitability			Implications	Actions to lessen/avoid threats	Actions to sustain position
	Low	Medium	High			
Rivalry among existing firms (e.g. number of competitors, industry structure, degree of product differentiation etc.)						
Threat of substitutes (e.g. degree of product differentiation, switch costs etc.)						
Threat of new entrants (e.g. barriers to entry, switch costs, access to distribution channels, degree of differentiation, capital requirements etc.)						
Bargaining power of suppliers (e.g. switch costs, supplier concentration, attractiveness of substitutes etc.)						
Bargaining power of buyers (e.g. switch costs, buyer concentration, product differentiation, buyers' costs etc.)						

Exercise 4.3
Assessing your market/industry future

1. Undertake a SLEPT analysis on your market/industry to identify key influences or events that might affect it over the next five years.

2. Using the market/industry analysis from Exercises 4.1 and 4.2, construct three scenarios – 'best', 'worst' and 'most likely' cases – that reflect how these influences or events might impact upon the trends in the industry. Remember to factor in the existence of your firm.
   - Will the industry expand or contract? Will it consolidate or fragment?
   - Are the main dimensions of competition changing and what is driving this change?
   - Will sectoral, performance and/or customer conventions change?
   - Will competition intensify or will products become more differentiated?
   - How will direct and indirect competitors be affected?
   - How might they react to your existence?
   - How will their reaction affect you?

3. Brainstorm to explore how you might react to these trends and competitors.
   - What strategies might you adopt?
   - Will you need to modify or change your product/service idea?
   - Will you need to identify and enter new markets?

4. List the critical success factors for your business – the things you need to get right to ensure your survival and success.

Visit http://www.palgrave.com/companion/burns-new-venture-creation for chapter quizzes to test your knowledge and other resources

New Venture Framework exercises

Provide a structured set of exercises that, chapter-by-chapter, allow the business idea to be explored and progressively built into a business plan

Visit www.palgrave.com/companion/burns-new-venture-creation to access the teaching and learning materials that accompany this book.

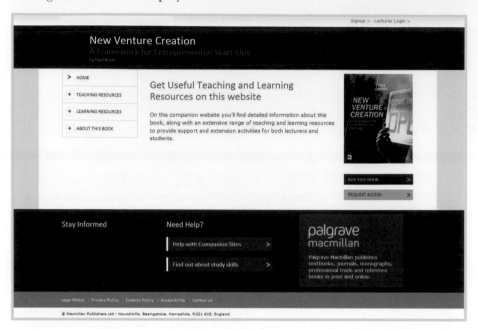

Resources for students

- Video interviews with the author relating to each part of the book

- Downloadable NVC Framework Canvas onto which you can plot your own business idea

- Downloadable and printable versions of the New Venture Creation Framework exercises which you can use to build your own business plan as you progress through the book

- A pro-forma business plan

- A glossary containing definitions of all the key terms, which appear in orange in this book

- Chapter-by-chapter quizzes

- Guides to sources of further information and laws and regulations for businesses in the UK

- Links to free online tests that allow students to assess their entrepreneurial character traits and their creativity

Resources for instructors

- Chapter-by-chapter PowerPoint slides, including relevant diagrams and figures, to use in teaching

- A chapter-by-chapter Instructor's Manual that includes:

  - case notes

  - links to useful websites

  - video links to support the teaching and many of the cases

I would like to thank all those who have helped me with this book, including the students and staff who inspired me to write it. Particular thanks go to Martin Drewe and Lauren Zimmerman at Palgrave, my editor, Ann Edmondson, the design team at emc design and, finally, Whittington (Chip) Vara from the University of Florida for his pertinent comments and suggestions at review stage. Thanks also to the other (anonymous) reviewers from around the globe.

Finally, I would like to thank my wife, Jean. She helps me with all my books, providing inspiration and insights and is an invaluable sounding board for new ideas. She is my rock when things go wrong. She also patiently helps with much-needed proof-reading. Any errors or omissions, however, remain my own.

The author and publishers are grateful for permission to reproduce the following copyright material:

Booz & Company Inc. for Figure 12.10 from J. Birkinshaw, 'The Paradox of Corporate Entrepreneurship', *strategy+business* magazine, Spring 2003. Copyright © 2003. All rights reserved.

Boston Consulting Group for Figures 8.3, 8.4, 8.5, 8.6, 8.7 (The Growth Share Matrix, adapted from the BCG Portfolio Matrix) from *The Product Portfolio Matrix*, © 1970, The Boston Consulting Group.

Gulf Publishing Co. for Figure 13.3 from R. Blake and J. Mouton (1978) *The New Managerial Grid*.

Harvard Business Review for Figure 12.1 (Greiner's Growth Model) from 'Evolution and Revolution as Organizations Grow', *Harvard Business Review*, 1972, 50(4), p. 41.

John Wiley & Sons for Figure 1.1 from A. Osterwalder and Y. Pigneur (2010) *Business Model Generation: A Handbook for Visionaries, Game Changers and Challengers*.

Taylor & Francis for Figure 6.2 from N.F. Piercy (2000) *Tales from the Marketplace: Stories of Revolution, Reinvention and Renewal*.

1

**THE
NEW VENTURE
CREATION
FRAMEWORK**

Contents

Learning outcomes

When you have read this chapter you will understand and be able to explain:
- What a business model is
- How it relates to a business plan
- How this book will help you develop your business model and draw up a business plan

The attraction of entrepreneurship

The twenty-first century has so far been characterized by turbulent change and disruption. The rise of terrorism led to wars in Afghanistan and Iraq. The banking crisis of 2008 plunged the Western world into recession. The so-called Arab spring of 2011 led on to disruption in many countries in the Middle East. We have seen corporate scandals such as Enron in the USA, Parmalat in Italy and Olympus in Japan that lead us to question corporate ethics. We have seen spectacular corporate failures such as Lehman Brothers in the USA and Royal Bank of Scotland (RBS) in the UK. Alongside this, we have seen unprecedented volatility in just about every market from commodities to exchange rates, from stock markets to bond markets.

Underpinning this volatility is the development of global connectivity – an increasingly complex world full of interconnections formed by a truly global market place linked by new technologies that allow instant communication with almost anywhere. Small changes tend to be amplified in highly connected systems. Actions in one part of a market can have unexpected and rapid consequences in another part of it. And nobody, not even sovereign states, seem able to control this. And the pace of change has accelerated. Change itself has changed to become a continuous process of often-discontinuous steps – abrupt and all-pervasive. Whilst large firms have increasingly found difficulty in dealing with this new order, start-ups and smaller ventures seem to find opportunities in the changes that these larger, more established firms find threatening. Even in this age of austerity they thrive, despite facing increasingly fierce competition. Never has it been easier to create a new venture. And never have the chances of success on a global basis been higher.

And as we look around for role models, we realize that so many of our most successful corporations have been founded since the 1970s. Bill Gates started Microsoft in 1975, the late Steve Jobs started Apple in 1976, Michael Dell set up Dell in 1984, Pierre Omidyar launched eBay in 1995 and Larry Page and Sergey Brin launched Google in 1996. And this was not just happening in the USA. In the UK Alan Sugar launched Amstrad in 1968, Richard Branson started his Virgin empire in 1972, James Dyson started selling his Dyson vacuum cleaners in 1976, the late Anita Roddick opened the first Body Shop in 1976 and Julian Metcalfe and Sinclair Beecham opened their first Pret A Manger in 1986. In India Sunil Mittal started the business that was to become Bhati Enterprises in 1976 and Kiran Mazumdar-Shaw started Biocon in 1978. These are now gigantic corporations that have made their founders into millionaires.

Over the last thirty years or so entrepreneurs establishing new ventures have done more to create wealth than firms at any time before them – ever! Ninety-five per cent of the wealth of the USA has been created since 1980. And small, growing firms create jobs from which the rest of society benefits. They have outstripped large firms in terms of job generation, year on year. At times when larger firms have retrenched, smaller firms continue to offer job opportunities. It has been estimated that in the USA small firms now generate half of GDP and over half of exports now come from firms employing fewer than 20 people. No wonder our governments and media are so fascinated by them. Entrepreneurs have finally been recognized as a vital part of economic wealth generation. They have become the heroes of the business world, embodying ephemeral qualities that many people envy – freedom of spirit, creativity, vision and zeal. They have the courage, self-belief and commitment to turn dreams into realities. They are the catalysts for economic, and sometimes social, change. They see an opportunity, commercialize it, and in doing so become millionaires themselves.

The **Entrepreneurial Revolution** is here to stay, having set the genetic code of the **US** and **global economy** for the 21st century, and having sounded the death knell for **Brontosaurus Capitalism** of yesteryear. Entrepreneurs are the **creators**, the **innovators**, and the **leaders** who give back to society, as philanthropists, directors and trustees, and who, more than any others, change the way people **live**, **work**, **learn**, **play**, and **lead**. Entrepreneurs create new technologies, products, processes, and services that become the next wave of **new industries**. Entrepreneurs create value with **high potential**, high growth companies which are the **job creation** engines of the US economy.

Jeffrey Timmons, New Venture Creation: Entrepreneurship for the 21st Century (1999) Boston: Irwin/McGraw-Hill)

💼 *Case insight*

Kiran Mazumdar-Shaw and Biocon

Millionaire entrepreneurs

Born in 1953 in Bangalore, India, Kiran Mazumdar-Shaw is one of the richest women in India. She is the founder of Biocon, a biotech company and India's largest producer of insulin. With a degree in zoology, she went on to take a postgraduate course and trained as a brewer in Australia, ahead of returning to India with the hope of following in her father's footsteps as a brew-master. Despite working in the brewing industry in India for a couple of years, she never achieved her ambition, finding her career blocked by sexism. Instead, in 1978, she was persuaded to set up a joint venture making enzymes in India.

Kiran Mazumdar-Shaw started Biocon India with Irishman Les Auchincloss in 1978 in the garage of her rented house in Bangalore with seed capital of only Rs 10,000. It was a joint venture with Biocon Biochemicals, Ireland. Eventually she found a banker prepared to loan the company $45,000 and, from a facility in Bangalore making enzymes for the brewing industry, started to diversify. Biocon India became the first Indian company to manufacture and export enzymes to the USA and Europe. This gave Kiran a flow of cash that she used to fund research and to start producing pharmaceutical drugs. The early years were hard.

In 1989, Kiran met the chairman of ICICI Bank, which had just launched a venture fund. The fund took a 20% stake in the company and helped finance its move into biopharmaceuticals. Shortly after this Unilever took over Biocon Biochemicals, and bought ICICI's stake in Biocon India, at the same time increasing it to 50%. In 1996 it entered the bio-pharmaceuticals and statins markets, then one year later Unilever sold its share in Biocon Biochemicals. Mazumdar-Shaw bought out Unilever and was able to start preparing Biocon India to float on the stock market, which it did in 2004 with a market value of $1.1bn.

In 2003 Biocon India became the first company to develop human insulin on a Pichia expression system. Since then it has obtained a listing on the stock exchange and entered into thousands of R&D licensing agreements with other pharmaceutical companies around the world. Today Biocon has a turnover in excess of Rs 24,000 million. It has Asia's largest insulin and statin production facilities and its largest perfusion-based antibody production facility. It produces drugs for cancer, diabetes and auto-immune diseases, and is developing the world's first oral insulin, which underwent Phase III clinical trials in 2013.

Kiran Mazumdar-Shaw has enjoyed many awards and honours. In 2010 *TIME* magazine included her in their 100 most powerful people in the world and the *Financial Times* had her in their list of the top 50 women in business, while in 2009 Forbes included her in their list of the 100 most powerful women. Passionate about providing affordable health care in India, she has funded the 1400-bed Mazumdar-Shaw Cancer Centre, a free cancer hospital in Bangalore. Every year, she donates $2 million to support health insurance coverage for some 100,000 Indian villagers.

BBC News Business 11 April 2011

> I was young, I was twenty five years old … banks were very nervous about lending to young entrepreneurs because they felt we didn't have the business experience … and then I had … this strange business called biotechnology which no one understood … Banks were very fearful of lending to a woman because I was considered high risk.

Kiran Mazumdar-Shaw Biocon

Biocon

4

Entrepreneurs are creating all sorts of new ventures, not just their own commercial businesses. They are creating new ventures for established, larger firms whilst remaining in salaried employment, content for the profits (and risks) of their work to go to their employers. We call them **intrapreneurs**. They are also creating new ventures for a range of motivations. Some have social or civic objectives and are willing to invest their own time and risk their own capital for little or no financial return, with profits being ploughed back to meet these objectives. We call them **social** or **civic entrepreneurs**. Sometimes these entrepreneurial projects do not even result in the establishment of a new venture but are subsumed within an existing organization, to change it subtly over time.

So, if entrepreneurship is not just about becoming self-employed, what is an entrepreneur? The notion of entrepreneur has been crafted over many centuries, starting with the Irish-French economist Cantillon (1755), and has seen many different emphases. In essence, entrepreneurs are best defined by their actions. They create and/or exploit change for profit, even if they do not take it themselves. In doing so, they innovate and accept risk to move resources into areas where they earn a higher commercial or social return.

But profit is not always the prime motivation for creating a new venture. For many people it is simply a badge of success and the attraction of being an entrepreneur lies in being their own boss, doing what they want to do rather than what they are told to do. Some people spot a business opportunity – a product or a service that they do not see offered in the market or a way of doing something better or cheaper. Some people might be frustrated by characteristics of current products or by services being offered that do not meet their needs. Some people, just a few, have a genuine 'eureka' moment when they come up with a new invention or have an idea that can revolutionize an industry. Whatever the source of their business idea, they feel motivated to do something about it – perhaps wanting to make a lot of money on the way. What defines the entrepreneur is their willingness to act upon the idea.

In fact most new ventures do not grow to become industry titans. More than 95% of small firms in Europe employ fewer than 10 people. Two-thirds employ only one other person. Many people choose to start up **salary-substitute firms** – ones that simply generate an income comparable to what they might earn as an employee (e.g. plumbers, store owners etc.). Others start up **lifestyle firms** – ones that allow them to pursue a particular lifestyle whilst enabling them to earn an acceptable living (e.g. sports instructors, artists etc.). In many cases self-employment is the conventional and accepted way of pursuing these life options. You might argue that the people starting these sorts of businesses are not 'true' entrepreneurs, and truly **entrepreneurial firms** are the ones that bring innovative ideas and ways of doing things to the market. They are set up to grow from the start. But both lifestyle and salary-substitute firms are the backbone of societies. And the risks associated with any new venture are high. One-third of businesses cease trading in their first year, although ceasing to trade does not always signify failure or the loss of money. And many of the challenges they face are similar. What is more, the business skills you need to survive can be applied to growth, so these distinctions are not absolute. Lifestyle and salary-substitute firms can become more entrepreneurial – with the right management and leadership.

Gazelles and economic growth

Young, high-growth firms – called 'gazelles' by academics – are few in number but have a disproportionate importance to national economies. Definitions of a 'gazelle' vary, but in the USA it has been estimated that they comprise less than 1% of all companies yet generate about 10% of new jobs in any year. Indeed, the top performing 1% of all firms generate about 40% of all new jobs (Strangler, 2010). In the UK they have been estimated to represent 2–4% of firms but were responsible for the majority of employment growth (BERR, 2008).

Middle-sized firms generally have a disproportionate impact on national economies. In the UK, whilst they represent just 1% of firms, they generate 30% of GDP and employ more than one-third of the workforce (GE Capital, 2012). And Europe lags behind the USA, where SMEs (small and medium-sized enterprises) were on average larger and expanded more rapidly (European Commission, 2008). Whilst a higher percentage of UK firms achieve high growth than European firms, the UK still lags behind the USA (BERR, op. cit).

BERR (2008) *High Growth Firms in the UK: Lessons from an Analysis of Comparative UK Performance*, Business, Enterprise and Regional Reform (BERR) Economics Paper 3, November.

European Commission (2008) *European Competitiveness Report 2008*, www.ec.europa.eu/enterprise.

GE Capital (2012) *Leading from the Middle: The Untold Story of British Business*, London: GE Capital.

Strangler, D. (2010) *High-Growth Firms and the Future of the American Economy*, Kauffman Foundation Research Series: Firm Growth and Economic Growth.

Macmillan

Julie Spurgeon and Material Pleasures

Life-style start-up

In her mid-forties, Julie Spurgeon graduated with a first in ceramic design from London's Central Saint Martin's College of Art and Design in the summer of 2008. As part of her final project to design a range of tableware she had to seek critical appraisal from retailers and industry experts. One of the firms she contacted was up-market retailer Fortnum & Mason, and they were sufficiently impressed to commission a range of bone china tableware, called Material Pleasures that was launched in August 2009.

The trade mark Material Pleasures, which goes on the reverse of each piece, is registered (cost £200) and Julie joined Anti Copying in Design (ACID), which allowed her to log her design trail as proof against copying. Julie has had to pay for tooling and manufacturing costs herself. The moulds cost £5000 and the factory in Stoke-on-Trent required a minimum order of 250 pieces. The contract with Fortnum's involved exclusivity for six months. All this was funded with a £5000 loan from the Creative Seed Fund and a part-time job.

> *Sunday Telegraph 12 July 2009*
>
> In the future I'd like to continue creating specialist tableware, as well as handmade pieces. Material Pleasures stands for individual design, not big-batch production.

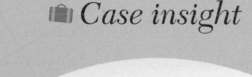 *Case insight*

John Bird and The Big Issue

Social enterprise start-up

The Big Issue is probably the most prominent example of social entrepreneurship in the UK. Initially started up as a non-profit organization by John Bird in 1991, and then backed by Gordon and Anita Roddick (of The Body Shop fame), it is now a limited company that donates its profits to the Big Issue Foundation, a charity that addresses the problems of the homeless. The scheme started in London, based on a similar idea in New York.

The Big Issue produces a magazine of the same name which is sold by homeless people on the streets of many UK towns and cities. Its aims are to allow homeless people to work to earn a living – enabling them to address their personal poverty and retake control of their lives – and to campaign on social exclusion issues. The magazine is sold to consumers on its quality rather than as a means of securing a charitable donation. However, the fact that it is sold by the homeless, exclusively on the streets, rather than in magazine stores or by volunteers, makes the nature of the transaction not altogether straightforward. When they are asked to buy, consumers come face-to-face with beneficiaries and can see that they are trying to help themselves out of their situation. Sellers are first given a small number of magazines and thereafter have to buy copies to sell on. One key aspect of the transaction is that the consumer is asked for a limited and relatively small financial contribution (the cover price was £2.50 in 2013). This legitimizes small donations. In this way giving small amounts to a morally justified and legitimate cause is made easy.

Case insight

Tony Fernandes and AirAsia (1)

Entrepreneurial start-up

Former Time Warner executive Tony Fernandes set up Asia's first low-cost airline, AirAsia, in 2001, buying the heavily indebted state-owned company from the Malaysian government for only 25p. He set about remodelling it as a short-haul, low-cost operator flying around Asia. Being first in the Asian market with an idea copied from companies in the West, such as easyJet, the company expanded rapidly from a fleet of only two planes in 2002 to 86 planes flying 30 million people around the world by 2010. It created a new Asian market in low-cost air travel. By 2007, UBS research showed it to be the lowest cost airline in the world. Now with hubs in Kuala Lumpur and Singapore, it has won the Skytrax World's best low-cost airline award in 2007, 2009, 2010 and 2011. It has also established associate airlines in Thailand and Indonesia.

Barriers and triggers to entrepreneurship

Creating a new venture is not easy. And running it can be even harder. It is an all-consuming, 24-hour, seven-day-a-week activity – at least until you have a management team you can rely on. You need commitment and dedication. You need stamina – '90% perspiration, 10% inspiration'. It can break up relationships and split families. It is risky, without guaranteed results. So, you need to be able to bounce back from set-backs, because there will be many. You need determination and persistence. You need to be emotionally self-sufficient – it can be lonely. You need to be task-orientated – motivated to deliver the best product or service to your customers. You need to be attuned to the opportunities generated by these customers and the market you operate in. Most of all you need to be able to live with a degree of risk and uncertainty. If you crave certainty, routines and regular pay, entrepreneurship is not for you.

For most people there are blocks or barriers that prevent them from creating a new venture, even if they have a good idea. These can come from situational factors. Your personal background and your commitment to others might create barriers – things like the need for a regular income to support a family or the lack of start-up capital. These barriers can also be psychological – lack of self-belief. It takes a degree of courage to risk the capital your family might rely on in an uncertain business venture. Fear of the unknown is a strong de-motivator, but increasingly paid employment is not seen as a guarantee of regular income. As

larger firms delayer, restructure and even just close, employees are increasingly realizing that there is no such thing as a 'job for life'. At least with self-employment you control some elements of your destiny.

Despite the barriers to creating a new venture, millions of people around the world do so every year. What is often needed is a 'trigger'. Some people are 'pushed' into setting up their own business because they are made redundant, they find they just do not fit into the company they work for or, simply, that they have no alternative, for example because they are immigrants to a new country. Typically these are situational factors that push you towards self-employment. Immigrants are often 'pushed' into being highly entrepreneurial. They have few alternatives.

The USA, famed for its entrepreneurial culture, was built by immigrants and many millionaire entrepreneurs are first- or second-generation immigrants. Sergey Brin, co-founder of Google, immigrated to the USA with his family from the Soviet Union at the age of six.

> **Bharat Shah, founder Sigma Pharmaceuticals Kenyan Jewels www.alusainc.wordpress.com**
>
> My wife didn't mind me working 14 hours a day on the business and not being at home to read the children bedtime stories. But we had, and still have, a good relationship. We have no regrets.

> **Tom Farmer, founder Kwik-Fit Daily Mail 11 May 1999**
>
> Neither my grandfather nor my father would be surprised if they could see me now. My success didn't just happen. As a young boy, I was always working. My parents and brothers and sisters all had high energy.

> **Mark Constantine, founder Lush RealBusiness 26 May 2009**
>
> We got the inspiration (for Lush) because we were broke. The previous business had gone bust. We had mortgages, three children and no money. So – make a living!

In the UK, six of the most successful wholesale medicine and drug supply companies were founded by Kenyan Asians who came to Britain in the 1960/70s as forced immigrants and are now millionaires (Navin Engineer, Bharat Shah, Bharat and Ketan Mehta, Vijay and Bikhu Patel, Ravi Kari and Naresh Shah).

Many people, however, are 'pulled' into starting up a business for more positive reasons. They yearn for independence and recognition of their achievements. This gives them drive and determination. They look for personal development. And the prospect of becoming rich might be attractive. Push factors are typically psychological – they derive from people's character traits and the influences on them. When 'push' and 'pull' factors combine it is little wonder that the result is a powerful trigger to potential entrepreneurs to create a new venture – as long as they have that all-important business idea. The combination of these triggers – the push and pull factors – and the barriers they face in setting up their own business are shown in Figure 1.1. It is no coincidence that the peak ages of entrepreneurs creating new ventures – in their early 20s or early 40s – match periods when barriers might be low because they have least to lose or have reducing family commitments as children leave home.

 UK

demarquette
fine chocolates

Marc Demarquette

Marc Demarquette

Sunday Times 24 May 2009

You need to have **nerves of steel** but it has been a fantastic experience. **I'm loving it.** I just wish I had a couple of extra hours in the day to enjoy my own life.

Demarquette

Case insight

Running your own business

Half-French and half-Chinese, Marc Demarquette was born and lives in London. He was a management consultant until a life-threatening accident caused him to reconsider his priorities. His interest in catering led him to the prestigious Maison Lenôtre in Paris to learn the art of making chocolate, and then to the Alps to work with a master chocolatier. In 2006, with the help of a £40,000 bank loan, he opened an up-market artisan chocolate shop, Demarquette, in Fulham, south west London, and a small production facility nearby. Since then the business has been entirely funded out of cash flow. He sells his range of high quality, award-winning chocolates through his store and through other retailers like Fortnum & Mason, but about one-third of sales come through his website.

Up-to-date information on Demarquette can be found on: www.demarquette.co.uk

BARRIERS TO START-UP
(SITUATIONAL AND PSYCHOLOGICAL)

- *Need for regular income*
- *Fear of loss of capital*
- *No capital*
- *Risk aversion*
- *Doubts about ability*

Business idea → Start-up

TRIGGERS

PUSH FACTORS (SITUATIONAL):

- *Unemployment*
- *Disagreements*
- *'Misfit'*
- *No other option*

PULL FACTORS (PSYCHOLOGICAL):

- *Independence*
- *Recognition*
- *Personal development*
- *Wealth*

F1.1 Barriers and triggers to entrepreneurship

New venture creation

Unless you are pushed, getting over the barriers to entrepreneurship may not be easy. The most fundamental fear of all is that of failure. So how might you improve the chances of success? Figure 1.2 summarizes the things you need, which this book will help you to develop.

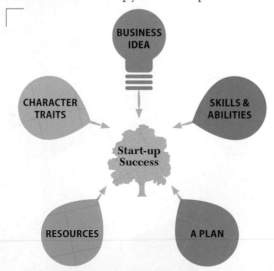

F1.2 New venture creation

- **Personal character traits that incline you towards entrepreneurship** – Not everybody is well-suited to self-employment. Some people get pushed into it reluctantly. But to make a success of it you need to be able to live with the stresses it produces and enjoy the challenges it presents. Even if you are pushed rather than pulled into starting a new venture, it is a lot easier if you have a positive psychological attitude towards it. We shall look at this in the next chapter.

- **A good business idea** – Finding good business ideas is not as difficult as many people think. Chapter 3 outlines a systematic process for finding them, rather than just relying upon the happenstance of having that 'eureka moment'.

- **The necessary skills to deliver your product/ service idea** – There is no point in starting out as a plumber without the necessary skills. Experience of an industry or sector can also be very valuable. It can provide knowledge of how the sector works and a network of contacts who could become customers or suppliers. It also helps to learn these things and make mistakes at somebody else's expense. So you do need to have some specific skills and knowledge about the business you want to set up. This book will give you a set of general business and management tools that will help you launch and grow your new venture based upon your specific skills. It will show you how to develop a business model that will improve your chances of success.

Ajith Jayawickrema, serial entrepreneur and business angel Sunday Times 2 June 2013

I want to see that the person who is doing it [the business] has a very clear grasp of what he or she is trying to accomplish. At this high risk, understanding the nuts and bolts goes a long way to reducing the risk.

- **A plan to launch and grow your business** – This book will help you plan the launch of your new venture and manage its growth. Whilst entrepreneurship is an uncertain activity, the act of planning helps you prepare for these uncertainties. It allows you to ask the 'what if?' questions and create options, rather than just reacting to situations as they arise. It also gives you the frameworks that make you better able to react to these unexpected threats and opportunities. Having a plan improves your chances of success.

- **The resources you need to launch and grow your business** – Whilst this book will not provide you with the financial capital, it will show you how to minimize the resources you need and assess how much and what sort of finance to look for. The business plan you produce will help attract that finance.

This book will help you create your new venture – whether it is a commercial or social enterprise – and reduce those risks of failure. It will help you assess whether you have an entrepreneurial character, find a business idea and develop a business model that will show you how it can best be delivered to the market.

Myths about entrepreneurs

Read et al. (2011) claim there are seven myths about entrepreneurs who 'see opportunities others don't, seize them faster, make better predictions and are brash risk-takers.' These lead to the usual objection to starting your own business – namely 'I don't have an idea, money, entrepreneurial skills – and I'm afraid to fail.' These seven myths are:

- Entrepreneurs are visionary – **Visions evolve** as opportunities emerge. You define your own vision and measures of success. These will change over time and may expand beyond your current imagination. An unrealistic vision can be just an illusion.
- Entrepreneurs have good ideas and you don't – Ideas are easy to come by, but you never know how successful they will be, and that includes entrepreneurs.
- Entrepreneurs are risk-takers – **They may be willing** to accept risk but they don't like it and limit and mitigate it in any way they can.

Academic insight

- Entrepreneurs have money and you don't – **Just not true.** Money does not guarantee success and many money-starved start-ups have blossomed.
- Entrepreneurs are extraordinary forecasters – **They are not.** They are just willing to live with uncertainty but then organize themselves to cope with, indeed influence, it.
- Entrepreneurs are not like the rest of us – **They are,** and entrepreneurial principles and skills can be taught.
- You don't know how to take the plunge – **Hopefully** books like this will show you how to do just that.

The message is simple: entrepreneurs are not special; find an idea; have a go but limit your loss. This book will show you how to do this.

Read, S., Sarasvathy, S., Dew, N., Wiltbank, R. and Ohlsson, A.V. (2011) *Effectual Entrepreneurship*, London: Routledge.

Business planning

The principles of planning are straightforward and translate directly into what you need to do to create a new venture:

- **Know where you are** – Understand your strengths and weaknesses, the skills you bring to the business, the resources you are able to mobilize, indeed whether you have what it takes to be an entrepreneur.

- **Know where you want to go** – Have a clear idea of the business opportunity and, more important, what you want your business to become in the future.

- **Plan how to get there** – Plan how to make this happen, how to get customers, combat competition and lead staff.

The business planning process is just like planning a route from A to B; you decide on where you are and where you want to go, and then you can start to plan your route. If you cannot decide where you are or where you want to go, you will never be able to find a route. If you know where you are and where you want to go, a good route increases the chance of getting there.

But starting a new venture is an uncertain exercise. So, you might decide not to go in a straight line because there are longer but faster routes; you might be forced to take diversions because unexpected road works upset your plans; you might not get to your destination as quickly as you expect because the car breaks down or you have an accident. Whilst nothing is certain, plans can be changed and planning should provide you with options about the best routes. Planning therefore needs to be a continuous process. If the unexpected happens you then have those options available. Planning the route will also help you estimate the petrol you will need and the money you will need to buy it – the

resources required. The business planning process is simple but systematic – just like planning a route from A to B.

The New Venture Creation Framework

The New Venture Creation Framework in Figure 1.3 provides a comprehensive framework to help you find, develop and refine a business idea. It takes you through the whole planning process for a new venture in a way that gives you the best chance of success. This book explains each stage in the process, and exercises at the end of each chapter help you to assemble and evaluate the information you need. These exercises build into a comprehensive business plan that can then be used to obtain finance.

This Framework has seven components. Each is covered by different parts of the book.

You and your business idea (Part 1) – You and your personal characteristics are critical to the success of a new venture. Are you really an entrepreneur? This section invites you to explore your personal aspirations and characteristics and the social, human and financial capital you bring to the new venture. If you need it, this section also helps you find a business idea that suits your aspirations.

Central to the New Venture Creation Framework is the development of a good business model. Indeed, an innovative business model can form the core of your business idea. The business model describes how you will go about delivering your business idea

> You jump off a cliff and you assemble an airplane on the way down
>
> Reid Hoffman, founder LinkedIn BBC News Business 11 January 2011

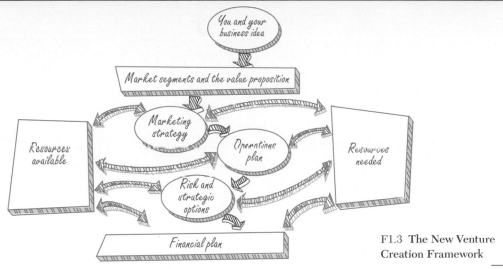

F1.3 The New Venture Creation Framework

to customers so as to achieve your business purpose and make a profit. Even if your core business idea has merit, unless you find and persuade customers to buy it and can then deliver it to them, you do not have a viable business. Even then, you have to persuade them that your product/service is so good that they want to buy it again and again. To do this you need marketing, operations and financial plans based on the resources you need and have access to. You also need to identify and minimize the risks you face.

Market segments and the value proposition (Part 2) – At the core of a business model is the identification of different groupings of customers with similar characteristics – called **market segments** – and the motivations each segment has for buying your product or service – called the **benefits** they are seeking. Pulling these benefits together for each segment is called your **value proposition**. Before you develop this you need to understand the structure of the market and industry you are entering and the value propositions they are currently offering customers.

Marketing strategy (Part 3) – Your marketing strategy describes how you will deliver your value proposition to each of the customer segments you have identified. The tool for delivering this is called the **marketing mix** – price, promotion/communication, service, distribution channels, branding etc. A good marketing strategy helps you develop **competitive advantage** against other companies in your market. This section needs to

cover your core strategy as well as your strategy for the launch and the subsequent growth of the business.

Operations plan (Part 4) – The operations plan highlights the practical things you need to do to launch a new venture. These range from legal to operating issues, including **partnership** opportunities. It should identify those key activities you need to undertake to ensure success.

Risk and strategic options (Part 5) – Launching a new venture involves taking risks, and the business model should tease out the major risks you face and how they might be mitigated or avoided entirely. It should identify the **critical success factors** that underpin the operations of the business and recognize different ways of doing things should circumstances change or differ from those anticipated – called **strategic options**. These are valuable because circumstances can, and do, change.

Resources available and needed (Part 6) – This defines the resources you bring to the business – **human**, **social**, **intellectual** and **financial** – and the resources you need. A major component of this is your ability to pull together and lead a management team.

Financial plan (Part 7) – This shows the **profit** the business should generate and how it will be used. It shows the **cash flow** of the business and the external finance that will be required. It is a set of **financial forecasts** – revenues, related costs and resulting financial structures of the business.

The Business Model Canvas

Osterwalder and Pigneur (2010) have developed what they call a 'Business Model Canvas' or generic business model that has been used as a model for consultants and trainers across the world. Designed for established businesses, the Canvas is described in *Business Model Generation: A Handbook for Visionaries, Game Changers and Challengers* which, the authors claim, strives 'to defy outmoded business models and design tomorrow's enterprises' that will 'turn visionary ideas into game-changing business models that challenge the establishment.'

The innovatively designed book certainly provides a stimulating pictorial structure for better understanding and developing business models. The authors give numerous examples of real business models for companies and/or products that translate onto the Canvas (e.g. Apple, Google, Skype, Amazon) as well as exercises and workshop scenarios.

The book provides a framework for developing a business model based upon a pictorial Business Model Canvas that comprises the nine building blocks shown in Figure 1.4. The left side of the canvas is driven by efficiency and the right side by value to customers. The idea is that you can use the canvas to sketch out (literally) and develop your business model.

Using real business examples, the book shows how business models can be sketched onto the Canvas so as to identify patterns:

- Unbundling the core business types or disciplines – product innovation, customer relationships and infrastructure management (low cost).
- The long tail – whereby a company offers a large number of small-volume, niche products at a relatively high price.
- Multi-sided platforms – bringing together different market segments that derive value from the presence of the other, called the network effect.
- Free product/services – where non-paying customers are financed by other parts of the business model or other customer segments.
- Open business models – where value is created through collaboration between partners.

Osterwalder and Pigneur encourage you to challenge conventional models by using six business model design techniques in conjunction with the Canvas:

- Customer insights – encouraging you to develop a deep understanding of customer needs, even if they are not always derived directly from the customers themselves.

Key partnerships:	Key activities:	Value proposition:	Customer relations:	Customer segments:
The network of suppliers and partners that make the business model work	The most important things you need to do to make the business model work	The product/service bundle that creates value for each customer segment	The types of relationships you aim to have with each customer segment	The different groups of people or organizations you aim to reach
	Key resources:		Channels:	
	The most important assets required to make the business model work		How you communicate with and reach each customer segment	

Cost structures:	Revenue streams:
All the costs that you will incur to operate your business model	The cash generated from each customer segment

F1.4 **Business Model Canvas**

- Generating new ideas – encouraging you not always to accept the 'dominant logic' of how to do things in a particular industry.
- Visual thinking – encouraging you to draw or sketch out the business model on the Canvas and use Post-it™ notes to explain it, thereby making abstract concepts more concrete.
- Prototype development – encouraging you to explore alternative business models that might add value for customers.
- Storytelling – encouraging you to be able to articulate the concept behind the product/service and how it creates value for customers.
- Scenario development – building on customer insights and development in the competitive environment to make future possibilities more tangible.

Finally, the book looks at how the Canvas can be used to develop strategy – constructively questioning established business models and strategically examining the business environment – changing drawings on the Canvas or adding Post-it™ notes. It describes the process an organization might go through to draw up and develop its Canvas, and how it might implement and manage the resulting changes.

The Business Model Canvas was designed for established businesses. Its great advantage is its simple pictorial presentation that facilitates creative but systematic analysis and development of a business model. *New Venture Creation* is about developing a business model and planning for a start-up, and the New Venture Creation Framework in Figure 1.3, along with the associated exercises, is essentially your Canvas on which you can plot and develop your start-up model.

Osterwalder, A. and Pigneur, Y. (2010), *Business Model Generation: A Handbook for Visionaries, Game Changers and Challengers*, Hoboken, NJ: John Wiley & Sons.

Each component of the New Venture Creation Framework is connected to and dependent on other elements of the Framework. For example, you need to operationalize your marketing strategy and to do that you need the appropriate resources. The Framework is therefore a holistic concept and its components may need to be modified or adapted as it is developed.

The exercises at the end of each chapter allow you to build up a New Venture Creation Framework for your venture and then evaluate and modify the components as you progress. These exercises encourage you to think innovatively. And the more innovative your business model, the more successful you are likely to be. Innovative business models can transform industry landscapes and create whole new markets. They create value for you, your customers and society. Apple transformed how music is sold with the launch of iTunes. eBay transformed how goods can be sold by pioneering online auctions. Grameen Bank transformed micro lending to the poor.

New Venture Creation concentrates on the particular needs of a start-up enterprise – encouraging you to think creatively about your product/service idea, how it translates into a business model and how it can be operationalized. The New Venture Creation Framework (Figure 1.3) provides a step-by-step approach to developing and improving your business idea, planning your start-up and developing a business plan that can be used to obtain finance. It can be applied in the same way as Osterwalder and Pigneur's Canvas (Figure 1.4) – using drawings and Post-it™ notes to develop your new venture model and plan. After all, the greatest value of producing a business plan is the planning process you go through, and anything that can help this must be worthwhile.

The business plan

Whilst the New Venture Creation Framework develops holistically, at some point it may need to crystallize into a formal, written business plan. The business plan is a document that sets out your business idea and the business model upon which it is based. It is your final route map showing what you need to do to launch and grow your new venture. Chapter 16 sets out a typical format, often used for external purposes, for example to raise finance.

The great advantage of developing a business plan using the New Venture Creation Framework in Figure 1.3 is that it forces you to think systematically and in detail about the future of the business. It forces you to think through the options that are open to you and justify the decisions you take, whilst thinking through the consequences of your actions. That is not to say that you can anticipate all the problems you will face, but it means that you will be better able to meet these challenges because you have a thorough understanding of the business and its market place. Remember, it is the process of planning that is really important and a true entrepreneur is constantly refining and modifying their plan – strategizing and developing strategic options – to meet changing opportunities and threats. In that sense, the skills you will learn in developing the plan are more important than the plan itself. Indeed, because circumstances change, most business plans have a shelf life of less than one year. Even a good business plan needs to be continuously updated to reflect the learning that takes place during the entrepreneurial process. And rather than rewriting the formal business plan all the time you can use the New Venture Creation Framework as an informal canvas onto which to plot the changes, think through the consequences and assess the strategic options you face as you grow.

16

🧳 *Case insight*

eBay

Developing the business model

The business model is crucial to success for all firms and central to the New Venture Creation Framework. The way internet firms make money largely defines their business model. Typically there are six ways of doing this:

- Direct sales model – where products or services are sold directly online (e.g. Amazon).
- Advertising model – where they are paid-for ads placed on their website (e.g. YouTube).
- Pay-per-click model – where they are paid-for clicks onto an advertiser's link (e.g, Google).
- Subscription model – where customers subscribe for the online product or service (e.g. *The Times* newspaper).
- Freemium model – where the basic service is free but there is a charge for extras or premium services (e.g. SurveyMonkey).
- Affiliate model – where the website hosting ads is paid commission on sales by online retailers or other people trying to sell things (e.g. eBay).

Arguably the most successful internet business – one that uses the affiliate model – is the online auctioneer, eBay. eBay was founded by Pierre M. Omidyar in 1995. The company has since expanded worldwide, claiming hundreds of millions of registered users, over 15,000 employees and revenues of some $8 billion.

eBay's high gross margin comes from being nothing more than an intermediary – fully automated software running on a web server. This keeps costs and risks low. Customers, both buyers and sellers, do all the work. Sellers pay to set up their own auction. Buyers use eBay's software to place their bids. Shipping and payment are arranged between the seller and buyer. eBay is simply the trading platform. It holds no stocks and its involvement in the trade is minimal. However, it takes between 7 and 18% of the selling price as commission for letting sellers use its software. After each transaction the buyer and seller rate each other. Next to each user's identification is a figure in brackets recording the number of positive comments – thus encouraging honesty and trust. It is a truly virtual business which also sells advertising space.

🇺🇸 USA

eBay developed a 'virtuous circle' in which more buyers attracted more sellers, which attracted yet more buyers and sellers – called 'network effects'. To achieve this, eBay needs to dominate its market. At the core of eBay's business is software rather than people. The company has bought software companies to gain exclusive use of their technologies and to make the auction process more efficient. It therefore faces enormous economies of scale in attracting as many auction transactions as possible and, with that in mind, has moved into new areas such as used cars and hosting storefronts for small merchants where 'buy-it-now' goods are offered. It has also started to supply private-label versions of its service to companies, for a fee.

In 2002 eBay purchased PayPal, the dominant provider of internet payments in the USA. The two companies are complementary but depend on each other. Indeed, auctions account for almost two-thirds of PayPal's business. PayPal allows customers to register details of their credit card or bank account so that when they buy something on the internet they just enter an e-mail account and an amount. Like eBay, it is fully automated, relying on software rather than people. Like eBay, it also relies on 'network effects'.

The company's business strategy involves achieving market dominance worldwide, often by acquiring competitors. It has already expanded into dozens of countries including China and India. The only countries where expansion failed were Taiwan and Japan, where Yahoo! had a head start, and New Zealand, where TradeMe is still the dominant online auction site. Another element of its strategy is to leverage the relationship between it and PayPal. eBay's basic business model generates revenues from sellers. Driving buyers and sellers to use PayPal means eBay also turns buyers into clients. For each new PayPal registration it achieves via the eBay site, it earns off-site revenues when the new PayPal account is used in non-eBay transactions.

Questions:

1. Why is efficiency important to eBay?
2. Why is market dominance important?
3. Why is it necessary to acquire other companies?

Summary

- Entrepreneurs are defined by their actions. They create and/or exploit change for profit by innovating, accepting risk and moving resources to areas of higher return.

- Starting your own business is hard work and many people face barriers that dissuade them from it – such as the need for a regular income or lack of capital. As well as the 'pull' of the attractions of self-employment they may also need a 'push' such as being made redundant.

- To successfully launch a business you need to have an entrepreneurial character, a good business idea, the necessary skills and knowledge, a plan and sufficient resources. This book will help you develop these things.

- The New Venture Creation Framework outlined in Figure 1.3 provides a comprehensive framework to help you find, explore, develop and refine a business idea. It takes you through the whole planning process for a new venture in a way that gives you the best chance of success. It translates into a formal business plan – a written document that can be used for internal as well as external purposes, for example to raise finance.

- At the core of the Framework is a holistic business model. The more innovative your business model, the more successful you are likely to be. The Framework exercises at the end of each chapter help you explore and develop this model.

- The process of planning is probably more important than the written business plan that results. It prepares you for the unexpected by getting you to think through the opportunities and risks that might present themselves and helping you to develop options. It also helps you develop the skills and frameworks that enable you to cope with those totally unexpected events that you did not think about, when they happen.

PART 1
YOU AND
YOUR BUSINESS
IDEA

2 **What you bring to** entrepreneurship

3 Finding **your business idea**

VIDEO

www.palgrave.com/companion/
burns-new-venture-creation

The New Venture Creation Framework

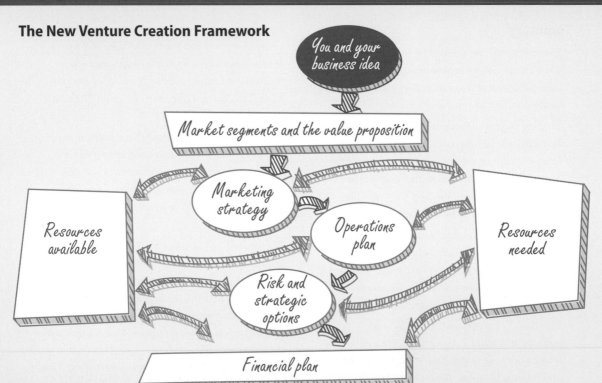

2
WHAT YOU BRING TO ENTREPRENEURSHIP

Contents

Learning outcomes

When you have read this chapter and undertaken the related exercises you will be able to:
- Understand your motivations for wanting to start your own business
- Critically assess the personal assets and liabilities you would bring to your business
- Critically assess whether you have an entrepreneurial character
- Critically assess the dimensions of your creative potential
- Understand the distinguishing characteristics of how entrepreneurs manage their business

Your personal drivers

The most important thing you bring to your new venture is you, which makes it important to understand what that means. You start by understanding your drivers – what motivates you to think about starting your own business? As we saw in the last chapter, people can start up many different kinds of organizations for many different reasons. You need to understand your own motivations for being an entrepreneur. Why are you considering it (push and/or pull)? What are your barriers? What are your personal drivers? What do you want the business to become – a salary-substitute, lifestyle or entrepreneurial business? Or do you want it to achieve some social or civic objectives? In other words, what is your business purpose?

Of course, entrepreneurs often start out thinking they want to achieve one thing and then change it later as new opportunities emerge. Many people start with a business that appears to have no growth prospects but go on to seize opportunities as they present themselves. John Hargreaves is a docker's son who left school at 14 and started a market stall in Liverpool selling M&S clothing seconds (i.e. less-than-perfect clothing). He went on to found the Matalan clothing chain in the UK, a venture he sold for £1.5 billion in 2009. Alan Sugar, now famous for his appearances on *The Apprentice* TV show in the UK, founded the computer companies Amstrad and Viglen and is a millionaire. He started out boiling beetroot to sell from market stalls in London's East End.

Nevertheless, you need to match your personal motivations and drivers with the business you intend to set up now – not in ten years' time. There is no point in setting up a business that is intended to grow rapidly unless you are willing and able to make the additional time and resource commitment. And you certainly will need to enjoy whatever your venture entails. You will spend a great deal of time working in it.

You also need to consider any personal constraints (barriers) that might affect your venture. These may come from family or other commitments. It is important that your business fits in with what you want from your life and lifestyle. You need to have a balance between work and personal life that suits you.

> **Fun** is at the core of the way I like to do business and has informed everything I've done from the outset. More than any other **element**, fun is at the core of Virgin's **success**.
>
> Richard Branson, founder Virgin *Losing my Virginity* (1988, London: Virgin)

Your resources

You also bring capital to your start-up. The **financial capital** you bring may be limited, but this can probably go further than you think. The important thing to remember is that you do not necessarily have to buy and own a resource to be able to use it. Using resources that you may not own is called **bootstrapping**. Entrepreneurs often commit only limited resources themselves – the resources they can afford to lose. They find ways of using resources that they do not own by partnering with others. Actually, minimizing your ownership of resources reduces your risks and gives you more flexibility – it allows you to commit (and de-commit) quickly to new opportunities. Chapter 10 will show you how you can expand the reach of your business by partnering with others.

However, capital is more than just financial. There is also **human capital** – such as education, training and previous managerial or industry experience. There is also **social capital** – derived from access to personal networks of friends and commercial contacts. All this is shown in Figure 2.1. The more capital you bring to the business – of any kind – the more likely you are to succeed.

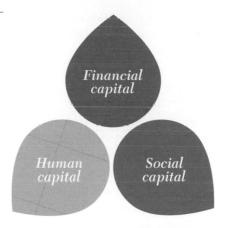

F2.1 **Start-up capital**

Human capital is vital for any business. Knowledge and experience of a business or industry can be an invaluable source of business ideas. It can also give you an insight into the problems that you will face in business and it is always better to make mistakes at somebody else's expense rather than your own. If you do not have that experience then education and training can alert you to the problems and give you the skills to overcome them. That is why so many people take training courses before they actually start up in business – it improves their chances of success. Human capital in the form of education and track record increases your credibility with financial backers. If you can demonstrate achievements, particularly in the industry that you want to start up in, it counts for a lot.

> Get as much **professional** training as you can before starting a business. Doing a **MBA** first really helped me.
>
> Andrew Valentine, founder Streetcar *Sunday Times* 15 November 2009

> You're constantly reading business **books** and constantly meeting people, (taking) **advice** from all sorts of people. I would recommend that.
>
> Mark Constantine, founder Lush *RealBusiness* 26 May 2009

Social capital is about your ability to get on with people – your social skills. It is built on relationships and this is at the core of the entrepreneurial approach to doing business – relationships with customers, employees, suppliers, the bank and your landlord. It is social capital that enables you to build your credibility with all these stakeholders in your business. It is the personal touch that distinguishes entrepreneurs from the faceless, grey-suited managers of large firms. These relationships can build into an invaluable network of contacts and goodwill that can be used to generate knowledge and information on new opportunities or threats. Networks can therefore increase your flexibility and reduce, or give you early warning of, the risks you face. Networks also might yield up partners or ways of bootstrapping resources. They might provide you with your first customer, or provide you with low-cost or free office space. They might provide professional advice and opinion, often without charge. They might even provide you with the cash that the banker is so reluctant to provide.

Chris Ingram, founder Tempus Sunday Times 17 March 2002

An entrepreneur is unfailingly enthusiastic, never pessimistic, usually brave, and certainly stubborn. Vision and timing are crucial. You have to be something of a workaholic, too. You have to be convinced that what you are doing is right. If not, you have to recognize this and be able to change direction swiftly – sometimes leaving your staff breathless – and start again with equal enthusiasm.

Character traits of entrepreneurs

Underpinning your personal motivations to start up a business is your personal character. This constitutes your psychological 'push' into entrepreneurship. Your character traits are mainly developed over time through your life and social experiences. They are the product of the many cultural influences that shape and develop us, from parents and nationality to education and the different groups of society we operate in. And some of these cultures and sub-cultures may encourage entrepreneurial activity whilst others discourage it. Research indicates that entrepreneurs have certain identifiable character traits or personality dimensions that incline them towards setting up their own business and help them navigate through the uncertainties of entrepreneurship.

F2.2 Character traits of entrepreneurs

Research into the character traits of entrepreneurs is substantial and goes back some forty years. Whilst facing many methodological issues, it has thrown up many overlapping personality dimensions. Figure 2.2 summarizes the five main entrepreneurial character traits, harvested from numerous research studies. Each is a necessary but not a sufficient trait. What is needed is the combination of all of them to be present. And even then you need to have the other factors mentioned in Chapter 1 in place.

Eddy Shah, founder Messenger Group The Times 16 March 2002

Entrepreneurs don't like working for other people … I was once made redundant by the *Manchester Evening News*. I had a wife who had given up a promising career for me, and a baby. I stood on Deansgate with £5 in my pocket and I swore I would never work for anyone else again.

Need for independence

Entrepreneurs have a high need for autonomy and independence. This is most often seen as the need to 'be your own boss' or an unwillingness to take orders. It has been said that, once you run your own firm, you cannot work for anybody else. This is the most often cited entrepreneurial character trait and supported by researchers and advisors alike. However, independence means different things to different people: doing things differently, being in a situation where you can fulfil your potential or controlling your own destiny.

Need for achievement

Entrepreneurs have a high need for achievement. However, people measure their achievement in different ways, depending on the type of person they are: for example, the satisfaction of producing a beautiful work of art, employing their hundredth person, or making the magic one million dollars. For many entrepreneurs, money is just a badge of success, validating their achievement. It is not an end in itself. What they are satisfying is their underlying need for achievement – a recognition of their success. And whilst they may have a 'need' for achievement, that does not necessarily mean that they are actually high achievers, only that this 'need' creates a drive within them.

Internal locus of control

Entrepreneurs have a strong 'internal locus of control' – a belief that they control their own destiny. They may believe in luck, but not fate. They believe that they can create their own destiny – their drive and determination (motivated by their high need for achievement) will lead them to achieve the outcome they want. This is underpinned by a high level of 'self-efficacy' – self-confidence in their ability to undertake a task.

So, entrepreneurs' internal locus of control and high levels of self-efficacy explain their high levels of drive and determination. However, in extremis, their strong internal locus of control can also manifest itself in a desire to control everything and everyone around them.

Because of this trait, entrepreneurs tend to be proactive rather than reactive, and more decisive. They act quickly and can be task-focused. However, this trait can have its down-side.

My **mother** gave me a **massive**
self-belief. I will always try things –
there is **nothing to lose**.

Richard Thompson, founder EMS
Quoted in Steiner, R. *My First Break:*
***How Entrepreneurs Get Started* (1999, Sunday Times Books)**

Chey Garland, founder Garlands Call Centres *Sunday Times* 27 June 2004

As a child I never felt that I was noticed. I never felt that I **achieved** anything or that there was any **expectation** of me achieving anything. So **proving** myself is something that is important to me, and so is establishing **respect** for what I have achieved.

Charles Muirhead, founder Orchestream *Sunday Times* 19 September 1999

Most of the **pleasure** is not the cash. It is the sense of **achievement** at having taken something from nothing to where it is **now**.

Part 1 You and your business idea

Elim Chew

Being an entrepreneur is like being a juvenile delinquent … The more you tell us we can't do it; the more we want to prove you wrong … If we were to listen to people who keep telling us not to do it, then 77th Street would never have happened. Because in the early days everyone was telling us we would fail … Today we have proved everybody wrong.

Elim Chew, founder 77th Street BBC News 20 December 2010

I think as entrepreneurs we are driven by ideas … When I have my free time, I like to go onto the internet and really explore the different things that people are doing; what are the different ideas popping all over the world.

Elim Chew, founder 77th Street
BBC News 20 December 2010

Often entrepreneurs can be easily diverted, for example by the most recent market opportunity. They also seem to do things at twice the pace of others, unwilling or unable to tolerate disagreement or wait for other people to complete tasks. They are often seen as controlling. They are restless and easily bored – patience is certainly not a virtue many possess. They seem to work 24 hours a day and their work becomes their life with little separating the two. It is little wonder that this can place family and personal relationships under strain. As a result, they can be difficult to work for and can be intolerant of those who do not share their enthusiasm. For example, the late Steve Jobs, founder of Apple, was notoriously difficult to work for and was well-known as a 'control freak' who was often accused of being rude and abusive and even bullying in order to get his own way. He believed he knew best and wanted things done his way – quickly.

Creativity, innovation and opportunism

The ability to be creative and innovative is an important attribute of entrepreneurs. But creativity can mean different things in different contexts. For entrepreneurs creativity is focused on commercial opportunities. They spot an opportunity and then use creativity and innovation to exploit it. They tend to do things differently. We shall explore measures of creativity later in this chapter, and show how creativity can be used to generate a good business idea in Chapter 3.

Acceptance of risk and uncertainty

Entrepreneurs are willing to take risks and live with uncertainty – things that can be very stressful for most people. They are willing to risk their money, reputation and personal standing if the business fails. However, that does not mean they are gamblers, and they will try to avoid or minimize the risks they face and insure against them. As we shall see later in this chapter, they have a distinctive approach to risk mitigation involving gaining knowledge and information from networks, partnerships and compartmentalization of risks. They have 'inside information' – real or imagined – that reduces the risk and uncertainty in their minds. They never really believe the business will fail and have complete faith that they will be able to affect the outcome – their high self-efficacy and 'internal locus of control'. They really do believe that they can succeed where others might have failed. The challenge is to ensure that the information on which this belief is based is real, verifiable and can be shared with others. The problem of different levels of knowledge is called 'information asymmetry' and is important when it comes to raising finance (see Chapter 14).

Gadget Shop *Sunday Times 17 March 2002*

You have to be **prepared** to lose everything and remember that the biggest risk is not taking any risk at all

Jonathan Elvidge, founder

Anne Notley, founder The Iron Bed Co. *Sunday Times 28 January 2001*

You have to have nerves of steel and be prepared to take risks. You have to be able to put it all on the line knowing you could lose everything.

Jonathan Elvidge

Cognitive development theory

Jean Piaget (1896–1980) is usually credited with the origination of cognitive development theory. He saw children's cognitive development as influenced both by biology and environmental experience. Children construct mental models (shortcuts or 'rules of thumb') of how the world around them operates, and these models change as they experience discrepancies between the real world and their mental models. Cognitive theory therefore shifts the emphasis from the individual towards the situations that lead to entrepreneurial behaviour. In particular, it seeks to understand how people think and react in different situations. It tries to understand the mental models (also called cognitive heuristics) that influence entrepreneurial behaviour and how they can be affected. Some strands of cognitive theory reinforce ideas about how traits may influence behaviour.

Chen et al. (1998) argue that it is self-efficacy that motivates entrepreneurs and gives them the dogged determination to persist in the face of adversity when others just give in. With this characteristic entrepreneurs become more objective and analytical but tend to attribute any failure to outside factors such as insufficient effort or poor knowledge. They argue that self-efficacy is affected by a person's previous experiences – success breeds success, failure breeds failure. And people can therefore be trained to change their beliefs.

Delmar (2000) outlines two other cognitive concepts. *Intrinsic motivation* suggests that people who undertake tasks for their own sake perform better than those motivated by external factors ('pull' factors compared to 'push' factors). This strong inner drive – type 'A' behaviour – amounts to almost compulsive behaviour. 'A' types tend to be goal-focused with high levels of drive, wanting to get the job done quickly. They also tend to try to proactively affect events (internal locus of control), focusing on the future when they are often not in control of the present. The second concept, *Intentionality*, suggests that people who intend to do things are more likely to do them than people who do not. This is the result of entrepreneurs' internal locus of control and is what underpins their drive and determination.

Chen, P.C., Greene, P.G. and Crick A. (1998) 'Does Entrepreneurial Efficacy Distinguish Entrepreneurs from Managers?', *Journal of Business Venturing*, 13.

Delmar, F. (2000) 'The Psychology of the Entrepreneur' in Carter, S. and Jones-Evans, D. (eds) *Enterprise and Small Business: Principles, Practice and Policy*, London: Prentice Hall.

Factors that influence the entrepreneurial character

The previous chapter showed how situational and psychological factors combined to push and/or pull us into self-employment, as well as create barriers. Situational factors also influence the development of our character traits that underpin these psychological factors. Cognitive development theory emphasizes the influence of our background on our character. The influences are many and varied. They are 'learned' through our experiences of life and our experiences are framed by the cultures and sub-cultures of the different groups that we operate within – such as nationality, family, religion, work background etc. (Figure 2.3). Culture is about the prevalent norms, basic values, beliefs and assumptions about behaviour that underpin that group. But it is not only cultures but also the situations and stages of our life that seem to influence our propensity to be entrepreneurial.

National culture

The most widely used dimensions of national culture are those developed by Hofstede (1981), who undertook an extensive cross-cultural study using questionnaire data from some 80,000 IBM employees in 66 countries across seven occupations. Although the survey was conducted some 40 years ago, it remains one of the most authoritative studies on national culture. From his research Hofstede established the four dimensions shown in Figure 2.4. This figure also shows the dominant culture he found in employees in particular countries, although this will probably have changed over the intervening period.

Individualism versus collectivism – This is the degree to which people prefer to act as individuals rather than groups. Individualistic cultures are loosely knit social frameworks in which people primarily operate as individuals. In these cultures the task prevails over personal relationships and the atmosphere is competitive. Collectivist cultures are composed of tight networks in which people operate as members of groups expecting to look after, and be looked after by, other members of their group. The atmosphere is cooperative.

Power distance – This is the degree of inequality among people that the community is willing to accept. Low power distance cultures endorse egalitarianism – relations are open and informal, information flows are functional and unrestricted and organizations tend to have flat structures. High power distance cultures endorse hierarchies – relations are more formal, information flows are formalized and restricted and organizations tend to be rigid and hierarchical.

Uncertainty avoidance – This is the degree to which people would like to avoid ambiguity and resolve uncertainty, and would prefer structured rather than unstructured situations. Low uncertainty avoidance cultures tolerate greater ambiguity, prefer flexibility, stress personal choice and decision-making, reward initiative, experimentation, risk-taking and team-play and stress the development of analytical skills. High uncertainty avoidance cultures prefer rules and procedures, stress compliance, punish error and reward compliance, loyalty and attention to detail.

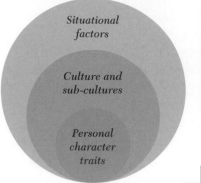

F2.3 Influences on our character traits

Situational factors

Culture and sub-cultures

Personal character traits

Nationality – National cultures do seem to vary widely, reflecting underlying core values. However, measuring them in any meaningful way is extremely difficult. The most widely used study of dimensions (see Academic Insight) shows that there are dominant, measurable cultures in particular countries. This is especially interesting because it allows us to describe the culture of what we might expect to be the most entrepreneurial country of all – the USA, an achievement-orientated society that values individualism and material wealth. We might assume that countries with similar cultures encourage entrepreneurship and those at opposite extremes of these dimensions probably inhibit entrepreneurship.

F2.4 Dimensions of national culture

LOW		HIGH
LOWER QUARTILE COUNTRIES		UPPER QUARTILE COUNTRIES
South America. Pakistan, Saudi Arabia	→ INDIVIDUALISM →	USA, UK, France, Germany, Canada, New Zealand
USA, UK, Germany, Scandinavia	→ POWER DISTANCE →	France, Malaysia, Philippines, Saudi Arabia, South America
USA, UK, Hong Kong, Singapore	→ UNCERTAINTY AVOIDANCE →	France, Greece, Portugal, Uruguay, Saudi Arabia
Northern Europe	→ MASCULINITY →	USA, UK, Germany, Austria, Italy, Japan

Academic insight

Masculinity versus femininity – This defines quality of life issues. Hofstede defined 'masculine' virtues as those of achievement, assertiveness, competitiveness and success. These cultures reward financial and material achievement with social prestige and status. 'Feminine' virtues include modesty, compromise and cooperation. These cultures value relationships, so issues such as quality of life, warmth in personal relationships, service and so on are important. In some societies having a high standard of living is thought to be a matter of birth, luck or destiny, rather than personal achievement (external locus of control).

At a later date Hofstede and Bond (1991) added a fifth dimension – short/long-term orientation. A short-term orientation focuses on past and present and therefore values respect for the status quo, including an unqualified respect for tradition and for social and status obligations. A long-term orientation focuses on the future and therefore the values associated with this are more dynamic. They include the adaptation of traditions to contemporary conditions and have only qualified respect for social and status obligations. Clearly an entrepreneurial culture is one with a long-term orientation.

Hofstede, G. (1981) *Cultures and Organizations: Software of the Mind*, London: HarperCollins.

Hofstede, G. and Bond, M.H. (1991) 'The Confucian Connection: From Cultural Roots to Economic Performance', *Organizational Dynamics*, Spring.

Education – One influence that comes through on many studies for both start-up and growth is educational attainment. Clearly there are problems measuring educational attainment consistently over studies. Nevertheless, particularly in the USA, many research studies show a positive association between the probability of starting up in business and high educational attainment. You might indeed question this, given that Bill Gates, Steve Jobs and Michael Dell all dropped out of university. However, similar research in other countries tends to support this result, albeit less strongly and not consistently.

Age and partnering – Although entrepreneurial activity is spread evenly over all age groups, research shows that middle-aged or very young entrepreneurs are most likely to be associated with growth companies. Youth brings creativity. Age brings experience and knowledge, and an invaluable network of relationships and contacts. Between the two, many people decide to bring up a family, with all the constraints that brings. Growth companies are also more likely to be set up by groups rather than by individuals, and these groups share in the ownership and therefore the success (or failure) of the business. Partnering with groups to set up a business can bring the same advantages as age, knowledge, experience and networks.

Imagesource

Immigration and ethnicity – Observation tells us that immigration to a foreign country is positively associated with entrepreneurship (a strong push factor) but evidence about ethnicity is mixed. Self-employment rates in the UK for ethnic minorities are not uniform. Those for Asians (Indian, Pakistani, Bangladeshi etc.) and Chinese are higher than those for white males, whilst those for black African and black Caribbean men are lower, typically more comparable to white women. With some 200,000 Asian-owned businesses in the UK, Asians are recognized as the most likely ethnic minority group in the UK to become entrepreneurs, and are represented across all sectors of business.

Gender – Although it is changing quickly, across most of the world women are less likely to start up businesses than men. In the UK, self-employment rates for women are almost half those of men and consistent research findings show women-owned businesses are likely to perform less well than male-owned businesses, however measured – turnover, profit or job creation.

Golden Krust (1)

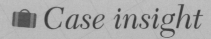 *Case insight*

Immigrant entrepreneurs

Lowell Hawthorne used to work with his family in his father's bakery in St Andrews, Jamaica. In 1981 he and many of his family emigrated to the USA where he joined the New York Police Department. Seven years later Lowell decided he wanted to start his own business, so he brought the family together and nine of them decided to start up what they knew most about – a bakery. However, the first problem was that they were unable to obtain any loan finance from the banks. Undaunted, the family pooled their resources (which involved family members having to re-mortgage their houses) to find $107,000 and Golden Krust was launched in 1989.

BBC News Business 20 June 2012

We have a 2020 **vision**: We want to make **Caribbean cuisine** mainstream by 2020.

Today Golden Krust is known for its Jamaican patties – flaky, yellow rectangles of dough filled with spicy meat or fish – and the sauces to go with them. But for the first three years of its existence, whilst the company produced a range of Jamaican bakery products, it bought in the patties from a West Indian restaurant chain. It was only when the supplier cut off supplies that Lowell was forced to find out about making patties himself – going to the UK to find out how to do it. Less than a year after the crisis, equipped with a baking method from Scotland, a chef named Mel and a new machine, sales exceeded $2 million for the first time. By 1996, as well as a bakery, the company had seven restaurants.

> 'As an immigrant, not understanding the system here made it more difficult … Had I lived there and understood how it worked I think we would have gone through it easier.'

Today Golden Krust remains a family business and has become the largest West Indian food chain in the USA. It still has its manufacturing base in New York, but it also operates as a franchisor and has a chain of more than 120 restaurants selling its patties in nine US states. Turnover exceeds $100 million. It now makes most of its money as a franchisor, which generates an up-front fee and a restaurant royalty of 5% on the turnover. The company also sells its patties wholesale to big distributors such as Wal-Mart and supplies New York's schools and prisons in an effort to expand the customer base beyond the West Indian communities.

More information on the company can be found on:
www.goldenkrustbakery.com

 USA

Measuring your personal character traits

The General Enterprise Tendency test (v2) is free and can be taken online at: www.get2test.net

The General Enterprise Tendency (GET) test (version 2) provides you with the opportunity to reflect on whether you have an entrepreneurial character. It is a 54-question instrument that measures your personal character traits in the five dimensions of entrepreneurial character highlighted previously. It provides an indicative, although not a definitive, measure of your enterprising potential. It can be taken online in only about 5 minutes. The results are automatically analyzed and a detailed report produced. The original test was developed by Sally Caird and Cliff Johnson at Durham University Business School in 1987–88 and has subsequently been updated and developed into an online resource by Sally Caird.

ImageSource

General Enterprise Tendency test

 Academic insight

Caird (1991a, b) established the construct validity and reliability of the GET test by testing it on entrepreneurs and comparing it to occupational groups including teachers, nurses, civil servants, clerical workers and lecturers and trainers. Overall, entrepreneurs were found to be significantly more enterprising than the other groups, but they were not the only group to score highly on *individual* measures.

Stormer et al. (1999) applied the test to 128 owners of new (75) and successful (53) small firms. They concluded that the test was acceptable for research purposes, particularly for identifying owner-managers, but it was poor at predicting business success. Either the test scales needed to be refined for this purpose or the test did not include sufficient indicators of success such as antecedent influences on the individual or other factors related to the business rather than the individual setting it up.

So, the GET scores need to be looked at overall rather than just individually in each of the five dimensions. Also, they do not predict business success – that involves too many other factors. However, the GET test does provide an indicative, although not a definitive, measure of your enterprising potential. As the website says, the test is best used 'as an educational aid to think about entrepreneurship'.

Caird, S. (1991a) 'Self Assessments on Enterprise Training Courses', *British Journal of Education And Work*, 4(3).

Caird, S. (1991b) 'Testing Enterprising Tendency in Occupational Groups', *British Journal of Management*, 2(4).

Stormer, R., Kline, T. and Goldberg, S. (1999) 'Measuring Entrepreneurship with the General Enterprise Tendency (GET) Test: Criterion-related Validity and Reliability', *Human Systems Management*, 18(1).

Measuring your creativity

The AULIVE creativity test is free and can be taken online:

www.testmycreativity.com

Creativity means different things to different people. And the GET test provides only a limited insight into your creative character. The AULIVE creativity test provides you with the opportunity to further reflect on this. It is a 40-question instrument that assesses you on eight dimensions against answers from others with similar backgrounds.

The dimensions are:

Abstraction – the ability to apply abstract concepts/ideas.

Connection – the ability to make connections between things that do not appear to be connected.

Perspective – the ability to shift one's perspective on a situation in terms of space, time and other people.

Curiosity – the desire to change or improve things that others see as normal.

Boldness – the confidence to push boundaries beyond accepted conventions. Also the ability to eliminate the fear of what others might think of you.

Paradox – the ability to simultaneously accept and work with statements that are contradictory.

Complexity – the ability to carry large quantities of information, and to manipulate and manage the relationships between such information.

Persistence – the ability to force oneself to keep trying to find more and stronger solutions even when good ones have already been generated.

How entrepreneurs manage

Studies on the personality traits of entrepreneurs have focused on their propensity to start and maintain a business successfully. Increasingly, however, the debate on entrepreneurship is moving to consider not only what the entrepreneur 'is' but what they actually 'do'. And successful entrepreneurs have a number of characteristic approaches to doing business and managing that have implications for you.

> *Jonathan Elvidge, founder Gadget Shop The Times 6 July 2002*
>
> Contacts are important but you have to get out there and meet people. It can be difficult when you are absorbed in running a business. But there is always something to learn from meeting someone new and a lot to learn from meeting someone old. The right contacts can become an invaluable source of learning as well as an inspiration and support.

Relationships

Entrepreneurs are good at developing relationships with customers, staff, suppliers and all the stakeholders in the business. This ability to form loyal relationships with customers has led to the development of techniques now called **relationship marketing**. They tend to manage their staff by developing strong personal relationships rather than relying on formal structures and hierarchies. Formality reduces flexibility, so they manage informally, setting an example by their behaviour. This ability to form strong personal relationships helps them develop the **partnerships** and **networks** that are part of the social capital they create. Relationships are based upon trust and respect and this takes time to build up. The implication of this is that, if you do not already have them, you need to develop strong **interpersonal skills**. We shall return to this in Chapter 14 as we explore entrepreneurial leadership.

Strategy development

Entrepreneurs develop strategy differently. They are often seen as being intuitive, almost whimsical, in their decision-making. Economists find it difficult to understand and to model their approach. It certainly does not fit well into 'logical' economic models such as discounted cash flow. The reason lies at the heart of any entrepreneurial venture – the greater degree of risk and uncertainty it faces. The result is a different approach to developing strategy and making decisions that is just as logical but little understood.

Successful entrepreneurs develop a **strong vision** of what they want their business to become (Chapter 6). Although they do not always know how they will achieve the vision because of the uncertain environment they face, they have strong **strategic intent**. This is accompanied by a loose or flexible strategy underpinned by continuous **strategizing** – assessing the options about how to make the most of opportunities or avoid risks as they arise. By creating more **strategic options** they improve their chances of successfully pursuing at least one opportunity and avoiding most risks. They keep as many options as possible open for as long as possible. The greater the number of strategic options, the safer they are in an uncertain environment. Make no mistake – entrepreneurs to a large extent create their own luck.

Decision-making

Entrepreneurs develop decision-making differently. In the same way as they develop strategy, entrepreneurs adopt an **incremental** approach to decision-making, despite their strong long-term vision. It is also part of their wide-ranging approach to risk mitigation. For example, successful entrepreneurs tend to keep capital investment and fixed costs as low as possible, often by sub-contracting some activities. They tend to commit to costs only after the opportunity has proved to be real, which

> *Lyn Lee, founder Awfully Chocolate BBC News Business 8 November 2010*
>
> I actually don't believe in luck...I don't know anyone who got anywhere without **hard work**.

Effectuation

Sarasvathy (2001) compared the approaches of entrepreneurs and managers to business decisions. She first undertook a study of 27 successful US entrepreneurs. The subjects all had at least 15 years of entrepreneurial experience, including successes and failures, and had taken at least one company public. They were presented with a case study about a hypothetical start-up with the founder facing 10 decisions. The rationale for these decisions was then explored in more detail. Some years later, the same research was conducted on a group of successful professional managers in large organizations, allowing contrasts to be made between entrepreneurs and managers.

The conclusion was that entrepreneurs relied upon something called 'effectual reasoning' or 'effectuation', which was quite in contrast to the causal or deductive reasoning used by the professional executives. Effectuation has gained popularity by contrasting itself with what might be called traditional principles of management. Sarasvathy came to five main conclusions about how successful entrepreneurs approach decision-making in their uncertain, rapidly changing environment.

1. Whilst the executives set goals and sought to achieve them sequentially and logically, the entrepreneurs' goals were broad and evolved on the basis of their personal strengths and resources, creatively reacting to contingencies as they occurred – reflecting the approach to strategy development outlined in this chapter. Entrepreneurs start with the resources they have and go to market quickly. They do not wait for perfect knowledge or the perfect opportunity. They learn by doing.

2. Whilst executives wanted to research opportunities and assess potential return before committing resources, entrepreneurs were far more inclined to go to market as quickly and cheaply as possible and assess market demand from that. This approach is labelled 'affordable loss' and reflects their attitude to learning and risk minimization, outlined earlier. Entrepreneurs set an 'affordable loss', evaluating opportunities based upon whether that loss was acceptable, rather than trying to evaluate the attractiveness of the predictable up-side. We explain this in more detail in Chapter 11.

may be prudent and reflect their resource limits, but then they run the risk of losing first-mover advantage in the market place – a difficult judgement call. Frequently, therefore, they will experiment with a **limited launch** into the market and learn from this. They also view an asset as a liability rather than financial capital in the balance-sheet sense, meaning that it may limit the flexibility that they need and commit them to a course of action that may prove unsound. Successful entrepreneurs find ways of reconciling these issues – ways of developing strategy without over-committing to one course of action and ways of minimizing their investment in resources. They start with the resources they can afford to lose and then move forward.

Risk mitigation

Whilst entrepreneurs are prepared to take measured risks, they always want to keep them to a minimum. Typically entrepreneurs adopt a number of approaches to mitigate risk. Primarily they do this through **knowledge and information**, often coming from the network of close personal relationships they have developed. They can also use this **network** to form **partnerships** that help them spread the risk of a venture, as well as leveraging the strategic skills of the partnership. They commit only **limited resources** – the resources they can afford to lose – to a new venture at any time and take an incremental approach to decision-making, assessing information and risks at each decision point. Finally, entrepreneurs are adept at **compartmentalizing risk**, for example by separating out business ventures into separate legal entities, so that the failure of one does not endanger the survival of the others. We shall return to risk mitigation in Chapter 11.

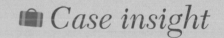

3. Entrepreneurs did not like extensive, formal research and planning, particularly traditional market research. This was explained in terms of them not believing that the future was predictable (and that the up-side could be evaluated), preferring instead to believe in their own ability to obtain the information needed to react quickly to changing circumstances. They believed that, whilst they could not predict the future, they could control it (internal locus of control), or more precisely, 'recognize, respond to, and reshape opportunities as they develop'. Entrepreneurs use uncertainty to their advantage by developing contingencies and remaining flexible rather than slavishly sticking to existing goals. However, it was significant that they did adopt more formal structures as their businesses grew and, as the study put it, they became 'causal as well as effectual thinkers'.

4. Also prominent was the entrepreneurs' propensity to partner with stakeholders – customers, suppliers and advisors – to help them shape the business, reflecting the importance of building relationships. They use networks of partnerships to generate knowledge, leverage resources and make the future become the reality. By way of contrast, the executives tended to know exactly where they wanted to go and then follow that set path without seeking partnerships.

5. It was noticeable also that the entrepreneurs were less concerned about competitors than the executives. This might be interpreted in terms of their inherent self-confidence, but the study explained it in terms of them seeing themselves as on the fringe of a market or creating an entirely new market through some sort of disruptive innovation. They believed they were different or better than competitors in a way that gave them a differential advantage.

Sarasvathy, S.D. (2001) 'Causation and Effectuation: Toward a Theoretical Shift from Economic Inevitability to Entrepreneurial Contingency', *Academy of Management Review*, 26(2).

Steve Jobs and Apple (1)

Entrepreneurial character

Steve Jobs died on 5 October 2011, aged 56, of pancreatic cancer. He was the epitome of an entrepreneurial leader who revolutionized three industries – computing, music sales and cinema animations. With Steve Wozniak, he co-founded Apple in 1976. Apple revolutionized the computer industry through its innovative designs: the Macintosh with its computer mouse, the iPod with its click wheel and the iPhone with its 'user-interface'. Apple also revolutionized how digital content, in particular music, could be sold rather than pirated. Through Jobs' animation studio, Pixar, films such as *Toy Story* (1995) completely changed our ideas about the use of computer-generated animations. And yet Steve Jobs was not an inventor. He was the bridge between the business idea and the market place – the entrepreneur. Not only did he start up Apple, he was also forced out of it in 1985 after an acrimonious boardroom battle. He returned in 1997 to turn it

around from near bankruptcy and, by 2011, had created the second most valuable company in the world, measured by market capitalization, with a cash mountain of some $80 billion.

The story of Steve Jobs is the story of a Silicon Valley hero. Born to a Syrian father and an American mother in San Francisco, he was the adopted child of a blue-collar couple and grew up in Mountain View, a suburb of San Francisco close to what is now known as Silicon Valley. The fact that he was put up for adoption by his birth parents was said to have left a deep scar. Whilst at high school, he met Steve Wozniak who was working on a summer job with Hewlett-Packard in Palo Alto. After high school Jobs reluctantly went to Reed, a liberal arts college in Portland, Oregon, but failed to attend his required classes and dropped out after one term. He grew his hair and did the sort of things that drop-outs at the time did, including visiting a guru in India. His engagement with Zen Buddhism, with a focus on stark, minimalist aesthetics and a belief in intuition, was to become ingrained in his personality. However, he never achieved the inner peace associated with Zen Buddhism, rather he was always driven by the particular challenges facing him at the time.

It was Steve Wozniak who had the talent for electronics and designing circuits with the minimum number of chips, and built the first Apple computer. At the time Wozniak was working for Hewlett-Packard and Jobs for Atari. Apple I was a hobbyist machine assembled by hand in Steve Jobs' parents' home and housed in a wooden box. The pair sold many of their personal possessions to get the start-up finance that was needed. Jobs' role was that of the businessman, the marketer who persuaded the local store to order 50, and then persuaded the local electrical store to give him 30 days' credit on the parts to build the computers. He also eventually persuaded Mike Markkula, a former Intel employee, to invest in the company and become its first chief executive. What followed was the beautifully designed, classic Apple II with its built-in colour graphics, easily accessible expansion slots and ability to connect to a TV set. Its simple design, understandable instruction manual and consumer-friendly advertising guaranteed it success until the launch of the IBM PC. Apple went public in 1980 with a market valuation of $1.8 billion only four years after being launched.

Steve Wozniak retired from Apple one year later following a serious plane accident. Jobs took over the development of the Apple II's successor, the Apple Macintosh. The Mac was intended to be the first mass-market, closed-box computer based on the now ubiquitous mouse and a graphic user interface. These ideas were not new. They were developed by scientists at Xerox Palo Alto Research Centre (PARC) and had been tried out in high-priced computers (Xerox Star and Apple Lisa), without commercial success. The launch of the Mac was the start of what became the signature Steve Jobs product launch. He appeared on stage with Bill Gates promising Mac versions of Word, Excel and PowerPoint. There were 20 full-page advertisements in major US magazines. But it was the TV commercial that had the biggest impact. Shown in the USA during the 1984 Super Bowl, it associated IBM with George Orwell's *1984* Big Brother. Despite the dramatic launch, the Mac failed to sell in the expected volumes, signalling the start of Apple's decline. In 1985 it closed three of its six factories, laying off 1200 employees. In the same year Steve Jobs was forced to leave Apple and by 1987 the Mac II was launched as a conventional three-piece computer system.

Jobs resented being thrown out of Apple, particularly by someone he had recruited two years earlier to the job of Chief Executive Officer – John Sculley, formerly president of PepsiCo. He took several Apple employees with him and set up another company (NeXT) to produce a powerful Unix workstation targeted at business and universities. It was very expensive and flopped, so the company switched to selling the operating systems, again without much success.

Steve Jobs bought the company that became Pixar in 1986 from Lucasfilm. Initially, the company produced expensive computer hardware. The core product was the Pixar Image Computer, a system primarily sold to government agencies and the medical market, but this was never particularly popular. The company struggled for years and, in an effort to demonstrate its capabilities, Pixar began producing computer-animated commercials. In 1991 this led to a deal with the Walt Disney Corporation to produce three computer animated films, the first of which was the ground-breaking *Toy Story*. Until this point Pixar had been in decline, having already sold off its hardware operations. Released in 1995, *Toy Story* was an outstanding box-office success, which was just as well because, as late as 1994, Jobs had considered selling off Pixar. After a series of highly successful, award-winning films such as *A Bug's Life* (1998), *Toy Story 2* (1999), *Monsters Inc.* (2001), *Finding Nemo* (2003) and *The Incredibles* (2004), the Walt Disney Company eventually bought Pixar in 2006 at a valuation of $7.4 billion, making Jobs the largest shareholder in Disney.

Meanwhile the PC market was again transformed in 1995 by the launch of Microsoft Windows 95 which really popularized the mouse and the graphic user interface. Apple was struggling to survive and the new Mac OS software development was not working. It was managed by committees and had lost its innovative flair. Apple knew it needed to buy in a new operating system, and fast, so it turned to Steve Jobs and paid a much inflated price for NeXT. In reality, this turned out to be a reverse take-over and Jobs took over as 'interim CEO' in 1997.

Jobs killed off weak products and simplified the product lines. He adapted NeXT's NextStep operating system to become the Mac OS X operating system. He also started the process of creating the distinctive eye-catching Apple designs with the teardrop shaped iMac, followed by the portable iBook. Explaining himself to the 1997 meeting of the Apple Worldwide Developers Association, Jobs said:

> Focusing is about saying **no** … and the result of that focus is going to be some really **great products** where the total is **much greater** than the sum of the parts … One of the things I've always found is that you've got to start with the **customer experience** and work backwards to the **technology** and try to figure out **where** you are going to try to **sell it**. I've made this mistake probably more than anyone else in this room, and I've got the scar tissue to prove it, and I know that it's the case.

But Apple's fortunes were really transformed when Jobs completely changed directions and launched the iPod in 2001 and the iTunes music store in 2003. This transformed the music industry, which was facing a decline in CD sales as more and more music was being pirated through online sites such as Napster, by allowing music to be easily downloaded, but at a price. Apple started on its growth path, which was reinforced in 2007 by the launch of the iPhone – a clever but expensive combination of cell phone, iPod and internet device. This was followed in 2010 by the iPad – a tablet computer without a physical keyboard. By 2011 Apple was selling more iPads than Macintosh.

Jobs was, of course, in the right place at the right time to capitalize on developments in computing and the change from analogue to digital technologies. But he shaped these developments to appeal to customers. The distinctive feature about Apple products was never the innovation – that normally came from elsewhere – but rather the application of an innovation to make the product easier and simpler to use, whether it be the physical product design or applications such as iTunes. All Apple products also enjoy a distinctive, eye-catching design. And they are never cheap. They were also supported by massive marketing campaigns with Jobs, dressed in black turtle neck, jeans and trainers, launching products himself with carefully choreographed, pseudo-religious stage presentations (known as 'Stevenote') that attracted adoring fans and received massive worldwide press coverage. In many people's eyes Jobs enjoyed the status of a rock star. At the same time the Apple brand had become iconic.

We'll look at Jobs' leadership style in more detail in Chapter 13.

Questions:
1. *What entrepreneurial qualities or characteristics did Jobs exhibit?*
2. *Why was he so successful? How much of this success was just good luck?*

Summary

- You need to define your personal drivers and constraints. These will influence what you want your business to become.

- You bring financial, human and social capital to your start-up. Financial capital for a start-up can be minimized through partnering with others and 'bootstrapping'. Human capital is derived from your education, training and previous managerial or industry experience. Social capital is derived from your social skills and access to appropriate professional networks. The more capital you bring to the business – of any kind – the more likely you are to succeed.

- The entrepreneurial character has five traits: a high need for achievement and autonomy together with an internal locus of control, high levels of creativity and a willingness to take measured risks. These traits are influenced by our background and upbringing, underpinned by the cultures of the different groups and societies we associate with.

- The quality of creativity can be measured in eight dimensions: abstraction, connection, perspective, curiosity, boldness, paradox, complexity and persistence.

- Entrepreneurs have a distinctive way of managing people through relationships rather than hierarchy. They develop relationships with customers and suppliers that enable them to build professional networks which, in turn, allow them to partner with other people to gain knowledge and information that helps them mitigate risk. They have a strong vision and strategic intent. They cope with their uncertain environment by strategizing continuously and generating strategic options. Because they operate in an uncertain environment their decision-making is incremental, with limited resources (affordable loss) being committed at any one time.

Exercise 2.1

Personal drivers

You need to decide whether being an entrepreneur suits you. What is more, do you want to start up a salary-substitute, lifestyle or entrepreneurial business that will grow rapidly? Or do you want a start-up that delivers social or civic objectives? It is important that your business fits in with what you want from your life and lifestyle. You need to have a balance between work and personal life that suits you.

1 List the things that you enjoy doing, and the things that you do not enjoy doing (e.g. hobbies and pastimes, figure-work, selling, meeting people, etc.).

2 List the things that motivate and drive you, and those that do not (e.g. family, money, social causes, green issues etc.).

3 List the things that you would want to avoid in a business at all costs (e.g. travel, too little free time, etc.).

4 Bearing these answers in mind, list the implications for your venture and for yourself and your lifestyle. Decide what sort of business you want to start up.

Exercise 2.2

Business purpose

You need to be clear about why you want to start up a business and what you want from it. Do you want a comfortable lifestyle or do you want to build a sizeable business that creates value? Do you want to work with your family or keep family life separate? Are you willing to commit time and resources to a growing business? Will you want to sell it on, and if so within what time scale, or would you want to grow it during your working life with the option then of selling or passing it on to other members of the family? These sorts of questions underpin the purpose of the business.

1 Write down what you want this business start-up to achieve for you.

Example:

To provide an adequate income for my wife and me whilst living above the shop

Now you are clear about the purpose of the business, you need to consider what targets or objectives you might want to set yourself to achieve this. Your objectives should be quantifiable (and therefore measurable), bounded in time and realistic. We shall return to this when your business idea has been evaluated.

2 Write down your business objectives for three years' time in ideal circumstances.

Example:

Sales of £1 million by the third year . . . and . . . profits before tax & my salary of £200,000

Exercise 2.3

Personal assets and liabilities

You need to know what resources you bring to a start-up. You also need to know the minimum amount of income you (and your family) need to live on, at least in the short term, and the maximum loss you are willing to accept if the start-up fails.

1 Write down the financial capital you could invest in the business. Are you willing to lose all this if the start-up fails?

2 List the elements of human capital you will be investing in the business.

3 List the elements of social capital you will be investing in the business. Make a list of your network of contacts and how they might be able to help.

4 List regular outgoings and the minimum expenditure that you (and your family) need to survive, at least in the short term. Total this up and add 10%. This is the minimum amount that you will need to take from the business.

5 Write down the maximum loss you are willing to accept if the start-up fails. Distinguish between the amount you are actually willing to invest (from Exercise 2.3.1) and how much might be lost in other ways, for example by providing personal guarantees.

Exercise 2.4

Entrepreneurial character

Do you have entrepreneurial character traits? You need to find out and decide whether entrepreneurship really is something that you will enjoy, or at least be comfortable with. Some traits are more difficult to manage around (e.g. risk-taking) than others (e.g. creativity – see below).

1 Take the General Enterprise Tendency (GET) test.

2 Review the results and reflect on whether you agree with the results by finding examples from your life that support or disprove them.

3 Decide on the implications of this result and list the things that you want to do as a result of this analysis.

Exercise 2.5

Creativity potential

Creativity is a key entrepreneurial skill but it is one that training can enhance and one that a business partner can supplement.

1 Take the AULIVE test.

2 Review the results and reflect on whether you agree with the results by finding examples from your life that support or disprove them.

3 Decide on the implications of this result and list the things that you want to do in the light of this analysis.

Exercise 2.6

Entrepreneurial management

We shall return to the characteristics of entrepreneurial management at various points later in this book, but you need to audit how you approach each of these four areas – relationships, strategy development, decision-making, risk mitigation – and the implications for you.

1 List your personal strengths and weaknesses.

2 Reflect on how you deal with other people. Do you consider that you have strong interpersonal skills? Are you good at forming relationships? Rather than just relying on your own opinion, check what other people think. Reflect on the implications of this compared to entrepreneurs and list the things that you want to change as a result.

3 Reflect on what motivates you and how you set yourself goals. Do you have a strong vision for what you (not the business) want to achieve? Check this is consistent with your answers to earlier exercises. Do you naturally strategize and develop options for your personal life? If you do this naturally for yourself you can do it for the business. Reflect on the implications of this compared to entrepreneurs and list the things that you want to change as a result.

4 Reflect on how you make decisions when faced with uncertain situations. How will this affect your decision on whether or not to become an entrepreneur? Reflect on the implications of this compared to entrepreneurs and list the things that you want to change as a result.

5 List the major risks of self-employment for you. Reflect on how an entrepreneur would mitigate them and list the things you might therefore want to do. Do they affect your answers to earlier exercises?

Visit www.palgrave.com/companion/burns-new-venture-creation for chapter quizzes to test your knowledge and other resources.

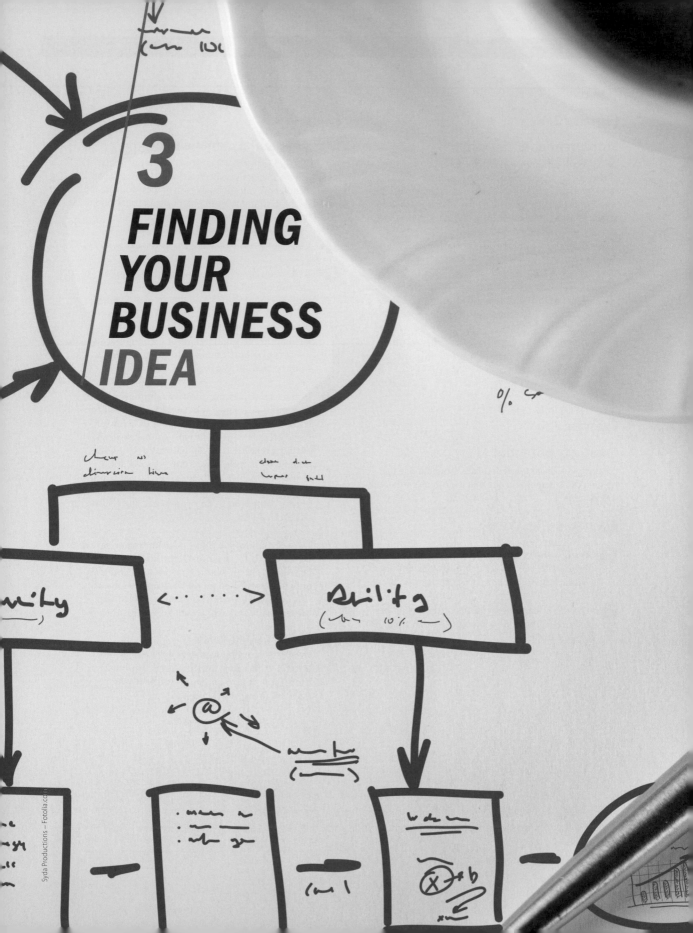

Contents

Learning outcomes

When you have read this chapter and undertaken the related exercises you will be able to:
- Develop your discovery skills
- Scan the environment for business opportunities
- Come up with a business idea by either creating or spotting opportunity
- Understand what characterizes a good business idea
- Critically evaluate whether the idea matches your aspirations

New venture typologies

There are six generalized types of new venture, shown in Figure 3.1. Each has implications for how you go about finding a business idea and each requires a very different business model, which influences the complexity of your business plan.

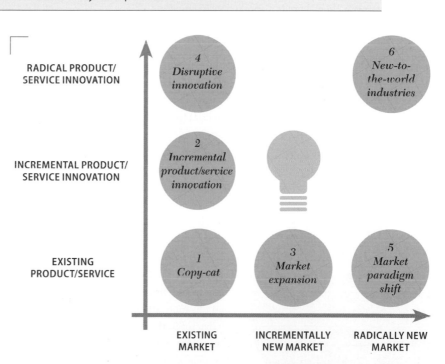

F3.1 New venture typologies

1. **Copy-cat** – You can introduce the same product or service into an existing market. Of course there is always room for competition in free markets but, unless you are significantly better than the competition in some way, you will probably be left to compete on price. This can be problematic if your competitors are large, well-established and able to capitalize on economies of scale since low price implies low costs. You may therefore struggle. Most copy-cat start-ups do compete primarily on price and therefore have low profitability and rarely grow. They are salary-substitute firms and comprise the majority of small, owner-managed firms. However, each new venture must be considered on its own merits. For example, a convenience/grocery store would be entering a highly competitive environment where large supermarkets have enormous economies of scale and will be able to compete more effectively on price. However, if this is the only store on a new estate, with the nearest supermarket 10 miles away, then there is a good chance of making a healthy profit … that is until another copy-cat store starts up because there are no barriers to entry in this market.

2. **Incremental product/service innovation** – If you want your new venture to avoid competing primarily on price, the thing to do is to try to spot gaps in the market, perhaps by altering the elements of the product/service in some significant way that adds value to customers. This avoids competing head-on with established businesses and should allow you to charge a higher price, at least until competitors appear. If you are able to safeguard your intellectual property on this innovation (Chapter 9) then you might sustain this strategy for longer. If you are able to create a market niche for your product/service, this could give you a sustainable competitive advantage and be very profitable – creating an entrepreneurial firm. Alternatively, it might allow you to establish a lifestyle business that lets you do the things you enjoy whilst generating an adequate income. The danger here is that you are, by definition, competing against established suppliers, with recognized brands and distribution channels. Competition will be fierce and they may be able to copy your incremental innovation.

3. **Market development** – Another option is to find new customers not currently served by existing suppliers, for example in different geographical markets (both national and international). This offers considerable opportunities for new ventures because new products or services that originate in more developed markets find their way into developing markets at a later date. Timing and local knowledge can be crucial when new products or services are introduced into any market. However, the danger here is always that the established supplier in the original market eventually moves into this new market and has sufficient resources and market presence to out-compete you. The challenge is therefore to move with sufficient speed that you dominate this new market before established suppliers try to enter it.

4. **Disruptive innovation or invention** – Introducing radically new products/services into existing markets will certainly confound the competition particularly if your innovation can be safeguarded, but it is not something that all of us are able to do. It is often linked to technological developments. Whilst most companies are continually making improvements and incremental innovations to their products and services, invention can be risky and takes both time and money. Unlike James Dyson and his now ubiquitous cyclone vacuum cleaner, many inventors fail to make their invention commercially viable. For example, Thomas Edison, probably the most successful inventor of all time, was so incompetent at introducing his

True **innovation** is rarely about creating something new. It's pretty hard to recreate the wheel or discover gravity; innovation is more often about seeing new opportunities for old designs.

Neil Kelly, founder PAV Sunday Times 9 December 2001

inventions to the market place that his backers had to remove him from every new business he founded. However, entrepreneurs are often able to make the connection between invention and market opportunity. As we saw in the Case Insight in Chapter 2, Steve Jobs never invented anything but he revolutionized three industries – personal computers, music and film animations – because he was able to find commercial applications for innovations.

5. **Marker paradigm shift** – This is when you create radically new markets by challenging the paradigms or conventions upon which an industry bases its whole marketing strategy. So, for example, the development of the low-cost airlines industry involved no inventions or innovations, only different ways of doing things that involved minimizing the costs, and therefore the price, of air travel. In doing this, companies such as Southwest Airlines in the USA and easyJet and Ryanair in the EU created whole new markets for air travel that never existed before. Tony Fernandes copied this business model very successfully in different markets with AirAsia (market development).

6. **New-to-the-world industries** – And just sometimes, radical new inventions create radically new markets. Tim Berners-Lee invented the world wide web in 1990, which in turn created new internet-based markets for information and changed the way we shop for many products and services. Like many inventors before him, the web did not make a fortune for Tim Berners-Lee. Others, like the founders of numerous 'dot.com' firms, such as Larry Page and Sergey Brin of Google or Jeff Bezos of Amazon, created businesses and made their fortune out of his invention. Again, it was the entrepreneur who saw the commercial application for the invention. New-to-the world industries have been created for centuries – water power, textiles and iron in the eighteenth century, steam, steel and rail in the nineteenth century and electricity, chemicals and the internal combustion engine in the early twentieth century. These innovations

are disruptive and difficult to predict, but cause enormous economic booms that eventually peter out as the technologies mature and the market opportunities are fully exploited.

The further you move away from being a copy-cat start-up (in either a vertical or horizontal direction) the higher the investment you are likely to need, but also the higher the profit you are likely to make. Whilst copy-cat start-ups can be very risky because of the strong competition, the greater the product/service or market innovation the greater the risks you are also likely to face. The 'dot.com' boom was rapidly followed by a 'dot.com' bust at the end of the twentieth century when many of the innovations were found not to have a viable market. Ideas that involve disruptive innovation or market paradigm shift are difficult to find and to launch as a business. We deal with them in greater detail below and throughout the book.

The 'eureka moment'

The 'eureka moment', when a business idea is born, rarely happens by chance. It has to be worked on and can be encouraged, particularly when you actively use the discovery skills we outline later in this chapter. Successful entrepreneurs are able to match opportunities in the market place with innovative ways of meeting those opportunities. They link opportunity with creativity and innovation. Successful entrepreneurial firms such as

Brian Jackson – Fotolia.com

Google or Samsung also go about seeking out ways of developing innovations that match commercial opportunities in a systematic way. Their success is not just down to good luck.

Generating good ideas is a numbers game: the more ideas you generate, the more are likely to see the light of day. Even at the development stage, it has been estimated that for every eleven ideas starting out on the process only one new product will be launched successfully, and perfecting that idea can take time. The idea is unlikely to be exactly right straight away, so you need to be willing to modify it before and after launch. This applies as much to the business model as to the product/service itself. This means that options need to be generated and considered at each stage of development and even after launch.

Often the only sure way of knowing whether the idea will make a lucrative business is to try it out – launch the business but minimize your risks in doing so. The more the business idea is original and different and without established competitors, the more a trial launch might be a good idea because there is incomplete information on the idea (see Academic Insight on Lean start-up (p. 66)). Market research is unlikely to yield an insight into the demand for a completely new product or service because customers do not understand how it might be used. Steve Jobs was famously disdainful of market research, in particular focus groups, preferring to rely on his own insight about what the market wanted. Just as famously, Henry Ford once said that if he had asked people what they wanted, they'd have said 'faster horses', rather than 'new-fangled' things called cars.

So how do you go about searching for these business opportunities? If you are looking for radical product/service innovation or to create radically new markets, you must **create** your opportunity, as it is unlikely that there is evidence of market need. If you are looking for incremental product/service innovation or to enter incrementally different markets, then you probably can **spot** an opportunity that meets an unfilled current or future market need. Spotting opportunity is easier than creating opportunity and can be just as profitable.

Creating opportunity

Creating a business opportunity that has not existed before involves radical product or market innovation and can lead to the development of new-to-the-world industries. It is more difficult and riskier than spotting an opportunity because there is no guarantee that the market need will finally materialize. It requires vision and self-belief aplenty, and is likely to take time and resources. It requires a high degree of creativity and innovation. However, the returns for success are likely to be high.

Bizarre start-up ideas from the USA

Bizarre ideas

Some business ideas do come from serendipity and their success would confound most of us. Here is a selection of some of its weirdest real business start-ups from the USA. It all goes to show that you can make money out of most things.

- **HappyBalls.com** of Cumming, Georgia, makes foam balls with colourful faces to be placed on top of car aerials. Do not mock – this is a million-dollar company.

 USA

📁 *Case insight*

- **Afterlife Telegrams** of New Athens, Illinois, offers to contact the dead. For a fee, they arrange for terminally ill patients to memorise a message that can be relayed to loved ones who have died when they themselves pass on.
- **eNthem** of San Francisco writes full length corporate theme songs.
- **Lucky Break Wishbone** of Seattle sells plastic wishbones so that all the family can have one despite the fact there is only really one in a chicken or turkey.

Disruptive innovation/invention – This is a step change in products, processes or the framing of markets. Generated by major inventions, they can have large-scale disruptive effects on markets, industries and even economies. For example, although Henry Ford did not invent the car, he did revolutionize the way cars were produced and sold, moving from craft-based to production-line methods and from wealthy customers to supplying an affordable car for everyman assembled on a production line. He created a new commercial market. This involved extensive incremental changes – to products and processes, component and factory design and in the way labour was organized in his factories. This disruptive innovation created the mass market for cars that we know today. But where did Ford get his vision of the future from? How was he able to break away from the established thinking of how a car should be made and who it should be sold to? When disruptive innovation creates radically new markets, fortunes can be made (and lost) quickly. This form of innovation can be highly profitable but very risky. It requires a leap in creative imagination, from mere possibility to commercial reality, that can be difficult for many people. And to stand any chance of seeing the light of day most inventors need to partner with an entrepreneur.

Patrick o Leary – Fotolia.com

If you are developing a completely new product or service, your business plan will need to explain what stage the development is at, and what further development is needed to take it to market. Basic ideas are unlikely to find funding. Even when there is a prototype, finding finance might prove difficult. The earlier the development stage, the more difficult this will prove. There is no guarantee the product will work and there is no guarantee that there will be customers for it. Even if it works, will you be able to stop competitors copying it? We outline the ways you can safeguard your intellectual property in Chapter 9.

Nicholas Valery (1999) 'Innovation in Industry', *Economist*, 5(28).

Innovation has more to do with the **pragmatic search** for **opportunity** than with romantic ideas about serendipity, or lonely pioneers pursuing their vision against all the odds.

- **SomethingStore** of Huntington, New York, will, for a payment of $10, send you something, anything – but no telling what.
- **WeightNags** of Austin sends mildly abusive weekly messages to dieters to encourage them to keep dieting.
- **Yelo** of New York City offers New Yorkers 20- or 40-minute naps in 'sleep pods'.
- **Throx** of San Francisco sells socks in packs of three – think about it.
- **Gaming-Lessons** of Jupiter, Florida offers video game lessons and coaching.

- **barefootlist.com** of Salt Lake City allows members to make up a list of things they want to do before they die, compare it to others' and track their progress.
- **Cuddle Party** of New York City offers 'structured, safe workshops on boundaries, communication, intimacy and affection … A laboratory where you can experiment with what makes you feel safe and feel good.'
- **Neuticles** of Oak Grove, Missouri, offers testicular implants for dogs that have been neutered.

Summly

Nick D'Aloisio

📄 Case insight

Creating opportunity

Born in London to well-off parents but brought up in Australia for his first seven years, Nick D'Aloisio became adept at using the computer at an early age. It was his hobby. He used it to make animations and films and even apps. Aged 15, he created an algorithm that formed the basis for an app called Trimit that summarized long articles down to tweet-lengths.

> I was using Twitter a lot on my phone, and was realizing there was a massive gap between the link on the tweet and the full story. If you could come up with a summary layer to show in Twitter, that would be awesome.

Trimit enjoyed mixed commercial success but attracted good reviews, wide publicity and thousands of downloads. It was this that attracted the attention of Horizon Ventures, a venture company led by Li Ka-shing, a Hong Kong billionaire and Asia's richest man. Horizon Ventures decided to invest $300,000 in the venture. This allowed D'Aloisio to recruit a small team in London to develop a completely redesigned version of the app, which was launched as Summly beta in December 2011.

Summly summarizes news articles for mobile phone users. If they are sufficiently interested, they can then read the full article on the original website. The idea is that the app generates traffic for these websites from users of mobile phones and creates a market for this content with a wider, younger demographic.

> There is a generation of skimmers. It's not that they don't want to read in-depth content, but they want to evaluate what the content is before they commit time. Especially on a mobile phone – you don't have the phone, or cellular data, or screen size to be reading full-length content.

The Guardian 9 March 2013

In 2012, D'Aloisio secured funding of £1 million to further develop the app. Working with partners such as Stanford Research Institute, D'Aloisio also managed to obtain the help and support of a network of technology experts and celebrities such as Ashton Kutcher, Wendi Deng, Mark Pincus, Brian Chesky, Stephen Fry and Yoko Ono. The full Summly app was launched in November 2012. It reached number nine in the free iPhone app chart in the same month and within one year attracted more than one million downloads and more than 250 publishers, including News Corp.

In 2013, still aged only 17, D'Aloisio sold Summly to Yahoo, reportedly for $30 million (£19 million). Yahoo intends to integrate the app into its own mobile services and therefore withdrew it from the App Store. They plan to apply the summarization algorithm to a wider range of web services, and Nick and his team have joined Yahoo to help with this development.

Market paradigm shift – Just like disruptive innovation, this happens when entrepreneurs challenge the conventional ways of marketing a product/service. In most sectors there are factors that managers believe are critical to the success of their business. These paradigms become part of the **dominant logic** of an industry. But circumstances and the environment can change and the managers running the industry may not adapt their way of thinking. To see an opportunity for market paradigm shift you need to be constantly questioning the status quo. You need to ask the question '*why* are things done this way?' followed by the question '*why not* do them a different way?' This willingness to continually question the status quo is one of the five fundamental 'discovery skills'

> We learned the importance of ignoring conventional wisdom … It's fun to do things that people don't think are possible or likely. It's also exciting to achieve the unexpected.

Michael Dell *Direct from Dell: Strategies that Revolutionized an Industry* (1999, New York: Harper Business)

exhibited by successful entrepreneurs that we shall discuss later in this chapter. Sometimes doing things differently can add value for the customer without involving extra costs – indeed sometimes doing things differently can reduce costs – whilst still giving you the opportunity to charge a high price. You can approach the task of challenging market paradigms by systematically looking at sectoral, customer and performance conventions and continually asking the questions 'why?' and 'why not?' (see Academic Insight).

To find disruptive innovation or ways of changing market paradigms you need to be able to think creatively 'outside the box'. You need to be able to generate new ideas and knowledge, a vision of the future that links market opportunities to your key capabilities. You need to be able to challenge conventions and be open to new ideas. You need to be able to deal with rapidly changing and disparate information in a wide range of new technologies and in diverse, fragmented and often geographically widespread markets. You need to be able to chart a way through often uncertain political and unstable regulatory environments. And in these circumstances knowledge and information are powerful sources of opportunity and innovation. But remember, creating opportunity can be risky because there is no guarantee that the market will agree with your vision of the future.

How to challenge market conventions

Based on a sample of 108 companies, Kim and Mauborgne (2005) estimated that, whereas only 14% of innovations created new markets, these innovations delivered 38% of new revenues and 61% of increased profits. So how might you go about creating completely new markets? Ian Chaston (2000) argues that you have to systematically challenge established market conventions and develop new solutions. Kim and Mauborgne call this 'blue ocean strategy'. Companies creating blue ocean strategies never benchmark against competitors, instead they make this irrelevant by 'creating a leap in value for both the buyers and the company itself'. Chaston's approach is simple: understand how conventional competitors operate and then challenge their approach by asking whether a different one would add customer value or create new customers – our 'why?' and 'why not?' questions. There are many conventions that can be challenged. Chaston suggests three categories:

1. **Sectoral conventions**: These are the strategic rules that guide the marketing operations of the majority of firms in a sector, such as efficiency of plants, economies of scale, methods of distribution and so on. Kim and Mauborgne talk about re-orientating analysis from *competitors* to *alternatives*. So, for example, in the UK insurance used to be sold through high street insurance brokers until Direct Line challenged the conventional wisdom and began to sell direct over the telephone, then on the internet. Now this is the norm.

2. **Performance conventions**: These are set by other firms in the sector and include profit, cost of production, quality and so on. Kim and Mauborgne argue that both value enhancement and cost reduction can be achieved by redefining industry problems and looking outside industry boundaries, rather than simply trying to offer better solutions to existing problems as defined by the industry. In the 1960s, Japanese firms ignored Western performance conventions en masse and managed to enter and succeed in these markets.

3. **Customer conventions**: These conventions make certain assumptions about what customers want from their purchases, for example price, size, design and so on. Kim and Mauborgne talk about re-orientating analysis from *customers* to *noncustomers*. The Body Shop redefined the cosmetic industry's 'feel-good factor' to include environmental issues. Companies like Southwest Airlines, Ryanair and easyJet pioneered low-price air travel and redefined the airline industry.

Chaston, I. (2000) *Entrepreneurial Marketing: Competing by Challenging Convention*, Basingstoke: Palgrave – now Palgrave Macmillan.

Kim, W.C. and Mauborgne, R. (2005) 'Blue Ocean Strategy: From Theory to Practice', *California Management Review*, Spring, 47(3).

Academic insight

Streetcar (now Zipcar)

Market paradigm change

Andrew Valentine studied modern languages and anthropology at Durham University. Whilst there, he and a friend set up a student radio station, Purple FM. After graduating he joined the shipping company P&O and worked for them for six years, doing a part-time MBA. But in 2002 Andrew got itchy feet and, together with a friend, Brett Akker, decided he wanted to set up his own business rather than work for other people. The problem was that he did not have a business idea. So he and his partner set about searching systematically for the right business. They spent 18 months researching many ideas from organic food to training courses, meeting twice a week, before coming up with the final idea.

We looked at hundreds of ideas. We were basically trying to identify gaps, so we were looking at how society was changing and what was missing. Our business had to have potential, be capable of being scaled up and play to our strengths. We kept looking until we found something that matched our criteria.

The final idea came from something Andrew read about in the USA – a car sharing club, but one with a commercial orientation. It piggybacked on environmental concerns about pollution and the problems city-dwellers face in driving and parking in their cities. The idea is that members of the car sharing club can rent a car for as little as half an hour, replacing the need to buy. There is a one-off membership fee with an annual renewal charge and members then rent the cars by the hour. Cars are parked in un-manned, convenient locations just off residential streets and are ready to be driven away using a smartcard to open the door and start – thereby eliminating the need to go to an office to collect and return keys. Members can make car reservations online or by phone at any time and cars are available 24 hours a day. The cars are kept clean, serviced and fuelled – ready to go.

'I read about a similar business overseas and immediately thought, what an amazing idea. There were a couple of other companies already running this kind of service in Britain but they weren't doing it the way we imagined we would be able to do it. We thought we could be more effective.'

Once they had the idea, Andrew and Brett spent four months holding market research focus groups to test out the business model and developing financial projections to estimate the resources they would need.

Sunday Times 15 November 2009

We were satisfying ourselves that not only would it work but that there was enough demand for it … Brett and I share a healthy level of permanent dissatisfaction with the service. This means that we are constantly working at making it better and improving everything. I really enjoy the creativity of growing a business.

Initially called Mystreetcar and based in Clapham, South London, the business was finally launched in 2004 on the back of their savings, £60,000 of outside finance and £130,000 of lease finance to purchase the first eight cars. They did not see their competition as car rental companies, but rather car ownership. It turns car ownership (a product) into a service and is seen by many as a 'greener' alternative because it encourages less road use. The business model challenges the basic paradigm of having to own a car to be able to use it at short notice, even for the shortest journey.

Initially Andrew and Brett did everything themselves, working almost a 24-hour day. They handed out leaflets at train and tube stations in the early mornings, eventually getting family and friends to help. They answered the phone and signed up members, meeting them to show them how to use the cars. They even washed and maintained the cars themselves. They offered a 24-hour service to members so, to start with, one of them had to be near to a phone all day, every day. After three months they had 100 members, each having paid a membership deposit and an annual joining fee, so they went out and leased 20 more cars at a cost of £300,000.

The company changed its name to Streetcar and, in 2007, Andrew and Brett gave up 43% of the business to Smedvig, a venture capital company, who invested £6.4 million. By 2009 Streetcar had a turnover of £20 million, with some 1300 cars based in six UK cities. In 2010, the US company Zipcar (a company launched

Scott Griffiths, chairman and chief executive Zipcar *The Guardian* 2 January 2013

> By combining Zipcar's **expertise** in on-demand mobility with Avis Budget Group's expertise in global **fleet** operations and vast **global network**, we will be able to accelerate the **revolution** we began in **personal mobility**.

Up-to-date information on Zipcar can be found on their website: www.zipcar.co.uk

in 2000) bought Streetcar for $50 million (£32 million), giving the founders $17 million (£11 million). Zipcar subsequently purchased similar businesses – Carsharing in Austria and Avancar in Spain. And in 2013 Avis, the third largest car hire firm, bought Zipcar for $500 million (£307 million) – a 50% premium on its share value. At this point Zipcar had 767,000 members in the USA and Europe.

Questions:

1. What benefits did Streetcar offer to its customers? How were these different from car ownership and traditional car hire?
2. How did Streetcar shift the paradigm of car ownership and car hire?
3. Why did Zipcar buy Streetcar, and why did Avis buy Zipcar?

Spotting opportunity

Creating opportunity is hard to do. Spotting opportunity in a systematic way is easier and there are tools and techniques that can help you. This may involve incremental product/service innovation and market expansion. The main source of opportunity is change. So, if you are looking for opportunity, look for change – changes in technology, law and regulation, market and industry structures, demographics, culture, moods and fashions all create market opportunities that entrepreneurs can exploit. As we have already observed, the internet is an enormous source of business opportunity. Reviewing the environment for change is therefore a prime source of business ideas, and a technique covered later in this chapter – SLEPT analysis – can help you with this.

Ning Li, founder Made.com BBC News Business 3 November 2011

> It's always an **opportunity** when you see a **big market** that hasn't changed much.

Of course, opportunity can also exist where markets are failing to meet customer needs – through laziness, ignorance or just because it takes time for the market information to be acted on. Entrepreneurs are often closer to customers and listen to what they say, and they recognize and act on market opportunity more quickly than established firms.

Analysis of the value chain (see Figure 3.2 overleaf) in an industry can also lead to opportunities

PRIMARY ACTIVITIES

INBOUND LOGISTICS — OPERATIONS — OUTBOUND LOGISTICS — MARKETING AND SALES — SERVICE

SUPPORT ACTIVITIES

Firm infrastructure | Human resource management | Technology development | Procurement

– particularly when market paradigms are questioned. Behind this is the idea that real advantages in cost or differentiation can be found in the chain of activities that a firm performs to deliver value to its customers. The value chain comprises five primary activities and four secondary or supporting activities, as shown in Table 3.1.

Each generic category can be broken down into discrete activities unique to a particular firm or industry. By looking at the costs associated with each activity and trying to compare them to the value obtained by customers from that activity, you can seek to identify any mismatches. Entrepreneurial opportunities exist when customers might derive greater value by changing the value chain, even if this involves increasing costs, or if costs can be reduced without affecting the value to the customer. For example, low-cost supply may be linked to proximity to a key supplier of raw materials or labour (see TutorVista Case Insight). Another example might be a high-quality product that was let down by low-quality after-sales service – the value to the customer not being matched by sufficient investment. Entrepreneurial firms can add value to the customer in a number of ways, not least by developing the close relationships they offer to both customers and suppliers. A particularly effective entrepreneurial strategy is to identify a sector in

T3.1 Activities of the value chain

Primary activities

1. Inbound logistics (receiving, storing and disseminating inputs)

2. Operations (transforming inputs into a final product)

3. Outbound logistics (collecting, storing and distributing products to customers)

4. Marketing and sales

5. After-sales service

Supporting activities

6. Procurement (purchasing consumable and capital items)

7. Human resource management

8. Technology development (R&D etc.)

9. Firm infrastructure (general management, accounting etc.)

which the relationships are weak, and to create value by tightening them up.

Another major source of inspiration are new business ideas introduced in other parts of the world. Good ideas take time to spread, and the window of opportunity to exploit an idea is not the same around the world. What might be a good idea today in one market might only be viable in another some years later. And the spread of the internet makes exploitation of overseas markets a real possibility for some start-ups. The Google equivalent in China is Baidu and in Russia it is Yandex. Both copied the Google model. In China, rather than Facebook, you would go to Qzone, RenRen, PengYou or Kaixin. All are copies of Facebook. It really is becoming a global market and opportunities exist everywhere.

TutorVista

Spotting opportunity – developing the supply chain

Based in India, Krishnan Ganesh launched TutorVista in 2006. It offers a very twenty-first century service. The company uses the internet to connect students in high wage-cost countries such as the USA and Britain with private tutors from low wage-cost countries such as India. It is completely dependent on the internet and the widespread availability of home computers. TutorVista is an intermediary. The part-time tutors are mainly employed full-time as teachers in schools and work from home for TutorVista – a remote business model that allows the company to keep capital and running costs to a minimum and minimize risks. Teachers are vetted and quality is monitored. The company markets the service directly using Google search advertisements. When somebody searches for tutor support in any subject an advertisement for

TutorVista comes up. When they click on the website they can talk to staff about the service. By 2011 the company had over 2000 students in the USA alone, and Pearson had acquired a controlling stake in the business.

And yet Krishnan had no experience of the education sector. He got the idea when he was travelling around the USA and was shocked to hear a media debate about 'the crisis in the US school education system'. He investigated (asking the question 'Why?') and realized that personal tutors in the USA were charging $40–$60 an hour and were regarded by most people as unaffordable. That got him to ask the question: 'Why not link teachers from India, where wage rates are lower, to the market demand in the USA?'

OnMobile

Spotting opportunity – the right time, right place

Arvind Rao was working in the financial services sector in New York when he tried to launch a business developing value-added services for mobile phones – ring tones, wallpapers and apps. Called OnMobile, it was originally incorporated in the USA in 2000, but failed to find a market. Not to be defeated, Arvind approached telephone operators in India with his ideas and found that his timing was perfect. India's mobile phone market was expanding rapidly. He quickly found one customer, then another and by 2011 OnMobile had become India's largest value-added services provider. Based in Bangalore, India, it now has offices around the world.

Sources of entrepreneurial opportunity

Academic insight

The management guru, Peter Drucker (1985), listed seven 'basic symptoms' of change that can be used to search systematically for entrepreneurial opportunities:

1. **The unexpected** – be it the unexpected success or failure or the unexpected event. Nobody can predict the future but an ability to react quickly to changes is a real commercial advantage, particularly in a rapidly changing environment. Information and knowledge are invaluable.

2. **The incongruity** – between what actually happens and what was supposed to happen. Plans go wrong and unexpected outcomes produce opportunities for firms that are able to spot them.

3. **The inadequacy in underlying processes** – that are taken for granted but can be improved or changed. This is essentially improving process engineering – especially important if the product is competing primarily on price.

4. **Changes in industry or market structure** – that take everyone by surprise. Again, unexpected change, perhaps arising from technology, legislation or other outside events, creates an opportunity to strategize about how the firm might cope and, as usual, first-mover advantage is usually worth striving for.

5. **Demographic changes** – population changes caused by changes in birth rates, wars, medical improvements and so on.

6. **Changes in perception, mood and meaning** – that can be brought about by the ups and downs of the economy, culture, fashion etc. In-depth interviews or focus groups can also often give an insight into these changes.

7. **New knowledge** – both scientific and non-scientific. This amounts to the disruptive innovation and challenges to market paradigms that we discussed previously.

Drucker, P. (1985) *Innovation and Entrepreneurship*, London: Heinemann.

Generating a business idea

So, all good business ideas are based upon commercial opportunities underpinned by market need. You can *create* opportunities through radical or incremental, product or market innovation, but when you do so there is probably little or no evidence of market need. Your innovation creates a need that did not exist before. However, you can *spot* opportunities by looking for situations which leave customer needs unmet. If you can introduce product or market innovations to meet this unmet need, you may have a viable business opportunity. As shown in Figure 3.3, to be successful both approaches must be linked to customer needs.

CREATE OPPORTUNITY
Product/market innovation: incremental to radical

Business idea

MARKET NEED

SPOT OPPORTUNITY
- *Changes in technology, law and regulation, market and industry structures, demographics, culture, moods and fashions*
- *Product/service deficiencies*
- *Unmet demand*

F3.3 Generating a business idea

Pieropoma – Fotolia.com

You can develop the skills to spot market opportunities and there are techniques to help with this. You also need to be creative. You measured your creativity with the AULIVE creativity test in the previous chapter. However, you can encourage your creativity by developing a certain way of thinking. These skills have been called 'discovery skills' – the skills of associating, questioning, observing, experimenting and networking (see Academic Insight). They involve being generally aware of and engaged with the world about you, but also being questioning and willing to experiment. Essentially, the process of generating ideas involves three stages:

1. Ensure that you are exposed to as many diverse and different ideas, influences and people as possible and that you are aware and alert to these influences. A general sense of awareness and openness is also important. Even when exposed to diverse influences, most people walk through life blinkered to what is happening around them.

2. Recognize market opportunities by observing how consumers go about their daily lives and questioning whether their needs can be met 'better' (or at all) in a different way. You need to practise the skills and techniques outlined in this chapter that encourage you to question ('why?' and 'why not?') and experiment. You need to think about things that are happening around you and how they might affect the future. You need to question the status quo and ask why things cannot be done differently.

3. Finally, formulate and reformulate your business idea so that there is a commercially viable business model. Not all products work to start with, and not all ideas are commercially viable to start with. Howard Head, the inventor of the steel ski, made some 40 different metal skis before he found one that worked consistently. Recognizing market opportunities by observing how consumers go about their daily lives and questioning whether their needs can be met 'better' in a different way is an important first step, but experimenting with the connection so as to perfect the product/service and the business model is vital.

All of this takes time. You need time to think and ponder, time to incubate ideas. Incubation time happens when you are engaged in other activities, including sleep, and you can let your subconscious mind work on the problem. Time is also needed to make the connections or associations between opportunities and your capabilities. There is an element of serendipity here, but the longer the time and the more the potential connections, the more likely the ideas are to germinate. The process is shown in Figure 3.4.

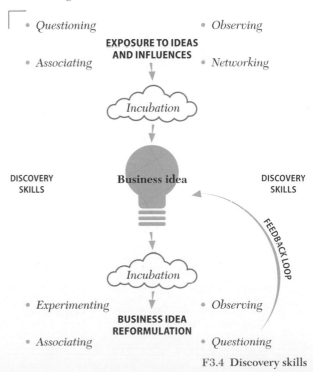

- *Questioning*   • *Observing*

EXPOSURE TO IDEAS AND INFLUENCES

- *Associating*   • *Networking*

Incubation

DISCOVERY SKILLS   **Business idea**   DISCOVERY SKILLS

FEEDBACK LOOP

Incubation

- *Experimenting*   • *Observing*

BUSINESS IDEA REFORMULATION

- *Associating*   • *Questioning*

F3.4 **Discovery skills**

Discovery skills

In a six-year study of more than 3000 US CEOs, contrasting 25 well-known entrepreneurs (such as Steve Jobs of Apple, Jeff Bezos of Amazon, Pierre Omidyar of eBay, Peter Thiel of PayPal, Niklas Zennström of Skype and Michael Dell) with other CEOs who had no track record for innovation, a research study found five 'discovery skills' that made these entrepreneurs particularly adept at linking market opportunity and innovation.

1. Associating

Innovative entrepreneurs connect seemingly unrelated questions, problems or ideas from many different fields. This often comes from mixing with people from diverse backgrounds and disciplines. The mind of the entrepreneur CEOs in the study was able to make connections between seemingly unrelated things, transferring questions, problems or ideas from one discipline to another. They capitalized on apparently divergent associations. What is more, this ability to associate seemed to be something that could be encouraged through stimulation: 'The more frequently people in our study attempted to understand, categorize, and store new knowledge, the more easily their brains could naturally and consistently make, store and recombine associations.' Associating links the attributes of connection, abstraction and perspective in the AULIVE test (Chapter 2).

2. Questioning

Innovative entrepreneurs have the curiosity to challenge conventional wisdom, asking 'why?', 'why not?' and 'what if?' The iconic Apple iPod was developed at a time when MP3 players were well-established. Staff developing Apple's iTunes software for use with MP3 players formed such a low opinion of the ease of use of MP3s that they decided to do better. Most of the entrepreneur CEOs were able to remember the specific question that inspired them to set up their business. They were also able to imagine opposites – apparent paradoxes – including some different future state and to embrace real-world constraints so that they became opportunities if they could be overcome. Questioning links the attributes of curiosity, paradox and boldness measured in the AULIVE test.

3. Observing

Innovative entrepreneurs observe common phenomena and people's behaviour, particularly that of potential customers. They scrutinize these phenomena, noticing fine detail and gaining insight into new ways of doing things. Ratan Tata observed a family of four perched on a moped and asked why they could not afford a car. In 2009, after years of product development which involved new modular production methods, Tata Group launched the lowest-priced car in the world – the Nano. Effective observing requires the ability to handle complexity and shift one's perspective – abilities also measured in the AULIVE test. Observing is a prerequisite to associating. It is part of how associations are made. You need to observe detail to be able to associate it across boundaries.

4. Experimenting

Innovative entrepreneurs actively try out new ideas, creating prototypes and launching pilots. Where these do not work, they learn from any mistakes and try to use the learning in different projects. The Apple iPod started life as prototypes made out of foam-core boards, using fishing weights to give them the right feel. All the entrepreneur CEOs engaged in some form of active experimenting, ranging from 'intellectual exploration' to 'physical tinkering.' One of their most powerful experiments was visiting, living and/or working in overseas countries. This was all part of being exposed to new ideas and mixing with people from diverse backgrounds. Experimenting is one aspect of curiosity.

5. Networking

Innovative entrepreneurs spend time finding and testing ideas with a network of diverse individuals in different countries. They do not just network with like-minded people. Networking in this context is just another aspect of observing and is therefore a prerequisite to associating.

Dyer, J.H., Gregersen, H.D. and Christensen, C.M. (2009) 'The Innovator's DNA'. *Harvard Business Review*, December.

 UK

MOMA!

Spotting opportunity – unmet demand

Tom Mercer was a management consultant with Bain & Co. in London. Before going to work, he would blend smoothies with oats for his breakfast in his flat. But it took time and he was often late for work. Then it suddenly struck him that his problem was actually a good business idea – pre-prepare the blend and then sell it to commuters from key points, like stations, around London. And so Moma was born in 2006.

Now you can see Moma's distinctively colourful carts around stations in London. They sell Oaties – smoothies and oats, Jumbles – oats soaked in apple juice and mingled with low-fat yoghurt and fruit, and Hodge-Podge – a layer of fruit cooked with spices, yoghurt and a packet of granola. Tom spent five months developing his recipes. The first products were sold in used plastic water bottles with labels glued on. Now the breakfasts are prepared in Deptford, South East London, then driven to central London to be sold from Moma's eight carts between 6.15 am and 10.45 am. In 2009, Tom had 25 people working for him, including 10 stall workers who were mainly students wanting to earn extra money. The driver picked up the stall workers and the leftovers at the end of the shift.

Moma products are also sold in Selfridges' food hall and served on Virgin Atlantic flights. Tom plans to open more stalls and extend the company beyond London by selling through Ocado, the internet grocer.

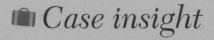 Case insight

Nuffnang

Spotting opportunity – matching with your skills

When he graduated from the London School of Economics, Cheo Ming Shen wanted to use his newly acquired skills to set up a new venture in his home country of Singapore, taking advantage of Asia's underdeveloped online market:

> I look for **business opportunities** that I think can work in the internet space and then I go **develop it**, and then **market it** and **sell it** as a business.

BBC News Business 16 November 2010
(www.bbc.co.uk/news/11757735)

He applied his business and internet skills in his home country where he had more local knowledge. His first venture was based upon his observation that there were a lot of blank spaces on blogs.

Founded with Cheo's partner, Timothy Tiah Ewe Tiam, Nuffnang acts as an intermediary between advertisers and bloggers. Bloggers are paid for each unique visitor and Nuffnang takes a percentage. The simple idea required little capital to establish as a business and became profitable within its first year. It has proved so successful that it has expanded to Malaysia, the Philippines and Australia. Cheo and Tiah now have four internet-based businesses in Singapore.

BBC News Business 16 November 2010

> In Asia there are hundreds of thousands of **blogs** … it's a fad that has taken off in such a way that … the West hasn't seen … This was a big chunk of internet space that wasn't being **monetised**. It represented a **huge audience** collectively but nobody could … effectively put them together … The blogs are a very **interactive medium** so it's a very personal medium as well … When someone sees **advertising** … they're more likely to **click**.

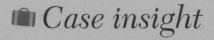 Case insight

Swarfega

Spotting opportunity – a product without a use

Not all ideas find a commercial application in the way they were originally envisaged, and observation and connectivity can change the direction of an invention. Swarfega is a green gel which is a dermatologically safe cleaner for the skin. It is now widely used to remove grease and oil from hands in factories and households. But the original product, developed in 1941 by Audley Williamson, was not intended for degreasing hands at all. It was intended as a mild detergent to wash silk stockings. Unfortunately, the invention of nylon and its use for stockings and tights rendered the product as obsolete as silk stockings. Watching workmen trying to clean their hands with a mixture of petrol, paraffin and sand which left them cracked and sore led Williamson to realize that there was a completely different commercial opportunity for his product. In 2004 he sold the business he set up to manufacture Swarfega for £135 million.

Connectivity and networking

Creativity underpins the generation of ideas. And a prerequisite of this is connectivity – a connection with and an awareness of what is going on in the world in general. It generates new ideas, knowledge and information. Reading newspapers, magazines, journals and books and surfing the web are passive forms of connectivity. But essentially it is a social process involving talking to people with different views of the world. Active connectivity means meeting a diverse range of people – networking. This might entail attending meetings, clubs, seminars and conferences. It is likely to involve travel. It is not just about being aware of different approaches or perspectives on a problem, but also about getting the brain to accept that there are different ways of doing things – developing an open and enquiring mind. Many people almost have to give themselves permission to be creative – to think the unthinkable.

Connectivity, therefore, extends beyond any industry or market context. Steve Jobs' interest in calligraphy is claimed to be the source for Apple's early development of a wide range of fonts on its computers. Some of the best business ideas have social origins, linking social need to commercial opportunity. Similarly, solutions to commercial problems or opportunities can come from unrelated disciplines. The ubiquitous Velcro fastening was conceived in 1941 by Swiss engineer, Georges de Mestral. He got his inspiration from nature. After a walk, he observed that there were burrs of the burdock plant sticking to his clothes and his dog's fur. He looked at them under a microscope and observed they had hundreds of tiny 'hooks' that caught onto 'loops' on clothing or fur. From this he conceived the possibility of two materials being bound together.

In other words, ideas that are commonplace for one group can spark insight for another. It is all about being open to ideas from all and every source and not being inward looking. Companies like LG and Hallmark have active programmes to encourage staff to expose themselves to ideas from a wide, and sometimes unusual, range of sources. This is one reason why partnering with other people can be so useful in stimulating innovation. One person exposes the other to different ways of doing things or different ideas, and from this comes the spark of creativity.

As shown in Figure 3.5, connectivity, linked with the discovery skills outlined earlier, combine to help make you more creative and innovative. These are the elements that will help you find a good business idea and sustain your competitiveness through innovation.

> Network. Meet people. Show a genuine interest in others. Don't talk too much. Listen more.
>
> Raoul Shah, founder Exposure *The Observer* 29 September 2013

> I believe opportunity is part instinct and part immersion – in an industry, a subject, or an area of expertise ... You don't have to be a genius, or a visionary, or even a college graduate to think unconventionally. You just need a framework ... Seeing and seizing opportunities are skills that can be applied universally, if you have the curiosity and commitment.
>
> Michael Dell *Direct from Dell: Strategies that Revolutionized an Industry* (1999, New York: Harper Business)

Connecting good ideas

Stephen Johnson's thought-provoking book *Where Good Ideas Come From* does an excellent job of dispelling the myth that good ideas come from a 'eureka moment':

'[Good ideas] come from crowds, from networks… You know we have this clichéd idea of the lone genius having the eureka moment… But in fact when you go back and you look at the history of innovation it turns out that so often there is this quiet collaborative process that goes on, either in people building on other people's ideas, but also in borrowing ideas, or tools or approaches to problems… The ultimate idea comes from this remixing of various different components. There still are smart people and there still are people that have moments where they see the world differently in a flash. But for the most part it's a slower and more networked process than we give them credit for.'

Johnson's central thesis is that new ideas rarely happen by chance. They take time to germinate and mature. Often the big idea comes from the collision of smaller ideas or hunches, and the chance of these 'accidental' collisions is increased with the exposure you have to more people and different ideas. This can come from many sources – reading, meetings, your network of contacts, the internet etc. – the more diverse the better. The more you are exposed to these influences the more likely you are to be innovative. Indeed, the driver of innovation over time has been the increasing connectivity between different minds. As he puts it: 'Chance favours the connected mind'.

Johnson, S. (2010) *Where Good Ideas Come From: The Natural History of Innovation*, London: Allen Lane.

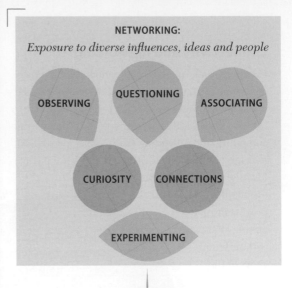

F3.5 Connectivity and discovery skills

Commercially, networks are important structures that can provide you with information about markets, professional advice and opinion, often without charge. Formal networks such as Chambers of Commerce and Business Links in the UK and the Small Business Development Centers in the USA and trade associations can be invaluable for this. Networks can also provide opportunities to form partnerships, either formally or informally, so as to better exploit an opportunity.

Techniques for generating ideas

There are many techniques designed to help generate new ideas. Generating ideas is a numbers game – the more ideas you come up with the more likely you are to find one that is viable. So it is worth distinguishing between those techniques designed to generate volume and those designed to improve quality. Some techniques are more applicable to spotting opportunity, others to creating opportunity.

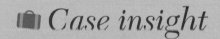
Great Ormond Street Hospital

Connectivity

Ideas for innovations can come from unusual sources. The Great Ormond Street Hospital for children took its inspiration from watching the McLaren and Ferrari Formula 1 racing teams take only six seconds to turn a car around at a pit stop. Doctors at the hospital were concerned by the time they took to move patients from the operating theatre to the intensive care unit where they recovered. Delays in emergency handover could cost lives, so they contacted Ferrari to see how the process might be improved. Ferrari explained that their pit-stop procedure was kept simple, with minimal movements all planned in advance. In fact, it was so simple that it could be drawn on a single diagram. From that plan, every member of the Ferrari team knew exactly what they had to do and when to do it in a coordinated fashion. Ferrari videoed the hospital's handovers. When the doctors watched it they were shocked at the lack of structure. Ferrari concluded that, with an ever-changing team and unpredictable demand, the hospital's handover teams needed a simple formula they could understand and work to – just like a pit stop. And Ferrari helped the hospital to design it.

Brainstorming

This is one of the most widely-used, basic techniques, designed to generate volume for either spotting or creating opportunity. It is practised in a group. In the session you do not question or criticize ideas. You suspend disbelief. The aim is to encourage the free flow of ideas – divergent thinking – and to come up with as many ideas as possible. Everyone has thousands of good ideas within them just waiting to come out. But people inherently fear making mistakes or looking foolish in front of others. Here making 'mistakes' and putting forward ideas which don't work is not only acceptable, it is encouraged. You might start with a problem to be solved or an opportunity to be exploited. You encourage and write ideas down as they come – there are no 'bad' ideas. All ideas are, at the very least, springboards for other ideas.

The Million Dollar Homepage

Brainstorming

The Million Dollar Homepage is a single web page that is divided into 10,000 boxes, each 100 pixels in size. Space was sold to advertisers at $1 for each pixel, providing a montage of company logos. Advertisers were promised that the page would remain online for at least five years. The idea for the page came to Alex Tew, a Nottingham Trent University student in the UK, in 2005. He had brainstorming sessions before he went to bed each night, writing ideas down on a notepad. The site took just two days to set up and cost £50. Alex sold the first blocks of pixels to his brothers and friends, and used the money to advertise the site. The site address began to appear in internet blogs and chat rooms and, following a press release, a BBC technology programme ran a short feature on the page in September 2005. By January 2006 Alex was a millionaire.

SLEPT Analysis

SLEPT analysis is a widely used tool to aid thinking about future developments in the wider environment. This in turn can be used to spot commercial opportunities that these developments generate. The analysis looks at the changes that are likely to occur in the areas spelt out by the acronym SLEPT:

Social changes such as an ageing population, increasing work participation often from home, 24-hour shopping, increasing participation in higher education, changing employment patterns, increasing number of one-parent families and so on.

Legal changes such as Health and Safety, changes in employment laws, food hygiene regulations, patent laws and so on.

Economic changes such as recession, growth, changes in interest rates, inflation, employment, currency fluctuations and so on.

Political changes like local or central government elections, political initiatives (for example on price competitiveness, new or changed taxes, merger and take-over policy) and so on.

Technological developments such as increasing internet bandwidth, the coming together of internet technologies, increasing use of computers and chip technology, increasing use of mobile phones, increasing use of surveillance cameras and so on.

The trick is to brainstorm about how these developments might create business opportunities that are not currently being met. Take, for example, the development of the internet. The ability to download films and music has questioned the viability of shops selling DVDs and CDs, but created opportunities for new devices (netbooks, tablets, smartphones etc.) and services (particularly niche services) linked to the internet. The development of internet shopping generally might cause developers to rethink the purpose and structure of our town centres. It might cause individual shops to re-engineer the way they meet customer needs – most shops now have websites and many offer internet shopping alongside conventional shopping.

Futures thinking

This is another technique that is often used to think about the future, and follows on from a SLEPT analysis. It helps develop further insight into the change that has been identified, ahead of defining the commercial opportunity. It tries to take a holistic perspective, developing a vision about the future state after the change has taken place. From this the commercial opportunities can be identified, again using brainstorming. So, for example, you might start thinking about the state of a particular form of retailing in five years' time, given the impact of the internet and smartphone. Will bricks-and-mortar retailing continue to exist? If so, how will it combine with these technological developments? What will it look like, where will it be located and what services will it need to offer? How will it attract customers? These and many more questions might help to 'flesh out' a picture of how it might look and what you need to do to survive and prosper in the future.

Current constraints to action are ignored and in this way the barriers to change are identified. Some barriers may indeed prove to be permanent or insurmountable, but many might not be. Objections are therefore outlawed and disbelief suspended at the initial ideas stage. Only later on might options be discarded, once the barriers are considered. The key to thinking about the future is not to assume it will necessarily be like the past. Change is now endemic and often discontinuous.

Mind maps

This is simply a map of related ideas from one original idea. It helps develop and refine a business opportunity, whether it is spotted or created. It can be used by individuals or in a group. As with brainstorming, you have to suspend disbelief and simply generate related ideas that might not have been encapsulated in the original. It can help you 'think outside the box' and generate relationships that might not initially have been apparent. Creativity is about making connections between apparently unconnected things, and this technique can be particularly helpful.

Figure 3.6 shows a four-stage, systematic process for spotting a commercial opportunity and generating a business idea based upon a SLEPT analysis, futures thinking and brainstorming and mind-mapping techniques.

Analogy

This is a product-centred technique that attempts to join together apparently unconnected or unrelated combinations of features of a product or service and benefits to the customer to come up with innovative solutions to problems. It is therefore designed to provide more focused ideas that create opportunity out of unsolved problems for customers. Analogies

1 *Brainstorm changes using SLEPT analysis*

2 *Develop a vision of the future after that change using futures thinking*

3 *Brainstorm commercial opportunities coming out of identified change*

4 *Develop and refine opportunity using mind maps*

Business idea

F3.6 **Spotting commercial opportunity arising out of change**

are proposed once the initial problem is stated. The analogies are then related to opportunities in the market place. It works in a similar way to brainstorming. Georges de Mestral's connection between the properties of burdock seed and the need to stick and unstick things is an example of analogy that led to the development of Velcro.

In building an analogy you need to ask some basic questions:

- What does the situation or problem remind you of?
- What other areas of life or work experience similar situations?
- Who does these similar things and can the principles be adapted?

Often the analogy contains the words '… *is like* …', so you might ask why something 'is like' another. For example, why is advertising like cooking? Because there is so much preamble to eating. Anticipation from presentation and smell, even the ambience of the restaurant you eat it in, are just as important as the taste and nutritional value of the food itself. They 'advertise' the food to be eaten.

Attribute analysis

This is another, more focused, product-centred technique designed to evolve product improvements and line extensions which is used as the product reaches the mature phase of its life cycle. It therefore can be useful in spotting opportunities arising from inadequate existing products or services. It uses the basic marketing technique of looking at the features of a product or service which in turn perform a series of functions but, most importantly, deliver benefits to the customers. An existing product or service is stripped down to its component parts and then you explore how these features might be altered, using brainstorming. You need to focus on whether those changes might bring valuable benefits to the customer. Nothing must be taken for granted. You can then develop and refine these changes using mind mapping.

Figure 3.7 shows a three-stage, systematic process for spotting a commercial opportunity and generating a business idea based upon analyzing the attributes of an existing product or service and using brainstorming and mind-mapping techniques.

So, for example, you might focus on a domestic lock. This secures a door from being opened by an

1 *List attributes of product/service*

2 *Brainstorm how these attributes can be improved*

3 *Develop & refine opportunity using mind maps*

Business idea

F3.7 Spotting commercial opportunity arising out of inadequate existing products or services

unwelcome intruder. The benefit is security and reduction/elimination of theft from the house. But you can lose keys or forget to lock doors, and some locks are difficult or inconvenient to open from the inside. A potential solution is to have doors that sense people approaching from the outside and lock themselves. You could have a reverse sensor on the inside – one that unlocks the door when someone approaches (which could be activated or deactivated centrally). The exterior sensor could recognize 'friendly' people approaching the door by means of sensors they carry in the form of 'credit cards' or the sensor could be over ridden by a combination lock. The lock could be linked to a door that opens automatically.

Gap analysis

This is a market-based approach that attempts to produce a 'map' of product/market attributes based on dimensions that are perceived as important to customers, analyzing where competing products might lie and then spotting gaps where there is little or no competition. Depending on scale, this can be used to spot or create opportunity, particularly in the form of redefining market paradigms. Because of the complexity involved, the attributes are normally shown in only two dimensions. There are a number of approaches to this task:

- *Perceptual mapping* places the attributes of a product within specific categories. So for example, the dessert market might be characterized as hot vs cold and sophisticated vs unsophisticated. Various desserts would then be mapped onto these two dimensions. This could be shown graphically (Figure 3.8). The issue is whether the 'gap' identified is one that customers would value being filled – and means understanding whether they value the dimensions being measured. That is a question for market research to attempt to answer.

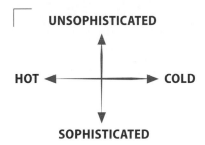

F3.8 A perceptual map for desserts

- *Non-metric mapping* places products in generic groups that customers find similar and then tries to explain why these groupings exist. A classic example would be its application to the soft drinks market where products might be clustered and then described simply in terms of the widely-used generic groups, 'still' vs 'carbonated' and 'flavoured' vs 'non-flavoured'. The key here is also finding the appropriate dimensions that create opportunities for differentiating the product. The mapping of soft drinks on the two dimensions of a perceptual map is unlikely to reveal any gaps in the market.

- *Repertory grid* is a more systematic extension of this technique using market research. Customers are asked to group similar and dissimilar products within a market, normally in pairs. They are then asked to explain the similarities and dissimilarities. The sequence is repeated for all groups of similar and dissimilar products. The explanations are then used to derive 'constructs' which describe the way in which people relate and evaluate the products. These constructs form a grid that can be used to map the products, using the words used by the customers themselves.

Figure 3.9 shows a three-stage, systematic process for spotting or creating a commercial opportunity and generating a business idea based on mapping the attributes of an existing product or service, using brainstorming and identifying gaps in the market.

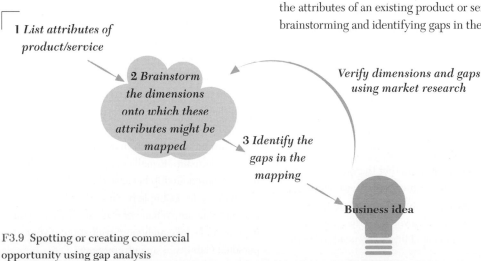

F3.9 Spotting or creating commercial opportunity using gap analysis

Boyd and Goldenberg (2013) believe that innovation can be pursued systematically. They identify five 'templates' that hold the key to innovation:

Subtraction – You can innovate by taking out features of a product that some segments of the market do not value. This is the approach taken by low-cost airlines.

Division – Dividing the functions of a product can be innovative. For example, dividing out the control features on many electronic products and placing them into a remote control provides more convenience and allows the products to become smaller/slimmer.

Multiplication – Taking some characteristic or feature of a product and duplicating it can be innovative. For example, 'picture-within-picture' TVs allow people to watch more than one programme at a time.

Task unification – Bringing together multiple tasks into one product or service can add value for customers. For example, sunscreen products added to facial moisturizers (and vice versa) to unify tasks.

Attribute dependency – Two or more apparently unrelated attributes can be correlated with each other. For example, smartphones now provide information that depends on your geographic location; the speed of your windscreen wiper or volume of your radio can be made to vary with the speed of your car.

Boyd, D. and Goldenberg, J. (2013) *Inside the Box: A Proven System of Creativity for Breakthrough Results*, London: Profile Books.

Is the business idea viable?

As we have seen, you can create opportunity or you can spot opportunity. In both cases your creative skills must be linked to customer need. The discovery skills and techniques for idea generation covered in this chapter can be combined to help both create and spot commercial opportunities. Often the first attempt at putting that product or service together in a marketable way fails, so a series of trial-and-error iterations – experimentation – may be necessary, all of which may take time. At some stage you need to think about whether you can safeguard the 'intellectual property' (IP) of your business idea. There are a number of ways you can do this, and these are covered in Chapter 9.

The next stage is to see whether the idea is viable, and whether it matches your aspirations. Does being an entrepreneur fit with your aspirations for your life at this time? Do you have the personal character traits and capabilities you need to be an entrepreneur? Do you have the skills and resources needed? Sometimes the idea might be very good, but you might not be the right person to take it to the market. In that case, you might be able to sell it on.

Most people base their business upon skills, experience or qualifications that they have already gained from a previous job or through a hobby. Often they think that their employer is not making the most of some opportunity. Sometimes they have an idea but cannot persuade their employer to take it up, so they decide to try it themselves. Often they have contacts in the industry they believe they can exploit to their own advantage. These are positive factors that 'pull' people into entrepreneurship. Equally people can be 'pushed' into entrepreneurship because they have few alternatives, for example because they have been made redundant. Whatever your motivations, you need to undertake an honest evaluation of your personal viability as an entrepreneur.

You need to assure yourself that there is a market for your product or service. And then there are your competitors. How will you compete against them? How are you different? Will you be able to capitalize on this idea as quickly as existing firms? You need to test your business model and be willing to modify it to best fit the market place. Finally, will those opportunities still exist in five years' time – is your business idea sustainable – or will it have to be redeveloped after a few years? A good business idea has a window of commercial opportunity. Too early or too late and it is unlikely to be successful, and it will only have a finite life cycle. You also need to evaluate the commercial viability of the business. Will it be profitable? Can it be funded? Although you might try to assess viability through various forms of market testing (see Lean start-up), ultimately the only way you can assess the commercial and financial viability is by drawing up a set of financial forecasts. Figure 3.9 shows this process.

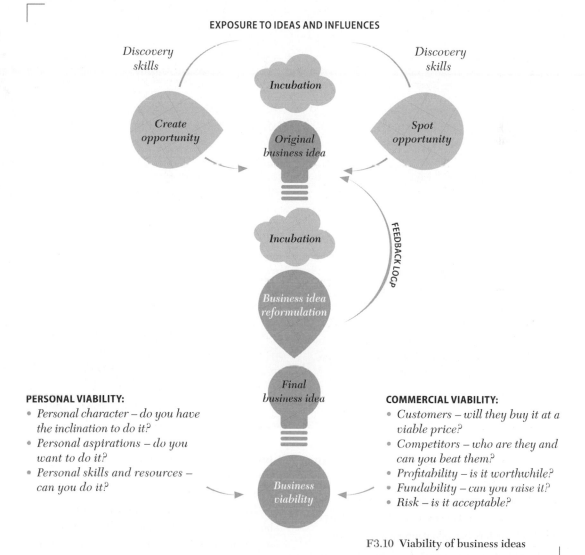

EXPOSURE TO IDEAS AND INFLUENCES

Discovery skills

Discovery skills

Incubation

Create opportunity

Spot opportunity

Original business idea

Incubation

FEEDBACK LOOP

Business idea reformulation

Final business idea

PERSONAL VIABILITY:
- *Personal character – do you have the inclination to do it?*
- *Personal aspirations – do you want to do it?*
- *Personal skills and resources – can you do it?*

Business viability

COMMERCIAL VIABILITY:
- *Customers – will they buy it at a viable price?*
- *Competitors – who are they and can you beat them?*
- *Profitability – is it worthwhile?*
- *Fundability – can you raise it?*
- *Risk – is it acceptable?*

F3.10 Viability of business ideas

Ries (2011) coined the phrase 'lean start-up' for new ventures that minimize the lead time as well as their investment in a new product/service launch. The idea is that the product/service is not launched in a 'perfect state', but rather in its 'minimum viable' state. Customer feedback is then used in an iterative fashion to further tailor the product/service to the specific needs of customers – a process Ries calls 'validated learning'. In this way, no valuable time and money are invested in designing features or services that customers do not value. This approach gives the company first-mover advantage and minimizes costs whilst, importantly, reducing market risks when the product/service finally reaches a wider market. The key to the approach is close customer relationships and developing mechanisms to receive their feedback.

Ries gives the example of the start-up strategy of Nick Swinmurn who founded the US online shoe retailer, Zappos. Instead of building a website and a large database of footwear, he tested his business idea by taking pictures of shoes from local stores, posting them online and selling them through his website, buying the shoes from the stores at full price. Although he did not make a profit, this method quickly validated his business idea, with minimum cost and risk.

The lean start-up idea was originally developed for high-tech businesses, based upon the way companies like Google develop new products, but has gained popularity generally. It reflects the 'parallel' new product development model – where product development and concept/market testing go side-by-side – and embraces elements of the 'lean manufacturing' philosophy. The approach mirrors entrepreneurs' incremental approach to decision-making – gaining knowledge as they proceed – and the way they limit their financial exposure as much as possible.

The idea of small-scale market entry and trial in order to gain market information prior to full product launch for a start-up is not new (Chaston, 2000). Nor is the idea that risk is related to the time taken to launch a new product/service – too early and you risk being ill-prepared and turning customers against it, too late and you lose first-mover advantage (Burns, 2005). Launch timing is critical. Ries says this depends upon having a 'minimum viable product' – one that 'allows a team to collect the maximum amount of validated learning about customers with the least effort'. But this is a matter of judgement. If the product/service is so underdeveloped that customers reject it, even a limited launch can spell disaster later.

The idea works well for some products – for example, software – where new features can be trialled on the back of the core product. This is an approach often taken by Google. However, if the core product does not function you risk customer rejection. For high-investment (often disruptive) innovations, the product must be substantially right first time. Imagine asking Apple if they would have been happy to launch a 'minimum viable' iPhone.

Burns, P. (2005) *Corporate Entrepreneurship: Building an Entrepreneurial Organization*, Basingstoke: Palgrave Macmillan.

Chaston, I. (2000) *Entrepreneurial Marketing: Competing by Challenging Convention*, Basingstoke: Palgrave Macmillan.

Ries, E. (2011) *The Lean Startup: How Today's Entrepreneurs Use Continuous Innovation to Create Radically Successful Businesses*, New York: Crown Publishing.

Characteristics of a good business idea

The best business ideas generate high profits and involve low risk. Unfortunately very few such opportunities exist. However, here is a checklist of twelve characteristics of a good idea:

1. **Identified market need/gap** – the idea must meet a clearly identified market need if it is to be commercially viable.

2. **Identified customers and marketing strategy** – if you don't know who you are selling to you won't know how to sell to them, which means you probably will not succeed. You need to go about building your business model systematically. And remember you may be selling to more than one market segment.

3. **No or few existing competitors** – the more innovative your product/service and markets, the fewer competitors, and the higher the price you are normally able to charge. However, remember it is always possible that there are no competitors because there is no viable market for the product/service.

4. **Not easily copied** – if it can be, protect your intellectual property. However, often getting to the market quickly and developing a brand reputation is the best safeguard.

5. **Growing market** – it is always easier to launch a business into a new or growing, rather than declining, market. Of course it may be that you are launching a business that will create a completely new market.

6. **High margins** – the more innovative your product/service and market, the higher your margin is likely to be.

7. **Low fixed costs** – low fixed costs mean lower risk should volume reduce; they give you flexibility. A combination of high margin and low fixed costs mean a low breakeven point. Breakeven measures the financial risk the business faces and the margin of safety (%) measures how far, proportionately, the business is above breakeven. These three financial characteristics are expanded in Chapter 11.

8. **Low funding requirements** – the lower the funding requirement, the easier it is to start up and the less you have to lose if the idea does not work.

9. **Financeable** – if you do not have sufficient resources yourself, the project needs to be able to attract finance.

10. **Identifiable risks that can be monitored and mitigated** – the future of a start-up is, by definition, uncertain. Identifying risks is the first step to understanding how they can be monitored and then mitigated.

11. **Management skill that can be leveraged** – you need to have the appropriate management skills and, if you do not, you need to acquire them or recruit or partner with others with the appropriate skills.

12. **Scalability** – small projects can usually get off the ground easily but bigger projects can be problematic because they are just 'too big'. In this case, you need to see whether the project can be broken down into smaller projects that can be implemented when the original idea is proved – scalability. The idea is to avoid as much risk as possible for as long as possible – but make sure you do not miss the market window completely. This is all a question of judgement and changing market conditions, so you need to remain flexible and think through how you will scale up the project when it proves successful.

Most of these characteristics will only become apparent as you develop your business model, which we do in Chapter 5. In doing this you need to be flexible and develop strategic options as you go through the process. If the preferred option turns out to be unattractive or impossible, you can then return to consider the other options you have come up with. Your business plan will put forward the best business model.

Summary

- There are six new venture paradigms: a copy-cat strategy, incremental product/service innovation, market expansion, disruptive innovation, market paradigm shift and new-to-the-world industries.

- A copy-cat strategy implies that you will have to compete primarily on price, and this means that the business is likely to have low profitability and limited growth potential. Any other paradigm involves product or market innovation – changing the product/service or its market to a greater or lesser degree.

- Good business ideas come from creating opportunities or spotting them. Creating opportunity involves product or market innovation – from incremental to radical.

- Radical innovation involves creating new business opportunities that have not existed before: developing disruptive innovation, market paradigm shift and/or new-to-the-world industries. This is difficult and risky.

- You can challenge industry paradigms by questioning sectoral, performance and customer conventions.

- You can spot opportunity by analyzing change. Change creates opportunities. These opportunities may involve incremental product/service or market innovation.

- Symptoms of change are: the unexpected, the incongruity, inadequacy in underlying process, changes in industry or market structure, demographic changes and changes in perception, mood and meaning.

- Opportunities also exist in questioning the value chain in an industry to see where additional value can be created (for customers and/or the firm) in some meaningful way.

- There are techniques that can help you to spot opportunities such as: brainstorming, SLEPT analysis, mind mapping, futures thinking, analogy, attribute analysis and gap analysis. Figures 3.6, 3.7 and 3.9 show how these techniques can be used systematically to generate business ideas.

- Developing ideas involves creativity. You can improve this by developing your discovery skills: associating, questioning, observing, experimenting and networking.

- Connectivity is a prerequisite to creativity. It generates new knowledge and information. Networking is an important element in developing this.

- Deciding whether a business idea is viable involves checking against your own aspirations and capabilities as well as evaluating the commercial viability of the idea.

Exercise 3.1

Business idea generation

To work through the rest of this book you need at least one business idea. Subsequent chapters will help you to evaluate and modify your business idea(s) and, if you end up with more than one, evaluate which is the one you want to pursue.

1 If you already have a business idea or ideas, go to Step 5.

2 If you have identified an inadequate existing product or service, go through the three-stage process outlined in Figures 3.7 or 3.9 to arrive at your new business idea. This is best done in a small group.

3 If you do not have a business idea, go through the four-stage process outlined in Figure 3.6 until you have at least three business ideas. This is best done in a small group.

4 Eliminate any ideas that do not meet any of the following three, simple criteria:
  - Practicability
  - Your ability to undertake the business idea
  - Whether it is likely to fit with your business purpose (Exercises 2.1 and 2.2)

  If none meet these criteria, repeat steps 2 and/or 3 until you have at least three more ideas.

5 Expand on the ideas, in the light of your mind maps and get feedback on them from your network of family, friends and any experts. This may take time, but it is part of the 'incubation' process.

6 Using the twelve criteria listed below, evaluate the attractiveness of each of your business ideas on a scale of 1 (not attractive) to 5 (very attractive). You can add your own criteria to the list. Total up the scores for each idea. At this stage some of these judgements will be based upon incomplete information. Make certain you jot down any reservations you have about this for consideration at the end of the exercise

Criteria	Business idea 1	Business idea 2	Business idea 3
1 Identified market need/gap			
2 Identified customers and marketing strategy			
3 No or few existing competitors			
4 Not easily copied			
5 Growing market			
6 High margins			
7 Low fixed costs			
8 Low funding requirements			
9 Financeable			
10 Identifiable risks that can be monitored and mitigated			
11 Management skill that can be leveraged			
12 Scalability			
13 Other (specify)			
TOTAL SCORE			

7 Reflect on the scores you have given to these business ideas and why the idea with the highest score was so attractive. Consider any reservations you may have about information that is available. Get feedback on your scores from your network of family and friends and jot down any insightful comment.

You should now have identified at least one attractive business idea that is worth evaluating. To evaluate this properly you need to develop a business model and business plan.

Exercise 3.2

Defining your business idea

Now you have come up with a business idea, we need to define more clearly what it is and who it would sell to. We shall return to this in Chapter 5 and specify things in more detail, but you need to write down your original idea before you start to modify it.

1 Write down as clearly as possible a description of your product or service idea. What are its features? What customer demands will it meet? What further development work still needs to be undertaken?

2 Which new venture typology in Figure 3.1 does your business idea most closely approximate? What are the implications of this for the business?

3 Describe as clearly as possible the types of customers (or segments) who you think will buy your product or service.

4 Write down the names of the competitors you will face. How does your product or service differ from theirs?

5 For each group of customers, write down the reasons why you think they will buy your product or service, rather than that of your competitors.

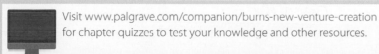 Visit www.palgrave.com/companion/burns-new-venture-creation for chapter quizzes to test your knowledge and other resources.

PART 2
MARKET SEGMENTS AND THE VALUE PROPOSITION

VIDEO

The New Venture Creation Framework

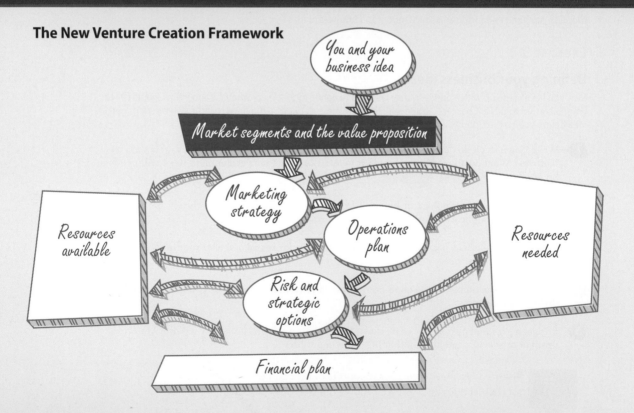

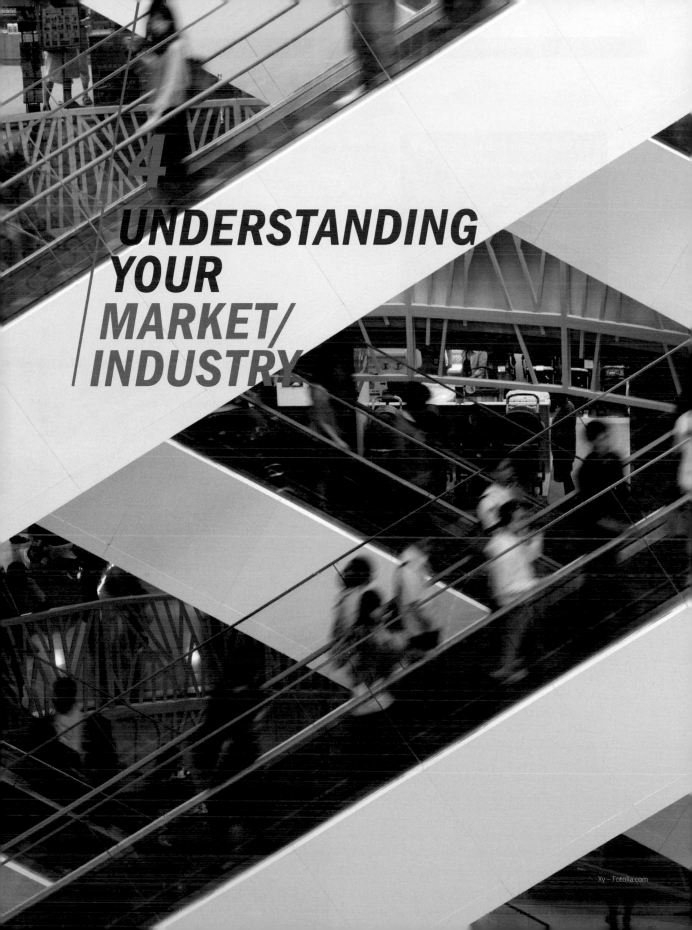

4
UNDERSTANDING YOUR MARKET/INDUSTRY

Contents

Learning outcomes

When you have read this chapter and undertaken the related exercises you will be able to:
- Define and describe your market or industry
- Assess the degree of competition in your market/industry and the effect on profitability
- Identify and evaluate the strengths and weaknesses of your competitors
- Review future trends in your industry and assess how they might affect you, and from this develop critical success factors for your business

Defining your market/industry

Unless you are creating a completely new-to-the-world industry as your new venture it is likely that there will be an existing market or industry that sells similar goods or services. Understanding this industry is vital because it will give you an insight into your potential customers, how to reach them and the competition you might face. Indeed, understanding the shortcomings of companies in an industry can yield business opportunities. Most industries have some underlying structural conditions that influence the degree of competition within them. However, the profitability of individual companies within an industry can vary widely, implying that your choice and, just as important, execution of strategy are probably more significant than your choice of industry. Copy-cat ventures facing established competition must find some distinctive competitive advantage.

The first step in industry analysis is to describe the key elements of the industry's structure.

However, defining the industry you are in can be more difficult than you think. An industry is any group of firms that supplies a market, but markets are rarely homogeneous. After all, they are made up of customers with a wide range of needs. The car industry comprises many market segments – hatchbacks, family cars, luxury cars, sports cars, SUVs etc. Do cars in each of these sectors compete against each other? Is Jaguar,

© manwolste – istockphoto.com

a UK producer of luxury saloon and sports cars, a competitor of Peugeot, a French producer of hatchbacks and family cars? There are clear market boundaries between segments and there is the question as to what extent a car and a car producer in one segment competes against a car and a producer in another. Similarly, a local convenience/grocery store might not be competing directly against large supermarkets, despite being in the food retail industry. So, geographic boundaries to a market might also apply. The criterion here is substitutability – are customers willing to travel to a supermarket?

So, an industry is likely to comprise a number of market segments. Drawing the boundaries of your industry and the market segments within it is therefore a question of judgement. It is an important judgement that will define who you think

you will compete with and, probably, the marketing strategies you will put in place. The judgement rests on an accurate identification of your customers, which we cover in the next chapter, and their willingness to buy similar products or services.

Describing your market/industry

In order to describe your industry and/or market, you need to understand some terminology. However, this is more than just terminology. The market/industry typologies below have implications for the firms within them and the opportunities they generate for newcomers.

It is usually easier to sell into an emerging or growing, rather than a declining, market, but can be hard going if your market is completely new. Backers may tend to prefer emerging rather than completely new markets, simply because they have proof that demand does exist.

F4.1 Market life cycles

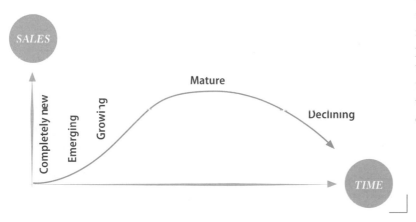

The first set of typologies refer to the stage the market/industry is at in its life cycle (Figure 4.1).

Completely new (market paradigm shift) – This is the new market emerging from a market paradigm shift or radical innovation. The market is not proven and demand is very difficult to estimate. Processes and procedures are yet to be developed. There are no competitors.

Implications:

- High risk, but also potential for high returns.
- Customers difficult to identify.
- No competitors.
- Gaining first-mover advantage very important.
- Opportunity to dominate the market.
- Likely to be high marketing costs (customers may not understand product/service benefits).

Emerging – This is a market where there is proven demand but its size is still uncertain. The market is growing. Processes and procedures have not yet become fully established. There are still no dominant brands or market leaders.

Implications:

- Few competitors.
- Customers starting to be identified.
- First-mover advantage still significant.
- Opportunity to redefine processes and procedures that are not operating effectively.
- Still opportunity to dominate the market.
- Marketing costs still likely to be high.
- Barriers to entry probably being established.

Growing – This is a market where there is proven and growing demand – market research would show it to be attractive. Processes and procedures are still developing as new competitors enter the market. Competition is fierce as companies battle to penetrate the market and gain market dominance. Dominant brands and market leaders are beginning to emerge at the same time as some companies are going out of business.

Implications:

- Growing number of competitors.
- Product/service extensions likely to be emerging.
- Buying patterns becoming established.
- Aggressive marketing strategies in a fiercely competitive market.
- Dominant brands beginning to emerge.
- Competitive pricing.
- Market looks good on paper, but entrants may be too late unless their product/service is based upon significant innovation.

Mature – This is an established market with well-documented characteristics. It is large but growth is slow or non-existent. There are established processes and procedures, buying and repeat-purchasing patterns. Few new customers are entering the market. Competitors are established. There is limited innovation. Industry might be fragmented or consolidated (see opposite).

Implications:

- Well-established competitors (market might be fragmented or consolidated).
- Defensive pricing possible (meeting or beating new entrants).
- Difficult to break into market, competition strong.
- Opportunity to innovate based on existing product/service.
- Opportunity to innovate based upon process or after-sales service.
- Opportunity to innovate based upon established marketing processes.

Declining – This is a well-documented, declining market with established processes, procedures and buying patterns. There is a declining number of customers and competitors. Product range is narrowing as weak lines are dropped. There is no innovation. Industry might be fragmented or consolidated (see opposite).

Implications:

- Market has a limited life expectancy.
- Declining range of products.
- Opportunity to consolidate market by becoming dominant player (probably by buying out competitors).
- May be opportunity to establish niche if reducing number of competitors means demand is still high.
- May be opportunity to cut costs by re-engineering production process to reflect reducing market demand.
- May be opportunity to buy stock at 'distress prices' from companies going out of business and sell on at a profit.
- Opportunity for radical product/service innovation.

The next set of typologies refer to the concentration of competitors.

Fragmented – This is a market where there are a large number of similarly-sized competitors, usually in a mature or declining industry.

Implications:

- Well-established competitors.
- Competitive pricing, limited profitability.
- Opportunity to consolidate industry and become market leader (probably by buying out competitors).

Consolidated – This is a market where there are a few, large competitors, usually in a mature or declining industry.

Implications:

- Well-established competitors.
- Defensive pricing possible (meeting or beating new entrants).
- Barriers to entry are likely to be high.
- Few entrepreneurial opportunities other than radical product or market innovation.

It is far easier to start up in a fragmented rather than a consolidated market. However, consolidation often happens as industries mature and decline, which is when some opportunities start to emerge.

The final set of typologies refer to the geographic extent of the market/industry.

Local, regional or national – This is often a new or emerging market that may become global in time.

Implications:

- Gradual geographic roll-out allows marketing mix to be fine-tuned, but at the expense of first-mover advantage.
- Market dominance easier in smaller geographic markets.
- Some markets (e.g. technology-based) can develop geographically over time from developed to developing countries.

Global – This is a market that is international from the start.

Implications:

- Competitors quickly become established in foreign markets.
- Opportunities for foreign start-ups where others have followed a local, regional or national strategy.
- Internet-based new ventures have the opportunity to 'go global' at start-up.
- 'Going global' at start-up can be very expensive.
- Opportunity to expand on a country-by-country basis, varying product/service offering as appropriate.

It is traditionally easier to start up in a local market and gradually spread your customer base but global start-ups are becoming easier to establish because of the internet, allowing products or services targeted at small, very specific customer segments to be sold globally. Sometimes thinking locally can also mean losing the window of opportunity for a good business idea by allowing competitors in.

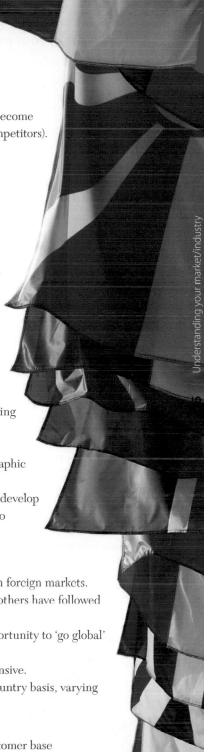

Understanding your market/industry

Researching your market/industry

You might intend to sell your product/service to private or business customers. Desk-based market research should help you estimate the size and growth of your market. It should also help you understand the profile of private or industrial customers. A private customer profile might include personal characteristics (demographics) such as age, gender, socioeconomic group, occupation, location of home, stage in family life cycle, and so on. Similarly, an industrial profile might include type of business, size, location, nature of technology, creditworthiness and so on. It might involve understanding why, where and when customers buy, the structure of established distribution channels and the nature of economic and other environmental trends that might affect the industry. Remember, you need to understand the conventions in a market or industry even if you intend to try to change them. Clearly, whilst you might be able to find this information for an established market/industry, research is far more problematic for new or emerging markets.

> If you ask me how we find new markets, the answer is research, research, research ... For us research is critical when it comes to opening new outlets. We put a lot of work into demographics and social indicators and really know our business. But they can fail: we put a store in Dewsbury, West Yorkshire, four years ago, everything looked good, we did the groundwork, but what the figures didn't show was that our site was in the middle of the town's devoutly Muslim centre. They ate only halal meat, and they certainly weren't eating pizza. We got it wrong and we had to shut the store.

Stephen Hemsley, Chief Executive, Domino's Pizza
Sunday Times **23 May 2004**

Desk-based research is cheap, quick to do and is usually good for getting background information. However, it will not be specific to your business, can be incomplete or inaccurate and may well be out of date. Information on markets, sectors and industries is published in newspapers, trade magazines, industry surveys and reports, trade journals or directories, many of which will be available on the internet. There are websites that provide all sorts of information but the prime source of information in the UK is the British Library, where most national and regional economic and business data and information are housed. Desk research can provide information on product developments, customer needs or characteristics, competitors and market trends. However, for many start-ups local information is of far more importance than regional or national information and that might come from Chambers of Commerce and other local sources of help and advice.

Estimating the size of a new market created by discontinuous innovation or by challenging a market paradigm can be almost impossible. However, as we have just discussed, even estimating the size of a segment of an existing market can be difficult. Market research can provide only so much data. If you wish to introduce a new smartphone app, the fact that there are over 1 billion smartphones worldwide is not entirely relevant. Your app might be in English, which limits the market size, and it might be developed for only one operating system. Then there is the question of the channels through which the app will be sold. All of these factors limit the market that you are attacking – even before you consider the question of whether you are likely to achieve your target market penetration.

You can measure a market size in either value or volumes (units), but you need to distinguish between the different types of market shown in Figure 4.2.

1. **Potential market** is the size of a general market that might be interested in buying a product (e.g. 1 billion smartphones).

2. **Total available market (TAM)** is the size of your prospective market – those in the potential market who might be interested in buying your particular product. This reflects the total sales of competing products (e.g. English apps for a particular operating system).

3. **Served available market (SAM)** is the size of the target market segment you wish to serve within the TAM (e.g. particular app function).

4. **Penetrated market** is the size of the SAM you capture.

SAM is the market segment(s) you are targeting, given any restrictions such as demographics, geography, language, technology etc. Your market share is therefore your penetrated market divided by SAM. If you are seeking funding, your backers will expect you to try to describe both your TAM and SAM, and to estimate their size and the trends within them. They will expect you to be able to explain and justify how you will achieve your penetrated market.

Porter's Five Forces can be a useful vehicle for looking at an industry's structures, assessing the degree of competition in it and, hence, its profit potential (see Academic Insight). Central to this is the rivalry between competing firms. This is based upon the number of competitors (fragmented vs consolidated), industry growth (point in life cycle) and the degree of product differentiation. The relative power of your customers (the fewer there are the higher their buying power) or your suppliers (the fewer there are the higher their power) in your market is important. If you are selling to the big supermarket chains they will squeeze your

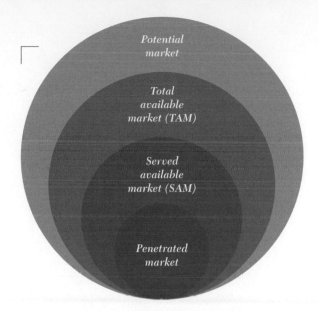

F4.2 Market size definitions

margins. Can competitors set up easily in this industry or are there barriers to entry? As well as the threat of new entrants to a market, there is also the threat of substitute products. How likely are customers to stop buying your product/service? Critical to Porter's analysis is the degree of product differentiation and inbuilt switch costs – the costs of switching to another product. You might question the wisdom of starting up in an industry that is highly competitive (and therefore with low profit potential). However, establishing yourself in an industry with low competitiveness might be very difficult because of the degree of concentration and market power of your competitors. How will they react to your entry? What is more, if the threat of new entrants and/or substitutes is low, how will you be able to enter the market?

Your backers will expect you to have a thorough understanding of your market/industry and the trends within it. If you are launching a new product, not only will they expect it to actually work as you say, but they will also probably expect some market testing to gauge customer reaction to it. They will expect an assessment of its strengths and weaknesses compared to competitors' products.

Porter's Five Forces – assessing industry competitiveness

Michael Porter developed a useful structural analysis of *established* industries which, he claims, determines competitiveness and goes some way towards explaining the profitability of firms within it.

1. Competitive rivalry in the industry
The competitive rivalry of an industry will depend on the number and size of firms within it and their concentration, its newness and growth and, therefore, its attractiveness in terms of profit and value added, together with intermittent over-capacity. Crucially important is the extent of product differentiation, brand identity and switch costs. The greater the competitive rivalry, the less the ability of the firm to charge a high price.

2. Threat of substitutes This revolves around a firm's relative price performance, switch costs and the propensity of the customer to switch, for example because of changes in tastes or fashion. The greater the threat of substitutes, the less the ability of the firm to charge a high price. So, for example, a small firm selling a poorly-differentiated product in a price-sensitive, fashion market would find it difficult to charge a high price.

3. Threat of new entrants Barriers to entry keep out new entrants to an industry. These can arise because of legal protection (patents and so on), economies of scale, proprietary product differences, brand identity, access to distribution, government policy, switch costs, capital costs and so forth. Switch costs are the costs of switching to another product. A firm whose product is protected by patent or copyright may feel that it is relatively safe from competition. The greater the possible threat of new entry to a market, the lower the bargaining power and control over price of the firm within it.

4. Power of buyers This is determined by the relative size of buyers and their concentration. It is also influenced by the volumes they purchase, the information they have about competitors or substitutes, switch costs and their ability to backward integrate. The extent to which the product they are buying is differentiated in some way also affects relative buying power. The greater the power of the buyers, the weaker the bargaining position of the firm selling to them. So, for example, if buyers are large firms, in concentrated industries, buying large volumes with good price information about a relatively undifferentiated product with low switch costs they will be in a strong position to keep prices low, as is the case with supermarkets.

5. Power of suppliers This is also determined by the relative size of firms and the other factors mentioned above. So, for example, if suppliers are large firms in concentrated industries, with well-differentiated products that are relatively important to the small firms buying them, then those small firms are in a weak position to keep prices, and therefore their costs, low.

Porter, M.E. (1985) *Competitive Advantage, Creating and Sustaining Superior Performance*, New York: Free Press.

Identifying your competitors

Of equal importance to knowing your market/industry is the identification of your competitors. You should be able to name them. There are three types of competitors:

- **Direct competitors** – those offering similar or identical products or services. These are the most important because they compete directly and you need to understand just how you are different and better than them, and how you will convince their customers to switch to you.

- **Indirect competitors** – those offering close substitutes. Where you have an innovative product or service you may have no direct competitors but you still need to persuade customers using the 'inferior' competitor offering to switch.

- **Future competitors** – those who could enter your market in the future. If your new venture is successful it will attract competitors. You need to think who they might be and how they might be countered.

Desk research might enable you to evaluate existing competitors in terms of their product/service offering, size, profitability, operating methods and distribution channels. Ultimately you will have to make some judgements about whether they are attacking the same customer segments as you and the quality of their value proposition. How are you different? How sustainable is your competitive advantage? These are issues we shall return to in the next chapter.

You should also assess the influence competitors have over the market. Customers sometimes face switch costs if they change the company they buy from. The higher these are the more they deter competitors from entering the market. Typically, the fewer competitors you face, the more likely your business is to succeed. However, few competitors can be a bad thing in some circumstances. If you are entering a market where there is high concentration, then it may be that these few competitors will combine to deter entry. High concentration can also mean bigger, more powerful companies as competitors and the cost of market entry rises with the dominance of existing players. You need to think carefully before entering a market dominated by big companies because they will have well-established market positions and the resources to fight off new entrants. Finally, it might just be that there are few competitors because the market is so small and/or unattractive.

Nevertheless, with discontinuous innovation or when you are challenging market paradigms with your product/service, it just may be that there is no real, direct competition – at least until new entrants to the market appear. This brings us back to looking at the barriers to entry in the market and, in particular, the legal protection your product/service might enjoy. Again, if you are seeking funding, your backers will expect you to have a thorough understanding of your competitors (real or otherwise) and their strengths and weaknesses compared to you. After all, you will be battling against them in the market.

> The **ability** to play your own game rather than playing the game of a **competitor** is exactly where you want to be as a **company**.
>
> Jeff Weiner, CEO LinkedIn Sunday Times 14 July 2013

Digital Vision/Punchstock

Industry futures

Ultimately, your interest in industry analysis is about trying to predict the future – the threats and opportunities you might face. Unless there are structural reasons, current levels of profitability in an industry are unlikely to be a good predictor of the future as competitors are likely to be attracted to the industry. So, you need to understand the current industry and market structures and then look at how they might change.

Some of the techniques we used in the last chapter to find a business idea can equally be applied to how your industry might look in, say, five years' time, after you have entered the market:

1. The SLEPT analysis can be used to identify the future influences on the industry (you should already have done this).

2. You can then apply these influences to the broad trends you have identified through research into the industry. Is the industry expanding or contracting? Is it consolidating or fragmenting? Is competition intensifying or are products becoming more differentiated?

3. The futures thinking technique can then be used to build up a scenario of how direct and indirect competitors might react to your entry into the market, and where future competitors might come from. How will all this affect the industry? How will this affect you?

4. You can then brainstorm to explore how you might react to these trends and competitors. What strategies might you adopt? Will you need to modify or change your product/service idea? Will you need to identify and enter new markets?

🧳 *Case insight*

Novo Nordisk — Diabetics and obesity 2025

Scenario planning

In 2006 the Danish multinational Novo Nordisk, the leading provider of diabetes treatments in the world, commissioned the Institute for Alternative Futures to produce four scenarios for what was seen as a looming twin epidemic of diabetes and obesity in the Western world. Currently 20.8 million Americans have diabetes. The study estimated that this number will more than double to 50 million by 2025 unless action is taken. The scenarios were designed to show the impact of various courses of action: how serious this twin epidemic could become if the West stayed on its current path, to illustrate the range of options available for averting the crisis, and to demonstrate how learning to meet the challenge of diabetes and obesity could play a major role in the evolution of the health-care system. Starting with a scenario that assumed a continuation of the status quo (which would result in 50 million diabetics in the USA by 2025), each of the subsequent scenarios progressively incorporated more diabetes control factors and laid out the consequences of these actions, with the fourth scenario showing the most comprehensive approach to control.

Novo Nordisk

 Denmark

Scenario planning is a technique that tries to assess how possible future situations might impact on a firm. Trends and drivers of change are identified from the SLEPT analysis and built into scenarios. These situations must be logically consistent possible futures, usually an optimistic, a pessimistic and a 'most likely' future, based around key factors influencing your firm. Optional courses of action or strategies can then be matched to these scenarios. In effect, the scenarios are being used to test the sensitivity of your start-up strategies. They also allow assumptions about the status quo of the environment to be challenged. After the financial crisis of 2008/9 Lego started using scenario planning as part of its annual budgeting process, allowing it to build contingency plans for each 'crisis' scenario that it identified.

This review of the future should generate a series of risks and opportunities that you may face in five years' time. You need to think through how you might cope with them. These in turn generate **strategic options** that you might undertake if the risks or opportunities actually materialize. The more strategic options you can identify, the more flexibility you have. They are sources of real value to you and potential investors. Companies that present many options and/or opportunities are more attractive than those with fewer. In the same way, resources that can be used in a number of different ways are more attractive to own, as opposed to rent or buy in, than those with limited use.

🧳 *Case insight*

Bill Gates and Microsoft

Looking to the future

In 1995, five years before he stepped down as CEO of Microsoft, Bill Gates wrote an internal memo that has become increasingly pertinent:

'Developments on the internet over the next several years will set the course of our industry for a long time to come … I have gone through several stages of increasing my views of its importance. Now I assign the internet the highest level of importance. In this memo I want to make it clear that our focus on the internet is crucial to every part of our business. The internet is the most important single development to come along since the IBM PC was introduced in 1981.'

By 2013, Microsoft had still not managed to focus on the importance of the internet and was falling behind competitors. With Windows and Microsoft Office sales falling sharply, it announced a 'far-reaching realignment of the company' to enable it to respond more quickly to change, 'focusing the whole company on a single strategy'. This involved disbanding product groups and reorganizing into functional lines such as engineering, marketing, advanced strategy and research. Will this be too little, too late? Only time will tell.

🇺🇸 USA

Your review of current and future competition should also start to generate a series of **critical success factors** – things you need to get right to ensure your survival and success. They might come out of your scenario planning and will certainly be amplified and developed as you develop your business model. The sort of questions you are seeking to answer are:

- What drives the competition?
- What are the sectoral, performance and customer conventions that competitors adhere to, and how important are they to customers?
- What are the main dimensions of competition?
- How intense is the competition?
- How can you be different and obtain competitive advantage?

The next considerations that will be critical to your success are: who will be your customers, what do they want and how will you persuade them to purchase your product or service? These are questions we shall address in the next chapter.

Defining a market

The boundary between markets and industries can become very blurred in the fast-moving technology-driven world of the internet, sometimes making the identification of competitors difficult. This is particularly the case when the real fight is for an emerging market that, as yet, is not formally defined. This is the case with the battle between the five US giants of the digital age – Amazon, Apple, Facebook, Google and Microsoft – that was ongoing at the time of writing (2013). In the past, these companies have provided hardware, software and various services, each content to 'stick to the knitting' and focus on its core market. However, new hardware, such as tablet computers and smartphones linked by wi-fi and 3G/4G, and new software in the form of apps are breaking down these barriers.

The battle is to become the sole provider of all our digital requirements, offering a vast range of services tailored to our 'needs', all day, every day, anywhere from the best online platform – a kind of digital utility. The reward is not just the profit from the goods or services that may be purchased but also the digital footprint of users (identified by their IP address) – their internet surfing and buying habits, likes and dislikes, including times of day on the internet and even their location. All of this is collected automatically in real time. It is very valuable to advertisers and salespeople alike, allowing them to offer targeted advertising at particular times of day in particular geographic areas. This has been popularized as:

- Amazon knows what you read;
- Apple knows what you buy;
- Facebook knows what you like;
- Google knows what you want;
- Microsoft knows where you live.

These firms aim to provide the best online platform for the delivery of 'universal internet services'. The more services these companies offer, the more customers they are likely to attract, and the more advertising revenue they are likely to earn. However, each of the Big Five is coming to this new market from different existing markets with new products and services and very different strengths and core competences.

Amazon started life selling books online and now sells almost everything. However, with the introduction of the Kindle, which allows the purchase and reading of books online, it entered the hardware market (it subcontracts production). The introduction of the colour touch-screen Kindle Fire, usefully preloaded with your Amazon account details, not only makes this easier, it also comes with social networking that connects you to others who purchase the same books and films. Amazon also offers a new app shop, online payment system, TV and film streaming and cloud computing facility.

Stockbyte

USA

Apple has become an iconic designer brand offering premium-priced electronic gadgets ranging from its computers to the iPod, iPhone and iPad. It recently integrated Twitter into all the Apple devices. Apple redefined how music sold through iTunes and sells books through iBooks. It also offers a range of apps for its devices. It intends to launch a web-enabled Apple TV shortly, selling films and TV programmes through iTunes. It has just launched iCloud, offering to store data and information on Apple servers. Apple is also sitting on $100 billion of cash – more than any of the other four companies.

Google has become not only the name of a company but also the verb describing what we do when we search the internet for information. As well as information searches, it offers maps, images and many other services. Google also has Gmail, which is well-established in the market, and Gmail+ is designed to make this more social, in direct competition with Facebook. It has its Chrome internet browser. In 2012, its Android operating system had more users than Apple's iPhones and accounted for over half of the worldwide smartphone sales. It makes mobile phones and tablets with a range of partners, including Samsung and HTC, and in 2012 purchased the consumer division of Motorola. It now makes its own smartphones and tablets under the brand name Google Nexus. It has Google Music, offering music downloads, and owns YouTube, where you can watch and now rent TV programmes and films, and has plans to launch Google TV. It has its own online payment system called Google Wallet.

Facebook, the ubiquitous social network site, has improved itself and now offers many of the features of Google+. At the time of writing (2013) it was about to launch a 'broader, more social' email system that (it said) would make Gmail 'old fashioned'. It was also about to launch its own Facebook phone, from which photos and status updates could be uploaded to a Facebook page at a click. In a strategic alliance with Netflix (the films and TV website), Spotify (the music streamer) and Zynga (the computer gamer), it intended to launch Facebook TV, Facebook movies, Facebook music and Facebook games. It even has Facebook credits, a virtual currency used to play computer games. It is exploring whether to offer its own internal search service, based on the data provided by Facebook subscribers rather than computer algorithms. These developments have been partly financed by Facebook's stock market launch in 2012, which was estimated to have brought in over $5 billion.

Microsoft predates the other four companies, starting as the supplier of the ubiquitous Windows Operating System and then the Microsoft Office suite of software. It also has the internet browser Outlook Express. Many computers come with its software already installed, including the Internet browser – which has been the subject of some anti-trust actions. It offers server applications and cloud computing services such as Azure. It has entertainment systems including the Xbox video gaming system, the handheld Zune media player, and the television-based internet appliance MSN TV.

Microsoft also markets personal computer hardware including mice, keyboards, and game controllers such as joysticks and gamepads. Arguably, it missed the internet revolution and since then has been playing catch-up by expanding, often by acquisition, into search engines such as Bing. It recently purchased the video communications company, Skype, and has entered into a strategic alliance with Nokia to produce smartphones with its own operating system – the Windows Phone. It is also imitating Apple and starting to open its own retail outlets.

All of this leads to the question of where this convergence of competition will lead. Will there be one winner? And what will we call this new industry?

Questions:

1. *What industries/markets do these five companies originate from?*
2. *Why are these markets converging?*
3. *What might this new industry/ market look like?*

Summary

- You need to identify and be able to describe the characteristics of the market or industry within which you will operate. However, drawing the boundaries of your industry can be difficult and is a question of judgement.

- Desk research is cheap and quick. It should help you to estimate the size of your market.

- Your total available market (TAM) is the size of your potential market – those who might be interested in buying your particular product. This reflects the total sales of competing products. Your served available market (SAM) is the size of the target market segment you wish to serve within the TAM. Your penetrated market is the size of the SAM you actually capture. Your market share is your penetrated market divided by SAM.

- Porter's Five Forces will help you assess the degree of competition within established industries.

- The profitability of individual companies within an industry can vary widely, implying that your choice and, just as important, execution of strategy is probably more significant than your choice of industry.

- Your interest in industry analysis is about trying to predict the future – the threats and opportunities you might face. You can use techniques such as SLEPT analysis, brainstorming, futures thinking and scenario planning to help you do this.

- Your analysis should generate a series of risks and opportunities, as well as strategic options that you might undertake if they actually materialize. The more strategic options that you can identify, the more flexibility you have. They are sources of real value to you and potential investors.

- Your analysis should also generate a series of critical success factors – things you need to get right in order to ensure survival and success. These will be amplified and developed as you develop your business model.

Exercise 4.1
Describing your market/industry

1 Research your general market/industry and your TAM at a macro level. Find out as much as you can about the size, growth and structure of the market, market trends, customer demographics, buying patterns, established channels of distribution etc. Which market/industry typologies characterize it? Note the implications of this.

2 How is the particular market you are targeting – your SAM – different (e.g. local vs national, other characteristics)? Repeat 1 for your SAM.

3 List your direct and indirect competitors. Against each, list their strengths and weaknesses as companies.

4 List the strengths and weaknesses of the products or services they produce that compete with yours. Combine the two lists.

Exercise 4.2
Assessing the degree of competition

The Five Forces model can be used to assess the degree of competition you face in an existing market/industry and, hence, the threat to your profitability. However, there may be things you can do to mitigate this threat.

Using the format opposite, for each of the forces:

1 Assess the threat to industry profitability.

2 Note the implications of this for you.

3 List the actions you need to take to ensure that you can avoid or lessen the effect of high threats to profitability.

4 List the actions you need to take to create a sustainable position that means others cannot copy these actions.

If there are no actions you can take in an industry with a high degree of competition, you may want to reconsider whether you want to enter it and return to the exercises in the previous chapter to find another business idea. However, if there is a low degree of competition you may equally need to consider why this is the case and whether it will stay the same after your entry. How will existing companies react to your entry? If the threat of new entrants and/or substitutes is low, how will you be able to enter the market?

Competitive Force:	Threat to industry profitability			Implications	Actions to lessen/avoid threats	Actions to sustain position
	Low	Medium	High			
Rivalry among existing firms (e.g. number of competitors, industry structure, degree of product differentiation etc.)						
Threat of substitutes (e.g. degree of product differentiation, switch costs etc.)						
Threat of new entrants (e.g. barriers to entry, switch costs, economies of scale, access to distribution channels, degree of differentiation, capital requirements etc.)						
Bargaining power of suppliers (e.g. switch costs, supplier concentration, attractiveness of substitutes etc.)						
Bargaining power of buyers (e.g. switch costs, buyer concentration, product differentiation, buyers' costs etc.)						

Exercise 4.3

Assessing your market/industry future

1 Undertake a SLEPT analysis on your market/industry to identify key influences or events that might affect it over the next five years.

2 Using the market/industry analysis from Exercises 4.1 and 4.2, construct three scenarios – 'best', 'worst' and 'most likely' cases – that reflect how these influences or events might impact upon the trends in the industry. Remember to factor in the existence of your firm.

- Will the industry expand or contract? Will it consolidate or fragment?
- Are the main dimensions of competition changing and what is driving this change?
- Will sectoral, performance and/or customer conventions change?
- Will competition intensify or will products become more differentiated?
- How will direct and indirect competitors be affected?
- How might they react to your existence?
- How will their reaction affect you?

3 Brainstorm to explore how you might react to these trends and competitors.

- What strategies might you adopt?
- Will you need to modify or change your product/service idea?
- Will you need to identify and enter new markets?

4 List the critical success factors for your business – the things you need to get right to ensure your survival and success.

Visit www.palgrave.com/companion/burns-new-venture-creation
for chapter quizzes to test your knowledge and other resources.

5
STRUCTURING YOUR BUSINESS
MODEL

Contents

Learning outcomes

When you have read this chapter and undertaken the related exercises you will be able to:
- Identify and describe your customer segments
- Define your value proposition for each customer segment
- Set your selling price(s)
- Describe how these value propositions fit into an overall marketing strategy

Identifying your market segments

The business model is at the core of the New Venture Creation Framework shown in Figure 1.3. The first step in developing your business model is to identify the market segment(s) and core value proposition(s) for your business idea – your customers, what they want and why they will buy from you. A business will only succeed if it offers customers a value proposition that meets their real needs or solves real problems for them. The initial target market should also be the group of customers that most need your solution to their problem because other solutions are less satisfactory. Whilst customers are all individuals, it is usually possible to group them in some meaningful way, for example by identifying their different group needs or problems. These are called market segments.

Normally, it is only possible to communicate with customers economically by grouping. The key for a start-up is to identify and focus limited resources on just three or four clearly defined, important and sizeable market segments. The marketing mix, marketing and communications strategy can then be tailored to the needs of customers in these different segments. Of course you will not turn away customers who don't fall into these segments, this is just about focusing your limited resources where they are likely to have the greatest return.

Clippykit (now Clippy) Daily Telegraph 6 February 2009

Vary your **markets**. Think about how your **product** could fit into different markets. Clippykit works for retail, the promotions industry and education.

Calypso Rose, founder Clippy

There are many ways of segmenting markets and there are no prescriptive approaches. Market segments match groups of customers with their product/service wants or needs – the benefits they are looking for. The segment can be any one, or a combination, of descriptive factors. The descriptive factors for private customers might include personal demographics (e.g. age, gender, socioeconomic group, occupation, stage in family life etc.), geographic location, channels of distribution used to get the product to market etc. For business markets, they might include type of business, size, location, nature of technology and so on. You are looking for groups of customers with similar needs who can be identified and described in some meaningful and useful way. You are looking for a gap in the market where the needs of a particular segment are not being met as well as they could be.

To be viable a market segment must be:

1. Distinctive with significantly different needs from other segments. Without this the segment boundaries are likely to be too blurred.

2. Sufficiently large, or willing to pay a high enough price, to make the segment commercially attractive. It may be that a gap in the market exists because it is not commercially viable.

3. Accessible. The gap in the market might not exist in reality because the segment cannot be reached through communication or distribution channels.

4. Defendable from competitors. If the segment is not defendable, for example because it is a commodity market, prices and profits will quickly reduce as competition increases.

Market segments vary in size. The slimmer the market segment that the product or service is tailored to suit, the higher customer satisfaction is likely to be; but so too is cost – and therefore price. We all like personal service and the ultimate market segment comprises just one customer.

However, this might not be a commercially viable segment. The trend is towards slimmer and slimmer market segments, particularly since the internet has made it easier to link customers with similar needs in different geographic areas. The danger facing firms selling to slim market segments is their overreliance on a small customer base. If tastes change the segment might disappear.

© Natikka – istockphoto.com

Defining your value proposition

Your value proposition is why customers buy from you rather than from another company. Customers buy a product or service because it provides a benefit or solves a problem for them. The features of a product or service must combine to deliver a benefit to customers, or they will not buy it. And different market segments might be looking for different benefits. The features of a car combine to provide the benefit of transport, but customers are looking for more than just transport and different customers want different things – which is why there are numerous types of cars and many producers.

One widely used technique for describing the features of a product or service is the marketing mix or the 'Five Ps', a convenient shorthand for: product/service (functional specification, design etc.), price, promotion (or communication), place of sale (including distribution channels) and people (or related service). Features included in this classification are shown in Table 5.1. Customers buy benefits not features, but all of the features can provide benefits to the customer and therefore enhance the value proposition. The customer buys the marketing mix as a package, and the mix must be consistent to reinforce the overall benefit that the customer is looking for. The marketing mix is only as strong as its weakest link. So, for example, a low price for a quality product might jeopardize sales because it sends a confused message and raises questions of credibility. A high price can be charged for a quality product, but the other elements of the marketing mix still need to be consistent with this.

For a start-up, which is likely to be short of money, the founding entrepreneur is central to the whole marketing mix. Of necessity, their approach to marketing will probably be very much hands-on and face-to-face. They might use their network of contacts to find customers and suppliers. They might develop strong personal relationships with customers to secure repeat sales. This can be a distinctive competitive advantage over larger firms that adds value to the customer. Indeed, one particularly effective entrepreneurial strategy is to identify a sector in which customer relationships are weak and to create value by tightening them up. In the longer term, this relationship can evolve into a distinctive brand. Customer relationships are an important part of the marketing mix and marketing strategy.

Whilst any individual element of the marketing mix may not be unique and can often be easily copied, elements of the mix can be combined to produce something unique and distinctive. It is the combination that is unique, not the individual elements, and this can provide a differential advantage over competitors (see Lush Case Insight). If the combination is sufficiently unique it may challenge existing market paradigms. Establishing a brand that captures the elements of uniqueness can itself add value to the value proposition. And building switch costs for customers into the value proposition can also enhance your competitive position by discouraging them from buying from competitors. Or, rather than building costs into your proposition, you could offer additional benefits for customer loyalty.

Product/service	Price	Promotion	Place	People
• Quality	• List price	• Communication	• Location	• Relationships
• Performance	• Discounts (volume, loyalty etc.)	• Advertising	• Layout	• Service
• Design		• PR	• Distribution channels	• Advice
• Newness or novelty	• Auction	• Word-of-mouth		• Support
• Colours	• Negotiated	• Fairs and exhibitions	• Retail/wholesale	• Partnerships
• Sizes	• Payment terms	• Sponsorship	• Internet	
• Specification	• Special offers	• Competitions	• Telephone	
• Customization	• Differential or segment pricing	• Point-of-sale displays	• Face-to-face selling	
• Packaging		• Brand		
• Convenience				

T5.1 The marketing mix

Service-dominant marketing logic

Academic insight

In their award-winning paper 'Evolving to a New Dominant Logic for Marketing', Vargo and Lusch (2004) seem to have changed the dominant logic of marketing academia. They argued that customers valued and purchased services rather than goods, and goods should therefore be viewed as a medium for delivering or 'transmitting' the firm's services. They defined service as 'the application of specialized competences (knowledge and skills) through deeds, processes, and performances for the benefit of another entity or the entity itself'. In this way companies manufacturing cars are not in the business of selling cars but in the business of providing 'mobility services' through the cars that they manufacture – a concept adopted by Andrew Valentine with Streetcar (see Case Insight in Chapter 3). Thus, all industries are service industries and it therefore becomes vital for firms to understand the service that consumers are seeking from them. It requires a shift in focus from the product to the consumer and an understanding of their needs and how these translate into a service they value.

Vargo, S.L. and Lusch, R.F. (2004) 'Evolving to a New Dominant Logic for Marketing', *Journal of Marketing*, 68(1).

Core value propositions

It has been argued that there are only three core value propositions that offer fundamental ways of achieving sustainable competitive advantage:

- **Low price/low cost** – This is where customers value low price more than anything. In this case low price can only be achieved through low costs and, if there are economies of scale to be achieved, a firm must achieve them quickly to survive. These sorts of products are virtually all commodities.

- **High differentiation** – This is where customers value the other elements of the marketing mix more than price and are therefore willing to pay a premium. Often quality of product/service is a key element of differentiation but the more product/service benefits you offer the more ways you will be different from competitors.

- **Customer focus** – This is where the fifth 'P' (people or service) is important, and ensures that customers are provided with a product/service that is more closely tailored to their specific requirements. The key to having a customer focus is the ability to have a close relationship with them, and it goes hand-in-hand with effective market segmentation.

Each of the core value propositions has different business imperatives, shown in Table 5.2. Business imperatives are the things that you need to keep on top of, or you risk failing to deliver your value proposition. They often translate into critical success factors for your business – things you **must** get right – and their achievement might be linked to key milestones. These imperatives can be conflicting, particularly between low cost/low price and the other two propositions. Because of this, some large companies with product ranges based on different value propositions, have unbundled their activities and set up separate organizations focused on those products with particular core value propositions. In this way, managers of these smaller organizations have clear imperatives.

Low price/low cost	High differentiation	Customer focus
• Maintain cost leadership through economies of scale	• Understand the basis for the differential advantage	• Maintain close relationships with customers
• Continually drive down costs	• Build on differential advantage	• Keep in touch with and understand changes in customer needs
• Achieve high sales volumes	• Build barriers to entry	• Maintain customer loyalty
• Improve efficiency	• Build the brand	• Maximize sales to existing loyal customers (economies of scope)
• Standardize	• Continuous innovation	• Build the brand
	• Encourage creativity and innovation	

T5.2 Core value propositions and business imperatives

🧳 *Case insight*

easyJet (1)

Low cost/low price strategy

One firm that has successfully followed the low cost/low price strategy is easyJet. It was founded by Stelios Haji-Ioannou, a MBA from London Business School, in 1995 with £5 million borrowed from his father, a Greek shipping tycoon. easyJet copied the business model of the US carrier Southwest Airlines, changing the marketing paradigm for the industry, and in doing so created a whole new market for low-cost airline travel in Europe. The company has transformed the European air travel market and has beaten off many rival imitators. Today it is a leading European airline. easyJet was floated on the Stock Market in 2000, making Stelios £280 million profit.

Only seven years after founding the company and still owning 29%, Stelios realized that he was not suited to managing a public company. He was better suited to being a serial entrepreneur, so in 2002 he resigned as chairman, aged only 35. He was to be replaced by Sir Colin Chandler, aged 62, previously part of London's financial establishment as chairman of Vickers Defence Systems, deputy chairman of Smiths Group and director of Thales.

> *Sunday Times 29 October 2000*
>
> You start the **business** as a dream, you make it your **passion** for a while and then you get **experienced** managers to run it because it's not as much **fun** as starting.

> *The Times 19 April 2002*
>
> Running a company that is **listed** on the Stock Exchange is different from building up and running a **private** company. The history of the City is littered with **entrepreneurs** who hold onto their creations for too long, failing to recognise the **changing needs** of the company. I am a serial entrepreneur … It is all part of **growing up**. I've built something and now it is time to move on.

A central strategy of being low-price is being low-cost and that has a number of implications for the way easyJet and its rivals are run. Aircraft are leased rather than owned. Low costs come from two driving principles – firstly 'sweating', or making maximum use of, the assets and secondly operating at high efficiency. easyJet flies 'point-to-point' (average trip length about 1000 kilometres), without the connecting flights and networks that the heritage carriers, like British Airways (BA), have to worry about. easyJet flies its planes for 11 hours a day – 4 hours longer than BA. Their pilots fly 900 hours a year, 50% more than BA pilots. In terms of operating efficiency, it means:

- Aircraft fly out of low-cost airports. These are normally not the major airport serving a destination and can be some distance from the destination.
- Aircraft are tightly scheduled. Rapid turnaround is vital. Low-cost airlines aim to allow only 25 minutes to offload one set of passengers and load another, less than half the time of heritage rivals.
- Aircraft must leave and arrive on time (they will not wait for passengers), because delays can have horrendous knock-on consequences for the timetable. Nevertheless, punctuality is varied, with the low-cost carriers just as good as more expensive airlines on some routes.
- There is no 'slack' in the system. easyJet admits to having 'one and a half planes' worth' of spare capacity compared with the dozen planes BA has on stand-by at Gatwick and Heathrow. If something goes wrong with a plane it can lead to cancellations and long delays.
- There are fewer cabin crew than more expensive rivals and staff rostering is a major logistical problem.
- All operations and processes must be slimmed down and made as simple as possible.

In terms of customer service, it means:

- Ticketless flights, without seat reservation.
- A single class, which means more seats on each plane but no 'frills' such as complimentary drinks, meals or assigned seats – all additional services must be paid for.
- Baggage allowances are lower than heritage carriers and there is no compensation for delays or lost baggage.
- Transfers not guaranteed, because the planes could be late.
- Aerobridges for boarding and disembarking are generally not used because these add cost.
- Concentration on point-to-point flights, whereas the heritage airlines tend to concentrate on hub-and-spoke traffic.

One of the fears about low-cost airlines has been that they will be tempted to compromise on safety for the sake of cutting costs. The British Airline Pilots Association has claimed that pilots of low-cost airlines have been tempted to cut corners to achieve flight timetables. The industry is all too aware that the low-cost US airline, Valuejet, went bankrupt after one of its planes crashed in 1996, killing all 110 people on board. However, by partnering with some of the best known maintenance providers in the industry, easyJet make safety their first priority. In common with other low-cost operators, it operates a single type of aircraft. This offers economies of purchasing, maintenance, pilot training and aircraft utilization.

easyJet has started to move away from being the lowest-cost carrier, and is adding customer value, for example by flying to airports nearer to major cities. AirAsia is now generally regarded as the lowest-cost airline in the world with Ryanair, a competitor of easyJet, not far behind. Interestingly Ryanair has so little faith in its timetable that it advises passengers not to book connecting flights.

easyJet is generally regarded as having an excellent branding strategy – originally based on PR around its founder – and having one of the best websites in the sector. It is aggressive in promoting its brand and running advertising promotions that maximize seat occupancy. It realizes that planes must have a high seat occupancy to be economic. To this end it is particularly inventive with pricing, encouraging real bargain hunters onto the less popular flights during the day and promoting early bookings with cheaper fares. easyJet has been at the forefront of the use of the internet for virtual ticketing, and now sells all of its tickets online. This means it does not have to pay commission to travel agents, and check-in can be quicker and more efficient. Its website has been held up as a model for the industry and many have copied it. easyJet also try to get more sales from every passenger visiting their website by offering other services such as airport car parking, car hire and hotel bookings.

The industry in Europe has seen some fierce price wars as competitors battled for market share in a fast-growing market where there were economies of scale to be had. easyJet has been aggressive in buying out competitors (e.g. Go in 2002) and purchasing new routes and landing rights – which can be difficult to secure – giving it a comprehensive European network and securing the economies of scale that it needed. These days the low-cost airline industry is well-established and far more difficult to enter. AirAsia entered the market in 2002, copying the successful low-cost model but in a new market without competitors.

Questions:

1. *From the information given, map out as much as you can of the business model for easyJet using the New Venture Creation Framework. What are the key elements of competitive advantage in their value proposition?*

2. *What are the operational imperatives for easyJet? Show how these are achieved.*

3. *Describe the market segments the core value proposition of easyJet is aimed at. Which market segments might it not appeal to?*

4. *How important is low cost compared to customer satisfaction? Which is more important and why? How do you go about compromising the core value proposition?*

5. *If you start to compromise your core value proposition, how far do you have to go before it is no longer core?*

Up-to-date information on easyJet can be found on their website: www.easyjet.com

Core value disciplines

A number of academic authors have claimed that there are only three core value propositions. Treacy and Wiersema (1995) call them value disciplines. These are consistent with the fundamental ways of creating sustainable competitive advantage popularized earlier by Michael Porter (1985) as 'generic marketing strategies'. The three value disciplines are:

- Operational excellence/Low price These companies have a good product/market offering but high fixed costs make large volumes essential to achieve the economies of scale needed to keep costs and prices low (e.g. McDonald's or Dell). Price is more important than other elements of the marketing mix. Fierce competition for market share will lead to a market with a few dominant big players. They are efficiency- and cost-focused. You enter an established market like this at your peril.
- Product leadership/Differentiation These companies offer the best quality or most innovative products (e.g. Apple or Rolls Royce). They are able to charge premium prices because other elements of the marketing mix are more important than price. They were early entrants to the market and moved quickly to establish themselves, often with premium branding. Small companies can thrive with this offering (e.g. Quad Electroacoustics).
- Customer intimacy/Focus These companies understand their customers' needs and develop close relationships with them, often based on good customer service (e.g. Coutts Bank). The fifth 'P' (people and service) is important to customers. Customer loyalty is high. Economies of scope are important so that the company can spread its costs over different products, for example by giving a range of products a prestige brand image. Despite the opportunity for economies of scope, small companies can thrive with this offering (e.g. Morgan Motor Company).

Treacy and Wiersema say there are four questions that you need to answer:

1. For each dimension, what proportion of customers focus on it as their primary or dominant decision criterion? In other words, how important is each value discipline to each market segment?
2. Which competitors provide the best value in each of these value dimensions? In other words, who is your major competitor in each discipline?
3. How do you compare to the competition on each dimension?
4. If you fall short of the value leaders in each dimension of value, how can this be remedied? Of course, if you do fall short the real question is whether you can compete at all, or whether you have constructed a sufficiently different value proposition to create a new market not currently catered for.

Porter, M. (1985) *Competitive Advantage: Creating and Sustaining Superior Performance*, New York: Free Press.

Treacy, M. and Wiersema, F. (1995) *The Discipline of Market Leaders*, Reading, MA: Addison-Wesley.

Different value propositions can exist side by side in the same industry if it is sufficiently large and heterogeneous. For example, the business model for low-cost airlines like Southwest Airlines, easyJet and AirAsia is very different from that of flagship carriers like Delta, British Airways and Emirates. Both Dell and Apple exist successfully in the personal computing market, but with completely different strategies serving different market segments. There is certainly no golden formula for success.

Competitors will, however, usually try to copy successful value propositions and today's novel business idea can often prove to be tomorrow's norm. So the question is, for how long can the elements of differentiation be sustained? Performance against competitors needs to be continually reviewed. Value propositions need to be continually reinforced but also improved. They might also need, eventually, to be changed, and doing this goes to the core of the skills, capabilities and competences a company has and the strategies it should employ.

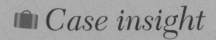
Dell Computers

Changing your value proposition

Dell has adopted both a low price/low cost and a customer focus value proposition (selling direct and allowing customers to configure their own computers). Dell were market leaders in the provision of value-for-money computers because they integrated their supply chain with their online retail operations. Their fully integrated value chain – a B2C2B business model – meant that customers could configure their own computers and order online whilst suppliers had real-time access to orders and deliveries, so that Dell could receive stocks on a just-in-time basis, keeping the assembly line moving and minimizing their costs. They patented many of the innovations in this integrated value chain but ultimately competitors were able to copy many of these technological developments and integrate their supply chains so as to achieve similar cost savings. This element of Dell's differential advantage is now less effective and the question is whether Dell's direct relationship with customers is now of higher value than their low price/low cost proposition. If it is, then Dell might also want to sell other digital consumer electronics and office automation equipment direct to customers. Indeed it has already started doing so. And why should it not sub-contract more of its assembly, focusing rather on the core strength that the customer values – the direct relationship? Again this is something it has started doing. This raises many questions about the scope of Dell's activities and the nature of its business domain. But this is nothing new. Amazon moved from the virtual sale of physical products produced by other people (books, CDs, DVDs etc.) to the virtual sale of virtual items (eBooks and music) and on to the sale of its own brand of eReader, the Kindle (which it does not manufacture), to use for the purchase and enjoyment of books and music. As we saw in the Case Insight in the last chapter, it is now one of the 'Big Data' companies competing to be the sole provider of all our digital requirements.

Niche marketing strategy

Companies that offer both high differentiation and customer focus are said to have a niche marketing strategy. Market focus involves understanding in depth the needs of relatively few customers and therefore there is more scope for differentiation. It often involves targeting smaller markets and therefore there are more opportunities for smaller businesses. This is the strategy that research tells us is most likely to succeed for a start-up since they can charge higher prices and are more likely to sustain their differential advantage because the smaller market segment does not attract competitors, at least initially. What is more, the internet has meant that market niches can be global and consequently, whilst there may be a clear identification of the needs of a few customers, the global size of this market segment could be quite large. And once the start-up dominates one market niche, it can move on to another.

There is usually a trade-off between price and the other elements of the marketing mix. The stronger or more distinctive and different these other elements, the higher the price you are normally able to command. Too many small firms compete primarily on price because they do not understand how the other elements might add value to the customer. They believe that the other elements of their marketing mix are insufficiently different from their competitors'.

> **Martyn Dawes, founder Coffee Nation Startups: wwwstartups.co.uk**
>
> If you set up a **company** selling widgets like the bloke down the road and the only **difference** is that yours are cheaper, you'll make a living but that's all you'll achieve. If you can be truly **differentiated** and **unique**, then you've really got something.

One small firm producing motor components found itself competing unsuccessfully against a large multinational that consistently undercut it on price. It decided that it could not survive with a value proposition relying on operational excellence/low cost and decided it needed a rethink. It researched its customers and the market and found there were many opportunities for products manufactured to a high technical specification in which quality and supplier reputation were more important than the price charged – a product leadership/differentiation value proposition – so it decided to switch its strategy. Low volumes and high price for specialist products proved to be a more sustainable strategy and, over time, it was able to develop close relationships with a few of its regular customers and became an established niche player in what otherwise might be seen as a highly competitive industry.

 UK

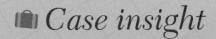 💼 *Case insight*

Quad Electroacoustics

Niche markets

In the UK one Huntingdon-based family company that has been very successful in differentiating its products and selling to a small but lucrative market segment is Quad Electroacoustics. Originally founded in 1936 by Peter Walker as an 'acoustical manufacturing company' to produce 'public address' systems, today its silvery grey, bizarrely sculptured audio equipment looks like no other. It sounds superb as well. When Japanese 'competitors' bring out new models every year, Quad's stay the same and last for ever. Its original electrostatic loudspeaker was in production for 28 years. Quads are a byword for quality, reliability and design originality – but they are not cheap. Current models sell for over £3000 and still 70% of Quad's sales are exported, especially to Europe, the USA and Japan.

Up-to-date information on Quad can be found on their website: www.quad-hifi.co.uk

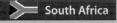 South Africa

💼 *Case insight*

Escape to the Cape

Niche markets

Escape to the Cape is a venture set up by Shaheed Ebrahim in 2010 in South Africa. The tourism industry is a fiercely competitive business in South Africa, but the company offers guided tours with a difference around Cape Town. Shaheed spent about $4000 to register his company and get a website, and then took out a mortgage of $32,000 to buy a 7-seater bus which he equipped with the latest internet technology. As well as having an expert guide, the bus is equipped with wi-fi and clients can borrow a complimentary tablet computer that then allows them to go online to email, Facebook or Tweet their family and friends with emails, photos or videos of their tour. They can even talk to them using Skype. Every seat has a facility to charge any mobile device. The bus has its own fridge offering a range of drinks including complimentary chilled water. Shaheed won the Emerging Tourism Entrepreneur of the Year award in South Africa for 2011/12.

BBC News Business 31 January 2013

There are hundreds of tour operators out in Cape Town but the difference is that we've taken technology that's available and put it onto our tours, thereby enhancing the tours.

Morgan Motor Company

Niche markets

One company, that arguably could make even higher margins by charging a higher price for its products, is the Morgan Motor Company. Founded in 1909, it is the world's oldest privately-owned car manufacturer, making a quintessentially British sports car. Every Morgan is hand-built and looks like it came from the 1930s. Each car is different, with a choice of 35,000 body colours and leather upholstery to match. It takes seven weeks to build a car and customers are invited to the factory to see the process. Morgan sells only about 500 cars a year, half overseas, and demand exceeds supply, cushioning the company from the vagaries of the market. Morgan is a unique car manufacturer in a niche market.

Morgan Motor Cars

Up-to-date information on Morgan can be found on their website: www.morgan-motor.co.uk

Setting your prices

Setting price is a crucial element of the marketing strategy, but it is an art rather than a science. You may have one list price for your product or different prices for different market segments. Alternatively, you may operate an auction or negotiate the price of your product. You may offer discounts for types of purchases such as volume or loyalty and even prompt payment. There may be special offers at sales times.

The underlying principle is that the price charged for a product or service ought to reflect the **value-to-customer** of the package of benefits. The value can be different to different customers and in different circumstances. Take, for example, the price charged for emergency, compared to routine, plumbing work. A premium price reflects the benefit to the customer of preventing the house being flooded. However, the features of that emergency service, as reflected in the marketing mix, must reflect the benefits the customer is looking for: ease of telephone call-out, 24-hour fast and efficient service, clear-up, facilitation of insurance claims and so on. Similarly, a low-cost airline such as easyJet is able to charge a range of different prices for what is essentially the same service, transportation from one place to another, for example by offering early booking or off-peak fares. However, there is usually a **going rate** that is charged by competing firms for a similar product or service.

One factor in the pricing decision is the costs you face. Many people use what is called **cost+** or **full-cost** pricing. This takes the total cost of producing a product or delivering a service and divides it by the predicted number of units to be sold to arrive at the average cost, to which a target mark-up is then added. Some costs, often called overheads, are **fixed**, and do not change with volume (e.g. depreciation of equipment, rent and some salaries). So what happens if predicted sales volumes are not achieved? The same fixed costs have to be spread over smaller volumes; implying that you need to charge a higher price to recover the overheads –

a strategy that itself is likely to lead to falling sales. The reverse is true if volumes are greater than predicted.

Another benchmark is the **variable cost** of the product or service – the cost of producing one additional unit (e.g. the costs of materials or components and piece-work labour). In general, you cannot charge just your variable cost because you are not recovering those fixed overhead costs. Unless price is above variable cost, there is no incentive to produce because each additional unit sold would incur an additional loss. However, if you are want to charge a range of prices to different market segments, these can be as low as your variable cost, so long as the average price you charge is above your full cost. The lower your variable cost, the greater discretion you have in pricing. This is why off-peak tickets on low-cost airlines can be so much lower than peak fares. The extra variable cost of taking a passenger off-peak, when the plane is not full, is very low.

Pricing is therefore a question of judgement. Figure 5.1 shows the pricing range. Minimum short-term price is set by the variable cost, but long-term viability is set by the full cost price. The average value-to-customer price needs to be above this. However, this can be made up of a range of prices to different segments, some of which might be bellow full cost (segments A, B and C).

PhotoDisc/Getty Images

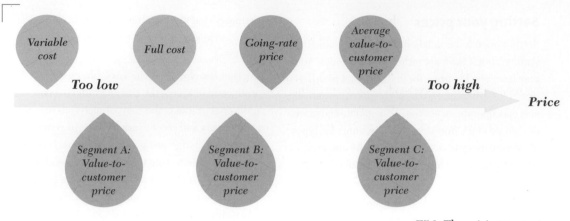

F5.1 The pricing range

Since it is always easier to lower prices than to raise them, it is important not to under-price your product/service. The price you charge should reflect the value-to-customer (Figure 5.1). However, if customers show resistance to this price you can always offer a one-off, introductory discount – but this needs to be consistent with your launch strategy (see Chapter 7). In this way you have established the market price and can remove the discount in due course. If you can do this on a customer-by-customer basis it should help you establish the actual value-to-customer. When you then try to remove the discount you can reappraise the effect on demand. However, for most products/services, the lower your price the higher your sales are likely to be. The question is whether that will lead to higher profit – and that is not always the case.

Price and volumes

How demand reacts to changes in price is determined by the cross elasticity of demand. The more differentiated the product or service, the more price inelastic is demand – the volume sold does not vary greatly with changes in price. The more the product or service is a commodity, the more price will be elastic – sales volumes will be affected by price changes. Price elasticity may

sound a highly theoretical concept, but the practical applications of it are important.

Table 5.3 shows the increase in sales volume required to maintain the same level of profitability as a result of a price reduction. This depends on the contribution margin (sales price minus variable cost, expressed as a percentage of the sales price) before the price cut. If the contribution margin is only 20% and you were tempted to cut prices by 15%, you would have to increase sales volume by a massive 300% – a quadrupling of sales – just to generate the same profit as before. The higher the margin the less the effect, but even at 40% margin, you would still have to increase sales by 60%.

		Contribution margin		
		20%	30%	40%
Price reduction	−5%	+33%	+20%	+14%
	−10%	+100%	+50%	+33%
	−15%	+300%	+100%	+60%

T5.3 The effect of price reductions on profit

In contrast, Table 5.4 shows the decrease in sales volume that could sustain the same level of profitability in the face of a price increase. The 20% margin could see a reduction in sales volume of 43% as a result of a 15% price increase, and would still generate the same level of profit. Of course, the effect is less the higher the margin. However, if you cut overhead costs at the same time (why maintain the same level of staff with less work?) you should see profits increase. Alternatively, you might decide to improve the level of service offered by redirecting these overheads so as to justify the higher price. Either way, lower volumes might mean that stock holdings and other capital costs will reduce, an important consideration if capital is scarce.

		Contribution margin		
		20%	30%	40%
Price	+5%	−20%	−14%	−11%
increase	+10%	−33%	−25%	−20%
	+15%	−43%	−33%	−27%

T5.4 **The effect of price increases on profit**

As you can see from these tables, if you are working on slim margins, lowering prices may well lead to increased sales volumes, but it may also lead to lower profits. On the other hand, increasing prices may lead to increased profits despite lower sales volumes. Tables 5.3 and 5.4 show how low profit margins make you very vulnerable to price competition and high profit margins give you greater price discretion, allowing you to price differentially (segments A, B and C in Figure 5.1).

These calculations underline the importance of understanding the costs related to your business. Your financial structure influences the business model, the funding you need and the risks you face. We shall return to this in Chapter 11.

Understanding your customers

Focusing on the needs of your market segments and delivering distinctive, differentiated value propositions to each of them is at the very core of developing your marketing strategy. The elements of the marketing mix, related to the customer segments they are targeted at, together make up the marketing strategy of the firm. The marketing strategy delivers the value proposition to the target market segment. Marketing strategy is just a series

of related tasks that, taken together, have coherence and give direction.

Let us take pens as an example. One type of pen is the cheap, disposable ball-point, bought simply as a writing implement. Clearly, its core value proposition to end-use customers is based upon low price/low cost, and the pen manufacturer needs to drive down costs and drive up volumes. Pens of this sort sell for a few pennies in volumes of 100+, but for much more (although still very cheaply) when sold individually. These pens typically have a low-cost, functional plastic shell, usually with a cap. Two end-use market segments might be private customers and organizations with employees needing pens. The characteristics of these segments and the routes to market are shown in Figure 5.2. Our pen manufacturer needs to understand the benefits these two segments are seeking. They are looking for a pen that writes satisfactorily and can be conveniently purchased, but is also cheap and therefore disposable. If new technologies produce cheaper, more convenient ways of writing or passing messages, these customers may stop purchasing pens altogether – which is happening because of smartphones and computers.

However, our pen manufacturer also needs to understand the routes to market, shown in the lower part of Figure 5.2. Channels of distribution are important for this product and each channel will be looking for different benefits – typically profit and product availability. If manufacturers do not get the benefits they are looking for, the end-use customers may never be offered the product, no matter how good it is.

Consider the route to market for the single-purchase private customer (segment 1A). Convenience of purchase is their primary consideration. No advertising or promotion is expected and service is non-existent, as pens are probably sold on a self-service basis. Other elements of the marketing mix are relatively unimportant, so there is strong price competition

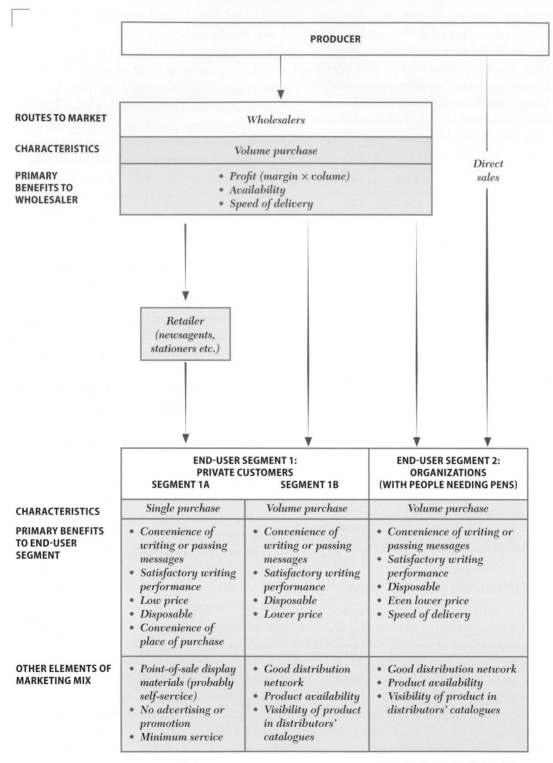

F5.2 Marketing a disposable pen

from manufacturers of similar pens. These customers purchase the pen through retailers like newsagents or stationers. Retailers buy in bulk through wholesalers. The benefit retailers, such as wholesalers are looking for is profit – which means the higher the margin to them, the more attractive the product and the more prominently they are likely to display the pen. Indeed they may be persuaded to stock only this pen rather than those of competitors (called **supply-push**). The margin must however be sufficient to satisfy both wholesaler and retailer. The retailers might be encouraged to purchase the pens because of 'free' point-of-sale displays. At the same time, just-in-time deliveries, with increased delivery reliability and improved distribution times, may allow wholesalers to both decrease their inventory costs and at the same time reduce stock-outs – real benefits that help differentiate this manufacturer from others.

Private customers (segment 1B) and organizations buying for their employees (segment 2) may buy these pens in bulk from wholesalers. They expect lower prices than those offered by the retailer as well as speedy, reliable delivery. Pens selling through this distribution channel will not need point-of-sale display materials but may need different packaging. There may be discounts based upon volumes purchased. The wholesaler may need to invest in a catalogue, website, advertising and a direct sales force. The pen must be prominently displayed, or at least easily found, in the catalogue or website. The pen manufacturer might also decide to sell direct to these end-users, but they would have to invest in a catalogue, website, advertising and a direct sales force – things that may not be their core activities.

One way of stimulating end-user demand is to advertise directly to end-users and persuade them to seek out the product from the distributor (called **demand-pull**). This only works if the product they are seeking is highly differentiated (e.g. through branding), so it is unlikely to work for this sort of pen. The less differentiated the product, the more likely this strategy is to work. However, an innovative start-up may decide to bypass the established distribution channels and sell directly to the end-customer. However, this is likely to involve extra costs (advertising, distribution, delivery etc.), which may not be commercially viable.

Channels of distribution

The disposable pen example underlines the fact that customers buy benefits, not features, and you need to understand the benefits offered to both end-use customers and distributors. You must tailor your marketing mix to suit the needs of customers and consumers at each stage in the chain. This is what your marketing strategy should articulate in a coherent, consistent way. Each element of the marketing mix needs to be consistent with the others. And your marketing strategy will have implications for other elements of your business model, from the operations plan to the resources you will need. It will determine costs and revenues and have implications for the risks you will face.

Your channels of distribution need careful consideration. Using retailers, wholesalers or agents may extend your market reach but each link in the chain is important and everyone is looking for benefits, of which profit is probably the most important element. You do not control your distribution channels directly, you influence them – and they eat into your profits. On the other hand, if you decide to sell directly to customers your revenues may be higher but so too are your costs. Direct sales costs might include: your own direct sales force, costs of developing your website, online and/or telephone sales team, advertising and mail/delivery costs. The typical channels of distribution for consumer goods and for business-to-business (B2B) sales are shown in Figure 5.3.

There is no one 'best' way to distribute a product or service and, as we have seen in the previous chapter, deciding to do it differently from the competition can prove profitable if the customers value the difference, and you can keep competitors from copying you for a sufficient length of time. easyJet and other low-cost airlines changed the way passengers bought their tickets by insisting that they could only book their flights online or by telephone, thus cutting out any intermediaries and the margin they might expect. Of course, other airlines have copied this direct route to market.

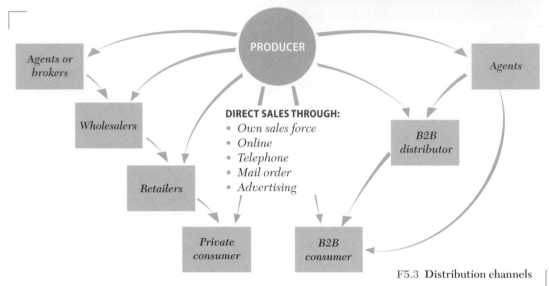

F5.3 **Distribution channels**

Understanding customer and consumer benefits

Not all pens are the same and not all customers are consumers of the product/service. Some pens are bought by a customer as a gift for the ultimate consumer. And, again, we need to offer benefits to both the customer and the consumer. Whilst a gift pen must perform the basic function of writing, it is likely to look very different and to have a very different marketing strategy, with a value proposition based upon high differentiation rather than low price. Two market segments and the benefits they are seeking are shown in Figure 5.4. The routes to market are likely to be the same as the disposable pen, although this time retailers are likely to be gift shops or department stores. Smaller gift shops might go through a wholesaler whilst

department stores might purchase direct from the manufacturer. As in the disposable pen example, retailers and wholesalers are looking for profit, but this time from smaller volumes at a higher price.

For both the customer and the consumer, the pens must be functional and well-made, high quality and elegantly designed. The other elements of the marketing mix are also important. The pen will have prestige branding with guaranteed quality performance. It will come in an attractive gift presentation case, and will be advertised and promoted at times of gift-giving as prestigious and something that values the 'worthiness' of the recipient. If sold in a shop, it will probably be kept in a glass display stand that can be accessed only with the help of a shop assistant. If sold to an organization, the company is likely to want the opportunity to be associated with the brand by having their name put on the pen, although they will probably still expect a discount if ordering in bulk.

The point here is that the customer wants to spend, say, £50 on a prestigious gift for the consumer; one that conveys a message to them about the feelings of 'worthiness' the customer has for them. The brand and what it conveys is probably more important than the functionality of the pen itself. This is the benefit they are looking for. A low price is not consistent with the message and the benefit sought. And a box of 500 cheap, disposable ball pens is not a substitute gift, even though they are likely to last longer than the expensive pen. They just do not provide the right benefits. Competition comes from other gifts costing £50 that convey a similar message.

Putting together a bundle of benefits through a consistent marketing mix for each target market segment is the key to an effective marketing strategy. It is not easy. There is no blueprint to work from since most products/services and their markets are different. And, whilst studying your industry can tell you how competitors currently do things, this is no guarantee for the future. Indeed, daring to do things differently can be very profitable.

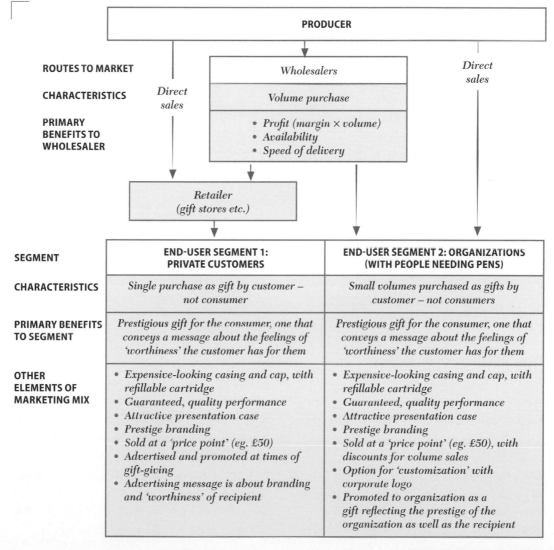

F5.4 Marketing a pen as a gift

The Pub*

Understanding customer value propositions

You might think that a pub (a bar selling food and alcoholic and non-alcoholic drinks) is a well-established and secure institution. However, it has to cope with all of the challenges facing any retail outlet. In particular, it faces high fixed costs related to its physical location and its serving staff. These costs need to be paid even if there are no customers. To compensate for this, gross margins can be high – 60 to 70% – so the operational imperative is to attract customers throughout the day.

To meet this challenge an English high street pub chain developed a two-level marketing strategy – one at the corporate level and one at the pub level to help local pub managers. Each pub was located in a prime, high street, town centre location, close to shopping centres and offices. Each was large, with different seating, lighting etc. in different areas, allowing it to change the ambience and target a number of different market segments. The pub chain needed to maximize the number of customers it attracted throughout the day. The local pub strategy summarized here was designed to target different market segments at different times of the day. It highlighted the value proposition for each segment and the main elements of the marketing mix needed to attract that segment.

Segments	Shoppers	Office workers
Time	11.00–17.00	12.00–14.00
Male/female	10/90%	40/60%
Value proposition	A comfortable, safe, value-for-money place to eat and drink	A quick, value-for-money place to eat lunch
Marketing mix		
Main products	Coffee, tea, soft drinks and food	Food, range of drinks
Service	Friendly	Fast
Price	Value-for-money	Competitive
Ambience	Safe, clean and comfortable	Clean and comfortable
Importance of location	High	High
Critical success factors	Safe, clean and comfortable environment	Rapid service. Value-for-money food

Lush (1)

High differentiation strategy

If you walk down any high street in the UK – and many in a wide range of overseas countries – you might suddenly have your attention taken by a very distinctive, honeyed smell that causes you to look around and notice the bright, inviting shop front from which it emanates – a shop called Lush. Despite its ubiquity, Lush was only started in 1994. Yet today it has over 800 stores in more than 50 countries and its founder, Mark Constantine, has become a multimillionaire. It remains a privately-owned family business and all seven shareholders work for Lush.

The story of Lush is intimately bound up with another very similar retailer called The Body Shop. In fact, you might, in passing, think that the shop front (if not the smell) bears more than a passing resemblance to The Body Shop, originally founded by Anita Roddick in 1976 and sold by her to the multinational L'Oréal (part of the Nestlé group) in 2006 for £652 million. And you would be right – not only the look but also the culture and ethics of the business are similar to The Body Shop, at least they were in The Body Shop's early years.

Pensioners and unemployed 14.00–17.00 90/10%	Office workers 17.00–19.00 60/40%	Students Any time 50/50%	Regulars 19.00–22.00 60/40%	Young, pre-clubbers 21.00–24.00 60/40%
A comfortable, value-for-money place to spend time	A lively atmosphere to meet friends after work	A relaxed, value-for-money place to meet friends	A friendly place to meet friends for value-for-money food and drink	A fashionable, lively place to meet friends
Alcoholic drinks	Wide range of alcoholic drinks	Alcoholic drinks	Food, range of drinks	Wide range of alcoholic drinks
Low priority	Friendly	Low priority	Friendly	Fast
Low-price beers	Attractive 'happy hour'	Value-for-money	Value-for-money	Low priority
Warm, TV, newspapers	Up-beat, lively	Relaxed, safe	Friendly, home-from-home	Lively, up-beat with music and promotions
Low	High	Moderate	Moderate	High
Low-price beers	Up-beat, lively ambience with 'happy hour'	Relaxed, safe environment with other students	Friendly service and ambience. Value-for-money food. Recognition as 'regulars'	Lively, up-beat ambience with music and promotions

*The Pub is a real company but the name is fictitious

💼 *Case insight*

The link between the businesses is the founder of Lush – Mark Constantine – and his is a typically entrepreneurial roller-coaster of a story. Born in 1953, Mark was thrown out of his home by his mother and stepfather at the age of 17 and initially lived rough in woods in Dorset, UK, before moving to London. He got a job as a hairdresser but started developing natural hair and skin products in his small bedroom. His ambition was to turn this into a business making and selling natural cosmetics, but it was not until he was 23 that he stumbled on his first success. He had read about The Body Shop in the press and sent Anita Roddick some samples, including a henna cream shampoo 'which looked a bit like you'd just done a poo'. She had just opened her second shop. They met, got on well together and she placed her first order for £1200 worth of products. That was the real start of his first company, Constantine and Weir. Mark set it up with his wife, Mo, and Elizabeth Weir, then a beauty therapist and now retail director and shareholder of

Lush. The company became The Body Shop's biggest supplier of cosmetics and Mark is credited for many of the elements of the ethical brand image that the company and Anita Roddick built up over those early years, in particular their opposition to animal testing.

However, The Body Shop became uncomfortable that the formulations for many of its products were owned by another company and, in 1988, it bought Constantine and Weir for £6 million. Mark put the money into a new company, Cosmetics to Go, a mail order company he had already started. The company never made a profit and went into bankruptcy in 1994. Faced with no money and a family to maintain, Mark started selling the bankrupt stock from a shop in Poole. This was the start of Lush.

Lush was set up with seven shareholders, including his wife, Mo, and Elizabeth Weir. New finance was injected by Peter Blacker, of British Ensign Estates, and his finance director, Andrew Gerrie, who now sits on the board of Lush. They put in 'modest sums' but, cleverly, Mark set the exit value of these investments at the time, so that they could be bought out. Mark never forgot his earlier ups and downs, and part of the firm's mission statement (prominent on the wall of its shops) states that 'we believe in the right to make mistakes, lose everything and start again'.

Lush does more than just make and sell cosmetics through its own shops. The distinctive elements of the marketing mix might be small individually but add up to give it a uniqueness that differentiates it from competitors. And, whilst cosmetics have always delivered a 'feel-good' mood, Lush has added an environmental and social responsibility dimension to this value proposition.

- Its range of hand-made soaps, shampoos, shower gels, lotions, bubble baths and fragrances are 100% vegetarian, 83% vegan and 60% preservative-free. They are made in small batches, based upon shop orders, from fresh, organic fruit and vegetables, essential oils, and safe synthetic ingredients in

factories around the world. Stores do not sell products that are older than four months. In addition to not using animal fats in its products, Lush is also against animal testing and tests its products solely with human volunteers. Moreover, Lush does not buy from companies that carry out, fund or commission any animal testing.

- The distinctive smell of a Lush shop is caused by their minimal use of packaging – which is environmentally sound – and Lush offer a free face mask for returning five or more of their product containers. The aim is to have 100% of their packaging recyclable, compostable or biodegradable.

- Lush shops are fun places, often with promotions and campaigns going on inside and outside. Lush supports many campaigns around animal welfare, environmental conservation, human rights and climate change.

- Some products, such as 'bath bombs', are stacked like fruit and others, such as soap, are sold like cheese, wedges stacked on shelves and sold by weight wrapped in greaseproof paper. These attractive, bright displays give Lush shops the feel of old-fashioned market stalls or sweet shops.

- The shops are staffed by enthusiastic young people who are trained not to 'sell' but to help people select products by providing comprehensive product information, which includes the name of the person at Lush who made the product.

- Lush donates around 2% of its profits to charity, supporting many direct action groups such as Plane Stupid, a group against the expansion of UK airports, and Sea Shepherd, a group that takes action against Japanese whaling ships. Often it launches products specifically to support these groups. Profits from the sale of 'Guantanamo Garden', an orange foaming bath ball, were donated to the human rights charity, Reprieve, which helped Binyam Mohamed, a British resident who was held at Guantanamo Bay. It launched a

Charity Pot moisturiser, giving the entire proceeds to charities such as the Dorset Wildlife Trust and the Sumatran Orangutan Society.

Lush never advertises. Its growth has been organic. It operates its businesses overseas in various joint ventures, including the USA, Japan and Australia. In 2001 Lush tried to buy The Body Shop, but the Roddicks turned down the offer. It is listed regularly in the *Sunday Times* 100 Best Companies to work for. The business is still based in Poole, Dorset, and run from a small office above the first shop. Mo still designs cosmetics. One son, Simon, is head perfumer and another, Jack, does the online marketing. Daughter, Claire, works for the charity Reprieve, to which Lush donates. The Constantines have lived in the same house now for 25 years. Mark does not hold a driving licence and has never owned a car. He often cycles to work. His hobby is bird songs and he recently published a book on the subject.

Up-to-date information on Lush can be found on their website: www.lush.co.uk

Questions:

1. From the information given, map out as much as you can of the business model for Lush using the New Venture Creation Framework. What are the key elements of competitive advantage in their value proposition?
2. List the ways in which Lush tries to differentiate itself.
3. What role does ethics play in this? Why is it important to Lush?
4. Bearing in mind that this is a retail business, what are the operational imperatives for Lush?
5. Review The Body Shop case (page 214). How does Lush differ from The Body Shop? What are the advantages and disadvantages of the two forms of business?

Summary

- The business model is how you go about delivering your business idea to customers so as to achieve your business purpose. The business model is at the core of the New Venture Creation Framework shown in Figure 1.3. You start to develop your business model by defining the market segment(s) and core value proposition(s) for your business idea. These feed into your marketing strategy.

- You need to define your value proposition to your identified market segment(s). This summarizes the benefits offered by the product/service, supported by its features and underpinned by the marketing mix.

- Core value propositions are: low price/low cost, high differentiation and customer focus.

- Different value propositions can exist side by side in the same industry, appealing to different market segments.

- The price you set for your product/service should reflect the value to the customer, but will be influenced by your costs and the 'going rate'. It may be possible to charge different prices to different market segments, reflecting the value to each of them of the product/service. In setting these prices you need to understand your cost structures and be able to estimate the price elasticity of demand.

- Marketing strategy is made up of elements of the marketing mix as they relate to the customer segments they are targeted at. It is just a series of related tasks that, taken together, have coherence and give direction. The marketing strategy delivers the value proposition to these target market segments.

- You can sell directly to customers or through distribution channels. If you sell through channels, you might gain wider distribution but you lose profit and may lose control over communication to customers.

- 'Supply push' occurs when you create incentives to intermediaries in your distribution channels to sell your product. 'Demand pull' occurs when you create incentives directly with end-use customers who then 'pull' the product through the distribution channels.

Exercise 5.1

Identifying your customer segments

You need to start to refine your ideas about the customers you will be selling to.

Customer segments	Benefits	Value proposition	Critical success factors (value drivers)	Communications media	Channels of distribution
1.					
2.					
3.					
4.					

Using the format above, and building on Exercise 3.2:

1 List and describe the customer segments you intend to sell to.

2 Alongside each customer segment, describe the benefits they are seeking from your product/service.

3 For each customer segment, describe the value proposition that will provide these benefits. Reflect on which of the three core value propositions most closely approximates to the propositions you offer.

4 For each of your value propositions, list the most important drivers of your value proposition – critical success factors. These are things you must ensure you supply in order to fulfil your value proposition and convince customers that you can deliver (Table 5.2). For example, speed of delivery might be one value driver to distributors if the value proposition is to maximize their profit margin. Similarly, design, product functionality and reliability might be value drivers of a high-quality value proposition.

5 Compare these drivers to the critical success factors from Exercise 4.3.4 and combine the lists.

6 Against each of the customer segments:
- List the best way of communicating your value proposition to them (communications media).
- List the possible channels of distribution, noting the implications of using each.

Exercise 5.2

Setting your prices

Estimating your best selling price is not a science. It involves judgement, based upon information from an iterative process. If you are charging different prices to different market segments, you should repeat this exercise for each segment price. When you have completed this exercise, decide the prices that you will be charging and reflect on whether this alters your responses in Exercise 5.1.

Reflecting on the results of Exercise 4.2:

1 Estimate and list your fixed, overhead costs in the first year. Total up these costs (FC).

Fixed overhead costs might include rent and rates, fixed wages and salaries, depreciation of fixed assets, gas and electricity, transport and travel, repairs and renewals, telephone, postage and stationery etc.

2 Estimate your variable cost of producing/selling one unit (UVC).

Variable costs might include material costs, variable wage costs (e.g. staff on piece-work rates), commissions, delivery charges etc.

These values will be used to complete the table opposite.

If there is a 'going-rate' price or you have an estimate of what the customer is willing to pay ('value-to-customer') complete the calculations shown in the table below by inserting the price (A), the estimated sales volume (B) and the calculations from the previous steps. You may want to charge different prices to different market segments. Estimate the effects on sales volumes of increasing these prices by 10% and then decreasing them by 10%. Complete the calculations to show the profit this will generate.

	Segment 1			Segment 2			Segment 3			Segment 4		
	Price	+10%	−10%	Price	+10%	−10%	Price	+10%	−10%	Price	+10%	−10%
'Going-rate' or 'value-to-customer' unit selling price (A)												
Estimated sales volume (B)												
Total estimated sales value (B × A)												
Total variable costs (B × UVC)												
Total contribution (B × A) − (B × UVC)												
Fixed overhead costs (FC)												
Profit (B × A) − (B × UVC) − FC												

If the resulting profit from one of these calculations does not meet your objectives, the next step allows you to estimate the change in sales volume or sales price to achieve your objective.

4 Complete the calculations below by starting with the profit target you have set (TP) and deducting fixed costs (FC) to arrive at your contribution target (CT).

Calculation 1 assumes the price you wish to charge (P) is decided and set, for example by the market. It shows you the volume of sales you need at this price to achieve your profit target (V). Calculation 2 assumes the volume of sales you will achieve is fixed and set, for example by capacity constraints. It shows you the sale price you need to set to achieve your profit target.

Profit target (TP)

Fixed overhead costs (FC)

Contribution target (£) (CT)
TP – FC

Calculation 1: Price decided/set

Set unit price (P)

Unit variable cost (VC)

Unit contribution (UC)
P – VC

Required sales volume
CT ÷ UC (above)

Calculation 2: Volume fixed/set

Set volume (V)

Unit contribution (UC)
CT ÷ V

Unit variable cost (UVC)

Required unit sales price
UC + UVC (above)

You now have the information you need to set your price(s).

Exercise 5.3

Assessing your performance against competitors

You need to start considering how you will respond to competitors using the following format.

Value Drivers:	Importance (%)	Your business		Competitor 1		Competitor 2		Competitor 3	
		Raw score	Weighted score	Raw score	Weighted score	Raw score	Weighted score	Raw score	Weighted score
1.									
2.									
3.									
4.									
5.									
Total weighted score									

Using this format, for each target segment:

1 List your value drivers from Exercise 5.1.

2 Estimate their relative importance to the customer in percentage terms (adding to 100%).

3 Give your product/service a score out of 10 (maximum).

4 Repeat the process for your major competitors, identified in Exercise 4.1.

5 Multiply the score by its percentage importance to arrive at a weighted score out of 10.

6 Reflect on the scores, in particular any implications for your business model. In which market segments is your competitive advantage greatest? If your business model needs to change for any market segments, repeat the previous exercises.

A comparison of simple, unweighted scores with competitors gives an informative map of different value propositions being offered in the market place. A comparison of the weighted score gives you an indication of how your product or service might be perceived by each market segment compared to competitive products or services.

Exercise 5.4

Assessing your competition

You now need to reflect on the implications of your final scores for Exercise 5.3 on your marketing mix and marketing strategy.

Customer segments	Product	Price	Promotion	Place	People	Critical success factors
1.						
2.						
3.						
4.						

Using the format above, for each target market segment:

1 Jot down the main elements of your marketing mix.

2 Decide which factors are the most critical to delivering your value proposition and differentiating you from the competition. Compare these to the critical success factors from Exercise 5.1.5 and combine the lists.

3 Write a brief report on how you intend to market your product or service and combat competition in each market segment.

Visit www.palgrave.com/companion/burns-new-venture-creation for chapter quizzes to test your knowledge and other resources.

PART 3
MARKETING STRATEGY

VIDEO

www.palgrave.com/companion/
Burns-new-venture-creation

The New Venture Creation Framework

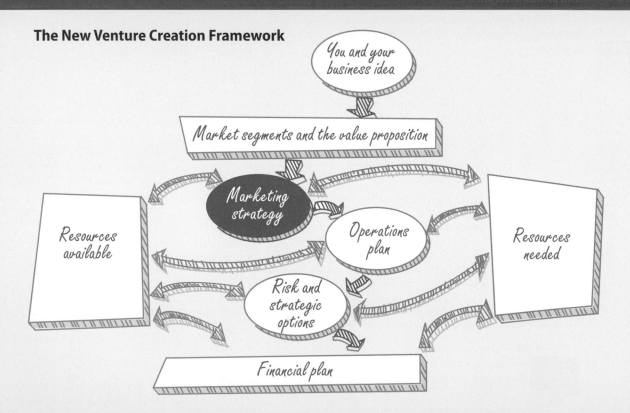

6
YOUR VALUES, BRAND AND CUSTOMER LOYALTY

Contents

Learning outcomes

When you have read this chapter and undertaken the related exercises you will be able to:
- Identify the values on which your start-up is based
- Develop a vision for your start-up and write its mission statement
- Understand the basis for value-driven marketing
- Understand how ethics and CSR can make good commercial sense and underpin the brand values of the product/service
- Understand how brand values can be communicated through your communications strategy

Your vision and values

Just as it is important that you understand why you want to start a business and what you want from it, it is also important that your business reflects your vision and values. After all, you will be spending much of your time developing it and, in many ways, it is an extension of you and your personality. Most people find it very difficult to live their lives within organizations that do not share their values and beliefs. Indeed this is often a reason for starting up your own business. This chapter will start to formalize the reasons why you want to set up a business, which we first considered in Chapter 2. It will develop the vision you have for the business and the values upon which it is based. It will also show you how strong, ethical values can add value to the business and be used as a valuable tool to create a clear brand identity. Later, in Chapter 13, we shall show how this is vital if you want to grow the business and become a successful entrepreneurial leader.

Values – Values are core beliefs. The values you set for your business set expectations regarding how you operate and treat people. They may well have an ethical dimension. Historically, many of the most successful Victorian businesses, such as Cadbury, Barclays Bank and John Lewis, were based upon Quaker values. Values form part of the cognitive processes that will help shape and develop the culture of your business. Shared values form a bond that binds the organization together – aligning and motivating people. Organizations with strong values tend to recruit staff who are able to identify with those values and thus they become reinforced. They also help to create a bond with customers and suppliers alike that can underpin a strong brand identity.

> One of the most important aspects of any business is its ethical code, a statement of the principles governing the way it operates and its employees behave.
>
> *Daily Telegraph 5 August 2009*
>
> *Duncan Bannatyne, serial entrepreneur*

You articulate values not only with words but also by practising what you preach – 'walking-the-talk'. It therefore follows that it is very difficult to pretend to have values that are not real. You will be caught out when you fail to practise them. Values are not negotiable and need to be reinforced through recognition and reward of staff. They need to be embedded in the systems and structures of your business, so that everybody can see clearly that you mean what you say. Every organization develops a distinctive culture that reflects certain underlying values, even if they are never made explicit. If you do not make your values explicit there is always the risk that they might be misunderstood and you end up with an organizational culture that you are unhappy with. This is why many successful companies actually write down their values. Your values also need to be reflected in the strategies you adopt when you launch the business – your ethical underpinning and policies for corporate social responsibility.

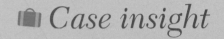 *Case insight*

Lush (2)

Values

We looked at Lush in the previous chapter. The founders have some strong ethical beliefs that are reflected in their lifestyle and the values of the company:

- We believe in buying ingredients only from companies that do not commission tests on animals and in testing our products on humans.
- We invent our own products and fragrances, we make them fresh by hand using little or no preservative or packaging, using only vegetarian ingredients and tell you when they were made.
- We believe in happy people making happy soap, putting our faces on our products and making our mums proud.

- We believe in long candlelit baths, sharing showers, massage, filling the world with perfume and in the right to make mistakes, lose everything and start again.
- We believe our products are good value, that we should make a profit and that the customer is always right.
- We also believe words like 'Fresh' and 'Organic' have an honest meaning beyond marketing.

 UK

© ghoststone – istockphoto.com

Go to: www.lush.co.uk/our-values

Vision – It is important to create a vision for what the business might become – important for your motivation and that of all the stakeholders. Your vision for the business should be based around and grounded in your business purpose. A vision is a shared mental image of a desired future state – an idea of what your enterprise can become – a new and better world. It must be attractive and aspirational and one that engages and energizes people, including yourself. However, it must be sufficiently realistic and credible that it is believable – stretching but achievable. It is usually qualitative rather than quantitative (that is the role of the objectives). Vision is seen as inspiring and motivating, transcending logic and contractual relationships. It is more emotional than analytical, something that touches the heart. It gives existence within an organization to that most fundamental of human cravings – a sense of meaning and purpose. It can be intrinsic, directing the organization to do things better in some way, such as improving customer satisfaction or increasing product innovation. It can be extrinsic, for example, beating the competition.

easyJet (2)

Mission

We looked at easyJet in the last chapter. Their mission statement is:

To provide our customers with safe, good value, point-to-point air services. To effect and to offer a consistent and reliable product, and fares appealing to leisure and business markets on a range of European routes. To achieve this we will develop our people and establish lasting relationships with our suppliers.

> I am often asked what it is to be an **entrepreneur** ... If you look around you, most of the largest companies have their foundations in **one** or **two** **individuals** who have the **determination** to turn a **vision** into **reality**.
>
> Richard Branson, founder Virgin, from Anderson, J. *Local Heroes* (1995, Glasgow: Scottish Enterprise)

🧳 *Case insight*

Starbucks (1)

Changing mission

Mission statements can also involve vision and do change over time. For example, as a start-up, Starbucks' mission statement was:

To establish Starbucks as the premier purveyor of the finest coffee in the world while maintaining our uncompromising principles while we grow.

It changed when the founder, Howard Schultz, came back in 2008 to turn around a struggling Starbucks:

To inspire and nurture the human spirit – one person, one cup and one neighborhood at a time.

USA

Mission – The formal statement of business purpose is called a mission statement. The mission statement says what the business aims to achieve and how it will achieve it. The mission statement, therefore, usually defines the scope of the business by including reference to the product/service, value proposition, customer groups and the benefits they derive. This stops you straying into markets where you have no competitive advantage, clarifies strategic options and offers guidance for setting objectives. Often it encompasses the values upheld by the organization. Like a vision statement, a mission statement should be short and snappy.

The vision and mission of your business must be consistent with your values. All three go hand-in-hand, each reinforcing the others and guiding your tactics. As represented in Figure 6.1, whilst strategies and tactics might change rapidly in an entrepreneurial firm, vision and values are enduring. Together, they form the 'road map' that tells everyone in the company where you are going and how you might get there, even when one route is blocked.

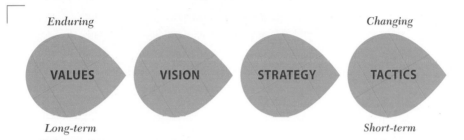

F6.1 Values, vision, strategies and tactics

Strategic intent and *kosryoku*

Hamel and Prahalad (1994) studied firms that had successfully challenged established big companies in a range of industries. They said that to reconcile this lack of fit between aspirations and resources the successful firms used 'strategic intent'. This necessitates developing a common vision about the future, aligning staff behaviour with a common purpose and delegating and decentralizing decision-making. They argued that 'the challengers had succeeded in creating entirely new forms of competitive advantage and dramatically rewriting the rules of engagement.' They were daring to be different. Managers in these firms imagined new products, services and even entire industries that did not exist and then went on to create them. They were not just benchmarking and analyzing competition, they were creating new market places that they could dominate because it was a market place of their own making.

Academic insight

Ohmae (2005) used the Japanese word *kosryoku* to describe what is needed to develop entrepreneurial strategy in an uncertain environment. Its meaning is a combination of 'vision' with the notions of 'concept' and 'imagination'. However, unlike imagination, it has no sense of daydreaming, rather than an ability to see what is invisible and shape the future so that the vision succeeds: 'It is the product of imagination based on realistic understanding of what the shape of the oncoming world is and, pragmatically, the areas of business that you can capture successfully because you have the means of realizing the vision.'

Hamel, G. and Prahalad, C. K. (1994) *Competing For the Future: Breakthrough Strategies for Seizing Control of your Industry and Creating the Markets of Tomorrow*, Boston, MA: Harvard Business School Press.

Ohmae, K. (2005) *The Next Global Stage: Challenges and Opportunities in our Borderless World*, Upper Saddle River, NJ: Pearson Education.

Golden Krust (2)

Mission, vision and values

We looked at Golden Krust in Chapter 2.

Their mission statement is to provide:

- Consumers with authentic, tasty Jamaican patties and relevant Caribbean cuisine in convenient settings and sizes.
- Customers with outstanding customer service and reliable predictability at every touch-point.
- Employees with an environment that is rewarding, fun and aspirational.
- Communities in which we operate with a corporate citizen of which they can be proud.
- Stakeholders with a superior return on their investment.

Their vision is that:

- Golden Krust exists to provide the taste of the Caribbean to the world.

Their values are:

- Our customers are at the core to our success.
- Integrity, value and fun are hallmarks to our approach to business.
- All stakeholders should benefit from their association with Golden Krust.

Encouraging customer loyalty

Your values and vision are tools that create identity for your business. And if this identity is attractive to customers it can create value. At the very least, a clear identity for the business means that customers know what they are buying and, if they like it, facilitates a repeat purchase. But identity can do more than this. As we have seen, customers buy a product/service because the marketing mix provides them with a range of benefits that they value. These benefits can be psychological as well as physical. For example, a successful sole trader might offer a *reliable, friendly* service that differentiates them effectively from the competition. The personal relationship they establish with their customers epitomizes the reliability and friendliness of the service they deliver. And this relationship underpins the customer loyalty that is generated. The challenge is to extend it beyond the single-person business.

This reflects a move away from seeing the customer as someone with whom to have an arms-length transaction – just somebody to sell to. It is part of the development called 'value-driven marketing' that seeks to actively use customers to help sell existing product/services and develop new ones. This is based upon establishing a good relationship with customers – one that is underpinned by mutual self-interest, where there is something in it for both the customer and the company with each helping the other in certain ways. Relationships are built on good communication – a topic we shall return to in the next chapter – and technology has made this easier on a mass basis. Indeed, the development of the internet and social media has made it possible and affordable on a global scale.

However, being able to communicate a message is only part of the challenge. The other part is having a message to communicate. This comes back to the value proposition you develop. But value propositions can be complicated. One way of shortcutting this is to develop a brand that encapsulates the value proposition and everything it, and also what the company, stands for. In this

way the customer's script is written for them and articulation is easier. This is the way to create sustainable competitive advantage and it is what companies like Apple have achieved with their brand identity. Value-based marketing involves having both a strong brand identity and good customer relationships. It uses these things to the mutual advantage of both customer and company. The advantages of branding are shown in Table 6.1.

To customers	To product/service producer
• Easier product/service identification • Clearer communication of value proposition • Aids with product/service evaluation • Reduction in risk when purchasing (homogeneity of offering) • Can create additional interest or character for the product/service	• Conveys emotional aspects of the value proposition • Promotes product/service loyalty • Helps target marketing • Defends against competitors (creates differential advantage) • Allows higher prices to be charged • Increases power in distribution channels

T6.1 Advantages of branding

Value-driven marketing

Piercy (2000, 2001) was one of the first academics to observe that, as customers become increasingly sophisticated, marketing will move away from just relationships to value-driven strategies that reflect customer priorities and needs: 'Achieving customer loyalty with sophisticated customers is the new challenge and we are only just beginning to realize what this means. It will mean transparency. It will mean integrity and trustworthiness. It will mean innovative ways of doing business. It will mean a focus on value in customers' terms, not ours. It will require new types of organization and technology to deliver value.' Piercy characterizes marketing strategy and the search for customer loyalty as progress from transactional and brand approaches to relationship and value-based strategies. These are illustrated in Figure 6.2.

Value-driven marketing (also called Marketing 3.0) has been characterized as a holistic approach to marketing based upon combinations of segmentation approaches. It places a *participative* customer at its centre – a customer that is not only king, but also market research head, R&D chief and product development manager – for example through open source innovation. Customers are actively involved as advocates of the product/service – for example through social network sites. In this way the customers' involvement is leveraged far beyond simple purchase of the product/service. This only happens if the organization is continually engaged in dialogue with customers through as many media as possible.

Piercy suggests that the sources for this value-driven strategy are:

- Management vision: Clarity in direction and purpose, effectively communicated through a wide range of communication media.
- Market sensing and organizational learning: Understanding and responding to the external world using all possible networks and channels of communication.
- Differentiating capabilities: Using core competences to build differential advantage.
- Relationship strategy: Managing the network of relationships and channels of communication used for market sensing to achieve superior performance.
- Reinventing the organization: Changing the organization's form and processes to sustain and renew this strategy.

Kotler et al. (2010) are keen advocates of value-driven marketing. Rather than seeing values as an 'add-on', they envisage marketing and values as being integrated, without separation. Companies need to focus on creating products/services and entire organizational cultures, which are customer *value*-driven at a more multi-dimensional, fundamental level, starting with their vision, mission and values. Customers are looking for products/services that not only satisfy their consumer needs, but also address their spiritual needs. You need to appeal to their head, their heart and their spirit. The key to this is customer participation and involvement, using all the channels of communication created by internet-based social media. Kotler et al. argue that to thrive in this interlinked world companies must collaborate with each other, with their shareholders, channel partners, employees and customers.

F6.2 Value-driven marketing

Academic insight

The book concludes with ten principles that the authors claim integrate marketing and values:

1. Love your customers and respect your competitors.
2. Be sensitive to change and ready to change yourself.
3. Guard your name, and have a clear identity.
4. Customers are diverse; first find those who benefit most from your product/service.
5. Always offer a good product/service at a fair price.
6. Always make yourself available and spread the news about your product/service.
7. Find your customers, keep and grow them.
8. Whatever your business, remember it is a service business.
9. Continually refine your business processes – quality, cost and delivery.
10. Continually gather information, but be wise in making your final decisions.

Kotler, P., Kartajaya, H. and Setiawan, I. (2010) *Marketing 3.0: From Products to Customers to the Human Spirit*, Hoboken, NJ: John Wiley & Sons.

Piercy, N. F. (2000) *Tales from the Marketplace: Stories of Revolution, Reinvention and Renewal*, Oxford: Taylor & Francis.

Piercy, N. F. (2001) 'The Future of Marketing is Strategizing' in S. Dibb, L. Simkin, W.M. Pride and O.C. Ferrell, *Marketing: Concepts and Strategies*, Boston, MA: Houghton Mifflin.

 USA

Case insight

Starbucks (2)

Using close customer relationships to innovate

When Howard Schultz returned to take control of Starbucks in 2008 he was keen to innovate. One of his approaches involved using close customer relationships to crowdsource ideas. By visiting the Starbucks ideas website anybody can post ideas about products, experience, service, location, community building and social responsibility. But the site is more than just a virtual suggestion box. There is a 'question of the day' which Starbucks uses to get market feedback on new ideas. Starbucks Ideas Partners manage the site, responding to people with questions and ideas. They change over time but are drawn from various teams involved in innovation, such as the Research and Development team that develop food and beverages, and the Mobile and Emerging Platforms team that develop new ways of communicating with customers, such as in-store digital signage or mobile phone apps.

Close customer relationships may be valuable to Starbucks but poor customer relationships can damage a brand and lead to lost sales. Revelations in 2012 that Starbucks had paid only £8.6 million in taxation in the UK since 1998 (against global net income of £253 million in 2012 alone) threatened to damage those relationships severely. An appearance in front of a UK Parliamentary committee and a customer boycott of its 700 British outlets led the company to alter the tax treatment of certain expenses which allowed it to channel profits to low-tax countries. As a result, it paid £10 million taxes in 2013 and estimated that it will make a similar payment in 2014. Starbucks listened and, although the row is still not over at the time of writing, the company has gone some way to re-establishing its relationship with customers in the UK.

Visit the Starbucks crowdsourcing website: mystarbucksidea.force.com

> When you've got single-digit market share – and you're competing with the big boys – you either **differentiate or die** ... The idea of building a business solely based on cost or price was not a sustainable advantage.

Michael Dell Direct from Dell: Strategies that Revolutionized an Industry (1999, New York: Harper Business)

Creating an identity

Differentiation means setting out to be unique in the industry along some dimensions that are widely valued by customers. These can be based upon the product or service and can be tangible (observable product/service characteristics such as function, quality, design, performance or technology etc.) and/or intangible (customer needs such as status, exclusivity etc.). Often differentiation is more sustainable when it is based not just on tangible factors, which are copiable, but also on intangible factors, which are not. So, for example, Mercedes Benz cars and Dom Perignon champagne differentiate themselves through product quality and status in their respective sectors. Hi-fi manufacturer Bang & Olufsen uses aesthetics of design as well as status. The UK retailer Lush differentiates itself through its bright, fun shopping environment, novel products and ethical values (Case Insight, Chapter 5). Even companies competing primarily on price attempt to differentiate themselves, and not just through brand recognition. Dell may not have differentiated products but it attempts to differentiate itself on speed of delivery, uniqueness of personal systems configuration and other elements of service, whilst still maintaining a competitive price (Case Insight, Chapter 5). McDonald's has a very recognizable brand associated with value-for-money meals but also tries to

> Basically any brand is an **assurance** to **customers**. It is an assurance of **quality**, an assurance of **consistency**. There is an **immediate recognition**, when you see the Cadbury signature on the front of the chocolate bar or box of Milk Tray, all those things are **guaranteed**.

Sir Adrian Cadbury The Times 8 July 2000

differentiate itself, in part, through consistency and quality of service (speed, cleanliness and so on). You can differentiate yourself therefore by 'bundling' these things in different ways – so long as the customer values the 'bundle' and cannot create the 'bundle' easily themselves.

Differentiation adds costs and it is essential that the benefits to the customers are seen by them as outweighing the costs. It is also essential that the product or service is clearly identified as being different. Design is an important element in this. Good design can help improve the functional performance of a product. It can also make the product distinctive. Good design is aesthetically pleasing and conveys emotions that functionality cannot.

Clear branding can do the same. A brand should be the embodiment of the product or service value proposition to customers. It tells you what you are buying, but it also reflects what you want from the purchase. So, for example, the Mercedes Benz, Jaguar and BMW brands tell you that you are buying a car but, more importantly, all convey quality and status. Virgin is the embodiment of Richard Branson: brash, entrepreneurial, different,

anti-establishment. Effective brands, therefore, are emotional, appealing to the heart as much as the head. However, many so-called brands fall far short of this instant recognition of values and virtues, being little more than expensive logos. What do the Barclays, Shell or the BT brands convey, other than the knowledge of what the firm sells? Brands should be more than just logos that identify the products sold. They should represent the very identity – the persona – of the product sold. And, just as you are more than a head, body, two arms and legs, so too any product/service should be more than the sum of its parts. The challenge is to create that brand identity.

Design and branding add extra layers to a differentiated product – shown in Figure 6.3. The functional qualities of the product/service can be enhanced through the aesthetics of design and reinforced by the emotional values associated with the brand. The more points of differentiation from competitors you have the more sustainable your competitive advantage. Apple combine a high-quality, easy-to-use product with elegant design, a fashionable, desirable brand – and a high price.

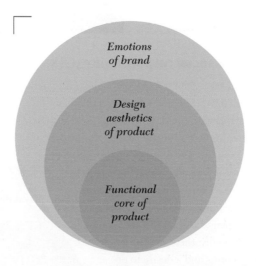

Emotions
of brand

Design
aesthetics
of product

Functional
core of
product

F6.3: Layers of differentiation

South Beauty

Creating an identity

Zhang Lan opened her first restaurant specializing in Sichuan cuisine in the 1990s in Beijing with $20,000 of savings. Today South Beauty is a chain of some 40 restaurants employing thousands of people. It offers high-quality, high-price dining in luxurious surroundings. From the first restaurant Zhang Lan realized that a restaurant was about more than just food. The presentation of the food was important – it had to look good as well as taste good. Service had to be first class. The design of the interior had to match the prices being charged and create the right ambience. Today, the flagship restaurant is the opulent Lan Club in Beijing, with an interior designed by the French designer Philippe Starck. Location is also important. The first restaurant was located near to government buildings and government officials frequently visited with important guests. However, creating a clear identity and branding were the key factors that would help Zhang Lan grow the chain. She has tried to create a brand that appeals to her target market – 'business, white-collar people'. She chose an opera mask as the logo for South Beauty, echoing the consistent theme of quality and luxury that she hopes is embodied in the brand.

© EmelErnalbant istockphoto.com

Ethical values and corporate social responsibility (CSR)

Ethical values in the corporate world translate not only into the culture of an organization and its brand, but also into strategies and actions that have an ethical and social, rather than just a profit, dimension. The areas of business ethics, social responsibility and environmental sustainability have now been subsumed within what is called corporate social responsibility (CSR). It is now widely accepted that many business practices can have negative social and environmental side effects. There is a hierarchy of virtue for companies practising CSR, shown in Figure 6.4. At its base is CSR that delivers profit to the company. Next is CSR that comes through compliance with the law. Finally, there is CSR that is discretionary, based upon ethical norms and a desire to do the best thing for the community and society as a whole. Fortunately this hierarchy is not always contradictory and there can be commercial benefit in many forms of CSR.

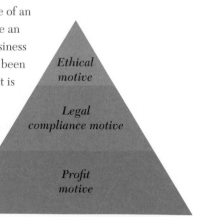

Ethical motive

Legal compliance motive

Profit motive

F6.4 CSR hierarchy of virtue

There are three sound commercial reasons for having a strong CSR policy:

1. **Increased sales, brand identity and customer loyalty** Whilst any product must first satisfy the customer's key buying criteria – quality, price etc. – a strong CSR brand can increase sales and customer loyalty by helping to differentiate it (see Abel & Cole Case Insight). Customers are increasingly drawn to brands with a strong CSR profile and CSR has become an element in the continuous process of trying to differentiate one company from another. A strong CSR brand can even create its own market niche for an organization. For example, the Co-operative Bank in the UK has a long history of CSR. It has set itself up as an ethical and ecological investor with an investment policy that is the most frequently-cited reason that customers choose the bank. On the other hand, a bad CSR image can severely damage sales, as BP found after the 2010 oil spillage in the Gulf of Mexico.

2. **Reduced operating costs and productivity gains** Sustainability is about measuring and controlling inputs, and many environmental initiatives therefore reduce costs (e.g. reducing waste and recycling, having better control of building temperatures or reducing use of agrochemicals). Yahoo saved 60% of its electricity costs simply by opening windows where servers are located so as to let the hot air out. General Electric started a programme of becoming more sustainable ('greener') in 2004. By 2008 this initiative had yielded $100 million in cost savings. Waste-reducing cost-savings can come from looking at raw materials usage, the manufacturing process, packaging requirements, transport needs, maintenance and the use of disposal methods. Actions to improve working conditions, lessen environmental impact or increase employee involvement in decision-making can improve productivity. For example, actions to improve work conditions in the supply chain have been seen to lead to decreases in defect rates in merchandise. Many social initiatives can increase

I think every business needs a **leader** that does not forget the **massive impact** business can have on the world. All business leaders should be thinking 'how can I be a **force for good**?' What I see is demand from our people to be a business that is **good**, makes a **profit**, but also does something for the **planet and humanity**. I think this is a trend we will see more of ... CSR in my mind is defunct now. Compartmentalizing the **social responsibility** is not the way to go. I think the model for starting **employee engagement** activities has to be embedded in everything you do.

Richard Branson
www.hrmagazine.co.uk 13 July 2010

employee motivation and cut absenteeism and staff turnover. An increasing number of graduates take CSR issues into consideration when making employment decisions. And caring for employees pays dividends. According to one newspaper, Southwest Airlines, the only airline in the USA never ever to lay off employees, was the largest domestic airline in the USA in 2010 with a market capitalization equivalent to all of its domestic competitors combined (Jeffrey Pfeffer, *Newsweek*, 15 February 2010).

3. **Improved new product development** A focus on CSR issues can lead to new product opportunities. For example, car manufacturers are striving to find alternatives to fossil fuels, whilst developing conventional engines that are more and more economical (see Ecotricity Case Insight). Innovation linked to sustainability often has major systems-level implications, demanding a holistic and integrated approach to innovation management. As well as reducing costs, General Electric's sustainability programme yielded 80 new products and services that generated $17 million in revenues between 2004 and 2008.

The value of CSR   📖 *Academic insight*

Is there evidence that CSR adds any corporate value? The quest to link corporate CSR directly to financial performance and/or share price performance spans some 40 years and the results have often been contradictory and confusing. Nevertheless, in a review and assessment of 127 empirical studies, Margolis and Walsh (2003) concluded that there was a positive relationship between CSR and financial performance, a result supported in a meta-survey by Orlitzy et al. (2003). Looking at investment portfolios, Ven de Velde et al. (2005) concluded that high-sustainability-rated portfolios (ones that integrated environmental, social and ethical issues) performed better than low-rated portfolios. What is more, an Economic Intelligence Unit Survey in 2008 showed that the vast majority of US business leaders and their boards of directors now accept a clear relationship between CSR and financial performance (Business Green, 2008).

More recently, in a review of the literature Carroll and Shabana (2010) concluded that on the whole a positive relationship exists between CSR and financial performance, 'but inconsistencies linger'. This is because financial performance is affected by many other internal and external variables, not all controlled by the firm. What is more, 'the benefits of CSR are not homogeneous, and effective CSR initiatives are not generic'. They concluded that CSR activities need to be part of a coherent and consistent strategy that is directed at improving both stakeholder relationships and social welfare. They talk about 'a convergence between economic and social goals' – where social good is crafted into creating economic value. Kurucz et al. (2008) summarized the four ways CSR can add value:

1. Reducing costs and risk (waste, hazards etc.).
2. Strengthening legitimacy and reputation, particularly through branding.
3. Building competitive advantage through reputation and branding.
4. 'Creating win–win situations through synergistic value creation' – linking economic and social goals.

Business Green (2008) 'US Execs: CSR Initiatives do Boost the Bottom Line', www.BusinessGreen.com.

Carroll, A.B. and Shabana, K.M. (2010) 'The Business Case for Corporate Social Responsibility: A Review of Concepts, Research and Practise', *International Journal of Management Reviews*, www.academia.edu.

Kurucz, E., Colbert, B. and Wheeler, D. (2008) 'The Business Case for Corporate Social Responsibility'. In A. Crane, A. McWilliams, D. Matten, J. Moon and D. Seigel (eds). *The Oxford Handbook of Corporate Social Responsibility*, Oxford: Oxford University Press.

Margolis, J.D. and Walsh, J.P. (2003) 'Misery Loves Companies: Rethinking Social Initiatives by Business', *Administrative Science Quarterly*, 48.

Orlitzy, M., Schmidt, F.L. and Rynes, S.L. (2003) 'Corporate Social Performance: A Meta-Analysis', *Organization Studies*, 24.

Porter, M.E. and Kramer, M.R. (2006), 'Strategy and Society: The Link between Competitive Advantage and Corporate Social Responsibility', *Harvard Business Review*, 84.

Ven de Velde, E., Vermeir, W., and Corten, F. (2005) 'Corporate Social Responsibility and Financial Performance', *Corporate Governance*, 5(3).

Abel & Cole

Using CSR to create differential advantage

Abel & Cole may be the UK's largest organic food delivery, but that was not how it started. In 1985 Keith Abel was studying history and economics at Leeds University, and selling potatoes door-to-door to make some money. He was a good salesman and that meant he could charge more for the potatoes than the supermarkets. Keith went on to City University, London, to study law. Unfortunately, he failed his bar exams and decided he might as well team up with a friend, Paul Cole, and go back to selling potatoes to make some money – no notion of organic food, just making money. A Devon-based farmer, Bernard Gauvier, approached them about selling his organic potatoes. They cost more, but after a week Keith realized that nobody asked the price. He decided to investigate the differences between organic and non-organic products, and went to see what his regular supplier was spraying on his potatoes. Keith was 'pretty appalled' at what he saw. The organic idea slowly started to creep into his consciousness and he began to 'push' the organic side of the business – after all he was good at selling, and he was delivering the produce to the door of the customers. The customers responded by buying more and asking for other things. Bernard persuaded Keith and Paul to start putting together organic vegetable boxes and by 1991 Abel & Cole converted to selling only organic vegetables, buying them directly from farmers.

Sales took off in the 1990s and they started to employ people. Unfortunately, whilst sales increased, the result was mounting losses. Things came to a head when unpaid debts caused the Inland Revenue to threaten them with bankruptcy. Paul decided to leave and set up his own wholesale company, while Keith decided to retake his bar exams – and passed. Then Keith realized that he could not practise law if he was declared bankrupt. Threatened with losing the family house, Keith's father-in-law, Peter Chipparelli, then chairman of Mobil Oil in South America, decided to bail him out. This may have focused Keith's mind because he started taking advice, first from his father-in-law then from social entrepreneur, Alan Heeks, who introduced him to his 22-year-old daughter, Ella. She came to do work experience and stayed, going on to become Managing Director only three years later.

The success of the company is due to the consistency of its marketing mix. Its ethical, eco-conscious profile is assiduously nurtured. Vegetables are organic, local (never air-freighted), seasonal and ethically farmed. They are delivered in a recycled cardboard box by a yellow bio-fuel van, together with a newsletter which includes lively vegetable biographies and hints on how to deal with some of the more obscure vegetables in the box. The company prides itself on employing the formerly long-term unemployed and offers them bonuses for cutting waste. It gives to charity. Customers can deposit keys with the company so that vegetable boxes are left safe and sound indoors. Prices are high, but not outrageously so since the 'middle-man' has been cut out of the distribution chain. Customers are middle class, and shopping from Abel & Cole is definitely fashionable.

In 2007 the private equity firm Phoenix Equity Partners bought a stake in the company, valuing it at over £40 million. However, the recession of 2008 took its toll and, as consumers tightened their belts, sales slumped dramatically. In 2008 Abel & Cole made a loss of £13.8 million. This led to the main holder of company debt, Lloyds Bank, taking control in a debt-for-equity swap. Keith Abel remained in managerial control and bought back into the company shortly afterwards. By 2011 it was again making profits – £2.5 million on sales of £9.3 million – and in 2012 the company was bought by the William Jackson Food Group, a 180-year-old family business that makes Aunt Bessie's Yorkshire puddings. Keith remains in managerial control.

Find out about Abel & Cole from their website:
www.abelandcole.co.uk

Ecotricity

Environmental opportunities

Dale Vince was once a New Age hippie who toured Britain and the Continent in a peace convoy. These days he is better known as a millionaire entrepreneur who owns the fast-growing company Ecotricity, which he founded in 1995. Ecotricity generates electricity from its wind turbines around the UK, as far apart as Dundee and Somerset, and sells the 'green' energy to domestic and corporate customers, including Sainsbury's, Tesco and Ford. The idea came to Dale on a hill near Stroud in Gloucestershire where his home – a former army lorry – was powered by a small wind turbine. Why not build a full-sized permanent wind turbine in the field?

Ecotricity is still based in Stroud and employs some 170 'co-workers'. It is very much a family business. Many of Dale's relations work in the business: his two adult sons, brother, sister, brothers-in-law and sister-in-law, and even his father. Ecotricity is involved in a number of other environmental projects. In 2013 it got the go-ahead to build the UK's fourth largest wind farm. It has also diversified into other sustainable energy areas such as 'sun-parks' and, in 2012, announced that it has invested in a pump-to-shore wave energy machine called Searaiser. It is also involved in building a UK national network of electric vehicle fast chargers, with a target of reaching 120 motorway service areas by the end of 2014.

Ecotricity reinvests most of its profits in renewable energy sources. Profits fluctuate with the weather. In 2010 it made a profit of £3.8 million but this dropped to £1.7 million in 2011 because of a mild spring and low winds.

Find out about Ecotricity from their website:
www.ecotricity.co.uk

Building the brand

As we have seen, in a world where products and services are often all too homogeneous, a good brand is a powerful marketing tool that must be the cornerstone of any strategy of differentiation. It also helps to cement customer loyalty. The brand must reflect the promise of your value proposition and the personality of the organization that offers it. Support for social and ethical causes can reinforce this, as well as often making good commercial sense. Building a brand takes time. It is built up through effective use of communication media and is recognized through the brand or company name and logo.

At this stage you may not have a recognizable brand like the ones cited, but you do have yourself and that can start to shape the identity of your start-up. In many ways shaping the identity of a start-up is easier the fewer people you have working with you. You have your personal values and beliefs to build on, underpinned by what the big companies call CSR. The trick is to understand what these values and beliefs are and to make them explicit and clear, to ensure that they are reflected not only in what you do, but how you do things. They need to be clear to customers, employees, distributors and suppliers alike. And they need to be sincerely felt values and beliefs, otherwise you will be quickly found out and any trust you may have built up will disappear quickly.

The identity of your business should reflect the culture within it – its personality. You create the culture of your business through your leadership and you need to ensure that you create the culture and identity you want. This involves being consistent in words and actions. It requires an emotional intelligence that does not always come naturally but can be nurtured. It will take time to develop, but you need to start immediately. We discuss these leadership skills and how they can affect the culture of your business in Chapters 12 and 13. Your brand should reflect this identity and one of the best ways to do that is to use yourself to promote the brand.

In Britain, probably the best known proponent of this is Richard Branson. His companies, under the Virgin name, are closely associated with him and what he personally stands for.

Brand and company names need to be distinctive and easy to remember, say and even spell across different cultures and nationalities. This implies short names are best. It is important that they do not have negative associations or that names do not mean bad things in other languages. Names should be supportive of your value proposition. This is not always easy or straightforward. 'Freeserve' was a good brand name for one of the first UK internet service providers – it was free. However, in 2004 it was changed to 'Wanadoo' because the name was easier to market across Europe. In 2006 it was again changed to 'Orange' as the company's product offering was expanded to include internet and telecommunications. Because it adds value to the company, your brand name and logo can and should be trademark protected if possible (Chapter 9).

There are no hard and fast rules about using the company name as a product name. Sometimes this works, particularly when it is a one-product company, but there are examples of successfully using different company and product names alongside each other. 'Burger King' is a successful company brand that describes at least the major part of the company's product range. It is associative – suggesting some characteristic or benefit of the product, albeit sometimes in an indirect way. In this way 'iPhone' is another associative product brand name, but this time is used alongside the company name 'Apple', which has a different set of brand associations. This is a freestanding name that has built brand value over a number of years. Some company names have been less successful in transferring across product ranges. For example the Dyson brand name is based upon the inventor/entrepreneur James Dyson, but is still very much associated with vacuum cleaners, although the company now offers a range of electrical products.

> Branding is **valueless** if consumers get home and are **disappointed** with the product.
>
> Simon Smith, Head of Brand, The Saucy Fish Co. The Observer 29 September 2013

Richard Branson and Virgin (1)

Building the brand

Richard Branson is probably the best known entrepreneur in Britain today, and his name is closely associated with the many businesses that carry the Virgin brand name. He is outward-going and an excellent self-publicist. He has been called an 'adventurer', taking risks that few others would contemplate. This shows itself in his personal life, with his transatlantic power boating and round-the-world ballooning exploits, as well as in his business life where he has challenged established firms like British Airways and Coca-Cola. He is a multimillionaire with what has been described as a charismatic leadership style.

Virgin is also probably the best known brand in Britain with 96% recognition and is well-known worldwide. The Virgin name has found its way onto aircraft, trains, cola, vodka, mobile phones, cinemas, a radio station, financial services, fitness studios and the internet. It is strongly associated with its founder, Sir Richard Branson – 95% can name him as the founder. Virgin believes their brand stands for value for money, quality, innovation, fun and a sense of competitive challenge. They believe they deliver a quality service by empowering employees and, whilst continuously monitoring customer feedback, striving to improve the customer's experience through innovation. According to Will Whitehorn, director of corporate affairs at Virgin Management:

> 'At Virgin, we **know** what the **brand** name means, and when we put our brand name on something, we're **making a promise**. It's a promise we've always kept and always will. It's **harder work** keeping promises than making them, but there is no **secret formula**. Virgin sticks to its principles and keeps its promises.' (1)

The brand has been largely built through Branson's personal PR efforts. He recognized the importance of self-publicity very early in his career when the BBC featured him in a documentary called 'The People of Tomorrow' because of his first venture, *Student* magazine. Since then he has become known for his often outrageous publicity stunts, such as dressing up as a bride for the launch of Virgin Bride.

According to Branson:

> 'Brands must be built around **reputation, quality** and **price**... People should not be asking "is this one product too far?" but rather, "what are the **qualities of my company's name?** How can I **develop** them?" (2)

As to what these qualities are for Virgin, Branson gives us a candid insight into at least one of them:

Virgin has a devolved structure and an informal but complex culture based upon the Virgin brand. It is the brand that unifies the different companies in the group. Branson believes that finding the right people to work with is the key to success and the Virgin brand is so strong that it helps to attract like-minded staff. He believes that it is not qualifications that matter in people, rather their attitude. He calls them 'Virgin-type' people – staff who will enjoy their work and are customer-focused. And their enthusiasm for the brand rubs off on the customers. As Branson says:

> '**Fun** is at the core of the way I like to do business and has informed **everything** I've done from the outset. More than any other element fun is the **secret** of **Virgin's success**.' (3)

> 'Our **brand values** are very **important**, and we tend to select people to work for us who share these values ... For as much as you need a **strong personality** to build a business from scratch, you must also understand the **art of delegation** ... I started Virgin with a philosophy that if staff are **happy**, customers will follow. It can't just be me that sets the culture when we recruit people. I have a really great set of CEOs across our businesses who live and breathe the Virgin brand and who are entrepreneurs themselves.' (4)

This case continues in Chapter 12.

Questions:

1. What is the essence of the Virgin brand? Why is it important to the company?
2. How is it developed and maintained?
3. How important is Richard Branson to the brand? What might happen when he retires?

Sources: 1. *The Guardian*, 30 April 2002. 2. Branson, R. (1998) *Losing my Virginity*, 1998, London : Virgin. 3. Andersen, J. (1995) *Local Heroes*, Glasgow : Scottish Enterprise. 4. www.hrmagazine.co.uk, 13 July 2010.

Summary

- Your values and beliefs should underpin the business. They set expectations for how to operate and treat people – customers, employees, partners and suppliers. They should be reflected in your value proposition to customers.

- Developing a vision for the future of your business is important. This is a shared mental image of a desired future state. It must be attractive but credible – acknowledging the tension created by a realistic appraisal of the current situation. It is communicated as a vision statement.

- A mission statement is a statement of purpose for your business. This should be underpinned by your values.

- Value-driven marketing seeks to develop customer relationships and is usually underpinned by a strong brand identity. It encourages customers to become loyal advocates of a product/service by involving them in aspects of marketing and product development.

- You can differentiate your product/service through its functional capabilities, its design and its brand.

- Branding identifies the product/service offering to the customer and is the start of developing a relationship based upon trust that mutually benefits the customer and company.

- Your brand identity should reflect the value proposition you present to customers and be underpinned by the values that you hold. Effective branding adds value for the customer and the organization.

- As well as being worthwhile in its own right, CSR can be used to underpin your brand identity by providing evidence of your values and beliefs. It can also make sound commercial sense in other ways.

- Your brand should reflect the personality of your organization – its culture – and this will take time to establish. You create the culture of your organization through your leadership and the culture of the organization is likely to reflect your personality.

Exercise 6.1

Values and beliefs

1 Building on Exercise 2.1, list details about your personality, your values, beliefs, social concerns, philosophies about life and other characteristics that you wish the business to adopt. Reflect on how these might be evidenced.

2 List the ways that your values etc. will be reflected in the value propositions for each market segment you intend to sell to. Review your answers to Exercise 5.1 to ensure that this is properly reflected.

3 List the way that your company will evidence these values and beliefs, for example through CSR policies etc.

Exercise 6.2

Mission and vision statements

1 Review Exercise 5.1 and write down the elements of your value proposition that are common to all customer segments.

2 Review Exercises 5.2 and 5.3 and write down what constitutes your competitive advantage.

3 Mission statements can take many forms. Building on Exercise 2.2.1, use the following framework (taken from P.A. Wickham (2001) *Strategic Entrepreneurship: A Decision-making Approach to New Venture Creation and Management*, Harlow: Pearson Education) to write a mission statement for your business.

(*The company*) aims to use its (*competitive advantage*) to achieve/maintain (*aspirations*) in providing (*product/business scope*) which offers (*value proposition*) to satisfy the (*needs*) of (*customer segments*). In doing this the company will at all times strive to uphold (*values*).

4 Write a vision statement consistent with your mission.

5 Review your objectives (Exercise 2.2.2) and restate them to ensure they are consistent with your mission and vision.

Exercise 6.3

Creating identity

The aim of this exercise is to reduce the elements of your corporate and/or brand identity to as few words as possible — words that reflect how you are and what you want your organization and/or your product/service to represent to stakeholders (customers, employees and other partners). You may wish to repeat this exercise for your 'corporate identity' and 'product/service identity' if they are different.

1 Based upon your mission statement (Exercise 6.2) underpinned by your values and beliefs (Exercise 6.1), write down words that convey the message you want your brand to convey – its identity.

2 Brainstorm how these words can be crafted into a simple, coherent message by linking the words to associated images and actions. Draw the images. Can any of these images be used to promote the brand? Write a single sentence that conveys your brand message.

3 Brainstorm how you might provide customers with evidence of the reality of this identity. Write down the actions you need to undertake to do this.

4 Brainstorm how you might best communicate your identity to customers. Review the results alongside the communications media you highlighted in Exercise 5.1. Write down the actions you need to undertake to communicate your identity effectively and ensure they are reflected in your marketing strategy.

Exercise 6.4

Company and product/service name

You need to decide on a name for your organization and/or the product/service it offers that is memorable and reflects the identity you wish to portray.

1 Reflect on the answers to Exercise 6.3 and consider whether the name you are considering is consistent with the identity you want to portray. Are there any images that could be incorporated into a logo that reflects your brand or company identity?

2 List the actions you need to undertake as a result of this exercise. The legal aspects of brand and company registration are covered in Chapter 9.

 Visit www.palgrave.com/companion/burns-new-venture-creation for chapter quizzes to test your knowledge and other resources.

7
LAUNCHING
YOUR
BUSINESS

Contents

Learning outcomes

When you have read this chapter and undertaken the related exercises you will be able to:
- Understand the customer buying process and how the marketing mix can be used to encourage customers to become an advocate of your product/service
- Understand how to find prospective customers throughout your distribution chain
- Enhance your face-to-face sales skills
- Write a press release
- Draw up a communications campaign that helps launch your business
- Develop a marketing strategy that launches the business

From prospect to advocate

Just because you've got a good business idea and a persuasive value proposition does not mean success is guaranteed. Customers will not queue up at the door of a start-up if they are unaware of its existence. Indeed, even if they are aware, they still might take some persuading to buy a new, untried product or service. As a newcomer to the market, you have little or no credibility or reputation. Even if you have a brand, customers will not initially recognize it. And then you still need to persuade them to purchase it again, and again. At least your brand should help them do this. But building the relationship that underpins an effective brand will take time.

This chapter is about trying to attract the customer segments you identified in Chapter 5 and persuading them to start the journey to become the valuable loyal customers we discussed in Chapter 6. It is not easy or straightforward, even if you have the best product/service in the world. To do this you have to use all the tools in your marketing armoury – price, promotion, place and people – and in different ways, at different times and in different circumstances. How you go about this all depends on who your customers are.

The journey a first-time purchaser takes in becoming a regular customer can be broken down into the four-stage process shown in Figure 7.1.

Levinson, J.C. *Guerrilla Marketing* (1984, London: Platkus Books)

In order to sell a product or service, a company must establish a relationship with the customer. It must build trust and support the customer's needs, and it must deliver a product that delivers the promised benefits.

Stage 1 Once your prospective customer becomes aware of your product they will evaluate the value proposition it offers. They need to be made aware that it is on the market and encouraged to make that all-important trial purchase.

Stage 2 Once they have purchased your product/service they will evaluate whether you have delivered the value proposition that you promised. Remember, it will be the whole marketing mix that they then evaluate, including service delivery and after-sales service. And whilst they will be evaluating your offering, you should also be checking to see they are happy with it.

Stage 3 If the value proposition that is delivered meets their expectations then they may be persuaded to repeat the purchase and become regular customers. Again, they will need some encouragement.

Stage 4 The objective is to move the customer up the loyalty chain from regular customer, to a supporter who thinks positively about the product/service, and ultimately to become an advocate. This is a customer who is so loyal that they are willing to recommend the product/service to others, and even bring in new customers or help with product development. Even at this stage their loyalty cannot be taken for granted. It must be encouraged and maintained.

As outlined in the last chapter, to convert your customers into advocates you should be aiming to build a relationship with them – a relationship based on shared values. To achieve this, you need to enter into a dialogue with your customers wherever they are on the loyalty ladder. The nature of that dialogue will depend where they are. Your communications strategy can help move customers up the loyalty ladder – creating product awareness, stimulating need, creating brand awareness and attitude, and facilitating dialogue.

Ideally, relationships are based upon one-to-one and face-to-face interaction, but they can be influenced by various media. Indeed in today's interconnected, knowledge-based society you can use a range of mass communications media to initiate, develop and maintain these relationships. And mass media becomes vitally important in communicating with mass markets, where the logistics of communicating face-to-face are problematic. Nevertheless, whether you are selling face-to-face or to mass markets, the objective is to build a long-lasting relationship with customers, rather than just selling them something on a one-off basis.

PhotoDisc/Getty/Images

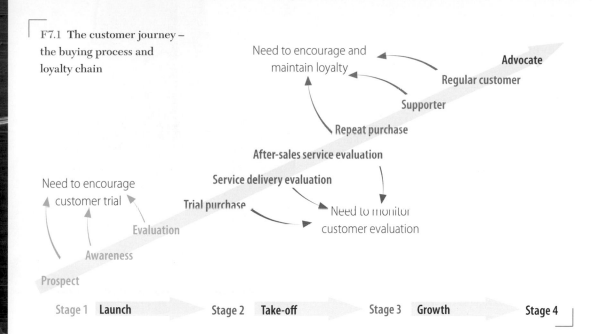

F7.1 **The customer journey –
the buying process and
loyalty chain**

Need to encourage and
maintain loyalty

Advocate

Regular customer

Supporter

Repeat purchase

After-sales service evaluation

Service delivery evaluation

Need to encourage
customer trial

Trial purchase

Need to monitor
customer evaluation

Evaluation

Awareness

Prospect

Stage 1 **Launch**   Stage 2 **Take-off**   Stage 3 **Growth**   Stage 4

Finding your first customers

Finding the first customer is crucial, and if
your network of contacts includes prospective
customers or family or friends who might introduce
you to them, use it. A ready-made network can
short-circuit the problem you have with a lack of
credibility. It all depends on who your prospective
customers are, and how you get to them.

Much of business-to-business selling is face-to-face,
particularly when you are looking for that first
order. Selling into distribution networks also often
involves face-to-face selling. You start by identifying
who specifically in the company you need to sell to.
You need to find out the name of the buyer of your
type of product/service and make an appointment
to see them. Even getting an appointment requires
a degree of 'selling' because these are busy people
with established suppliers. They need a reason to
see you. And then you need to master some basic
selling skills to turn these prospects into customers.

Face-to-face selling can be necessary for mass
consumer markets but, because there are so
many people, finding prospective customers that
meet your marketing segmentation profile can
be extremely time-consuming. Of course you
can sometimes buy in lists of prospects that meet

your marketing segmentation profile and contact
them directly – by phone, email or text. You may
need to 'qualify' these leads – assess their real
potential – before you commit too much time to
trying to sell to them. You might be able to obtain
referrals. This can be particularly valuable once
you are established and satisfied customers are
willing to help. However, you need to persuade
these prospective customers to show some interest
in your product/service so they can be sold to. And
this is particularly the case if you are counting on
prospects contacting you rather than the other
way round. There are many communications
techniques you can use, and there is a wide range
of communications media. What media to use
depends on the target market you wish to reach and
the product/service you are offering. For example,
if your target market is young males, digital new
media, using the internet and smartphones, can
be very effective and good value. However, these
methods will not work if your target market does
not use the internet or consume online content.
Sometimes, old-fashioned media such as flyers
and posters can be more effective. Once you have
identified the channels, you need to decide on the
message. Why should the prospect contact you,
even if they see your message?

Developing your sales skills

Most entrepreneurs will have to sell face-to-face – either to other businesses or to consumers. To sell face-to-face you need to identify the prospective customer by name and then be able to meet with them. This is easy to say but usually more difficult to arrange. Corporate buyers have busy schedules and established suppliers. Personal buyers often try to avoid sales people. They need a reason to meet you – a hook that offers them something that they need.

It sounds obvious, but the first thing is to make certain you have identified the benefits this specific customer is looking for and thoroughly understand your value proposition. You must do some basic research on the prospect and, if relevant, the company they represent. The larger the potential sale, the more important the research and the longer you should spend on it. You want to build a relationship quickly. Knowing a few personal details about the prospect can help break down barriers quickly. But a professional relationship is based on mutual self-interest – you both want something – and trust that you both can deliver what you promise (in your case, the value proposition and, in their case, cash payment). If possible, send them information on your company and your product/service in advance. A brochure can be very useful. At the meeting you need to establish what they want – the 'problem' they have – and how your product/service can solve it for them. You need to be able to:

- Ask questions and listen to the answers.
- Be clear about how your product/service will solve their specific 'problem' and be able to demonstrate its features either directly or with the help of photographs or brochures.
- Back up the claims you make about your value proposition with proof, for example by providing references or testimonials from satisfied customers.
- Handle objections and concerns.
- Close the sale.

Corbis

Some objections are fundamental – the customer does not want your product/service. But some are concerns that you might be able to solve. There are six of these other types of objection, some of which can be dealt with. They are:

- **Feature objection** – Some of the features do not meet the customer's approval. This might be overcome by emphasizing the positive reasons for these features.
- **Information-seeking objection** – The customer wants more information about the product/service, often about proving your claims for it. This gives you the opportunity to expand on your product's benefits.
- **Price objection** – This might be fundamental or it might be a signal that the customer is considering buying and, therefore, the start of negotiations. If they are seeking a lower price, try stressing the product benefits compared to competitors' and value-for-money. If this does not work, try offering a discount, but only in exchange for something such as a larger order.
- **Delay objection** – The customer wants to put off making a decision. This is difficult if the delay is genuine so you need to find out the reason. If necessary, arrange a return visit.

- **Loyalty objection** – The customer may have an established relationship with a competitor. Stress the benefits of the product, do not 'knock' the competitor but try to find reasons why they should change supplier, for example, because they are not receiving the service they ought to. Always keep in contact as it may just take time to convince them to try you.

- **Hidden objection** – The buyer prevaricates for no obvious reason. It is important to get to the unstated objection and deal with it, so ask questions.

Some people have problems recognizing buying signals and can continue relentlessly through a sales pitch long after the customer was ready to buy the product or service. Buying signals can be many and various – the customer becoming interested and animated, positive body language such as leaning forward or wanting to pick up or try the product. If interest is confirmed by asking a few questions, the whole process can be short-circuited and you can go to the most important stage of all – closing the sale. There are six well-known techniques for closing the sale:

- **Trial close** – You can try this one immediately you see a buying signal. This close uses the opportunity of an expression of interest to ask a further question which implicitly assumes a sale. For example, 'It is the quality of the product that has convinced you, hasn't it?' The trial close ends with a question and if the answer is positive then you can proceed straight to closing the sale.

- **Alternative close** – This forces the customer to a decision between options. For example, 'Do you want an initial order of 1000 or 2000?' or 'Can we deliver next month or would you prefer next week?'

- **Summary close** – This is useful if the buyer is uncertain about the next step. It summarizes what has been said and sets out the next steps. For example, 'So those are the advantages our service offers over the one you are using at the moment and I think you can see that we are better in every respect. Do you agree?'

- **Concession close** – Concessions are usually on price. They may secure orders but should not be given away too early, only at the end of the meeting when you judge it necessary to tip the balance in your favour. Always try to get something in exchange for a price concession. For example, 'And if you place an order this month, there is a special 5% discount.'

- **Quotation close** – Often you have to provide a formal quote at the end of the sales interview. If this is the case, then it should be followed up with another visit to the customer to clarify the main points, answer any queries and secure the sale.

- **Direct close** – Just sometimes it is actually necessary to ask for the order directly – and then remain silent and listen to the answer. If the answer is 'no' a follow-up question should elicit some objections that you might still be able to overcome.

Selling to well-informed customers can be particularly difficult. They may have sought out online reviews or gathered expert advice from independent sources rather than relying on what you might tell them. They come to a sales meeting with a decision already half-made and, after clarifying a few points that confirm they want to buy your product, often try to go straight to a price negotiation. The approach to take here is called **insight selling** and involves trying to disrupt these pre-meeting decisions. Firstly, it means trying to establish relationships with prospective customers well ahead of the meeting, in their 'learning' phase, so that you are seen as an expert consultant with valuable knowledge. Secondly, it involves using this position to disrupt and 'reset' customer thinking by challenging their assumptions, perhaps by identifying undisclosed problems. In this way the buying decision is a joint one, with the salesperson adding value by action as an expert consultant in the process.

Communications media

This brings us back to the importance of building relationships with prospective customers – not an easy task for a brand-new start-up. And you can use a range of mass communications media to initiate, develop and maintain these relationships. Indeed, there has never been a greater choice of communications tools and it grows every year. Some of these are listed in Table 7.1.

Word-of-mouth	Newspaper advertising	Posters
Relationships and networks	Radio advertising	Flyers
Social networks and media	TV advertising	Hoardings/billboards
Blogging	Internet advertising	Direct mail
Guerrilla marketing	Sponsorship	Email
Publicity and public relations	Telephone	Texting

T7.1 **Communication tools**

> *Dieter Burmester, founder Burmester BBC News 23 February 2012*
>
> I believe that one of the most important things is to **spread the word** in your personal network. Get your personal network working for you. A personal **recommendation** is so much more valuable than any kind of advertisement you can make.

Word-of-mouth recommendations, spread through your **relationships and networks,** can be a very effective way of promoting a local start-up. It is a low-cost option that involves personal time and effort. It is extremely effective because, essentially, you are using advocates to promote your business. Family and friends might be able to help you initially but, once you are established, unpaid customer recommendation is very powerful. And, where word-of-mouth works well within a limited geographic location, social networks can take over to spread the word to a wider audience.

Social networks and media is a term that covers any communication hosted on the internet or on smartphones, such as texting, tweeting or blogging. It includes social networking sites such as Facebook, Twitter and YouTube. Social media can spread word-of-mouth recommendations very cheaply. It is extremely fast and can reach enormous audiences. The word 'viral' has been used to describe how messages can get passed around, causing revolutions in some countries. It is therefore a powerful tool.

Social media sites can be used in a number of ways, for example by establishing a presence and creating a community around your product/service. Usually linked to your own website, it can be used to establish a dialogue with customers, solicit feedback from them, building brand awareness and even generating sales leads. If used effectively, it can help harness the 'advocate effect' by building a 'community' of interest around you product/service. You can generate interest by constantly providing new topics for discussion or by organizing events or contests. Blogging is one way of familiarizing people with your product/service and building an emotional bond with them. For a blog to work, it must be continually refreshed with new content. It must be interesting, informative and fun. It must deal with more than just your company's product/service and reach out to address other lifestyle or industry issues of more general interest. It is unlikely to work if used as a medium

> *Raoul Shah, founder Exposure The Observer 29 September 2013*
>
> **Personal** recommendation still counts for a lot. As my first boss told me: 'Make one person **happy** and they'll tell four others. Make one person **unhappy** and they'll tell seven others.' Never underestimate the power of **word of mouth.**

for straightforward advertising. Chat-rooms and discussion forums can also be cheap ways of developing relationships with customers. You might even email friends and family and ask them to promote your business. Many larger organizations now expend considerable resources on developing an internet presence through blogging and other social networking sites, generating artificial excitement and web traffic around their message.

Some social media sites also take advertising, which can be a useful way of reaching your target market. For example, Facebook allows start-ups to deliver targeted advertisements based upon key words in personal profiles and geographic location. But remember, if you are using the internet to promote your business, you need to have a good website for customers to look at (see Chapter 10).

Another approach to using social media to promote your product/service is to offer a free phone app that that is useful or entertaining. If an app is something your target market uses it can be extremely effective because it will be shared and talked about. For example, in 2010 Volkswagen launched the new Golf GTI in the USA using a mobile platform exclusively, targeting young males. It offered a free app for a game featuring the new car. Within five days the app had been downloaded 800,000 times and had become the number one free app download on Apple's iTunes App Store in 36 countries.

Guerrilla marketing is a term used to mean any low cost approach to creating awareness of a product/service using any of the above media. It relies on time, ingenuity and novelty, rather than cash, to get the message taken up and passed on. It might adopt unconventional ways to do this, such as publicity stunts, graffiti, flash mobs etc. For example, BMW notoriously attached a Styrofoam copy of a Mini Cooper to the side of a skyscraper in central Houston, Texas, as part of a guerrilla marketing campaign. The idea is to create a 'buzz' around the product/service so that potential customers want to find out more and are eager to search out where it can be seen and/or purchased. One approach is to encourage the spreading of

rumours related to a product/service. The campaign might use social networks and mobile technologies to encourage the buzz or the rumours to 'go viral'. The whole idea is to involve prospective customers in promoting the product/service by doing something unusual and memorable, at the same time building a relationship with them.

Publicity and public relations (PR) involves getting media to recognize what you are doing and write news articles or record radio or TV features about it. It is therefore likely to reach a wider audience than your network of relationships. The key is to find something that is newsworthy or interesting. You must prepare press releases and be prepared to give interviews. A major advantage is that PR is free and, because you do not pay for them, these articles or programmes will have greater credibility than advertising. However, the problem is that you do not control the content of the article or feature, and prospective customers may be left interested in the product/service but not knowing how to purchase it or contact you. Worse still, there is a danger that the published article or feature might be negative or critical. If you have the cash, one option is to hire a professional PR company to manage your message. You also take the chance that your story will not be run because other, more newsworthy, events have happened on that day.

You can get PR from the human-interest story associated with your start-up, promoting yourself as a successful local entrepreneur. The combination of an interesting personality and a 'David and Goliath' story of taking on larger competitors can be irresistible. Richard Branson has been particularly good at this, ever since he launched his first magazine – *Student* – at the age of 18. He used PR to establish the Virgin brand. Branson is outward-going and an excellent self-publicist. He has been called an 'adventurer', taking risks that few others would contemplate, such as his transatlantic power boating and round-the-world ballooning exploits. He launched Virgin Atlantic by identifying himself with the brand and positioning himself as the entrepreneur competing against the established competitor, British Airways – a 'national carrier' that had government backing and a near-monopoly on transatlantic air travel from the UK.

You might be able to get PR because of the novelty of your new product/service. Another approach is to ask a celebrity to launch the product or open new premises. You might also get specialist media to review your product by sending them a free sample. Apple use PR by getting respected computer and technology experts to review their new products prior to launch.

Advertising a new product/service launch can be done through a range of media such as newspapers, magazines, radio, TV, internet, flyers, posters, hoardings, direct mail, emails etc. Advertising can be expensive, but it should guarantee a wide audience. Most start-ups are unlikely to enjoy a large advertising budget, so extensive media advertising of the sort often seen for a new car model launch is unlikely to be an option. However, low-cost advertising such as posters and flyers – delivered to homes or placed under car windscreen wipers – can be extremely effective for a locally-based business. They can create product/service awareness and tell customers where you are located and, if combined with a message that encourages a trial purchase, can quickly stimulate sales.

Highly focused advertising can be very cost-effective, for example through trade press or the focused pay-by-click advertising offered by Google and Bing. Pay-by-click allows you to advertise on the screen only when certain search words are used. It also allows you to place adverts on other peoples' websites where they offer related products or services. With pay-by-click you only pay when your advertisement is clicked on.

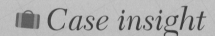

Case insight

Bicycle Space

Building customer relationships as a retailer

Jordan Mittelman opened his Bicycle Space cycle store in Washington DC in 2010. But with so much competition, this set out to be a cycle store with attitude, indeed passion, aiming to build 'a cycling community' around the shop using social networks. The retailer organizes regular group maintenance workshops and bike rides, such as the monthly 'full-moon' rides and a Halloween 'night of the cycling undead' attended by hundreds of bikers. These are organized as social outings and are accompanied by music and food and refreshments.

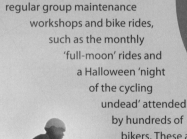

USA

BBC News Business 3 March 2013

People can find all the products we sell online, and are often so well-read and knowledgeable. They've looked up every detail and come in knowing so much. To sell to those people you have to appeal to something greater – we're selling a lifestyle and an experience. People want to be part of something and come to a place where they'll be taken care of. We're really a social gathering spot and an essential place to learn about bikes, use them and have a good time.

Visit the website on:
www.bicyclespacedc.com/

Case insight

The Fabulous Bakin' Boys

Building customer relationships as a manufacturer

Gary Frank set up a company called the Delicious Doughnut Company in 1989, but performance was lacklustre and in 1997 he decided to create a new image and re-brand the company with the name Fabulous Bakin' Boys. He also changed his packaging and invested heavily in marketing and promotion to help persuade the supermarket chains to 'push' his products. Being a small company means that he has to rely mainly on in-store promotions, but the internet has enabled him to open direct links with the consumers of his products. The Fabulous Bakin' Boys website contains a database of jokes, cheeky postcard advertisements and online games such as Muffin Munchin and Cake Invaders that can be downloaded or 'mailed to a mate' as part of a viral marketing campaign. However, you can only do all this after you have registered. Once registered you receive regular mail-outs. Online ordering is also possible. The Fabulous Bakin' Boys have become one of Europe's leading muffin makers.

Visit their website on: www.bakinboys.co.uk

Developing a communications campaign

You need to develop a communications campaign as part of your launch strategy. This can be aimed at your end-use customers as well as your distribution channels. Your campaign needs to be slightly different at each stage in Figure 7.1. However, underpinning it is the need to develop sustainable customer relationships and create a clear brand identity. Your strategy must both deliver and receive communications with customers, but ultimately it should be designed to open up a dialogue. Customer listening is important at all stages. The major aims at each stage are:

Stage 1 This is the launch stage of the business where creating awareness of the product/service and persuading your first customers to purchase it are important. You need to get the customer to understand what the product/service does for them and create a desire to at least try it. It is about:

- Creating brand awareness – getting customers to recognize that your brand, among others, meets their needs and should be considered.
- Stimulating brand purchase – persuading customers to buy your brand.

Stage 2 This is the take-off stage of the business when you are still trying to persuade more customers to try your product/service at the same time as persuading those who have tried it to repeat purchase. It is about:

- Creating brand attitude – getting customers to recognize how your brand is different from others.
- Facilitating brand purchase – having decided to buy your brand, the customer needs to know where the product can be purchased and at what price.

Stage 3 This is the growth stage of the business. It is about:

- Continuing to facilitate brand purchase.
- Restating brand attitude and identity – reinforcing your value proposition so that regular customers are convinced that they are making the right purchase decision.

Stage 4 This is the final stage of creating brand advocacy. It is about:

- Cementing the relationship with the customer – involving them in prospecting.
- Encouraging new customers and product/service development.

You need to develop a communications campaign that integrates with your overall launch strategy and moves customers through these four stages. Remember that, whilst there may be short-term objectives at each stage, the longer-term aim is to develop close customer relationships based on shared values. Developing such a campaign involves six steps:

1. Identifying the target market you wish to communicate with.

2. Identifying the media that reach this target market.

3. Defining your communications objectives.

4. Developing and refining your communications message – words and images.

5. Setting the budget (money and other resources). Deciding whether the medium that reaches your target market is appropriate for your message and is within your budget.

6. Preparing your communications plan – media, dates, times etc.

If your communications campaign is expensive, you would be well-advised to test it out through focus groups before you launch it. And once the campaign is over you should evaluate it against the objectives you set in step 3.

The swift rise of new **communication** channels such as Facebook and Twitter have caused many executives to reassess how they stay in touch with their customers, employees and, increasingly, with the media itself. People no longer want to be sold to; they want companies to help them find an informed way to buy the **right product** or service at the **right price**. They will watch ads, but often **online** rather than on TV, and they're much more likely to view ads that friends have recommended. When something goes wrong with a product, they want to be able to reach the company **instantly** and get a **quick solution**. How companies adapt to this **energetic** and sometimes **chaotic** world will define their **future success**. The website, Facebook page, blog and Twitter feed are no longer add-ons to a business's communication budget. They should be central to its marketing strategy, and used in coordination with other marketing efforts.

Richard Branson

www.entrepreneur.com/article/218098, 8 February 2011

Kowloon, Hong Kong

Creating product awareness

Whilst all start-ups need to create product awareness, how you approach this will depend on the type of business you are launching. Refer back to the start-up typologies in Figure 3.1 (p. 41). The more radical the product/service innovation, the more likely the start-up is to create genuine public interest. You are also likely to be able to use PR when you are introducing a product/service that exists elsewhere into a new market. Such developments are newsworthy in their own right and mean that you can use PR to your advantage. But even here, few companies would trust the public to beat a path to their door on the back of a news story. There is no guarantee that it will be accurate, nor is there any guarantee that they will explain where potential customers can buy the product/service. So it is important that you provide the media with information on what the product/service is and why it is newsworthy. This involves producing and distributing a press release and possibly organizing a press conference or launch event. This can be supported by a range of other activities that utilize as many of the communication media as time and money permit.

Few product launches enjoy the same level of anticipation and pre-ordering as Apple products – and certainly Apple plan these launches meticulously. Even before the launch of a new product Apple ensure that it is being promoted, normally through a mix of free PR (pre-launch feature leaks, pre-launch product reviews etc.) and a theatrical launch event supported by media advertising. But then Apple have a brand that is recognized for its design and innovation and has an established band of loyal customers and advocates – something that takes time to create and is not an option for a start-up. But the lesson is clear – you need to create awareness of your product or service before the customer will even consider purchasing it – and you do not leave it to chance. You need to consider all the communications media discussed in the previous section.

With any product/service launch it is important to get the right message to prospective customers. The message you want to convey to your target market segment is that you have a value proposition that meets some, as yet unmet, need they have or meets it better than other products or services. They should be told about your product/service, what it can do for them – the benefits – and where they can buy it. However, if your product or service is entirely novel you may have to limit the awareness message to what the product does, explaining the benefits offered. In both cases you want to create sufficient curiosity that prospective customers will consider purchasing it when they see the product or service on sale.

For those start-ups where the product innovation is incremental the job of creating awareness is more difficult because the launch is less newsworthy. That means PR is less likely to be effective and you might focus more on the other communications media. However, you still have options that might get results. Some businesses are lucky enough to be able to have a celebrity launch their product/service – sometimes free and often found through their network of contacts. Celebrity launches can be extremely effective, particularly for shops because they attract potential shoppers. A celebrity might also be persuaded to endorse the product/service, but do remember that they are putting their reputation on the line. Alternatively, never under-estimate the newsworthiness of your personal entrepreneurial story. Many newspapers run regular small business pages and are looking for inspiring stories to fill their pages.

As we have already discussed, social media can be a very cheap way of generating interest in a new business, but you need to have a 'hook' to get people interested even with this medium, and you need to find a way of finding the addresses to send your message to. Posters and flyers can do the same thing for local businesses. One way to short-circuit the early stages in the process outlined in Figure 7.1 is to get customers to jump straight to the evaluation or trial 'purchase' stage by offering them free or discounted samples or trials. This is only appropriate for low-price product/services that generate repeat sales. And it is most appropriate for product/services that are only incrementally different to those offered by existing competitors. In many cases it needs to be linked to incentives offered to the distributors offering the product/service.

Good Hair Day

Start-up marketing strategy

Good Hair Day (GHD), part of Jemella Group, was started by Martin Penny in 2001. Based in West Yorkshire, the company has revolutionized the hair styling industry with an iron that straightens hair between two heated ceramic plates. But when Martin first took the idea to his bank, asking for a £50,000 loan, the bank manager was sceptical, seeing the product as 'just another set of hair tongs'. Martin only got the money on the strength of his track record running an environmental consultancy.

Martin decided on two important strategies that were to underpin the subsequent success of his business:

1. Not to manufacture the product himself, but to have it manufactured in Korea where costs were lower. In this way, he could focus on sales and keep his fixed costs to a minimum.

2. Not to sell through the high street but to target up-market London West End hair salons first, and then salons across the UK. The 'hair styling irons' were sold both for salon use and to customers by the salons themselves. Customer prices were high but so too were the margins for the salons. Despite product costs being relatively low, using this route to market differentiated GHD's product from 'just another set of hair tongs'. It was seen as professional, special and up-market.

Since they used hair stylists, many celebrities such as Madonna, Victoria Beckham, Jennifer Aniston and Gwyneth Paltrow used GHD tongs, and the company benefited from celebrity endorsements. These helped to give it a certain exclusive cachet that then helped sell GHD products to the general public. The company claims that the iron is now used in more than 10,000 UK salons – 85% of the market. Based on this success, GHD is diversifying into other hair-care products such as shampoo, conditioner and styling gel, and has launched a new brand called 'Nu:U', aimed at the mid-price, mass salon market.

Up-to-date information on Good Hair Day can be found on their website: www.ghdhair.com

Getting customers to buy

Figure 5.3 (p. 102) outlined the different ways of getting your product/service in front of customers. Selling through a distribution chain such as shops, agents or distributors eats into your profit margins but allows you to expand your reach, benefiting from your partners' strengths. Getting end-use customers to buy your product means incentivizing each stage of your distribution chain. Whilst you might be able to contact distributors directly to create awareness of your product, they will need an incentive to stock it. They will be interested in the uniqueness of your product and will also react to whether customers are already seeking it out because of your customer awareness campaign (**'demand-pull'**). 'Demand-pull' communication strategies focus on your end-use customer. They create demand for the product and pull it through the distribution chain.

Ultimately these channels are interested in profit, so they might be persuaded to stock your product, particularly if initially it is offered on a sale-or-return basis. Indeed they might help promote your product if you offer them an extra initial discount or bonus (**'supply-push'**). With 'supply-push' your launch strategy will need to influence each link in the distribution chain. However, unless accompanied by other promotional activity, such as point-of-sale displays etc., this can leave decisions about promotion activity entirely with the distributor. This can lead to unintended consequences, such as distributors entering into local price promotions that are not consistent with other elements of your marketing mix. This underlines the important point that your launch strategy must be consistent with your overall strategy and should seek to coordinate 'push' and 'pull' incentives.

'Demand-pull' can be stimulated using all the communication media covered earlier. The message is different from an awareness campaign (although the two can be linked) because you now want to get people to try out and evaluate your product/service. The first customers to buy a new product/service have been characterized as '**innovators**' – people who think for themselves, like novelty and try things. Innovators constitute only two or three per cent of the market.

You can also encourage people to try out your product/service through pricing. For example, if the product or service is relatively low price and customers are likely to repeat purchase, free samples/trials or special introductory price offers may persuade customers to try it and then, if they like it, buy it again. Offering introductory discounts, rather than offering your product/service at a low price, allows you to re-establish your market price more easily after introduction. Customers will accept the removal of a discount far more easily than an increase in price. This strategy is usually necessary when differences to existing product/services are not great and customers need an incentive to switch.

By way of contrast, if your product/service is sufficiently unique or novel, it may be possible to premium price at launch, particularly if customers are unlikely to repeat the purchase quickly. This creates a certain status associated with ownership of the product or service. You can then effectively lower the price later by including more features but keeping the price the same. This is the strategy used by Apple, with new versions of its products carrying new and better features. With this sort of product you can also afford to be selective about distribution, going into new channels as the product ages. So, for example, a film is shown first in cinemas, then on pay-to-view channels and finally it becomes available on video or through download, usually with the price reducing progressively over time.

Once a customer makes a purchase they will evaluate your product/service against the promises you held out to them. Are the value propositions you advertised real? Does the product/service meet their expectations? Is the service delivery at each stage of the distribution chain appropriate?

Remember the customer may not repeat buy if just one of your channels of distribution does not meet their expectations in some way. So, as well as making your first sales, you need to start evaluating your customers' reactions to your product/service and correcting any weaknesses in your value proposition. Indeed, doing this effectively could be your first step in establishing a relationship with customers. You can use face-to-face trials, evaluation questionnaires or feedback sheets. If you can get a contact address then, if there are weaknesses, communicate to them when they are corrected. If there are no weaknesses then these are prospective repeat-buy customers.

Penetrating your market

Your business will grow through a combination of repeat sales (for appropriate products) and new customers. Repeat sales will be built on the relationship you develop with customers, particularly as competitors emerge. New customers will come from a combination of promotional activity (including face-to-face selling), finding new distribution channels and using existing customers who are willing to act as your advocates in some way. Reputation spreads, but it can take time.

Whilst your first customers have been characterized as innovators, they will be followed by second-wave customers characterized as **early adopters** – people with status in their market segment and opinion leaders. These constitute about 14% of the population. They choose new products carefully. They adopt successful products, making them acceptable and respectable. As your product/service attracts more customers, it will attract more attention from competitors. They may adapt their marketing strategy and even change their product/service characteristics so as to compete more directly with you. So, your marketing strategy may need to adapt and change to combat this threat.

The appropriate strategy to adopt at this stage depends, in part, on the competitive position you find yourself in. Referring back to the start-up typologies in Figure 3.1, the more radical the product/service innovation or market you are creating, the more likely you are to be in a dominant market position at start-up. This should reflect itself in the low level of competition you identified in Exercise 4.2.

Strong competitive position

If you are in a strong competitive position you need to expand as rapidly as possible, investing in whatever is the basis for value that you are offering and developing your brand identity. There is a window of opportunity for you to capitalize on your first-mover advantage before competitors copy you. In terms of the core value propositions outlined in Chapter 5:

- If your core value proposition involves high differentiation then you should further differentiate yourself from the competition, creating and building your brand. You will probably have been able to charge a premium price at launch and you should have been investing those profits in increasing your differentiation from the start. Despite your high differentiation, as competitors emerge your price may need to come down, either directly or, more likely, by improving the product's value in some way. Second-generation electronic products are typically better than their predecessors (e.g. storage capacity for computers) but at the same price.

- If your core value proposition involves cost leadership (low price) then you must obtain the necessary economies of scale as quickly as possible to gain that dominant position. This involves investing in ways of keeping your costs low and, at the same time, expanding your sales through aggressive marketing, including price promotions.

So, the key to success is gaining rapid market dominance, at the same time as building those close customer relationships. To attract more innovators and early adopters you need to make an intensive push on distribution. This might involve organizing frequent sales promotions, continually finding new channels of distribution, expanding into new geographic areas etc. Agents and distributors love to sell products or services that have proved successful elsewhere. It reduces their risk. Whilst some, particularly high technology, start-ups are international from the start, most move into overseas markets more gradually, starting by exporting products through independent channels like sales agents. We shall return to the issue of international expansion in the next chapter.

Weak competitive position

If you are not in a strong competitive position then your expansion needs to be more cautious. Your answers to Exercise 4.2 should give you the actions you need to take to combat competition, with a view to increasing profitability. One attractive option is to find a market niche within a competitive industry. Often in these circumstances a start-up is better advised to ignore the mass market, trying instead to carve out a smaller but distinctive market niche for itself – at least in the short term. This often avoids the high fixed costs usually associated with mass markets. It also means that a higher price can be charged for the product/service, albeit on a smaller volume which, as we saw in Chapter 5, can result in higher profits. And frequently that niche is bigger than the founder ever imagined. Serial entrepreneurs go on to found one business with 'limited' potential after another, often selling them on.

Whilst competition will certainly show itself at this stage, the real battle will come later. The **early and late majority** of customers each make up about one-third of customers and are more conservative, with slightly higher status and are more deliberate, thinking purchasers. They only adopt the product after it has become acceptable and will shop around and compare different product/service offerings. By this stage some competitors will have become established, whilst others will have fallen by the wayside. Those remaining will compete aggressively. This is the stage where your dominant market position and a well-recognized brand will really start to pay dividends. We shall address some of the challenges of marketing at this stage in the next chapter.

10 practical tips for a successful start-up

1. **Don't run out of cash** – only cash pays the bills so plan your cash flow so that you do not run out of it. We look at this in Chapter 15.

2. **Understand the mechanics of your business** – what it takes to make the product or service, and make certain you can deliver. We look at this in Chapter 10.

3. **Understand yourself** – what your strengths and weaknesses are, and make sure you play to your strengths and avoid (or compensate for) your weaknesses. You covered this in Chapter 2.

4. **Understand your customers** – who they are (name names), and why they should buy from you. You covered this in Chapter 5.

5. **Understand your competitors** – who they are (name names), and why customers will buy from you and not them. You covered this in Chapter 4.

6. **Don't be afraid to be different** – but understand why customers value it. You covered this in Chapters 5 and 6.

7. **Don't be afraid to charge as high a price as possible** – but be able to justify doing so and make certain customers agree. You covered this in Chapters 5 and 6.

8. **Keep your fixed costs as low as possible** – and for as long as possible. We look at this in Chapter 11.

9. **Plan ahead** – but any plan should not constrain you, it should allow you to think through and plan for contingencies, and don't be afraid to change it if circumstances change. This book is all about preparing a plan – with strategic options.

AND (JUST IN CASE YOU FORGET)

10. **Don't run out of cash** – too many profitable businesses have failed because of insufficient cash.

Jack Wills — University Outfitters

Low-cost marketing

Launched only in 1999 by Peter Williams and Rob Shaw, the Jack Wills brand has an old-world university association. It was originally known for selling hoodies (emblazoned with the names of universities), tracksuit bottoms, rugby shirts, pyjamas and party dresses – primarily to well-off youngsters.

Using the trademark 'Jack Wills – University Outfitters', the brand has a 'public school' or 'preppy' image – and prices reflect this, although they do offer a 25% discount to registered students. However, the business started life as a simple shop in the seaside town of Salcombe in Devon – a town without any university but plenty of well-off visitors. The founders invested £40,000 in the venture, taken mainly from their credit cards, which left them little spare cash for anything else. So, they lived above the store.

Today, the founders are millionaires. With annual sales of over £120 million and more than 60 stores in the UK and some 20 overseas in the USA, Ireland and Hong Kong, the Jack Wills brand is now better known for selling a modern 'take' on traditional 'British' clothes such as men's blazers and women's tweed jackets – 'playing off the tensions between old and new, formal and casual'. These often incorporate aspects of traditional British military and sporting design. The company uses navy blue and pink colour schemes in its packaging and for some of its products. They still sell sports-orientated clothing (for sports such as polo, rugby and rowing) but the shops have evolved to also sell expensive designer clothes and hats – often developed in collaboration with well-known partners like Liberty or Fox Brothers – as well as toiletries, cushions, bed linen and towels.

With many stores located in university towns, the shops are often housed in historical buildings. The interiors feature dark wood tables and display cases, faded Persian rugs and yellowed posters, designed to mirror the image of all-things-British. And products like bowler and pork-pie hats, and silk headscarves help

> I had just left university and I thought the years between 18 and 21 were amazing because you've got all the independence and freedom of being adult but you haven't quite entered the adult world. I looked back and realized I didn't appreciate how amazing those years were and I wanted to create a brand that epitomised that – for the person who has an aspirational response to that 18–21 British university thing.

emphasize the eccentric and 'dandyish' Britishness of the brand. The company logo features a pheasant with a top hat and walking stick, known as Mr Wills.

Curiously, Jack Wills' approach to marketing today can look remarkably similar to its approach when the founders opened the first store – an approach that sets the brand apart from competitors. Back in 1999 the founders could not afford an expensive advertising campaign. Instead they gave away branded hoodies and rugby shirts to 'influencers' in the town – kids that others would admire – and would pay them to go around giving away branded t-shirts. Jack Wills clothes became 'cool'. Overt advertising would have detracted from the brand image.

Today the company employs teams of 'seasonnaires' to roam beaches, ski resorts and university campuses and spread the brand – but never to sell. They rely on word-of-mouth and viral marketing. A year before the Jack Wills store opened in Nantucket, off Cape Cod in the USA, a team of 'seasonnaires' spent the summer 'seeding' the market.

> They are the mouthpieces of the brand. They have often worked in stores and their job for the summer is to make friends, throw parties and be in the right places to seed the brand.

The company sponsors certain more exclusive university sports events (and related entertainment) such as polo between Cambridge and Oxford, Harvard and Yale, Eton and Harrow. It also hosts exclusive 'events' such as the annual seasonnaires party. The company website lists its brand values as:

British – 'Britishness anchors all that we do; we're inspired by its history and tradition, blending old and new to create something that's distinctly ours. Wherever we go in the world, we'll always stay true to our British roots.'

Entrepreneurial – 'The business began with two friends taking a risk. That pioneering approach and commercial instinct remains. And we will retain it, however large we become.'

Innovative – 'Creativity, and the desire to be leading edge, drives us. It makes our day jobs more exciting, and ensures that we keep inspiring our customers too.'

Case insight

Responsible – 'Integrity and decency is at our core; it's inherent in us to act properly and treat everyone, whether our people, our suppliers or our customers, with respect.'

Excellence – 'It's not just about our high quality product: we believe in excellence in everything we do, it's that simple.'

Today t-shirts are old-hat. Instead they give away bright yellow, 'party pants' branded with different locations.

Questions:

1. From the information given, map out as much as you can of the business model for Jack Wills using the New Venture Creation Framework. Is the marketing mix consistent? Why is this important?
2. What are the brand values?
3. Why has the company's original approach to creating brand awareness, translated so well into a longer-term advertising/promotions strategy?
4. What are the advantages and disadvantages of this approach?

The product is **amazing** but if you kind of boil it down to what's really special – and what people talk about – it's **the party pants** … They sort of define us because it's not just a bunch of clothes, it's the **best summer** they've ever had, the best university experience or just the best winter trip because we're embedded in their **lifestyle** … There's an inherent naughty rebelliousness in everything that we do.

Peter Williams Sunday Times 16 September 2012

Find out more about the company on: www.jackwills.com

Summary

- You must make prospective customers aware of your product/service then persuade them to purchase it. Once they have purchased your product/service they will evaluate whether you have delivered your value proposition. They may then be persuaded to repeat purchase and become regular customers. Eventually they may become supporters who think positively about the product/service, and ultimately they may become advocates of it. You need to encourage this progression through building a relationship with your customers.

- You can build this relationship through face-to-face contact and through your communications strategy. Communications media include your personal networks, internet and social media, PR and advertising.

- The more radical your product innovation or the more novel the market you are creating, the more likely your start-up is to be of interest to the general media. However, they can also be interested in the human interest side of a business start-up. Media need to be made aware of the launch of your business. You can do this through a press release and a product launch event.

- You can sell directly to customers or through distribution channels. If you sell through channels, you might gain wider distribution but you lose profit and may lose control over communication to customers.

- 'Supply-push' is when you create incentives to intermediaries in your distribution channels to sell your product. 'Demand-pull' is when you create incentives directly with end-use customers who then 'pull' the product through the distribution channels.

- Price incentives can be effective in stimulating trial purchases of low-priced, repeat-purchase products, particularly when the differences from existing products are small.

- If your product/service is sufficiently unique it may be possible to charge a premium price at launch.

- Your strategy for market penetration may involve further sales promotions, expanding into new geographic areas, finding new channels of distribution and so on.

- The more innovative your product or market the more important it is to capitalize on your first-mover advantage and maintain your market dominance through rapid market penetration and growth. Building brand loyalty is the ultimate aim as the regular customer becomes an advocate for your product/service.

Exercise 7.1

Developing a marketing strategy for your business launch

The aim of this exercise is to build on the core marketing strategies in Exercises 5.1, 5.2, 5.3 and 5.4 to start to develop your launch strategy; creating awareness, encouraging customers to make their first purchase, then to repeat the purchase and become regular customers.

Customer segments	1.	2.	3.	4.
Creating awareness				
Encouraging trial purchase				
Encouraging repeat purchase				
Finding new prospective customers				
Evaluating service delivery				
Building relationships				

Using the format above, for each of your target market segments identified in Exercise 5.1:

1 List the ways that you will create awareness of your product/service both directly with end-use customers and distributors.

2 List the ways that you will encourage customers (including distributors) to make a trial purchase.

3 List the ways you will encourage repeat purchases from existing customers.

4 List the ways you will find new prospective customers.

5 List the things you need to do to ensure that the customer will make a positive evaluation of your service delivery and how you will monitor this.

6 List the things you need to do to ensure that customers work their way up the loyalty chain and how you might use them as advocates. How will you build and use a close customer relationship?

7 Estimate the costs and resources associated with the above.

Exercise 7.2

Developing your communications campaign

The aim of this exercise is to draw up a communications campaign for the launch of your business. This should reflect the communications elements coming from the lists generated in Exercise 7.1. Remember that, whilst there may be short-term objectives coming from Exercise 7.1, the longer-term aim is to develop close customer relationships based on shared values that reflect your brand identity (Exercise 6.3).

Customer segments	1.	2.	3.	4.
Target media				
Communications objectives				
Communications message				
Budget				
Communications plan (media, dates etc.)				

Using the format on the previous page, for each target market segment identified in Exercise 5.1:

1 Identify the target media.

2 List your communications objectives.

3 Develop your communications message (word and images).

4 Decide on your budget (money and other resources).

5 Write down your communications plan (media, dates etc.).

Exercise 7.3
Writing a press release

Write a press release concerning some aspect of your business. It should be no more than 100 words and contain two quotes. Make certain there is some newsworthy or human-interest aspect to it. Try to reflect your brand identity (Exercise 6.3) in your press release.

Exercise 7.4
Marketing strategy for your business launch

The aim of this exercise is to consolidate Exercises 7.1 and 7.2 and develop the launch strategy for your business.

Customer segments	1.	2.	3.	4.
Target media				
Communications objectives				
Communications message				
Budget				
Communications plan (media, dates etc.)				

1 Using the format above, write down the main elements of the marketing strategy for the launch of your business and identify the critical success factors.

2 Write a brief report on how you intend to launch your product or service.

Exercise 7.5
Selling skills

The aim of this exercise is to improve your selling skills. However, in doing this you may gain some insight into your value proposition and business model and wish to modify elements of it. Review your answers to all exercises in Chapters 5, 6 and 7 in the light of your experience.

Team up with two other students; one to act as a buyer (end-use customer or distributor) and one as an observer. Conduct a role-playing sales meeting lasting 5 minutes.

Seller: Provide the buyer in advance of the meeting with a one-page summary of your product/service and its value proposition (Exercise 5.1 and 7.4). Plan your meeting using the outline in this chapter. Try to close the sale.

Buyer: Make certain you understand your role. Remember you have been identified as a prospect and therefore you are interested in the product/service. However, prepare some objections that the seller will have to counter.

Observer: Observe the sales meeting and give feedback on what worked or did not work and how it might be improved.

 Visit www.palgrave.com/companion/burns-new-venture-creation for chapter quizzes to test your knowledge and other resources.

8 GROWING YOUR BUSINESS

Thinkstock

Contents

Learning outcomes

When you have read this chapter and undertaken the related exercises you will be able to:
- Understand which broad strategies are most likely to lead to successful growth
- Critically evaluate the strategic options for growth and understand the implications for a start-up
- Critically evaluate the effects of product life cycles on marketing strategy and how the life cycle can be lengthened through product expansion and extension
- Use the Growth Share Matrix to communicate marketing strategies for a portfolio of products
- Show advanced knowledge of the effects of the product portfolio on cash flow and how the product portfolio can be managed
- Critically evaluate the use of acquisition as part of a growth strategy and the advantages and disadvantages of diversification

Growth options

The previous chapter looked at ways in which you could increase sales by penetrating the market you have identified for your product or service. You will probably already have started to move from a selective distribution network to a more intensive network. At the same time you may already be adopting a more aggressive promotion and pricing strategy that encourages further market penetration ahead of the rapidly emerging competition. Alongside this, you will be building the brand as a vital part of the promotional message. This chapter will look at how you can build potential by considering new or different markets and think through how the product or service might be developed as you move into selling to the middle and late majority of customers and the product or service itself starts to age and move through its life cycle.

However, before doing this it is always worth having a moment of reflection, looking back on what has worked and what has not, understanding how you have modified your original value proposition to better meet the needs of customers. It is also important to understand

> After you've **launched** your business, while you are still privately-owned ... what you have to do is **grow very fast**, so that some day when you have to really drop a lot of dollars to the bottom line, you've laid in a base that can still **grow** at maybe 10% or 20% a year ... Five years into being a public company, you can never do that again.
>
> Kevin Surace, founder Serious Materials BBC News Business 20 June 2010

Strategies that build potential: playing the odds

© Kenishirotie – istockphoto.com

Does research tell us which strategies are most likely to deliver sustainable competitive advantage and growth? As we saw in Chapter 5, Porter (1985) wants us to select cost leadership, differentiation or focus. On the other hand, Hamel and Prahalad (1994) want us to focus on core competences and Treacy and Wiersema (1995) want us to select operational excellence, product leadership or customer intimacy. Which theory do you choose?

Differentiation – The answer is that all the evidence points to differentiation having a greater potential than low cost for producing sustainable competitive advantage. Differentiation takes more time to copy. For example, just one element of differentiation, quality, has been shown by many studies to be more likely to lead to growth than competing simply on price (Burns, 1994; Harrison and Taylor, 1996; Ray and Hutchinson, 1983; Storey et al., 1989). Strategy should therefore emphasize something that makes the firm as unique as possible and delivers as much value to the customer as possible today and, more importantly, tomorrow.

Speed of market dominance – Speed of execution is also important, particularly in new markets. Whilst first-mover advantage may disappear rapidly if the product/market offering proves unattractive or too many elements of the market offering prove inappropriate, delay can attract unwelcome competitors. Many surveys show that rapid domination of a market niche is likely to lead to sustainable growth (3i, 1993; Birley and Westhead, 1990; Harrison and Taylor, op. cit.; Macrae, 1991; Siegel et al., 1993; Solem and Steiner, 1989; Storey et al., op. cit.). There is also a strong relationship between market share and financial return (Boston Consulting Group, 1968, 1972; Buzzell et al., 1974; Buzzell and Gale, 1987; Yelle, 1979).

Continuous innovation – Frequent product or service innovation is also seen as important by many researchers, particularly for manufacturing businesses (Dunkelberg et al., 1987; Solem and Steiner, op. cit.; Storey et al., op. cit.; Woo et al., 1989; Wynarczyk et al., 1993).

Execution – Nohria and Joyce (2003) provide a postscript. They report the results of a ten-year study of 160 companies and their use of some 200 different management techniques. They conclude what we all know: it does not really matter so much which technique you apply but it matters very much that you execute it flawlessly. They claim flawless execution is something too many management theorists have forgotten. Attention to detail is important.

The conclusions, therefore, are obvious. Whilst nothing in this world is guaranteed, the strategy with the best chance of generating sustainable growth and the highest profits is to differentiate with the aim of dominating your market as quickly as possible, and to continue to innovate around that differential advantage. Gaining rapid market dominance is important. It can come from internal growth but might also involve acquisition of competitors.

3i European Enterprise Centre (1993) *Britain's Superleague Companies*, Report 9, August.

Birley, S. and Westhead, P. (1990) 'Growth and Performance Contrasts between Types of Small Firms', *Strategic Management Journal*, 11.

Boston Consulting Group (1968) *Perspectives on Experience*, Boston, MA: Boston Consulting Group.

Boston Consulting Group (1972) *Perspectives on Experience*, Boston, MA: Boston Consulting Group.

Burns, P. (1994) *Winners and Losers in the 1990s*, 3i European Enterprise Centre, Report 12, April.

Buzzell, R.D. and Gale, B.T. (1987) *The PIMS Principles – Linking Strategy to Performance*, New York: Free Press.

Buzzell, R.D. Heany, D.F. and Schoeffer, S. (1974) 'Impact of Strategic Planning on Profit Performance', *Harvard Business Review*, 52/2.

Dunkelberg, W.G., Cooper, A.C., Woo, C. and Dennis, W.J. (1987) 'New Firm Growth and Performance', in N.C. Churchill, J.A. Hornaday, B.A. Kirchhoff, C.J. Krasner and K.H. Vesper (eds) *Frontiers of Entrepreneurship Research*, Babson College, Boston, MA.

Hamel, G. and Prahalad, C.K. (1994) *Competing For the Future: Breakthrough Strategies for Seizing Control of your Industry and Creating the Markets of Tomorrow*, Boston, MA: Harvard Business School Press.

Harrison, J. and Taylor, B. (1996) *Supergrowth Companies: Entrepreneurs in Action*, Oxford: Butterworth-Heinemann.

Macrae, D.J.R. (1991) 'Characteristics of High and Low Growth Small and Medium Sized Businesses', paper presented at 21st European Small Business Seminar, Barcelona, Spain.

Nohria, N. and Joyce, W. (2003) 'What Really Works', *Harvard Business Review*, July/August.

Porter, M. (1985) *Competitive Advantage: Creating and Sustaining Superior Performance*, New York: Free Press.

Ray, G.H. and Hutchinson, P.J. (1983) *The Financing and Financial Control of Small Enterprise Development*, London: Gower.

Siegel, R., Siegel, E. and MacMillan, I.C. (1993) 'Characteristics Distinguishing High Growth Ventures, *Journal of Business Venturing*, 8.

Solem, O. and Steiner, M.P. (1989) 'Factors for Success in Small Manufacturing Firms – and with special emphasis on growing firms', paper presented at Conference on SMEs and the Challenges of 1992, Mikkeli, Finland.

Storey, D.J., Watson, R. and Wynarczyk, P. (1989) *Fast Growth Small Business: Case Studies of 40 Small Firms in Northern Ireland*, Department of Employment, Research Paper No 67.

Treacy, M. and Wiersema, F. (1995) *The Discipline of Market Leaders*, Reading, MA: Addison-Wesley.

Woo, C.Y., Cooper, A.C., Dunkelberg, W.C., Daellenbach, U. and Dennis, W.J. (1989) 'Determinants of Growth for Small and Large Entrepreneurial Start-Ups', paper presented to Babson Entrepreneurship Conference.

Wynarczyk, P., Watson, R., Storey, D.J., Short, H. and Keasey, K. (1993) *The Managerial Labour Market in Small and Medium-Sized Enterprises*, London: Routledge.

Yelle, L.E. (1979) 'The Learning Curve: Historical Review and Comprehensive Survey', *Decision Sciences*, 10.

what your real strengths and weaknesses are and whether the environment has thrown up any new opportunities or threats, and finally, whether experience has changed your views about your core competences. You need to build on your strengths and shore up your weaknesses. Threats create new risks that need to be countered. And new opportunities should never be ignored.

Figure 8.1 presents a simple framework for looking at your growth options in a systematic way. The previous chapter was concerned with market penetration – selling your original or existing product or service to the customers you originally identified. Once you have proved that you can succeed in this, the next stage is moving to new markets and developing new products/services. At each stage the objective is to achieve market dominance. Combining new product/service development with new markets is called diversification.

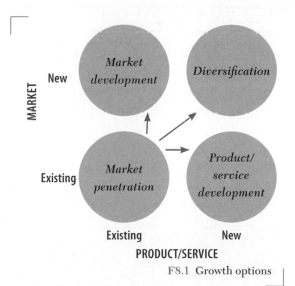

F8.1 Growth options

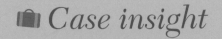

Web 2.0

Fast, high-growth businesses

Some of the fastest and highest-growth start-ups since 2000 have been based on the development of interactive websites, where users can generate their own content and interact with each other to form a virtual community – called Web 2.0. This contrasts with websites that limit the user to viewing the content. Examples of Web 2.0 include social networking sites, wikis, blogs, video hosting sites, hosted services, mash-ups etc. Fast, high-growth start-ups face particular problems. Because of their accelerated development they need to plan for growth and often require considerable finance at inception. The Lean Start-up techniques outlined in Chapter 3 can help mitigate the risks they face. Nevertheless, there are many examples of highly successful Web 2.0 start-ups that have made their founders millionaires.

Facebook is arguably the best known Web 2.0 start-up. Founded by **Mark Zuckerberg** in 2004, it is an online social networking site based in Menlo Park, California. Its famously oversubscribed initial public offering in 2012 raised $16 billion, although share prices subsequently slumped. It now has more than one billion active users, and revenues in 2012 were some $5.1 billion.

LinkedIn is another social networking site, but one targeted at professional occupations. Now headquartered in Mountain View, California, and Dublin, Ireland, It was founded by **Reid Hoffman** in 2002 and launched in 2003. Its initial public offering in 2011 was also oversubscribed but shares subsequently doubled in value. It now has more than 225 million users, and revenues in 2012 were some $972 million.

Twitter is a social networking and microblogging site that enables users to send and receive text message 'tweets'. Based in San Francisco, it was launched by **Jack Dorsey** in 2006. By 2013 it had more than 500 million registered users (some 213 million active) who post some 340 million tweets a day and generate revenues of some $317 million, although after seven years the company had still not made a profit. For everybody using the site, Twitter generates annual sales of $1.45, about one cent for each character in a Tweet. It has attracted considerable private and venture funding and was floated on the stock market in 2013, attracting $1.82 billion – a company valuation of over $14 billion.

Dropbox is a file hosting service founded by **Drew Houston** in 2007 and launched in 2008. It is based in San Francisco. It allows files to be stored 'in the cloud' – free up to a certain size and for a fee beyond this. It now has more than 100 million users, and revenues in 2011 were some $240 million.

YouTube is the well-known widely used video-sharing website based in San Bruno, California. It was launched in 2005 by **Steve Chen**, **Chad Hurley** and **Jawed Karim**. The venture-funded start-up was purchased by Google only 22 months later, in 2006, for $1.65 billion.

PhotoDisc

Market development

Market development is the natural extension of market penetration. Instead of selling more of the same to your existing customers, you find new customers for those products or services. There are three reasons for selecting market development as a route for expansion:

1. To achieve economies of scale of production. This is particularly important if cost leadership is your core value proposition and is dependent upon achieving these economies.

2. Your key competence lies with your product, for example with technology-based products in which you have some intellectual property (IP) and you need to exploit your IP by finding new markets within a limited window of opportunity. Most technology-based companies follow this strategy – opening up new overseas markets as existing markets become saturated – because of the high cost of developing new products. By way of contrast, many service businesses such as consultancies have been pulled into overseas markets because their clients operate there.

3. The product is nearing the end of its life cycle in the existing market and you need to develop new markets, if you can find them, to continue to grow.

Any growing firm will have to find new customers and the key to doing so is to understand the customers it already has – who they are and why they buy – and then try to find more customers with similar profiles. Many firms start out by selling locally and gradually expand their geographic base by selling regionally and then nationally. However, it is one thing to find new customers in a market that you are familiar with, but it is quite another to enter completely new markets, even when you are selling existing products or services that you know well. Nevertheless, if you want to grow you will have to do so. These new markets might be new market segments – the ones you originally identified but did not have the resources to target. They might be new geographical areas – often foreign markets. The low-risk option is to seek out segments in these countries that are similar to the ones you already sell to.

BBC News Business 11 December 2012

We have always very carefully managed growth against profitability. Cash is king.

Eileen Gittins, founder Blurb

As we saw in Chapter 4, the structure of any new market – its customers, suppliers, competitors – and the potential substitutes and barriers to entry determine the degree of competition, and therefore the profitability you are likely to achieve. Porter's Five Forces analysis is a valuable tool and the exercises at the end of Chapter 4 can equally be applied to help assess the potential of a new market.

Trying to sell the same product or service to new market segments usually involves reconfiguring the marketing mix in some way so as to 'fine-tune' your value proposition. The exercises at the end of Chapter 5 can help you with this. Sometimes market development and product development might go hand in hand, since the move into a new market segment may involve the development of variants to the existing product offering by altering the marketing mix or making minor changes to the product range. However, we are talking about incremental and minor changes rather than brand-new products.

Fat Face

Market development

Tim Slade and Julian Leaver began selling their own printed t-shirts in a shop in the ski resort of Méribel, France in 1988. They were skiers, but had run out of money and sold their belongings, including a Volkswagen camper van, to purchase plain t-shirts on which to print logos. The whole idea was to finance their lifestyle as 'ski-bums'. The first Fat Face store was opened in the UK in 1993. It has now become a cult brand for sports enthusiasts and the company has shops worldwide, which made the pair into millionaires.

In 2000 Julian Leaver explained what they were trying to achieve:

> *Sunday Times 27 February 2000*
>
> When you buy a Fat Face product, you are not just buying the fleece, you are **buying** the **experience** – the chat in the shop about the snow in Val d'Isère – or surfing in Cowes. Staff are selected because they are **passionate** about the **lifestyle**.

In 2000 the company raised £5 million expansion capital from Friends Ivory & Sime Private Equity to finance their expansion, but they were careful to manage the brand as they expanded. Julian Leaver explained once more:

> We could easily wholesale the hell out of it and be in every ski and surf shop and department store inside a year. Within two years, we would have trashed the brand.

Slow, planned expansion came through increasing the number of shops in Britain and Europe and eventually the rest of the world, making certain that the right sort of staff, with the right sort of personality, were recruited. Initially Fat Face entered new markets based upon intuition and on an experimental basis, later they undertook more professional market research. Across all their markets their typical customer is a well-off professional in their mid-30–40s who enjoys skiing or water sports. And they try to keep close to their customers by getting feedback by email and having regular face-to-face focus meetings. The key to this successful expansion has been good brand management. All Fat Face shops have the same 'fun' feel, with enthusiastic young staff. And whilst the product range has been expanded into shoes, bags and jewellery, they all have the same lifestyle, sporty image. Whilst Fat Face products are premium priced, the shops have frequent sales or promotions that encourage passing customers to enter, browse and make 'impulse' purchases.

In 2005 Tim and Julian sold the major shareholding in the company to Advent for £100 million. Advent in turn sold it on to Bridgepoint Capital in 2007 for £360 million. Tim and Julian are millionaires and retain a minor stake in the company. They both still enjoy skiing.

Up-to-date information on Fat Face can be found on their website: www.fatface.com

Entering foreign markets

There are many ways to enter a foreign market. If your competitive advantage is based on resources located in your home country then the form this takes should be exporting. Exporting is also often a low-cost, low-risk way of finding out about a market. It can take the form of spot sales – one-off sales to individual customers, now much easier with the advent of the internet.

CREATAS

However, if you need to achieve market presence in foreign distribution channels you will probably need a local sales agent. A good agent should have valuable local knowledge and might suggest changes to the product or other elements of the marketing mix to better suit local needs. They might expect you to finance or contribute to advertising and promotion – and with no certainty of a profitable return. Finding an agent can be difficult enough but if, for whatever reason, they do not meet your sales targets then there is little you can do other than change your agent, if you can terminate the contract.

Another approach is to offer a local firm a licence to make your product or a contractual agreement, such as a franchise, to deliver your service. This allows them to capitalize on their local knowledge but requires them to take on many of the business risks. Their local market knowledge and dedication is vital if the market is to be effectively penetrated. For a service or retail business, the equivalent is to appoint a head franchisee who will be responsible for the franchise roll-out in their country (Chapter 10). They might operate some franchises themselves and also extend it to others. Franchises offer a fairly standard format to the particular market in which they operate. If the franchise roll-out is successful the head franchisee shares in the success. To be effective, the firm and their franchisee or distributor must have a symbiotic relationship, one based upon mutual trust and with effective incentives to ensure success.

The Body Shop's rapid growth over thirty years owes much to its successful global roll-out using a franchise format. In most countries a Head Franchisee was granted exclusive rights as user of the trademark, distributor and, after an initial trial of running a few shops themselves, the right to sub-franchise. In this way The Body Shop built upon local market knowledge and minimized its risks. The model was not successful in every country; for example, The Body Shop had to take back control of the franchise in France because the Head Franchisee was not delivering the volume of sales expected.

The next stage in involvement in a foreign market is to form a strategic alliance, partnership or joint venture, whereby the partner brings different resources to the joint venture and shares the profits as well as the risks. This is covered in more detail in Chapter 10. In some developing economies, only joint ventures with local firms are allowed.

The final stage is direct investment. This entails setting up a wholly-owned subsidiary which may involve simply marketing and distribution or be fully integrated into the operations of your company. Clearly this is an expensive option, normally only taken by larger companies. These different degrees of involvement in foreign markets, and the increasing risk associated with them, are shown in Figure 8.2. There is no prescriptive 'best' approach and often the degree of involvement in the foreign market increases with the success of the product or service.

INCREASING RESOURCE COMMITMENT

F8.2 **Degree of involvement in foreign markets**

B&Q China

Penetrating foreign markets

British retailers have a history of failure in overseas ventures, and the experience of B&Q, the UK do-it-yourself (DIY) store chain, in setting up in China is interesting. B&Q opened its first store in China in 1999. Up until 2005, when China joined the World Trade Organization, foreign retailers were prevented from opening more than three stores in any one city and some towns were completely off limits. What is more, they had to work with Chinese partners. B&Q did deals with a number of Chinese organizations, normally giving them a 35% stake in the business, but making it very clear that B&Q intended to buy them out as soon as it could – which it typically did in 2005. Also in 2005, it acquired 13 stores of OBI China for an undisclosed sum, all of which have been converted to the B&Q format.

The stores were initially a huge success and the Beijing store boasted the highest average customer spend of any of its stores in the world (over £50). But it is the cultural similarities and differences and how they affected the retailer that are really interesting. The stores look very similar to those in the UK, although they are usually considerably bigger. At 20,000 sq. ft, the Beijing Golden Four Season store is the largest of its kind in the world. Like their UK counterparts, staff wear orange overalls. The products offered are also very similar, although the space devoted to garden products is considerably smaller and the Chinese B&Q also sells soft furnishings.

But the big difference is that Chinese customers do not want to 'do it themselves' at all; they prefer to get

It is important to undertake a thorough market and country analysis before deciding to get involved in a foreign market with any degree of investment (anything beyond a sales agent). You are assessing the opportunities there but also the risks you will face. You need to undertake an economic analysis of the environment of the country – domestic demand, local laws and regulations, government policies, exchange rates, related and supporting industries etc. Try using the SLEPT analysis from Chapter 3. You can use Porter's Five Forces analysis to assess profit potential but, as well as entry barriers, consider the exit barriers you face. Exit barriers can arise from legal constraints and/or high costs associated with exit. Just as high entry barriers increase profit potential (because they discourage new competitors), high exit barriers increase the risks you face because, if you do not find the market profitable, exiting it might be expensive or even prohibited.

Every country needs to be evaluated in its own right – and not just using strict economic criteria. Cultural differences can greatly affect consumer preferences. Some of the most economically attractive countries can prove the most difficult to penetrate. For example, China has turned out to be particularly resistant to Western retailers' efforts. In 2013 the UK's largest supermarket, Tesco, announced that 80% of its Chinese operation would be bought by the state-run China Resources Enterprise Ltd., the country's second largest supermarket chain. Earlier that year Germany's Metro AG announced it was pulling out of consumer electronics, and in 2012 the US Home Depot Inc. announced the closure of a number of stores across China.

Product development

Product/service innovation is a characteristic of successful growth companies. It can take four forms.

Product modification – This involves the modification of existing products where the changes are small and evolutionary. They might be modified in terms of quality, function or style so as to address

others to do it for them. The Chinese customers are typically middle-class and wealthy. They come to the store to select what they want and get it installed by a professional. The reasons for this are partly cultural and partly economic. Labour is significantly cheaper than in the West, but also things like painting would be regarded as a major DIY job in China. What is more, if you buy one of the thousands of apartments being built in Beijing you buy a concrete shell – with no garden – and customers will then purchase everything else they need – plumbing, lighting, kitchens, bathrooms and furnishings – from one store. B&Q therefore started to offer more services to customers – designers and contractors to install its products. The Beijing store has a room full of designers working at computer terminals, ready to design the customer's living room, kitchen or bathroom. Teams of workers then deliver and install the products. Twenty-five per cent of all B&Q sales in China now involve some kind of B&Q service.

However, in 2008/09 sales at B&Q China fell dramatically and continued to fall into 2013. The ensuing losses resulted in B&Q closing almost one-third of its stores and reducing floor space in others. Local press comments indicated that local price competition was a major factor in this decline. Time will tell whether B&Q can succeed where other British retailers have failed, but even with 39 stores, B&Q remains one of the largest Western retailers in China.

Up-to-date information on B&Q can be found on their website: www.kingfisher.com

any weaknesses or to suit local markets. Service levels might be improved. This is usually necessary when competition increases as the middle and late adopters start to buy the product/service and other firms start to produce 'better' products. This can be a particular problem if you are pioneering a product in a market with low barriers to entry, especially if the product is developing into a commodity. However, even successful products such as the iPhone need constant modification to keep up with the competition.

Product expansion – This involves developing product variations that meet the needs of different market segments. Most business will start to offer a range of products or services quickly after launch as they spot new market opportunities. So, for example, a car manufacturer might start offering sports, estate or fuel-efficient variants of a model. A soft drinks manufacturer might start to offer 'light' variants or new flavours for a successful brand. A tablet-computer manufacturer might offer 7 inch and 11 inch screens.

Product extension – This is where a successful brand is extended to similar but different products or services that might be purchased by the same customers. For example, a number of chocolate bar manufacturers have successfully extended their brand into ice cream. The key to success here is having a strong brand, one that actually means something to customers, with values that can be extended to the other products. Thus Timberland, a company well-known for producing durable outdoor footwear, extended its product range to include durable outdoor clothing. Virgin and Saga are good examples of brands that have been applied to a wide range of diverse products, mainly successfully, linking customers and their lifestyle aspirations. Virgin, however, rarely undertakes 'production', relying instead on partners with existing expertise. On the other hand Mercedes Benz is a brand that has a strong association with quality and the company has capitalized on this by producing an ever wider range of vehicles, always being able to charge a premium price for its product. This has allowed it to move into new and different segments of the vehicle market.

163

Growing your business

Completely new products – It may be that you introduce completely new products because you spot new market opportunities. These might be innovative products to either replace or sell alongside your existing product range. This is most successful when you have built up a loyal customer base and you have a close relationship with customers – a customer focus – and a good reputation for quality or delivery that can be built upon. A customer-focused firm will have an advantage in developing new products because, if it understands how its customers' needs are changing, it ought to be able to develop new products that meet them. What is more, if there is a relationship of trust, customers are more likely to try your new product, provided of course they perceive a need for it. The key to this strategy, therefore, is building good customer relationships, often associated with effective branding.

One advantage of this approach is that it is frequently far more cost-effective to increase the volume of business with existing customers than it is to go out looking for new ones. What is more, good relationships often result in customers becoming advocates who bring in new customers and are willing to help with product development. However, developing new products, even for existing customers, can be expensive and risky.

American Giant

🧳 *Case insight*

The problems of too-rapid growth

Established in 2012 and only eighteen months into business, everything was going according to plan for the online clothes retailer American Giant. The San Francisco-based company was founded by Bayard Winthrop and sells better-quality sweatshirts and other items of clothing produced in the USA from US cotton. With limited resources, the company had relied upon word-of-mouth marketing and had estimated that it would be at least two years before growth really started. It had built this into its business plan. It only took pre-orders on its most popular styles, like the zipped hooded sweatshirt, while recognizing that it was not possible to restock the other less popular styles quickly. It bought and stocked prudently so as to manage its cash flow.

But growth does not always go according to plan, and unplanned success can cause as many problems as failure. It was December and the firm was actually a little overstocked, when the online magazine *Slate* ran an article saying that the company's hooded sweatshirt was 'the greatest hoodie ever made'. Within two days the company received over $500,000-worth of extra orders, clearing out the stocks of hoodies. The company had neither the manpower nor the materials to meet demand. Because the company's supply chain went all the way back to the US cotton fields, with fabric specially woven and dyed for American Giant, it could not simply pick up a phone and order more material. At the same time the factory was set up to make hundreds of sweatshirts – not thousands. All the company could do was to apologize to customers and hope they would be patient and wait for orders to be fulfilled – not the best situation for a company relying on quality of product and service and repeat sales.

Some customers agreed to wait but many did not. Nevertheless, the open and honest way the company dealt with the problem was appreciated by customers. And running out of stock proved to be further good PR – everybody likes to have something others cannot. So American Giant survived the crisis and sales continued to increase, although they never peaked in the same way again.

> **BBC News Business 10 March 2013**
>
> Commitment to quality comes first … we're going to ask our customers to be patient because we believe in the quality and the pay-off is worth it … it's an acceptable thing for a customer to fall out of the queue.

🇺🇸 USA

Development must be grounded firmly in the needs of the existing market. And even then, if done too rapidly, it can mean resources are spread too thinly across an unbalanced portfolio.

Developing a product portfolio

As you develop more product/service offerings you will probably need to follow different strategies for each. One important reason is that each of the offerings may be at different stages in their life cycle in different markets. So, for example, McDonald's may have a different marketing mix for its products in developing countries, where it is at the introductory phase of its life cycle, compared to the USA, where it is a mature product.

All products have a limited life and, as we have seen, attract different types of customers at different stages of their life. The added complexity of having a portfolio of product/market offerings, each at a different stage of its life, can be handled

using a technique adapted from the Growth Share Matrix. This is also known as the 'Boston Matrix' after the Boston Consulting Group that first developed it, and is shown in Figure 8.3. The vertical axis measures market attractiveness – the growth and profit potential of the market. The horizontal axis measures the strength of your product/service in the market – its sales, relative market share etc. You launch a product/service into an attractive market (otherwise why do it?), but you are likely to be weak in the market. This is called a 'Problem Child'. Sometimes the market proves to be unattractive – then its life is very short as it becomes a 'Dog'. More often, if the market continues to be attractive, sales will grow and your market position will strengthen. This is called a 'Star'. Eventually, however, the market will mature, becoming less attractive, and your product/service will become a 'Cash Cow' – a market leader with a lot of stability but little additional growth because it is at the end of its life cycle.

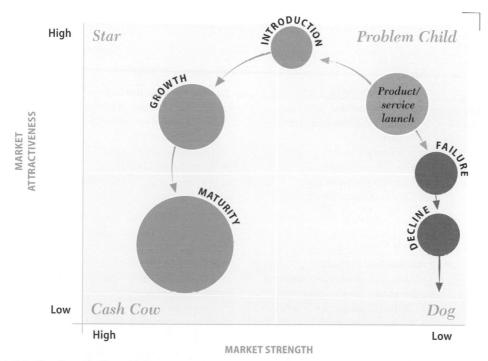

F8.3 The Growth Share Matrix

Source: Adapted from The BCG Portfolio Matrix from
The Product Portfolio Matrix, © 1970, The Boston Consulting Group

Different business skills are valued at different points in the matrix. Entrepreneurial skills are of most value in the problem child phase. Once the product is in its mature phase it needs to be managed as a cash cow – milked for all the cash flow it can generate. That means high levels of efficiency are needed, probably achieved through a high degree of control and direction. The cash cow is likely to be best managed by an accountant. And, if we are to characterize the discipline needed to manage the star, it would probably be marketing. In other words, as the product works its way around the matrix the imperatives of management change. In a one-product company this presents a challenging but manageable problem. In a multi-product firm the problem is more complex.

There are a number of measurement issues with the framework. How do you define your market so that you can measure market share or market growth? You might use just one factor on each axis or a number of them weighted in some way. Nevertheless, the problem of measurement remains. The Growth Share Matrix is probably best used as a loose conceptual framework that helps to clarify complexity. Anything that simplifies complexity and thereby helps our understanding must be of value.

Marketing strategy and product portfolios

The Growth Share Matrix allows us to make some broad generalizations about marketing strategy for product/service offerings in the different quadrants. These are shown in Figure 8.4. If you can place the product/market offering within its life cycle on the matrix, these would be the elements of marketing strategy you would, a priori, expect to see. But remember that, whilst this framework reflects product life cycles, it does not reflect Porter's generic marketing strategies, which need to be superimposed on them. Nevertheless, as a product nears the end of its life, and becomes a cash cow, it is more likely to be on its way to becoming a commodity and therefore having to sell on price.

Star
INVEST FOR GROWTH
- *Penetrate market*
- *Accept moderate short-term profits*
- *Sell and promote aggressively*
- *Expand geographically*
- *Extend product range*
- *Differentiate product/service*

Problem Child
DEVELOP OPPORTUNITIES
- *Be critical of prospects*
- *Invest heavily in selective products/services*
- *Specialize in strengths*
- *Shore up weaknesses*

Cash Cow
MANAGE FOR EARNINGS
- *Maintain market position with successful products/services*
- *Differentiate products/services*
- *Prune less successful products/services*
- *Stabilize prices, except where temporary aggressive stance is required to deter competitors*

Dog
GENERATE CASH
- *Monitor carefully – judge when to discontinue*
- *Live with low growth*
- *Improve productivity*
- *Reduce costs*
- *Look for 'easy' growth segments*

F8.4 **Strategy implications of the Growth Share Matrix**

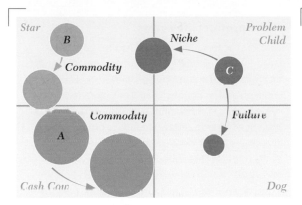

F8.5 **Presenting strategy using the Growth Share Matrix**

F8.6 **Product development options shown on the Growth Share Matrix**

The Growth Share Matrix also allows us to present complex information more understandably, particularly when linked to forecasting future market positions and strategies involved in getting there. For example, Figure 8.5 represents a hypothetical three-product portfolio. The size of each circle is proportionate to the turnover each achieves. The circles marked A, B, C represent the present product positions, the related unmarked circles represent the positions projected in three years' time. The portfolio looks balanced and the diagram can be used to explain the strategies that are in place to move the products to where they are planned to be. Again, one essential added complexity is the generic marketing strategies. If products A and B are commodities selling mainly on price with low margin under intense pressure, it has implications not only for strategy but also for the cash flow available to invest in product C, particularly if this is a niche market product needing heavy investment. As a result, product C might fail and have to be killed off.

Product modification, extension and expansion opportunities can also be represented in the Growth Share Matrix. Again this is a useful visual aid to understanding strategy options. An example is shown in Figure 8.6.

Financing implications of product portfolios

The structure of the product portfolio has implications for your cash flow. The problem child consumes cash for development and promotional costs at a rate of knots, without generating much cash by way of revenues. The star might start to generate revenues but will still be facing high costs, particularly in marketing to establish its market position against new entry competitors. It is therefore likely to be cash neutral. Only as a cash cow are revenues likely to outstrip costs and cash flow likely to be positive. There are two kinds of dogs. One is a cash dog that covers its costs and might be worth keeping, for example if it brings in customers for other products or services or it shares overheads. The other is the genuine dog which is losing money – both in cash flow and profit terms – and should be scrapped. It is from this model that phrases like 'shoot the dog', 'invest in stars' and 'milk the cow' came. These implications are shown in Figure 8.7.

Ideally you should have a balanced portfolio of product/service offerings so that the surplus cash from cash cows can be used to invest in the problem children. However, that situation may take many years to achieve. These surplus funds can be used

Star		Problem Child	
Revenue	+++	*Revenue*	+
Expenditure	---	*Expenditure*	---
Cash flow	neutral	*Cash flow*	--
Cash Cow		Dog	
Revenue	++++	*Revenue*	+
Expenditure	--	*Expenditure*	-
Cash flow	++	*Cash flow*	neutral

F8.7 Cash flow implications of the Growth Share Matrix

almost as venture capital to invest, selectively, in new products and services. This ideal firm – if it exists – is self-financing. The problem that arises with an unbalanced portfolio is that there is either a surplus of cash (no new products) or a deficit (too many new products). If you have too many problem children and stars in your portfolio (too many good, new ideas) then you will require cash flow injections which will only be forthcoming if you can either borrow the capital or raise more equity finance.

Crocs

Niche product life cycles

The Croc can be found in more than 125 countries, having sold more than 150 million pairs by 2011. And that means that about 1 person in every 500 on the entire planet has bought a pair. The Colorado-based company was founded only in 2002 by George Brian Boedecker Jr. and two friends to produce and distribute a plastic clog-like shoe, now available in all the colours of the rainbow, at a relatively cheap price. It was an instant success at the Florida Boat Show, where it was launched. It sold 76,000 pairs in its first year and 649,000 in its second. The brightly-coloured Crocs are made from Croslite, a durable, soft, lightweight, non-marking and odour-resistant material which was originally manufactured by Foam Creations, a Canadian company that Crocs purchased in 2004. Crocs are now manufactured in Mexico, Italy, Romania and China, having closed their Canadian facility in 2008.

Crocs was a 'fairy-tale' entrepreneurial story, if the press were anything to go by in the early days. *Business 2.0* magazine (3 November 2006) summarized the story:

> 'Three pals from Boulder, Colorado, go sailing in the Caribbean, where a foam clog one had bought in Canada inspires them to build a business around it. Despite a lack of venture capital funding and the derision of foot fashionistas, the multicolored Crocs with their Swiss-cheese perforations, soft and comfortable soles, and odor-preventing material become a global smash. Celebrities adopt them. Young people adore them. The company goes from $1 million in revenue in 2003 to a projected $322 million this year [2006]. Crocs Inc.'s IPO (Initial Public Offering) in February was the richest in footwear history, and the company has a market cap of more than $1 billion.'

The company went public in 2006 with a hugely successful $200 million stock market float (the biggest float in shoe history). Its initial strategy can be summarized as selling a relatively cheap product to as many people as possible, as quickly as possible. The company used the money to diversify and acquire new businesses, such as Jibbitz, which made charms designed to fit Crocs' ventilating holes, and Fury Hockey, which used Croslite to make sports gear. It built manufacturing plants in Mexico and China,

©clovercity istockphoto.com

opened distribution centres in the Netherlands and Japan, and expanded into the global market place. A foray into Croslite clothing in 2007 fell flat and was quickly scaled back. The company liquidated Fury Hockey in 2008.

And herein lies the paradox. Popularity breeds contempt in the fashion business. Arguably, the backlash started in 2006, almost as soon as the company went public, with a *Washington Post* article that said: 'Nor is the fashion world enamored of Crocs. Though their maker touts their "ultra-hip Italian styling", lots of folks find them hideous.' A blog named 'I Hate Crocs.com' followed Croc opponents. The shoes and those who wore them – from US ex-President Bush to Michelle Obama and stars such as Al Pacino, Steven Tyler (Aerosmith) and Faith Hill – became objects of satire on US television shows, and, by 2009, over 1.4 million people had joined a Facebook group which had the single purpose of eliminating the shoes. The site even featured a ritual Croc-burning.

Nevertheless in 2008, Crocs was ranked by the NPD Market Research Group as the number one casual brand in the athletic specialty sporting goods channel for men, women and children. However, having had a bumper year in 2007, the company made a $185 million (£113 million) loss in 2008 and had to cut 2000 jobs. It suddenly began to look very fragile. In late 2008 the company replaced chief executive Ron Snyder, who had been at college with the company's founders, with John Duerden, an industry veteran who ran a consulting firm focused on brand renewal. He believed there was life yet in Crocs and what the company needed was new products to which he could extend the brand.

By 2009 the company was stuck with a surplus of shoes it could not sell and a mountain of expensive debt. The new business lines it had purchased – often at a premium – failed to prosper. As a result the share price plummeted. By this time the company produced a range of different products, mainly plastic clogs and sandals, but also a range called 'Bite', aimed at the golf market. The problem was that Crocs were hitting saturation point and the company had failed to successfully diversify. With a nearly indestructible product and about one in every five hundred people owning a pair, how many more could the company sell? And the company had invested enormous amounts into meeting a demand for a product that then seemed endless but now seems ridiculous as the shoe's ubiquity put off even the most ardent Crocophile. In May 2010 *Time* Magazine rated Crocs as one of the world's 50 worst inventions.

But behind the scenes the company brought in Italian designers and started producing a new range of attractive Crocs, albeit at much higher prices than the original clogs, that celebrities such as Brad Pitt, Ryan Reynolds and Halle Berry, once more, started wearing. These new shoes and sandals played to the strengths of the Croslite material from which the sole was made and targeted mainly beach- and boat-wear ('so light, they float' – 'vents let air and water flow through' – 'grooved rubber outsole improves grip'). As well as diversifying their range of shoes, Crocs diversified into retailing by opening their own branded stores. And just to prove that the fashion business can be fickle, in 2011 Crocs sold $1 billion (£630 million) worth of shoes, with one-third of the revenue coming from sales of the original clogs. The 'I Hate Crocs.com' blog gave up and closed in that year. Pondering the turnaround and the ugliness of the original Croc, the *Sunday Times* (22 April 2012) said: 'In the history of retail, has a brand ever thrived so well on adversity? It seems the more the loathers loathe them, fans go wild. While for under-10s (a core market) they're a straightforward sell, grown-up clog wearers appear torn between love and hate.' It seems that having an ugly product polarizes opinion and this can give a brand its uniqueness.

Up-to-date information on Crocs can be found on their website: www.crocs.eu

Questions:

1. *From the information given, map out as much as you can of the business model for Crocs using the New Venture Creation Framework. What are the key elements of competitive advantage in their value proposition?*

2. *Where is the original Croc clog now in its life cycle? How reliable are future sales?*

3. *What went wrong at Crocs and how was it put right?*

4. *What is the company's current strategy? What do you think of it?*

Diversification

Diversification involves moving away from core areas of activity into completely new and unrelated product/market areas. Whilst it is central to the process of corporate evolution, it is only something to be undertaken after very careful consideration because it is high risk. Developing either new products or new markets is always risky. Developing both at once is even riskier – akin to another start-up. And it has been suggested that a strategy of diversification has probably caused more value destruction than any other type of corporate strategic decision. What is more, it has been shown that conglomerates – diversified companies with interests in a range of different industries – that are quoted on the stock exchanges create no additional shareholder value by being diversified. Indeed they often trade at a discount on the value of their component parts because of their complexity. And yet growing firms often seem to 'diversify', so the question is why? The answer probably lies in two parts.

1. **To gain market dominance in newly emerging markets or industries** – Companies do this by moving into related areas, often through acquisitions. Most importantly, it is a way of redefining the scope of any newly emerging industry, for example in technology. It is therefore worth considering if your start-up involves disruptive innovation, market paradigm shift or new-to-the-world industries (quadrants 4, 5 and 6 in Figure 3.1). The risks associated with it can be reduced if it is done in incremental moves, constantly bundling new products and services whilst extending the newly developing market. Incremental diversification is generally into related areas, where you have some product or market knowledge and/or expertise. **Related diversification** is therefore less risky than **unrelated diversification**. However, the distinction between related and unrelated areas is not always clear, shading into grey particularly in the areas of rapidly developing new technologies in which new markets are being created where none existed before.

As we saw in the Case Insight in Chapter 4, five of the most successful entrepreneurial companies since 2000 – Apple, Amazon, Facebook, Google and Microsoft – have adopted strategies of related diversification that are starting to redefine their business scope – linking hardware, software and internet services. This is happening through a combination of organic growth, internal product/ service development and external acquisitions. Their moves into new areas have been incremental, bundling additional services to sell to existing customers, finding out about market acceptance of their new products experimentally – a form of market testing. Often they have used acquisition to buy new customers as well as new services. Incremental, related diversification means lower risks. It is also a way of mitigating the risks of introducing disruptive innovation by using an incremental approach to test markets and obtain product/service and market information.

There are three types of related diversification. When companies move into complementary or competitive areas, as above, it is called **horizontal integration**. When companies move into their supply chain, for example to become a manufacturer, it is called **backward vertical integration**. When they move into their distribution chain, for example to become a retailer, it is called **forward vertical integration**.

2. **To reduce risk in privately owned businesses** – By having business interests in a range of different markets or industries you spread the risk of a business downturn in any one. However, this only works in companies that are owned by individuals or families where the main wealth of the individual or family is tied up in the business. If the company is quoted on a stock market and owned by the general public, the public can simply spread their risk by buying shares in a range of companies in different markets or industries. They do not value diversification as it does not reduce their risk. It only adds to the complexity of managing the business.

Diversification and the formation of conglomerates therefore remains a powerful driver of strategy for private, unquoted companies. For example, the Virgin Group is a private conglomerate whose scope of business reaches into markets across the world and covers many different industries from transport (airlines, trains and buses) to media (TV, radio, mobile phones and internet), from health and lifestyle (health programmes to gyms) to financial services (credit cards, pension and insurance products and banking). Richard Branson withdrew Virgin from the stock market some years ago, buying back its shares.

However, publicly quoted conglomerates do continue to exist and prosper, particularly in developing economies (see Case Insight on Reliance Industries). This may be because of local stock market inefficiencies such as high share transaction costs and consequent low level of trading, but is more likely to arise from the high concentration of share ownership in family hands.

Sticking to the knitting

A focus on core business at corporate level was emphasized in the 1980s by researchers such as Abell (1980). A firm's core business is the one in which it has a distinct advantage by adding the greatest value for its customers and shareholders. Many studies have shown that firms which are focused on their core business perform better than diversified ones (e.g. Wernerfelt and Montgomery, 1986). This was popularized by Peters and Waterman (1982) as 'sticking to the knitting'. Although some studies were subsequently disputed (e.g. Luffman and Reed, 1984; Michel and Shaked, 1984; Park, 2002), Peters and Waterman (op. cit.) concluded:

> **Organizations** that do branch out but stick to their knitting **outperform** the others. The most successful are those that diversified around a single skill ... The second group in descending order, comprise those companies that **branch out** into related fields ... The least successful are those companies that **diversify** into a wide variety of fields. **Acquisitions** especially among this group tend to wither on the vine.

Nevertheless, several studies have found that diversification is associated with improved performance up to a point, after which continued diversification is associated with declining performance (e.g. Palich et al., 2000). Robert Grant (2010) suggests that diversification has probably caused more value destruction than any other type of strategic decision. He describes diversification as being 'like sex: its attractions are obvious, often irresistible. Yet the experience is often disappointing. For top management it is a mine field.'

Developments in financial theory in the 1970s, in particular the Capital Asset Pricing Model (CAPM), also showed that conglomerates did not create shareholder value in stock markets by reducing risk (Levy and Sarnat, 1970; Mason and Goudzwaard, 1976; Weston et al., 1972). This is because diversification does not reduce systematic risk – that part of risk associated with how the share price performs compared to the overall market (measured by the company's beta coefficient). Shareholders can simply buy shares in undiversified companies representing the diversified interests of the conglomerate. This spreads their risk, probably with lower transaction costs. Therefore at the corporate level diversification does not create shareholder value.

Abell, D.F. (1980) *Defining the Business*, Hemel Hempstead: Prentice Hall.

Grant, R.M. (2010) *Contemporary Strategic Analysis*, 7th edn, Chichester: John Wiley & Sons.

Levy, H. and Sarnat, M. (1970) 'Diversification, Portfolio Analysis and the Uneasy Case for Conglomerate Mergers', *Journal of Finance*, 25.

Luffman, G.A. and Reed, R. (1984) *The Strategy and Performance of British Industry*, London: Macmillan.

Mason, R.H. and Goudzwaard, M.B. (1976) 'Performance of Conglomerate Firms: A Portfolio Approach', *Journal of Finance*, 31.

Michel, A. and Shaked, I. (1984) 'Does Business Diversification Affect Performance?', *Financial Management*, 13(4).

Palich, L.E., Cardinal, L.B. and Miller, C.C. (2000) 'Curvi-linearity in the Diversification–Performance Linkage: An Examination of Over Three Decades of Research', *Strategic Management Journal*, 22.

Park, C. (2002) 'The Effects of Prior Performance on the Choice between Related and Unrelated Acquisitions', *Journal of Management Studies*, 39.

Peters, T.J.

Waterman, R.H. (1982) *In Search of Excellence*, London: Harper & Row.

Wernerfelt, B. and Montgomery, C.A. (1986) 'What is an Attractive Industry?', *Management Science*, 32.

Weston, J.F., Smith, K.V. and Shrieves, R.E. (1972) 'Conglomerate Performance Using the Capital Asset Pricing Model', *Review of Economics and Statistics*, 54.

Reliance Industries

Family-owned conglomerates

Reliance Industries is the largest publicly traded company in India (by market capitalization). It is a family-run conglomerate and was started by Dhirubhai Ambani, the son of a poor Gujarati school teacher who began work at a Shell petrol station in Aden. To make extra money he traded commodities and, at one time, even melted down Yemeni Rial coins so as to sell the silver for more than the currency's face value. He returned to India and started a yarn-trading company in 1959 which, by the end of the 1990s, had become an integrated textiles, petrochemicals and oil conglomerate that then diversified into telecommunications and broadband, power, biotechnology, retail business and even financial services. Initially the business grew primarily through exploiting contacts with Indian politicians and bureaucrats. However, in the wake of the changes caused by economic liberalization in the early 1990s, it started to do things differently – it built production sites that were competitive in global markets. Dhirubhai also popularized share ownership in India – which is where financial services comes in – and the two holding companies now have over 3.5 million shareholders.

Dhirubhai died in 2002 and the business is now run by his two sons Mukesh and Anil. Both have MBAs from the USA and have been involved with the business for some 20 years, managing the company increasingly since their father had his first stroke in 1986 and having a strong role in forging it into the world-class company that it is today. Although little known outside its native country, Reliance has high brand recognition in India. According to a 2010 survey conducted by Brand Finance and *The Economic Times*, Reliance is the second most valuable brand in India and the 2011 Brand Trust Report ranked it the sixth most trusted brand in India.

Growing your business

173

© MaryAnnShmueli – Istockphoto.com

Using acquisition for market and product development

Obtaining rapid market dominance can be very important for certain types of new venture. And sometimes acquiring rivals – just as Zipcar bought Streetcar – is a way of consolidating your market position at home and buying market share in foreign markets. One of the reasons for the early success of Lastminute.com was its aggressive acquisition strategy in European markets after its launch in 1995. It purchased similar online businesses as well as a wide range of related travel and holiday firms such as Lastminute.de in Germany, Dégrif-tour in France, Destination Holdings Group, Med Hotels, First Option and Gemstone. These acquisitions helped it to gain international market dominance as well as scale in both product categories and geographic markets. In this way it consolidated its brand across Europe very quickly.

Clearly this strategy requires access to funds – acquiring another successful new venture in another country can be expensive. It is really therefore only an option for high-growth businesses, that have proved their business model and where economies of scale or scope are vital. **Economies of scope** is the term used when less of a resource is used because it is spread across multiple activities – also called **synergy**. This can arise when an intangible asset such as a brand can be extended across more than one product (brand or product extension). This is the claim made by Virgin. It can also arise when organizational capabilities, such as sales or technological management and their related fixed costs, can be extended across more products or services. This is why eBay bought PayPal. Many technology-based firms such as Apple, Amazon,

Facebook, Google and Microsoft have used this strategy extensively to expand both their product/ service offering and customer base (Case Insight, Chapter 4).

When large companies 'buy in' product development by acquiring smaller companies it is called **corporate venturing**. It happens in a wide range of sectors from telecommunications to consumer goods to engineering and is particularly common in the pharmaceutical industry and in the USA, where it represents a very significant proportion of venture capital investment. The reason for mentioning corporate venturing at this point is that, in the future, this may be a way of realizing your investment by selling on your business.

Generally, a strategy of using acquisition for market and product development should be approached with caution – it is expensive and very risky. Acquisitions have a high failure rate. The larger the acquisition compared to the acquiring company, the riskier it is because the acquired business will be more difficult to integrate. It should only be used where there is a newly emerging market and it is the only way to gain rapid market dominance in what otherwise might become a fragmented industry. If you are considering it as part of your strategy you will need professional advice.

A cheaper and less risky alternative to acquisition is strategic alliances and joint ventures (Chapter 10). These do not require funding and keep the management of the businesses separate. Although you have to share the profits with your partner, you also share the associated risks. And, for the founder, it can mean that they do not have to spread themselves too thinly.

Summary

- The strategy with the best chance of generating sustainable growth and the highest profits is to differentiate with the aim of dominating your market as quickly as possible, and to continue to innovate around that differential advantage. Gaining rapid market dominance may come from internal growth but may also involve acquisition of competitors. So the advice is to differentiate, dominate and innovate.

- Growth comes from market penetration, market and product/service development and/or a combination of both – diversification.

- Market development is about finding new markets. This can be geographic – going from local to regional to national and on to global. It might also be about going on to sell to different market segments.

- One reason for finding new markets is to achieve economies of scale of production. Another is that your key competence lies with the product, for example with technology-based products, and therefore the continued exploitation of the product by market development is the preferred route for expansion. A final reason might be that the product is nearing the end of its life cycle in the existing market.

- Porter's Five Forces is a useful tool to help assess competitiveness in new markets. It can be used to assess foreign markets but the risks associated with exit barriers also need to be considered.

- There are a number of ways to enter a foreign market, each one increasing your degree of commitment and investment: to export, to appoint an agent, to license/franchise, to set up a joint venture or to set up or acquire a wholly-owned subsidiary.

- Product development might include product modification, extension and expansion, leading to the development of completely new products.

- The Growth Share Matrix is a loose conceptual framework that helps to clarify the complexity of managing a portfolio of products. It has implications for the appropriate marketing strategy for each product and the cash flow it generates.

- Diversification involves moving from core areas of activity into completely new and unrelated product/market areas. It is central to the process of corporate evolution as new markets and industries are created.

- Diversification is high risk, but if done incrementally by constantly bundling new products and services together whilst extending the newly developing market, the risks can be reduced.

- Acquisitions can be used to help companies gain rapid market dominance early in the life of a product. They can also help develop a more comprehensive offering to customers.

- Diversification does not reduce shareholder risk in a publicly quoted company, and hence does not increase shareholder value – unless new markets or industries are being created. It does, however, reduce risk for the individual or family owning an unquoted company by spreading risk across different sectors.

- Any strategy of using acquisition for market and product development should be approached with caution – it is expensive and very risky. It should only be used where there is a newly emerging market and it is the only way to gain rapid market dominance in what otherwise might become a fragmented industry.

Exercise 8.1

Product/market development

The aim of this exercise is to get you to think about the future potential of your venture: how it might affect your strategy in the first three to five years and the options that you might highlight in your business plan for consideration in the future.

1 Using the matrix below, list the strategies that you intend to use to grow the business through market and product development and diversification (quadrants 1, 2 and 3).

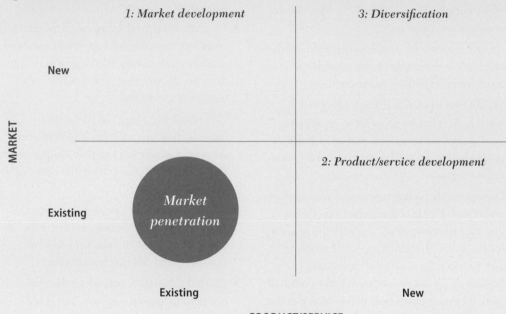

1: Market development   *3: Diversification*

New

MARKET

2: Product/service development

Existing

Market penetration

Existing   New

PRODUCT/SERVICE

2 If your growth strategy includes diversification (quadrant 3), jot down:
- The justification for the strategy;
- How it will be achieved;
- How the associated risks will be mitigated.

3 Note the time scale that applies to these strategies and the critical success factors.

4 Amend your launch strategy, as appropriate, to reflect these developments (Exercise 7.4).

5 List the strategic options you wish to consider in 3–5 years' time that may need to be covered in your business plan.

Exercise 8.2

Developing foreign markets

1 If your market development involves foreign markets, jot down the ways you intend to penetrate these markets over time, noting any things you need to find out before making final decisions about these strategies.

2 Note the time scale that applies to these strategies and the critical success factors.

3 Amend your launch strategy, as appropriate, to reflect these developments (Exercise 7.4).

4 List the strategic options you wish to consider in 3–5 years' time that may need to be covered in your business plan.

Exercise 8.3

Strategy implications of your future product portfolio

1 Map the product or service developments you are planning onto the Growth Share Matrix below.

Star	*Problem Child*
Cash Cow	*Dog*

2 List the marketing strategy and cash flow implications of these developments.

3 Note the time scale that applies to them and amend your launch strategy, as appropriate, to reflect these implications (Exercise 7.4).

4 List the strategic options you wish to consider in 3–5 years' time that may need to be covered in your business plan.

 Visit www.palgrave.com/companion/burns-new-venture-creation for chapter quizzes to test your knowledge and other resources.

PART 4
OPERATIONS
PLAN

9 Legal **foundations**

10 Organizing **operations**

VIDEO

www.palgrave.com/companion/
burns-new-venture-creation

The New Venture Creation Framework

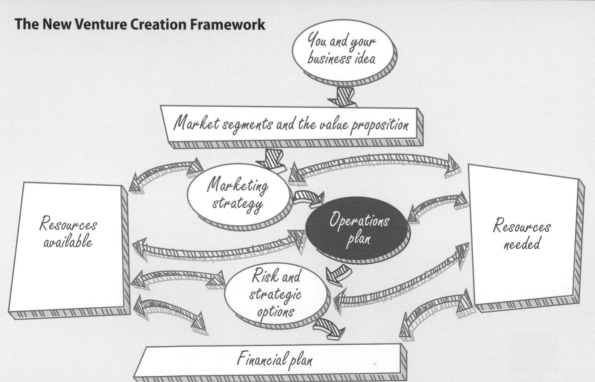

You and your business idea

Market segments and the value proposition

Marketing strategy

Operations plan

Resources available

Resources needed

Risk and strategic options

Financial plan

9
LEGAL FOUNDATIONS

Contents

Learning outcomes

When you have read this chapter and undertaken the related exercises you will be able to:
- Understand the ways you might be able to safeguard your business idea
- Decide on the appropriate legal form for your business or social enterprise
- Understand the responsibilities of the board of directors of a company

Safeguarding your business idea

One of the important things you need to think about is whether you can safeguard the 'intellectual property' (IP) of your business idea. There are a number of ways you can do this: patents, trademarks, copyrights, industrial design rights and, in some countries, trade secrets. However, strong intellectual property rights (IPR) can also have some disadvantages. In particular, if yours is a technology-based start-up that needs constant input of external knowledge, for example through various forms of partnering or networking, strong IPR gets in the way because it can inhibit collaborative working. Secrecy may be just as strong a tool as IPR. Indeed sometimes, if they can be maintained, trade secrets, such as the formula for Coca Cola, are more effective than any form of legal safeguard since, by definition, if you register a 'secret', it is no longer secret. Only if your product can be 'reverse-engineered' by competitors in some way so as to expose its 'secret' is registration probably the best option.

Nevertheless, for a start-up the IP you have on your business idea may be one of the few real assets available to you and, in seeking finance for your idea, you will have to expose it to many people, some of whom may be less scrupulous than others. In this case you would be well-advised to seek the maximum IPR you can find. Nevertheless, being first to market is sometimes more effective in creating competitive advantage than establishing IPR on an idea that then misses its window of commercial opportunity.

IP law varies from country to country. It is complex and usually comprises a multiplicity of individual pieces of legislation generated over a number of years. Because of this, if you think IP is important to your business, take legal advice. With the exception of copyright, if you want to protect your IP in other countries you will generally need to apply for protection in that country. The World Intellectual Property Organisation, an agency of the United Nations, produces the *Guide to Intellectual Property Worldwide* (available at www.wipo.int). In the UK information on regulations and laws can be obtained from the Intellectual Property Office (IPO) (www.ipo.gov.uk). Detailed UK legislation can be viewed on this site, as well as practical help with searches and registering your IP.

Generally, however, four fundamental methods of protection are offered in most countries: patents, trademarks, industrial design rights and copyright. A simplified guide to these is given below, but details may vary from country to country.

Patent

A patent is intended to protect new inventions. It covers how they work, what they do, how they do it, what they are made of and how they are made. It gives the owner the right to prevent others from copying, making, using, importing or selling the invention without permission. The existence of a patent may be enough on its own to prevent others from trying to exploit the invention. However should they persist in trying to do so, it gives you the right to take legal action to stop them exploiting your invention and to claim damages. And herein lies the problem for cash-strapped start-ups. Can you really afford the legal fees involved in pursuing such a claim? Nevertheless, the patent does allow you to sell the invention and all the IP rights, license it to someone else but retain all the IP rights or discuss the invention with others in order to set up a business based on the invention.

The IPO says that for the invention to be eligible for patenting it must be *new*, have an *inventive step* that is not obvious to someone with knowledge and experience in the subject and be capable of being *made* or *used* in some kind of industry. If a patent is granted, it lasts for 20 years but must, in the UK, be renewed every year after the fifth year. Patents are published by the IPO online after 18 months, which makes people aware of patents that they will eventually be able to use freely once the patent protection ceases. This also can be seen as a disadvantage, and you should remember that there is no legal requirement for you to file a patent; you can always decide to keep your invention secret. This is undoubtedly cheaper but if the invention enters the public domain then you may lose your rights to it. However, in dealing with individuals, such as prospective partners, suppliers or financial backers, you can always ask them to sign a confidentiality agreement (also known as a non-disclosure agreement) which legally binds them not to disclose company secrets. You can also require employees to sign such an agreement.

The IPO lists some things for which a patent cannot be granted such as:

- a scientific or mathematical discovery, theory or method;
- a literary, dramatic, musical or artistic work;
- a way of performing a mental act, playing a game or doing business;
- the presentation of information, or some computer programs;
- an animal or plant variety;
- a method of medical treatment or diagnosis;
- anything that is against public policy or morality.

Trademark

A trademark is a sign – made up of words or a logo or both – which distinguishes goods and services from those of competitors. The IPO says that a trademark must be *distinctive for the goods and services provided*. In other words, it can be recognized as a sign that differentiates your goods or service from someone else's. Once registered, a trademark gives you the exclusive right to use your mark for the goods and/or services that it covers in the country in which you have registered it. You can put the ® or ™ symbol next to it to warn others against using it. In the USA you can use the ™ symbol without a registration process, but it limits the 'exclusivity' to your local market. To get national exclusivity for specific categories, formal registration ® is required and you must prove a formal transaction has taken place within six months of registration. In all cases, trademark registration must be renewed every ten years and cannot be maintained if it is not being used on a continuous commercial basis.

As with a patent, a registered trademark may put people off using the trademark without permission and allows you to take legal action against anyone who uses it without your permission. However, in the UK a trademark also allows Trading Standards Officers or the Police to bring criminal charges against counterfeiters illegally using it. As with a patent, you can sell a trademark, or let other people have a licence that allows them to use it. In the UK, even if you don't register your trademark, you may still be able to take action if someone uses your mark without your permission, using the lengthier and onerous common law action of 'passing off'.

It is worth mentioning that registering a company name does not mean that that name is a registered trademark – company law is different from trademark law. Similarly, being the owner of a registered trademark does not automatically entitle you to use that mark as an internet domain name, and vice versa. This is because the same trademark can be registered for different goods or services and by different proprietors. Also, someone may have already registered the domain name, perhaps with its use being connected with unregistered goods or services. To search or register a domain name you should apply to an Accredited Registrar (available from the Internet Corporation for Assigned Names and Numbers, www.icann.org).

The IPO says that trademarks cannot be registered if they:

- describe goods or services or any characteristics of them, for example, marks which show the quality, quantity, purpose, value or geographical origin of the goods or services (e.g. Cheap Car Rentals or Quality Builders);
- have become customary in this line of trade;
- are not distinctive;
- are three dimensional shapes, if the shape is typical of the goods you are trading, has a function or adds value to the goods;
- are specially protected emblems;
- are offensive;
- are against the law (e.g. promoting illegal drugs);
- are deceptive.

Registered design

If you are creating products or articles which are unique because they look different from anything else currently available, then you might want to protect the look by registering it as a design. A registered design is a legal right which protects the overall visual appearance of a product in the geographical area you register it. The registered design covers the things that give the product a unique appearance, such as the lines, contours, colours, shape, texture, materials and the ornamentation of the product (e.g. a pattern on a product or a stylized logo). It is a valuable asset that allows you to stop others from creating similar designs. It does not offer protection from what a product is made of or how it works.

Registering a design gives you exclusive rights for the look and appearance of your product. This may be enough on its own to stop anyone using your design, irrespective of whether they copied it or came up with the design independently. Once a design is registered you can sell or license it and sell or retain the IP rights.

The IPO says that to be able to register a design it must:

- be new – in the UK a design is considered new if no identical or similar design has been published or publicly disclosed in the UK or the European Economic Area;
- have individual character – this means that the appearance of the design (its impression) is different from the appearance of other already known designs.

In the UK, Design Right and Community Design Right may also give you automatic protection for the look of your product.

Copyright

Copyright allows you to protect your original material and stops others from using your work without permission. It can be used to protect any media:

- literary works such as computer programs, websites, song lyrics, novels, instruction manuals, newspaper articles and some types of database;
- dramatic works including dance or mime;
- musical works;
- artistic works such as technical drawings, paintings, photographs, sculptures, architecture, diagrams, maps and logos;
- layouts or typographical arrangements used to publish a work (e.g. for a book);
- sound or visual recordings of a work;
- broadcasts of a work.

Copyright does not protect ideas, only how you 'publish' your ideas, for example in the case of writing, words cannot be copied. This happens automatically in most countries, which means that you do not have to apply for it so long as it falls within one of the categories of media that is protected, but it also means there is no official copyright register. Although not essential, you should mark the material with the © symbol, the name of the copyright owner and the year in which the work was created (e.g. © 2014 Paul Burns). Copyright owners may also choose to use technical measures such as copy protection devices to protect their material. In the UK, in addition to or instead of copyright protection, a database may be protected by the 'database right'. Trademarks can be both registered designs (for the artwork) and copyright. You can only copy a work protected by copyright with the owner's permission, even when you cross media boundaries (e.g. crossing from the internet to print).

As copyright owner you have the right to authorize or prohibit any of the following actions in relation to your work:

- copying the work in any way (e.g. photocopying, reproducing a printed page by handwriting, typing or scanning into a computer, and taping live or recorded music);
- renting or lending copies of the work to the public, although in the UK some lending of copyright works falls within the Public Lending Rights Scheme and this does not infringe copyright;
- performing, showing or playing the work in public (e.g. performing plays and music, playing sound recordings and showing films or videos in public);
- broadcasting the work or other communication to the public by electronic transmission, including transmission through the internet;
- making an adaptation of the work (e.g. by translating a literary or dramatic work, or transcribing a musical work or converting a computer program into a different computer language).

If you have copyright of a work you can sell or license it and sell or retain your ownership. You can also object if your work is distorted or mutilated. As with other forms of IP protection, the existence of copyright may be enough on its own to stop others from trying to copy your material. If it does not, you have the right to take legal action to stop them exploiting your copyright and to claim damages – that is if you can afford to go to court. Copyright infringement only occurs when a whole work or substantial part of it is copied without consent. However, what constitutes a substantial part is not defined and may therefore have to be decided by court action. Copyright is essentially a private right and therefore the cost of enforcing it falls to the individual.

🧳 *Case insight*

Trunki

Combating counterfeiters

The Trunki is a fun suitcase that looks like an animal, designed for children. It is estimated that 20% of three-to-six-year-olds in the UK own one. It was an idea that Rob Law came up with in 1998, but it has proved so successful that it has attracted many imitations. In 2013 his company, Magmatic, finally won a lawsuit in the UK against PMS International, a Hong Kong company that had been selling a Trunki-style product. The UK High Court ruled that PMS's Kiddee Case, breached Law's design rights in that the 'overall impression' created by the Kiddee Case, including the horn-like handles and clasps resembling the nose and tail of an animal, was similar to the designs underpinning the Trunki. As a result of this, Magmatic can take out an injunction preventing the sales of Kiddee Cases throughout Europe and force PMS to destroy remaining stocks. PMS may also be liable to damages to compensate Magmatic for lost sales.

Rob Law

trunki.com

The Trunki product range can be viewed on: www.trunki.com

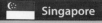

Case insight

Combating counterfeiters

Ryan Lee set up Xmi in Singapore to manufacture and sell small, portable speakers he had developed that were capable of filling a room with high-quality music. His first product, the X-mini, was launched in 2006:

> There was no other small speaker that was better than this at the time. That is why we demanded the (price) premium. Customers are willing to pay for quality.

Lee minimized the costs he faced in his new venture. Even today he operates from what used to be a bar in Singapore's central business district. He also sub-contracted manufacture to companies in China, having considered companies in Indonesia and Vietnam:

> Not everything can be done in these countries, and on top of that they are not even as good at assembly. So you're going to pay more for an inferior product.

Despite the high price, demand was high and the product proved successful. However, within six months Lee started receiving calls from distributors in Europe asking for a discount because they had been offered what looked like identical X-mini speakers at a much lower price. Upon investigation he found that,

although these imitations had plastic casings that were identical to the X-mini, they had far poorer sound quality, different packaging and did not carry the company's serial numbers. Once he had convinced his distributors that these were fake, inferior products the problem disappeared, but it did make Lee aware that there was a black market for fake X-minis. His reaction was to change suppliers to ones with a reputation for trustworthiness. He also started to manufacture some of the highly sensitive components himself as well as splitting up components among different suppliers. But ultimately he feels that the only way to combat these fakes is to keep one step ahead by constantly innovating and improving the product.

> I'd rather throw my money to the engineers, not to the lawyers. You innovate faster than your fakes. That's how you play the technology game.
>
> BBC News Business 25 March 2013

By 2012 Xmi had turnover of $26 million (33 million Singapore $).

Information about the X-mini can be found on the website: www.x-mini.com

Legal forms of business

 The UK government provides guidance on legal forms of business and an interactive guide on any permits or licences you might need (click on 'Licences') on: www.gov.uk/set-up-business-uk

In the USA the Small Business Administration provides information on the laws and regulations you need to adhere to on: www.sba.gov

Starting up in business is inherently risky, and how you structure your business has implications for how much risk you face personally. The three most popular legal forms of business are: sole traders (almost 60% of businesses), partnerships and limited liability companies. Their advantages and disadvantages are summarized in Table 9.1. In many countries a business needs a licence to operate, which can normally be obtained from the local council. In the UK certain types of business, such as those selling food or alcohol, employment agencies, minicabs and hairdressers need a licence or permit.

Sole traders

This is a business owned by one individual. The individual is the business, and the business is the individual. The two are inseparable. A sole trader is the simplest form of business to start – all that is needed is the first customer. It faces fewer regulations than a limited company and there are no major requirements about accounts and audits, although the individual will pay personal taxes which are based upon the profits made by the business.

There are two important limitations, however. The first is that a sole trader will find it more difficult to borrow large amounts of money than a limited company. Lending institutions prefer the assets of the business to be placed within the legal framework of a company because of the restrictions then placed upon the business. It is, however, quite common for a business to start life as a sole trader and incorporate later in life as more capital is needed.

The second disadvantage is that the sole trader is personally liable for all the debts of the business, no matter how large. That means creditors may look both to the business assets and the proprietor's assets to satisfy their debts. However, this disadvantage may be overcome by placing family assets in the name of the spouse or another relative.

Partnerships

Some professions, such as doctors and accountants, are required by law to conduct business as partnerships. Partnerships are just groups of sole traders who come together, formally or informally, to do business. As such it allows them to pool their resources; some to contribute capital, others their skills. Partnerships, therefore, face all the advantages of sole traders plus some additional disadvantages.

The first of these disadvantages is that each partner has unlimited liability for the debts of the partnership, whether they incurred them personally or not. Clearly partnerships require a lot of trust. The second disadvantage is that the partnership is held to cease every time one partner leaves or a new one joins, which means dividing up the assets and liabilities in some way, even if other partners end up buying them and the business never actually ceases trading.

Generally, if you are considering a partnership you would be well-advised to draw up a formal partnership agreement. It is very easy to get into an informal partnership with a friend, but if you cannot work together, or times get hard, you may regret it. If there is no formal agreement, then in the UK the terms of the Partnership Act 1890 are held to apply. Partnership agreements cover such issues as capital contributions, division of profit and interest on capital, power to draw money or take remuneration from the business, preparation of accounts and procedures when the partnership is held to 'cease'. Solicitors can provide a model agreement which can be adapted to suit particular circumstances.

Frank Gärtner – Fotolia.com

Limited liability companies

A company (registered in accordance with the provisions of the Companies Acts in the UK) is a separate legal entity distinct from its owners or shareholders, and its directors or managers. It can enter into contracts and sue or be sued in its own right. It is taxed separately through corporation tax (in the USA this is an election). There is a divorce between management and ownership, with a board of directors elected by the shareholders to control the day-to-day running of the business. There need be only two shareholders and one director, and shareholders can also be directors.

The advantage of this form of business is that the liability of the shareholders is limited by the amount of capital they put into the business. However, banks are likely to ask for personal guarantees from the founder to get around this problem. A company also has unlimited life and can be sold on to other shareholders. Indeed there is no limit to the number of shareholders. Therefore a limited company can attract additional risk capital from backers who may not wish to be involved in the day-to-day running of the business. Also, because of the regulation they face, bankers prefer to lend to companies rather than sole traders. However, in reality, the founder of a start-up business is unlikely to avoid having to give personal guarantees for the loans a company raises. Clearly this is the best form for a growth business that will require capital and will face risks as it grows.

Nevertheless there are some disadvantages to this form of business. In the UK under the Companies Acts, a company must keep certain books of account

	Advantages	Disadvantages
Sole trader	• Easy to form • Minimum of regulation	• Unlimited personal liability • More difficult to borrow money • Pays personal tax
Partnership	• Easy to form • Minimum of regulation	• Pays personal tax • Unlimited personal liability for debts of whole partnership • More difficult to borrow money • 'Cease trading' whenever partners change
Limited liability company	• Limited liability • Easier to borrow money • Can raise risk capital through additional shareholders • Can be sold on • Pays corporation tax (which can be lower than personal tax)	• Must comply with Companies Acts • Greater regulation • Greater disclosure of information

T9.1 **Advantages and disadvantages of different forms of business**

and appoint an auditor. It must file an annual return with Companies House which includes accounts and details of directors and shareholders. This takes time and money and means that competitors might have access to information that they would not otherwise see. Companies whose shares are traded publicly on a stock market are called public (as opposed to private) limited companies and face additional regulation.

The easiest and cheapest way to set up a company is to buy one 'off the shelf' from a Company Registration Agent. This avoids all the tedious form-filling that is otherwise required. It also saves time. In addition, agents will show you how to go about changing the company's name if you want to. To find out more, simply Google 'Company Registration Agent'.

In the USA there are also 'corporations'. These are also separate legal entities but organized under the authority of the state as either 'C Corporations' (C Corp) or 'Subchapter S Corporations' (S Corp). These are broadly similar to limited liability companies. The major difference between a C Corp and an S Corp is their tax treatment. C Corps are subject to double taxation at both the corporate and shareholder level. S Corps do not pay tax, instead all profits or losses are passed through to individual shareholders. Therefore losses in a C Corp reside with the company and cannot be deducted from shareholders' other sources of income – unlike an S Corp (a limited liability company can elect for different tax treatments). Because of this, private investors tend to prefer these two legal forms if there are losses at start-up. However, most venture capital funds will not invest in S Corps because the number of investors is restricted to 100 – unlike C Corps or limited liability companies, where there is no restriction. So, your planned funding structure may affect the legal framework you adopt, although a company can change its legal form later in life.

Cobra Beer

Company failure

Cobra Beer was set up in 1990 by Karan Bilimoria, the son of an Indian army general and a former accountant, to sell a different type of beer to Indian restaurants.

I entered the most **competitive** beer market in the world against long established brands. The product itself was **innovative** – an extra smooth, less gassy lager that compliments all cuisine and appeals to ale drinkers and lager drinkers alike ... Deciding to **import** the beer in a 650ml bottle was important in positioning the product within the market and raising the profile among restaurant owners. It also promoted a **new, shared way** of drinking ... The brand's point-of-sale items, such as unique and different glasses, were another effective way of establishing **brand awareness** ... Also [the glass] is embossed with six icons telling the story of Cobra beer, from concept and production to growth and development, and this is the **first time in the world** that, to our knowledge, the brand has incorporated its story directly into its packaging.

The Times
23 May 2004

By 2009 the company had sales of £177 million, but there was one problem. It had yet to make a profit. Indeed in the financial year to July 2007, the last year for which accounts are publicly available, Cobra lost £13 million. Instead of tracking profits, Cobra had focused on sales growth, spending £40 million on marketing since its launch. Sales growth had indeed been spectacular, showing 20% year-on-year growth in a falling market.

Unfortunately, the 2008 recession took its toll. While growth stalled, the banking crisis made it impossible to secure fresh funding. In the autumn of 2008 Bilimoria tried to find a buyer for the business but the big brewers were not interested and the credit squeeze prevented a sale to a private-equity firm. He cut costs. Four directors stood down and staff numbers were cut from 150 to 50.

Bilimoria called in the accountants PriceWaterhouseCoopers in the spring of 2009 to work on a company voluntary arrangement (CVA). This would have given all creditors some money back, but one creditor, Wells & Young's, which brewed Cobra under licence in Bedford, vetoed the proposal. Bilimoria therefore decided to restructure Cobra in what is called 'pre-packaged sale'. In this arrangement the business was acquired by a joint venture company comprising Molson Coors, the US brewer of Carling lager, and the former owner, Bilimoria. Molson paid £14 million for its 50.1% share. Karan Bilimoria kept 49.9% and remained as Director.

Unfortunately the nature of this form of administration in the UK means that, whilst the secured creditors, largely banks who were owed some £20 million, were paid back in full, unsecured creditors, who were owed almost £70 million, got nothing. These debts included £57 million to investors, £6 million to the government in taxes and £6 million to 330 small unsecured trade creditors. These included many small businesses such as Spark Promotions UK, owed £62,018 for developing a beer pump for Cobra, Pop Displays, owed £31,129 for producing printing and packaging for Cobra promotions and MicroMatic, another pump maker, which was owed £60,143. They were not happy:

> **Brian Flanagan, MD Spark Promotions UK Sunday Times 2 August 2009**
> [Bilimoria] has **risen** from the ashes like a **phoenix** while people like us, the creditors, have been **burnt alive.**

> **Chris Hall, MD Pop Displays Sunday Times 2 August 2009**
> How can someone **dump** all their **debts** on creditors and then the next day walk into what is, effectively, the same business with a **49%** stake?

Whilst the unsecured creditors may have lost out, observers suggest Molson Coors have landed a 'fantastic' deal. Bilimoria, who was made a Lord in 2007, said he lost the £20 million he invested in the firm and insists he is committed to repaying as many debts as possible:

> **Sunday Times 31 May 2009**
> We had **no choice** but to go down this route. I feel **terrible** about that. I feel gutted that the unsecured creditors aren't going to be **paid.**

The story of Cobra Beer can be found on: www.cobrabeer.com

Questions:

1. From the information given, map out as much as you can of the business model for Cobra using the New Venture Creation Framework. What are the key elements of competitive advantage in their value proposition?
2. Up to 2009, was Cobra successful? Was their strategy prudent?
3. Who has paid for the growth of Cobra? Is this fair? If not, what are the alternatives?

Corporate governance

If you decide to establish your start-up as a limited company, corporate governance – that is, the responsibility for overseeing strategy and ensuring its efficacy – rests legally with the company's board of directors. Its legal duties and responsibilities arise out of common law and statute, varying from country to country, and may also be detailed in the bylaws of an organization.

Directors have a fiduciary duty – a legal duty of loyalty and care – to act honestly and in good faith, exercise skill and care and undertake their statutory duty. They must act in the best interests of the company and its shareholders. This may seem an academic distinction if there are only two shareholders (e.g. yourself and your spouse) and one of these is the sole director of the company (e.g. yourself). However, even if this is the case, you must realize that you have certain legal responsibilities. If your start-up is larger, or you have aspirations for it to grow, then your board of directors may comprise more than just yourself. It might include other key members of your executive management team, who might also be shareholders, and even non-executive directors – outside directors who are not employees and part of your executive management team. Often, if you have obtained equity funding for your start-up, one of the conditions will be the appointment of specified non-executive directors. For example, if you obtain funding from a 'business angel', they will normally expect to be appointed a non-executive director. In fact non-executive directors have a valuable role in bringing different skills, an independent and objective perspective and a new network of contacts that can contribute to organizational knowledge and learning. They can also act as an early warning system for potential future difficulties and can be particularly valuable in helping to resolve conflict in family firms.

The broad functions of the board are summarized in Figure 9.1, using the dimensions of inward/outward looking and past/future orientation.

GETTY

Future orientation – Arguably the prime function of the board is to be outward looking and future orientated – to review and guide corporate strategy and policy. This might include overall strategic planning, approval of strategies or investments in key areas, changes in the scope or nature of operations, major company decisions and so on. The board is also responsible for how these translate into internal policies for the organization such as annual budgets, performance objectives, changes in organizational structure, compensation policy for key objectives, risk policy and so on.

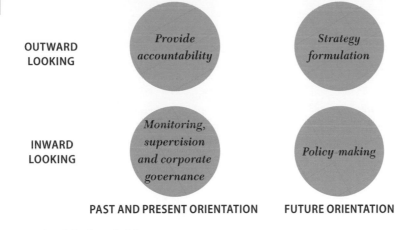

OUTWARD LOOKING	*Provide accountability*	*Strategy formulation*
INWARD LOOKING	*Monitoring, supervision and corporate governance*	*Policy-making*
	PAST AND PRESENT ORIENTATION	**FUTURE ORIENTATION**

F9.1 Role of the board of directors

Past and present orientation – The board then monitors performance against these strategies and policies and the ensuing risks it faces, as well as compliance with the law. These responsibilities include ensuring the integrity of the company's accounting and financial reporting systems, monitoring and supervising management performance, planning for management succession, providing proper accountability to other stakeholders in the firm, for example, by appointing auditors and approving the annual financial statements, as well as ensuring that the company complies with all aspects of the law.

Whilst establishing corporate strategy and policy may be the most important job for the board, it is unlikely that it will be given the appropriate weighting in terms of time allocation. Most boards, particularly in larger companies, spend too much time on the other functions, particularly monitoring management performance and legal compliance.

The board becomes more important where there is separation between day-to-day management and ownership of the firm and there are multiple stakeholders. Their role therefore becomes key once a company grows to the point where it is floated onto a stock market. Once this happens the board needs to function in a more formal way. For example, in Europe separating the role of Chief Executive or CEO from that of the Board Chairman is considered good practice – to help avoid potential conflicts of interest between stakeholders and executive directors. For the same reason most of the *Financial Times* Stock Exchange (FTSE) companies comply with the recommendation that they have non-executive directors, although in small unquoted companies the proportion is much smaller. In the USA, the Sarbanes-Oxley Act imposed new standards of accountability on US public companies that made directors directly responsible for internal control, facing large fines and prison sentences in the case of accounting crimes.

To help boards develop and operate more effectively, the UK Institute of Management published a set of best practice checklists based upon a model of board-level competences. Twenty-three board-level skills were identified, grouped together under the four key headings shown in Figure 9.2. These generic competences need to be balanced and tailored to particular circumstances and specific functional board roles.

> Elizabeth Gooch, founder EG Solutions *Sunday Times* 23 November 2008
>
> **Floatation** gives a public face to your business and access to **finance** that is so often the key to development. But there needs to be a lot more **attention** to **strategy**.

<table>
<tr><td>

Strategy
GUIDING STRATEGIC DIRECTION
- *Strategic thinking*
- *Systems thinking*
- *Awareness of external environment*
- *Entrepreneurial thinking*
- *Developing the vision*
- *Initiating change*
- *Championing causes*

</td><td>

Operations
EXERCISING EXECUTIVE CONTROL
- *Governance*
- *Decision-making*
- *Contributing specialist knowledge*
- *Managing performance*
- *Analyzing situations*
- *Awareness of organizational structure*

</td></tr>
<tr><td>

Culture
DEVELOPING ORGANIZATIONAL CULTURE
- *Customer focus*
- *Quality focus*
- *Teamwork focus*
- *People resource focus*
- *Organizational learning focus*

</td><td>

People
PRACTISING 'HUMAN' SKILLS
- *Communicating*
- *Creating a personal impact*
- *Giving leadership*
- *Promoting development of others*
- *Networking*

</td></tr>
</table>

F9.2 Institute of Management model of board-level competences

Legal forms of social enterprise

 The UK government provides further information on social enterprise on: www.gov.uk/set-up-a-social-enterprise

You can run a commercial limited liability company and still have social objectives. Many have them as part of their corporate social responsibility (CSR) commitments. However, in the UK if the primary aim of your start-up is social good and *all* the profits will be ploughed back into these activities then there are six legal forms of social enterprise that provide certain different benefits.

Unincorporated associations

These are informal associations of individuals that can form (and reform) quickly – similar to sole traders or informal partnerships. They enjoy great freedom as they are not regulated. They are not registered with anybody, but they can apply for charitable status, which means they have to comply with the regulations of the Charity Commission (www.charity-commission.gov.uk).

They can trade but cannot own assets because an association has no legal status. However, it may be possible to set up a trust to legally hold ownership of property and assets for the community they are intended to benefit. Because these associations are unincorporated, each individual in the association is personally liable for any debts or loans.

Trusts

These are run according to the social objectives set out in the trust deed. Many organizations in health care and education are structured as trusts. Trusts are unincorporated bodies. Trustees manage the trust on behalf of the community for which it was set up, which will be laid down, along with the trust's social objectives, in the trust deed. The trust can hold assets but it cannot distribute any profits. However, trustees are personally liable for any debts or loans. Trusts may need to register with Companies House (www.companieshouse.gov.uk) and, since they have social objectives, they can apply for charitable status through the Charities Commission.

Maggie's Centres

(The Maggie Keswick Jencks Cancer Caring Centres Trust)
Social enterprise

Called Maggie's Centres, this trust was set up with a charitable donation by Maggie Keswick Jencks, a landscape designer with an international reputation, just before her death from breast cancer in 1996. Maggie's has 6 centres and 3 'interim centres' and dealt with 77,000 visitors in 2008. Each centre is located next to a NHS cancer hospital. All of the centres are designed by leading architects, such as Frank Gehry, based upon the belief of the Trust founder that design affects how we feel. Each is unique, being built around a kitchen on an open-plan basis – no closed doors – and designed to be friendly and welcoming. Each is staffed by health professionals, including a cancer nurse and a psychologist, and a fundraiser. Maggie's is piloting online support groups, managed by psychologists.

maggie's
People with cancer
need places like these

Maggie's, Nottingham UK

Maggie's Cancer Care

193

Lego Foundations

Charitable social enterprises

These are set up wholly for charitable purposes that benefit the public. They must be registered with Companies House or the Financial Conduct Authority (www.fsa.gov.uk). They are regulated by Charity Commission regulations (HM Revenue & Customs in Northern Ireland and the Office of the Scottish Charities Regulator in Scotland). Trusts benefit from tax and rate relief and any surplus must be reinvested. The founder of a charity shapes its creation but not its strategic direction or operation. The charity is run by directors or trustees, who cannot be paid for their work. They shape its strategic direction.

Community benefit societies (BenComs)

These are incorporated 'industrial and provident societies' – legal entities set up with social objectives, which conduct business for the benefit of their community. They are run and managed by their members but profits cannot be distributed among members and must be returned to the community. BenComs can raise funds by issuing shares to the public and can be registered as charities. They are regulated by the Financial Conduct Authority and must submit annual accounts. BenComs differ from cooperatives in that cooperatives operate for the mutual benefit of their members – which is not necessarily the same as the community – and therefore cannot be registered as charities.

Community interest companies (CIC)

These are essentially limited liability companies, registered with Companies House or the Financial Conduct Authority, but with extra requirements. They can be limited by shares or by guarantee. They must demonstrate their social and environmental impact each year by issuing an annual community interest company report alongside the annual accounts. They must operate transparently and not pay directors excessive salaries. Profit distribution is also regulated; companies limited by guarantee may not distribute profits, whereas those limited by shares can do so under certain circumstances. CICs must have an asset lock, which means that profits or assets cannot be transferred for less than their full market value. People who start a CIC can steer the business as they see fit because they will be directors. More information can be found on www.bis.gov.uk/cicregulator/.

A CIC cannot be a charity. However, it is common for it to run alongside one. So, for example, it is common for a social organization to have two forms: a CIC, which runs in a business-like way while giving the community a stake in how it is run, and a charitable social enterprise to which the CIC's profits are transferred and which decides how they are spent. This dual form can maximize tax advantages. It also means that the charity can apply for grant funding that will help to get projects up and running, while the income generated by the CIC means that the organization is not totally dependent on these grants or the goodwill of donors or government.

Charitable incorporated organizations (CIO)

These are a new form of incorporated organization that is set up for charitable purposes and therefore reports to the Charity Commission rather than Companies House or the Financial Conduct Authority. Like CICs they must benefit local communities and have an asset lock. They are not able to distribute profits or assets to their members. Unlike CICs which have directors, CIOs have charity trustees. CICs and charitable social enterprises can convert into CIOs.

Taxation

All commercial businesses are liable for tax and there are a number of different taxes all organizations may have to deal with. All new businesses need to inform the tax authorities of their existence but particularly those with employees, where arrangements to deduct tax from wages may have to be made.

Value Added Tax   This is a form of sales tax that is common throughout the European Union. If your turnover is above a certain level you must register for VAT (in 2014 in the UK the level was £79,000). If your turnover is above this, VAT must be charged on all goods or services you supply, but at the same time VAT on the goods or services you receive can be deducted from the amount you pay to the government. Different countries have different rates and there can be different rates for different sorts of products or services (in 2014 in the UK the standard or main rate of VAT was 20%). Certain goods or services may also be 'exempt' from VAT, which means that VAT is not charged on the goods or services you supply, but you cannot claim back VAT on exempt goods or services you receive.

Corporation tax – Limited liability companies pay corporation tax on their profits (in the USA this is by election). This can be imposed at country and/or state level. There are rules about how profit is calculated for tax purposes and these vary from country to country. Some expenses are not tax deductible and normally there are set rates of depreciation for fixed assets. The rate of corporation tax also varies from country to country and can increase with taxable profit (from 1 April 2015 the rate will be 20% in the UK). Shareholders receiving dividends from the company (paid out of profits) are charged income tax. In the UK this is calculated in such a way that this income does not face corporation as well as income tax. In the USA, C Corps are subject to double taxation.

Income tax for sole traders and partnerships – Sole traders and partnerships pay income tax on their business profits. Although the expenses that can be deducted are similar to corporation tax, in many countries the detailed regulations and rates of tax can differ. Personal income tax rates are usually higher than corporation tax rates.

Local taxes – Most countries have local taxes. In many countries this takes the same form as corporate or income tax. In the UK it is a lump-sum tax based on the size of your business premises and is called 'Business Rates'.

You can get more information on business taxation.
For the UK: www.hmrc.gov.uk
For the USA: www.sba.gov

Income tax on employees – In many countries businesses are responsible for collecting income tax from employees and remitting it to the government (in the UK this is called the Pay As You Earn or PAYE system).

Charities – Registered charities are normally exempt from tax on their income and exempt from VAT, but they have to pay income tax on employees.

imageSource

Summary

- You may be able to safeguard the IP on your business idea through patent, trademark, registered design and copyright. However, this can be expensive and time-consuming. Sometimes being first to market is more effective in creating competitive advantage. You can get employees or third parties to sign a confidentiality or non-disclosure agreement which prevents them from disclosing your idea.

- There are three legal forms of business: sole trader, partnership and limited liability company.

- Responsibility for corporate governance legally rests with the board of directors. Directors have a fiduciary duty to act honestly and in good faith, exercise skill and care and undertake their statutory duty. They must act in the best interests of the company and its shareholders.

- There are six forms of social enterprise in the UK: unincorporated associations, trusts, charitable social enterprises, community benefit societies, community interest companies and charitable incorporated organizations.

- All commercial businesses are liable to tax and there are a number of different taxes all organizations may have to deal with.

Exercise 9.1

Intellectual property

Decide whether you wish to and whether you are able to safeguard any IP related to your business. List the actions you need to take to safeguard it.

Exercise 9.2

Legal form of business

1 Decide on the legal form your new ventures will take. List anything you need to do to register the business. List the operating implications of this decision.

2 If you decide to establish a limited company:
- Decide who might be on the board of directors
- Decide whether you are willing to share equity in the business with others and describe the skills and competences of those who might be on your board of directors now, and in three to five years' time.

3 If you want to establish a social enterprise, decide who else needs to be involved and what will be their status

Visit www.palgrave.com/companion/burns-new-venture-creation for chapter quizzes to test your knowledge and other resources.

10
ORGANIZING
OPERATIONS

Contents

Learning outcomes

When you have read this chapter and undertaken the related exercises you will be able to:
- Identify the key activities needed to launch and operate your business and their implications
- Understand the value of partnerships, joint ventures and strategic alliances
- Understand the advantages and disadvantages of franchising and what is involved in establishing a business as either a franchisee or a franchisor
- Prepare Gantt charts and undertake critical path analysis
- Prepare a 'high level' operating plan for your business that highlights your critical success factors

Identifying key activities

Key activities are the most important things that you need to get right to make your business model work. They have implications for all aspects of the business, including the resources you need. Every business has its own key activities upon which its competitive advantage probably hinges. Some of these will need to be completed prior to your business launch, for example selecting an appropriate location for a retail business or obtaining the necessary licences. Others are key operating activities for the life of the business, for example keeping an up-to-date and engaging website or maintaining service levels. These may change over time as the business develops. But they are the day-to-day operating issues that you need to get right to deliver your customer value proposition. Some will be critical success factors. However, key activities cascade down an organization and what might be important or critical for a department within a larger business might not be of the same importance for the business

overall. Paying salaries and wages on the due date is very important to employees but is unlikely to feature on the key activities or critical success factors list for your business. It is all a matter of judgement.

Key pre-launch activities – If you hope to sell an innovative product, you probably will need to at least have a working prototype before trying to get finance and you certainly need to have refined that prototype and be able to deliver the product in the required volumes before you go to market. However, you do not necessarily need to manufacture or even assemble the final product, just as you do not, necessarily, need to retail it directly to customers yourself.

Some key pre-launch activities have implications for future operations. For example, eBay's business model requires them to have an efficient and effective web platform. This was needed at start-up, but the platform continues to be developed so the company can maintain its competitive position. Google's original business model required a working word-search algorithm. Today they need to keep at the forefront of internet-based search and retrieval technology and developments. Dell set out to be a low-cost provider of computer equipment and developed an innovative B2C2B integrated supply chain to facilitate this. Now this is commonplace they are struggling to differentiate themselves.

Key operating activities – These are specific to each business, but there are some generalizations that can be made for specific industries – retail, internet, manufacturing and service. The location of a bricks-and-mortar retail business is a vital decision, just as the effective operation of the website is a vital activity for a virtual retail business. Many service businesses such as consultancies are based around some key skills, knowledge or problem-solving abilities and training might therefore feature as a key updating activity. Production activities that underpin quality or efficiency might dominate the key activities for a manufacturing firm. We shall return to these sectors later in this chapter.

Your business model and the operational imperatives associated with the three core value propositions have important implications for your key operating activities (Table 5.2 is reproduced below as Table 10.1). For example, Amazon originally set out to be a low-cost online retailer of books, so it located in Seattle, a major distribution hub for several large publishers. easyJet, like other low-price airlines, must also keep its costs low, and this has numerous operations implications – from ticket pricing to luggage allowance, turn-around time to staff rostering, website design to branding. Companies with a differentiated product, like Apple, continuously

innovate whilst building their brand based upon what they see as their differential advantages, such as design simplicity. Companies with a strong customer focus work on expanding their customer offering – Virgin continually seeks out new opportunities for brand extension, whilst reinforcing its brand through the image of its founder, Richard Branson. Dell has a low-cost focus, so one of its key activities includes supply chain management. Should this focus change, as it is doing, then the importance of the supply chain is reduced and other imperatives will emerge.

Every business is different and you need to identify your key activities and which of these are your critical success factors. Deciding on which factors are critical and which are not involves making a judgement. It is not just about urgent tasks – most are urgent for a start-up. It is not just about identifying factors that might set you back – there will be many of these. It is about deciding which things might fundamentally affect the success of the venture.

You will need to have completed some activities prior to your business launch. For example, you might need a working prototype or your business model might have implications for the assets you need to own (licences, patents etc.) or you might need to secure key contracts with both partners and/or customers. Some will be key operational activities that derive from your business model and its core value proposition that help focus your day-to-day managerial attention. The crucial question to ask yourself is whether this will cause the start-up to fail or succeed? You start by considering how the generalized business imperatives in Table 10.1 translate into key activities for your business.

Low-price/low-cost	High differentiation	Customer focus
• Maintaining cost leadership through economies of scale • Continually driving down costs • Achieving high sales volumes • Improving efficiency • Standardization	• Understanding the basis for the differential advantage • Building on the differential advantage • Building barriers to entry • Building the brand • Continuous innovation • Encouraging creativity and innovation	• Maintaining close relationships with customers • Keeping in touch with and understanding changes in customer needs • Maintaining customer loyalty • Maximizing sales to existing loyal customers (economies of scope) • Building the brand

T10.1 Business imperatives of the core value propositions

Retail imperatives

Launching a retail business – a shop, restaurant, bar etc. – poses a particular set of challenges. For any retailer, the 'place' element of the marketing mix is very specific and very important. The location must provide access to your target market. If you want the casual shopper or diner, you might locate in the high street or at a transport hub (like Moma! in Chapter 3) – wherever there is high footfall. High-footfall locations are called prime sites and can be expensive. However, just because there are lots of people passing a location, it does not mean that those people are potential customers for the product/service offered by your business. If you are selling something that customers will seek out and you can rely on it 'pulling' them into the shop or restaurant, then you can afford to be located at a secondary site, with lower footfall. You often see stores relying on in frequent purchases (furniture, cars, do-it-yourself etc.) located in secondary locations. Secondary locations have much lower rent and rates than primary locations. However, there may be additional costs associated with 'pulling' customers into that location.

- Size of population in local area
- Demographic and nature of population
- Footfall outside specific location
- Visibility of site
- Proximity of 'magnets' such as anchor stores or transport hubs
- Strength of competition
- Consistency with customer value proposition
- Site costs
- Availability of parking
- Availability of public transport
- Potential for expansion
- Nature of legal agreement (e.g. lease term, rent reviews etc.).

T10.2 Factors affecting the location decision of a retailer

Sometimes small retailers group together in areas which have lower rent and rates and establish their own customer 'pull' because of the charm the area has or because of the variety offered. Retailers offering similar products/services can also group together to establish specialist 'quarters' such as a jewellery quarter or restaurant quarter.

For any retail outlet the frontage is the equivalent of a huge advertising hoarding for the products/services sold. It therefore needs to reflect the value proposition to customers. The ambience is also very important – design, hygiene, layout etc. – and must also reflect the value proposition (see for example South Beauty Case Insight on page 124). It must be consistent with the rest of your marketing mix. If you are selling on price – for example like the Poundland stores – you do not need an expensive frontage or point-of-sale displays because it is not consistent with the low-price value proposition. On the other hand, you may still need to locate in prime sites.

The launch of a new retail outlet needs to attract potential customers into the building. They therefore often have opening events, perhaps with celebrities or even bands, trying to generate a party atmosphere with banners, balloons, special decorations etc. Shops often have opening sales. Whilst shoppers might just browse, drinkers or diners will want to try out the products on sale, so special opening price discounts might be offered. Rather than relying on price offers, exclusive bars or restaurants might have special opening events to which only selected people are invited, creating an atmosphere of exclusivity. And whilst prime-site shops might rely on attracting passing customers, other retailers will need to promote their opening event.

Whilst, increasingly, transactions are electronic, any business handling cash needs to ensure that there are safeguards in place to prevent theft. Staff theft is particularly problematic in bars. Increasingly cameras are being used to supplement electronic cash registers. Cameras are also used extensively to discourage shoplifting. Table 10.3 provides a checklist of possible key activities for a retailer.

Restaurants will need to develop attractive menus and make certain they have the chefs to deliver them. Waiting staff will need to be trained.

Pre-launch

- Location
- Licences and leases
- Layout, design and fit-out
- Merchandising and stocking
- Internet sales and website
- Sales staff recruitment and training
- Credit/debit card merchant account
- Launch event

Operations

- Merchandising
- Stock control
- Promotions
- Security (cash and shoplifting)
- Service levels

T10.3 **Key activities checklist for a retailer**

Hygiene will be an important consideration and the restaurant will need to obtain a hygiene certificate from the local authority. Any retailer selling alcohol needs to obtain a licence from the local authority. Table 10.4 provides a checklist of possible key activities for a restaurant or bar.

Pre-launch

- Location
- Licences and leases
- Restaurant/bar design and fit-out
- Menu design
- Chef recruitment
- Staff recruitment and training
- Credit/debit card merchant account
- Website
- Launch event

Operations

- Hygiene
- Promotions
- Cash control
- Stock control (food and drink)
- Staff rostering
- Menu rotation
- Service levels
- Customer security

T10.4 **Key activities checklist for a restaurant or bar**

Internet business imperatives

Many businesses trade on the internet and that can get you access to international markets immediately. According to IMRG, the industry body for global e-retailing, in 2011 British consumers spent £68 billion on online goods and services, and this is growing rapidly. Selling on the web offers the opportunity to do business 24 hours a day, seven days a week – worldwide. It also offers you the chance to build relationships and develop an understanding of individual customers' buying patterns. The pure internet firm does not require the major fixed costs of a retail business like the high street site and the shop-floor staff – but many traditional bricks-and-mortar businesses are

now also trading on the internet, trying to offer customers the best of both worlds. At the moment internet-based retail is most successful for branded products where the features are already understood, or for 'low-touch' products or services such as music downloads, books, airline or theatre tickets where, once again, customers understand precisely what they are buying. Almost 50% of computers are now sold online, compared to less than 10% of clothing and footwear.

The key to successful trading here is a good website – one that gets people to visit and then revisit. Of course you can trade on other ready-built e-tail platforms such as eBay. However, you may want to control content and presentation and to have your own web presence

imageSource

will find many, but try asking friends and colleagues for recommendations.

Your website should enable customers to order quickly and easily. A site with a difficult sales process is likely to lose customers before they reach the checkout. It should also be easy to navigate so customers do not get frustrated and leave without even attempting to make a purchase. Security should also be a priority, and potential customers should be assured that their details will be kept safe. The content of the website needs to be updated regularly so as to maintain customer interest. It should also present a 'human face' and, better still, build a community of interest that encourages the visitor to communicate with you, ideally leaving their email address. You can then communicate with them directly. Just as in the real world, you should try to build a relationship with your customers. We saw in Chapters 6 and 7 that the internet can be an important part of a communications campaign that helps build a loyal customer base around your brand.

You need to get customers to visit your site in the first place; just as with bricks-and-mortar businesses, you need to create awareness. Internet businesses often seem to forget this. You can create awareness of your site by using all the media mentioned earlier, including advertising in print media or on other websites. As we have seen, services such as Google AdWords can be very cost-effective because they operate on a 'pay per click' basis. Social media such as blogs, chat-rooms and discussion forums can also be cheap ways of getting customers to become aware of your website.

All internet businesses need to ensure that potential customers searching the web for products such as theirs get links to their site as quickly as possible. Search engines thrive on content and the more relevant content with keywords or phrases the more likely your site is to be featured on a list of search results. Few people searching the web look beyond the first couple of pages of results. Search engine optimization (SEO) ensures that you catch any potential customers searching for your type of

– and anyway eBay charges for its service. Indeed your Microsoft® software contains a basic website writing tool on Microsoft® Office Live, where you will find links to free web design tools. If you do not want to build your own website from scratch you can buy skeleton sites that you customize yourself or employ professional web designers. You can spend as much as you want on designing and setting up your own website. A basic one might cost as little as £500 but a good one could easily cost £20,000. If you search online you

Calypso Rose, founder Clippy Daily Telegraph 6 February 2009

Optimize your website. Keep driving customers to your website using PR and marketing and make your site **sticky**. It's your **portal** to world markets.

product on search engines such as Yahoo or Google as quickly as possible. However, it can be expensive if you employ a company to do it. On the other hand, you can learn how to do it yourself with the help of a good book or an online course. There is also specialist software that can help you monitor the traffic on your own website. Table 10.5 provides a checklist of possible key activities for an internet business.

 Search engine optimization (SEO) software is available to download.

Google offers a free tool for analyzing your website traffic: www.google.com/analytics

This is a key-word research tool: www.compete.com

These sites offer guides and tips on SEO: www.seochat.com www.seoforum.com

This site offers free SEO tools: www.seolite.com

Pre-launch
- Web design and navigation
- Search engine optimization
- Website advertising and promotion
- Credit/debit card merchant account
- Transaction security
- Merchandising and stocking
- Launch advertising and promotion

Operations
- Promotions
- Social media promotions (e.g. blogs, chat-rooms and discussion forums)
- 'Community' building activities
- Website update
- Stock control

T10.5 Key activities checklist for an internet business

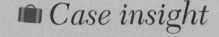 *Case insight*

Figleaves

Using the internet to penetrate markets

Michael Ross, Chief Executive of Figleaves, a UK online retailer of women's lingerie, has managed to penetrate one of the most difficult markets in the world – the USA. Launched in 1999 as easyshop.co.uk, the company changed its name the following year after it decided to focus on lingerie. But Figleaves' secret was that, when it launched in the USA, it was already its second largest market because it sold on the internet and American women were not concerned that the lingerie they ordered came from Britain.

Figleaves has negotiated a number of online marketing deals and web links to maximize the exposure their site enjoys. US deals are negotiated by somebody who flies out once a month from the UK. The company even has a concession within Amazon.com. Its 'Shock Absorber' bra was launched in the USA by holding a tennis match between Amazon's founder, Jeff Bezos, and the tennis star Anna Kournikova. One feature of the Figleaves website is the facility to purchase in a number of different currencies. Figleaves now claims to be the global leader of 'multi-brand intimate apparel e-tailers'. The website features 250 brands and more than 30,000 items of lingerie, swimwear, sleepwear, active-wear, menswear and hosiery.

Up–to-date information on Figleaves can be found on their website: www.figleaves.com

 UK

Reasons for international start-ups

Academic studies tell us that the increasing number of new ventures that establish as international start-ups generally do so because they derive some other significant form of competitive advantage from going international (Oviatt and McDougall, 1994). These firms start with an international business strategy, for example at the outset making international product/market offering decisions or making use of international sourcing of components. They deploy their assets internationally. Typically, they use alliances and networks to overcome resource deficiencies. One good reason to start up internationally is that you own certain valuable assets, particularly IP, that can be exploited in or transferred to a foreign location (Oviatt and McDougall, op. cit.). Another reason is that you have international experience and/or a network of contacts that allow you to capitalize on international market opportunities or imperfections by linking resources from around the world (Oviatt and McDougall, 1995). The systematic and effective exploitation of this key asset is seen as the prime reason for early internationalization.

Many international start-ups are in high technology niche markets (Aggarwal, 1999). This is because economies of scale are important and the high cost of R&D precludes a purely domestic orientation if costs are to be recouped (Coviello and Munro, 1995; Litvak, 1990; Oakley, 1996). What is more, the ever accelerating pace of technological innovation means that product life cycles are shortening and first-mover advantage in all markets becomes vital. Rapid international expansion is designed to counter competitive reaction. In a review of the literature and a study of twelve high technology international start-ups, Johnson (2004) found many factors influencing the decision to internationalize. He concluded that the principal factors influencing this decision were:

- The international vision of the founders;
- Their desire to be international market leaders;
- The identification of specific international opportunities;
- The possession of specific international contacts and sales leads.

Aggarwal, R. (1999) 'Technology and Globalisation as Mutual Reinforcers in Business: Reorienting Strategic Thinking for the New Millennium', *Management International Review*, 2(1).

Coviello, N.E. and Munro, H.J. (1995) 'Growing the Entrepreneurial Firm: Networking for International Market Development', *European Journal of Marketing*, 29(7).

Johnson, J.E. (2004) 'Factors Influencing the Early Internationalisation of High Technology Start-ups: US and UK Evidence', *Journal of International Entrepreneurship*, 2.

Litvak, I.A. (1990) 'Instant International: Strategic Reality for Small High-Technology Firms in Canada', *Multinational Business*, 2 (Summer).

Oakley, P. (1996) 'High-Tech NPD Success through Faster Overseas Launch', *European Journal of Marketing*, 30(8).

Oviatt, B.M. and McDougall, P.P. (1994) 'Towards a Theory of International New Ventures', *Journal of International Business Studies*, 25 (First Quarter).

Oviatt, B.M. and McDougall, P.P. (1995) 'Global Start-ups: Entrepreneurs on a Worldwide Stage', *Academy of Management Executive*, 9(2).

Manufacturing business imperatives

There are five types of operations processes involved in manufacturing or production:

Project – This is the production of one-off, large-scale products to meet the specific requirements of a client, for example buildings. Normally the project is built or manufactured on-site around the needs of the client, because it is not practical to move it once it is produced. Operational issues include effective resource delivery to and allocation around the site and the coordination of a large number of interrelated activities. The challenge is to deliver the project on time and on budget. Because it is one-off, specialist knowledge of these sorts of project and accurate costing are vital.

Jobbing – This is one-off production to meet the specific requirements of a client, but the process can be undertaken in a factory and then shipped to the client. This would normally make the organization of operations easier. The challenge is still to deliver the project on time and on budget, and specialist knowledge and accurate costing is vital.

Batch – This is where there is sufficient volume of production to justify organizing production in the most efficient and effective way. There is a degree of task repetition, but volumes rarely justify the investment of time in task analysis. An example is the manufacture of components that go on to be assembled into a bigger, more complicated product.

Line – This is where there is a further increase in volume, with a regularity of order that justifies the investment in task analysis and dedicated resources. Assembling sub-components (which may come from sub-contractors) to form the final product is usually an important part of the process. Organizing these processes in the most efficient and effective way is important.

Continuous – This is where volumes have increased to such an extent that an inflexible, dedicated process is in place to run all day, every day, with a minimum of shutdowns. This is something that a small business would not normally be involved in.

Manufacturing and assembly can be complicated and often require expensive machinery. So the first question to ask is whether you need to undertake the task yourself or whether you might have the process undertaken more cheaply, more quickly and to a higher standard by sub-contracting the operation to a specialist? The answer lies in the particular knowledge, skills and capabilities upon which your business is based. If these are not based in manufacturing then looking for a subcontractor might be a good idea.

Most manufacturing businesses require specialist machinery and equipment of some sort. You can use trade magazines to search out suppliers. Quality control is likely to be an important operating issue and there are quality standards that may help (BS/ISO 9000 series). You will need to source raw materials. Business-to-business directories such as Kelly Search (www.kellysearch.co.uk), Kompass (www.kompass.co.uk) or Applegate (www.applegate.co.uk) can help you source suppliers from around the world. All these things might need to be mentioned in your business plan.

Operating imperatives in manufacturing vary considerably. Project and jobbing manufacture requires a high degree of specialist knowledge and skill and may require expensive specialist equipment. Project management skills are also important. There is the opportunity to differentiate and brand the business based upon this. Small businesses seem attracted to batch manufacturing, probably because the batches are not sufficiently large to warrant pursuing efficiencies and economies of scale. However, batch can involve high volumes and a relatively wide range of products with different orders competing for the same processes and therefore control can be complex. Line manufacturing involves the ability to organize assembly and manage repetitive, routine operations efficiently and effectively. Cost control, plant utilization and economies of scale are likely to be important. Table 10.6 provides a checklist of possible key activities for a manufacturer.

Service business imperatives

The most important imperative for a service business is the ability to deliver that service, and that depends upon the knowledge, skills and abilities of those delivering it. All service businesses involve people and their training is important. This training might reflect the specialist nature of the service – for example in consultancy and training. It might reflect the service process – for example where efficiency and effectiveness are important. Where direct contact with the client is involved it should help develop the interpersonal skills of staff and their ability to manage client relationships as well as other staff.

Perhaps surprisingly, service delivery has some similarities with manufacturing. Larger consultancy assignments take the form of projects and require the same degree of coordination and control. A tailor made, training programme is similar to jobbing. A computer bureau that processes different clients' work is, in effect, a batch manufacturer. A fast-food restaurant has more than a passing similarity to line manufacturing. Table 10.6 provides a checklist of possible key activities for a manufacturer and service business.

Pre-launch
- Premises lease
- Licences
- Premises design and layout
- Equipment purchase
- Staff recruitment and training
- Materials and stocks
- Safety procedures

Operations
- Quality control
- Stock control
- Safety checks

Project and jobbing
- Project management
- Knowledge and skills update

Batch
- Scheduling and processing of orders
- Handling complexity

Line
- Staff control
- Efficiency studies

T10.6 **Key activities checklist for a manufacturer or service business**

Environmental sustainability and waste reduction

Scott (2010) argues that what is good for the environment can also be good for business. Furthermore, sustainability means reducing costs for business – doing more with less. Scott gives the example of Wal-Mart which demanded that its 60,000 suppliers reduce packaging by at least 5% with the expectation of reducing solid waste by 25% and shaving $3.4 billion off operating costs. General Electric decided to become 'greener' in 2004. By 2008 'green' practices had reduced costs by $100 million and yielded a portfolio of 80 new products and services that generated $17 billion in annual revenues. Here are Scott's ten guidelines to reduce product waste:

1. Carefully design the product to minimize resources so as it can be re-used in a closed-loop system.
2. Design products so they can be disassembled easily.
3. Reduce the use of hazardous inputs.
4. Switch to non-hazardous manufacturing methods.
5. Reduce the amount of energy required in manufacturing and use sustainable energy.
6. Use newer, cleaner technologies.
7. Use sustainable re-manufactured, recycled or scrap materials in the manufacture.
8. Improve quality control and process monitoring.
9. Find ways to get the product returned for disassembly and harvesting of parts.
10. Reduce packaging or use recycled materials.

Scott, J. (2010)
'The Sustainable Business',
Global Focus, 4, EFMD.

Kirsty's

Brompton Bicycle

Growth through focusing on core activities

The Brompton folding bicycle was invented by Cambridge University graduate Andrew Ritchie in 1976. He produced small volumes of the cycle himself from a small, cluttered factory in West London. It became a style icon and a profitable niche business, selling at a price premium. By 2002 the company was still producing only about 6000 cycles each year and employing 24 people. And demand exceeded supply.

That all started to change when Will Butler-Adams joined the firm as Managing Director aged only 28. He brought in new ways of working, introducing budget plans and sub-contracting parts of the process, such as the manufacture of wheels and frame, to other UK manufacturers. This allowed more space to become available in the small factory for assembling the cycles.

> The idea was to outsource the non-core stuff, so that we could then lavish more attention on the core things, and do them better. And we could make more bikes.

By 2013 Brompton had become the UK's largest cycle-maker, producing 40,000 cycles a year and employing 190 people. With a turnover of £28 million, it now exports 80% of its cycles to some 44 countries. This growth has been achieved entirely organically and without outside finance. Will has no plan to relocate any production to the Far East to take advantage of cheaper labour costs.

BBC News Business 15 July 2013

What we are doing by **making** the bikes in London is **protecting** our intellectual property. It's brilliant, and it really works. Of course we sell bikes in **China**, so someone could buy one and try to reverse engineer it. But it is not that simple – the **complexity** of our manufacturing process is such that it is **not easy**.

Kirsty's

Breaking down operations through partnering

When Kirsty Henshaw went to appear on *Dragons' Den* (a television show in which entrepreneurs pitch their ideas to investors) in 2010 to get equity backing she knew exactly what she wanted. She asked for £65,000 in exchange for 15% of the business, but was happy to give away 30% because she wanted the involvement of two Dragons with experience and a network of contacts in this sort of business – Peter Jones and Duncan Bannatyne.

Kirsty was a 24-year-old single mother from Preston, Lancashire who left university before completing a Sports Therapy degree some two-and-a-half years before her appearance on *Dragons' Den*. She started her business, working from her kitchen, less than a year before appearing on television. Her son suffers from severe food allergies and intolerances and could not even eat an ice cream without becoming ill. Kirsty wanted a healthy, additive-free frozen dessert for her son, but found that there was nothing available from the supermarkets. Over a couple of years she developed two sorts of frozen dessert that not only tasted good but were low fat, low calorie and free from dairy, sugar, gluten, artificial additives, soya, cholesterol and nuts. One was eventually branded Coconuka and the other Coconice. She invested some £20,000 of her own money whilst holding down two jobs. Producing food for sale in the UK is not straightforward, and she took advice from her local Business Link, the Trading Standards Institute and the Food Standards Association. She had her packaging and a website developed through a £3000 government grant. And she only started producing her first products after she had secured distribution through a national wholesaler of health foods in December 2009. She also sold her products direct to customers through her website. But this was relatively small volumes which she batch produced in her own kitchen.

She knew that when she went to *Dragons' Den* looking for equity investment she would need, not only a track record of sales, but also evidence of potential and plans for how to meet predicted demand. She believed these products were unique and had national sales potential. But she also realized that she would face big problems with production and distribution on this scale. She therefore made two important operational decisions. Firstly, she decided that, to really make an impact, she must sell into the national supermarket chains and, secondly, that the only way she could meet this sort of demand would be to sub-contract production. Kirsty had no expertise in this sort of large-batch/line production and sub-contracting would allow her to focus on two important aspects of the business where she did have expertise – product development and sales. She also realised that, if (or when) the product was successful, competitors would soon copy her, so gaining market share with a branded product in the supermarkets as quickly as possible was vital.

Kirsty's sales in the months up to her *Dragons' Den* appearance had been some 2,500 units, giving her a profit of over £2,500. But the business plan she produced for the *Den* showed a profit projection of £300,000 for the year. The difference was a supermarket contract. Over a period of months Kirsty had visited buyers at Tesco, the largest supermarket chain in the UK, who tasted the product and liked it, confirming that it was indeed unique to the UK market. At the same time, it emerged that some staff at Tesco liked the product so much that they had been purchasing it online. Tesco offered to give the product a trial in their stores, so long as Kirsty could guarantee availability. Tesco would trial the product in 400 stores and each store would take 4 cases per week. Each case has 12 units and each unit has a margin of just over £1. The potential was obvious. So the next thing was to find somebody to produce the dessert for her. Always thinking big, Kirsty approached the largest ice cream manufacturer in Europe to see if they could manufacture these sorts of volumes. Using the name of Tesco to the full, the company agreed to produce the product, so long as she would guarantee the volumes.

So all the elements of the jigsaw puzzle were in place, but she decided that she now needed, not only some venture capital, but also some commercial expertise to help put these deals together and roll out the product – which is where the Dragons came in. Kirsty was looking not only for cash, but also some commercial and industry experience. Peter Jones provided the food

manufacturing, distribution and retailing experience she needed whilst Duncan Bannatyne, through his fitness clubs, provided an opening to a health food market that she had not yet tackled.

The first thing Peter Jones did was to negotiate the sub-contract deal with her manufacturer. They re-estimated first-year sales at some 1.5 million units, giving a turnover of £5 million. Sales have taken off since then and Kirsty's products are now available in all five leading UK supermarkets. Indeed, in 2013 her product range was extended to include a range of healthy ready-meals. The company also changed its name from Worthenshaws (the name it appeared under in the *Dragons' Den*) to Kirsty's.

You can find out more about Kirsty's on: www.kirstys.co.uk

Questions:

1. *From the information given, map out as much as you can of the business model for Kirsty's using the New Venture Creation Framework. What are the key elements of competitive advantage in this value proposition?*
2. *List the partnerships the company has and evaluate their importance.*
3. *Identify Kirsty's key operating activities and the risks the company faces. List the critical success factors.*
4. *What are Kirsty's growth options? How would you change the business model, going forward?*

Kirsty Henshaw

Kirsty's

The benefits of partnerships and strategic alliances

Numerous academic studies have shown that there are real benefits from strategic alliances and partnerships for organizations of all sizes. A government survey in the UK concluded that: 'in both the UK and the US, we observe that the highest growth firms rely *heavily* on building relationships with other firms, either through supply chains or through formal strategic alliances' (DBER, 2008, emphasis added). Alliances can create economic advantage by leveraging market presence (Lewis, 1990; Lorange and Roos, 1992; Ohmae, 1989). An example is Oneworld, a strategic alliance of a dozen airlines including British Airways and American Airlines whose primary purpose is to encourage passengers to use partner airlines. Alliances can also provide vertical integration and scale economies at a greatly reduced cost (Anderson and Weitz, 1992). In its simplest form this is the arrangement a distributor has with a manufacturer when they have sole distribution rights.

Anderson, E. and Weitz, B. (1992) 'The Use of Pledges to Build and Sustain Commitment in Distribution Channels', *Journal of Marketing Research*, 29 (February).

DBER (Department of Business, Enterprise and Regulatory Reform) (2008) 'High Growth Firms in the UK: Lessons from an Analysis of Comparative UK Performance', *BERR Economic Paper*, 3 (November).

Lewis, J.D. (1990) *Partnerships for Profit: Structuring and Managing Strategic Alliances*, New York: Free Press.

Lorange, P. and Roos, J. (1992) *Strategic Alliances: Formation, Implementation and Evolution*, Oxford: Blackwell.

Ohmae, K. (1989) 'The Global Logic of Strategic Alliances', *Harvard Business Review*, March/April.

Partnerships, strategic alliances and joint ventures

Partnerships, strategic alliances and joint ventures are ways of exploiting a business opportunity where you may not have all the skills or resources to pursue it yourself. In its simplest form, you might decide to sub-contract manufacturing or use a sales agent or distribution channels to sell your products. These are all forms of partnerships – where there is mutual advantage to be gained from some form of collaboration. The actual form of these collaborations can vary from informal to formal, underpinned by legal contract.

Partnering with others or organizations in setting up a new venture simplifies the operating tasks you face and mitigates your risks. Since assets are owned or contributed by all the partners, the financial resources needed and the associated risk are spread and flexibility is increased. True partners can become part of a team pursuing a particular opportunity, even though not part of the same legal entity. They can help you in unexpected ways and you can often leverage their capability and resources – to your mutual advantage. So, just as you try to develop relationships with customers, you should try to develop them with other business entities. View your suppliers as partners, rather than just suppliers of a resource. But there are a wide range of partners and partnerships.

imageSource

Strategic alliances are a form of partnership whereby separate organizations come together to pursue an agreed set of objectives. They can be an effective way of sustaining competitive advantage and are particularly important in relation to innovation, where the partners have different competences that they can apply in pursuing a commercial opportunity. There are often explicit strategic and operational motives for alliances, such as gaining access to new markets. Jaguar partnered with the Williams racing team in 2011 to produce a new hybrid electric/petrol supercar. Nokia partnered with Microsoft to rejuvenate its smartphone offering in 2012 with the Lumia. Some start-ups have based their international expansion strategy almost entirely on foreign alliances.

A more formal strategic partnership is called a joint venture. This usually has a degree of direct market involvement and therefore needs to be underpinned by some form of legal agreement that determines the split of resource inputs and rewards. Often the joint venture takes the form of a legal entity that is separate from either of the parties involved. Richard Branson has been particularly adept at using joint ventures as a basis for rolling out new business ideas. He partnered with Deutsche Telecom to create Virgin Mobile, and Singapore Airlines owned 49% of Virgin Airlines. Some developing countries do not allow foreign companies to set up in their country, only allowing joint ventures with local organizations.

The opticians and hearing-aid specialists, Specsavers, operate a contract-based, joint venture approach to retailing, tailored to professional practitioners, in this case opticians. It offers all the advantages of a franchise but gives the local operator greater professional autonomy and responsibility. Specsavers is now the largest chain of opticians in the UK and expanding rapidly in other countries.

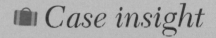 *Case insight*

Specsavers

Rapid roll-out through partnering

Specsavers was founded in 1984 by Doug and Mary Perkins. They started the business in their spare bedroom in Guernsey where they had moved after selling a small chain of West Country opticians. In the early 1980s the UK Government deregulated professional services, including opticians, allowing them to advertise for the first time. Doug and Mary seized the opportunity to try to launch a national chain of opticians. They opened their first stores in Guernsey and Bristol, followed rapidly by stores in Plymouth, Swansea and Bath. They wanted the company to establish its brand so that it would be seen as offering a wide range of stylish, fashionable glasses at affordable prices. They wanted Specsavers to be seen as trustworthy, locally-based but with the huge buying power of a national company that meant savings could be passed on to the customer. Now with over 1600 outlets worldwide and a turnover of £1.5 billion, Specsavers is the largest privately-owned opticians in the world, and the Perkins family are believed to be billionaires.

Specsavers has used an interesting joint venture approach to grow its business, a strategy which minimizes its capital requirements and the risks it faces. It enters into joint ventures with individual opticians, meaning that each joint venture is a separate legal entity. When the new company is formed, an equal number of 'A' shares and 'B' shares are issued. All the 'A' shares in the company are issued to the practice partners. All the 'B' shares are issued to Specsavers Optical Group. If there is more than one director in the business, for example an optometrist and a dispensing optician or retailer, then the 'A' shares are divided between the two parties. 'A' shareholders are delegated responsibility for the day-to-day running of the store. As 'B' shareholder, Specsavers provides supporting services, expertise, experience and information. As the number of practices has grown, so has the range of support services provided to practices, so that partners receive full support in all aspects of their business, tailored to their requirements. These can include property services, practice design, practice start-up, buying and distribution, retail training, professional recruitment as well as support in producing accounts, audits and tax returns. Individual opticians can sell on their 'A' shares, subject to certain conditions.

A typical joint venture start-up may cost in excess of £150,000, depending on location and practice size. In an equal partnership between two optician partners, each would be expected to provide the business with a loan of at least £20,000. Specsavers will match this loan. Specsavers Finance will provide a further 5-year loan for the remainder of the capital. Personal collateral is not required by Specsavers Finance to secure this loan. Specsavers and the partners sign a specific finance agreement. Loans are repaid from practice profits, sometimes within three years.

Specsavers claim the following advantages for opticians from this joint venture approach:

- A lower level of financial commitment from the opticians compared to a franchise.
- If targets are met the initial loan can be repaid from operating surpluses.
- Unlike a brand partnership, a joint venture partnership gives the partner the possibility of selling their shares in the future.
- The partner can end the relationship when they want.

Visit the website on:
www.specsavers.co.uk

Questions:

1. List the advantages and disadvantages of this form of joint venture to both Specsavers and their partners.
2. How is this different from a franchise? Is this important?

Franchising

Franchising is another form of partnership. A franchise is a business in which the owner of the name and method of doing business (the franchisor) allows a local operator (the franchisee) to set up a business under that name offering their products or services. For franchisors it is a way of rolling out a business format rapidly without the need for large amounts of capital. It is popular with franchisees who are less entrepreneurial but wish to run their own business.

Franchisors need a proven, robust business model with an infrastructure to support local franchisees. One key principle is that the franchisor shall have operated the business concept with success for a reasonable time, and in at least one pilot unit before starting the franchise network. In exchange for an initial fee (anything from a few thousand to hundreds of thousands of pounds) and a royalty on sales, the franchisor lays down a blueprint of how the business is to be run; content and nature of product or service, price and performance standards, type, size and layout of shop or business, training and other support or controls.

Franchisees expect a detailed operations manual and operating systems and hands-on help in their start-up. They pay all the costs of establishing the business locally. Since the franchise is usually a tried and tested idea, well-known to potential customers, the franchisee should have a ready market and a better chance of a successful start-up. Indeed only about 10% of franchises fail.

There are hundreds of franchises in the UK and tens of thousands of franchisees. Franchising can be an effective way of rolling out a business model quickly by leveraging the capabilities and capital of franchisees. Most established franchisors are members of the British Franchise Association, which has a code of conduct and accreditation rules, based on codes developed by the European Franchise Association. Table 10.7 summarizes the advantages and disadvantages of being a franchisee and a franchisor.

	Franchisee	Franchisor
Advantages	• Business format proved; less risk of failure • Easier to obtain finance than own start-up • Established format; start-up should be quicker • Training and support available from franchisor • National branding should help sales • Economies of scale may apply	• Way of expanding business quickly • Financing costs shared with franchisees • Franchisees usually highly motivated since their livelihood depends on success
Disadvantages	• Not really your own idea and creation • Lack of real independence • Franchisor makes the rules • Buying into franchise can be expensive • Royalties can be high • Goodwill you build up is dependent upon continuing franchise agreement; this may cause problems if you wish to sell • Franchisor can damage brand	• British Franchise Association rules take time and money to comply with • Loss of some control to franchisees • Franchisees can influence the business • Failure of franchisee can reflect on franchise • May be obligations to franchisee in the franchise agreement

T10.7 Advantages and disadvantages of being a franchisee or franchisor

Case insight

Ahmed Khan and McDonald's

Franchisees

In 2011 the average McDonald's in Britain turned over £1.5 million per annum. A McDonald's franchise costs £125,000–325,000 depending upon size and location (the average cost of a franchise in Britain is about £50,000) plus an additional one-off fee of £30,000. Monthly charges include rent, based on sales and profitability, a service fee of 5% of sales plus a contribution to national marketing (4.5% of sales in 2011). Terms are for 20 years (most franchises are for five), franchisees are not permitted to hold other franchises and there is a compulsory nine-month, unpaid, training programme for new franchisees.

Ahmed Khan left school at 18 to work in McDonald's in his home town of Southend-on-Sea. He became a supervisor and progressed until, at the age of 33, he bought his first McDonald's franchise for £240,000, using £60,000 of his own money and borrowing the balance from the bank. By the age of 44 he had five outlets in Newcastle-upon-Tyne.

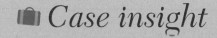

Having worked for McDonald's, I knew what someone could achieve by owning a franchise. The most appealing thing is the near-guaranteed profits, and the potential to expand. My dream is to own 10 or 15 stores.

Sunday Times 24 July 2011

The Body Shop

Rapid roll-out through franchising

Although The Body Shop is now owned by L'Oréal, the first store was opened by Anita Roddick in a back street in Brighton in 1976. It sold only about a dozen inexpensive 'natural' cosmetics, all herbal creams and shampoos, in simple packaging. Anita thought it would only appeal to a small number of customers who shared her values. Her husband, Gordon, even went off to ride a horse across the Americas about a month after it opened. But Anita was wrong. It proved to be a huge success. However, whilst this idea was novel at the time, it was easy to copy. The firm's initial roll-out owed much to Anita and Gordon Roddick's clear focus on where their competitive advantage lay. They realized that their idea could be easily copied and success would only come from developing the brand and a rapid expansion. Unfortunately they had little cash to do either. It was Gordon who had the idea of making The Body Shop a franchise, which meant that franchisees purchased the rights to open a The Body Shop store and manage the shop themselves. The Roddicks initially decided not to manufacture their products or even invest in a distribution system, but rather to concentrate on getting the franchise formula right, developing the brand and protecting it from imitators.

Today, The Body Shop remains an international franchised chain of shops. The Body Shop International Ltd is the franchisor. Traditionally, franchisees paid an initial fee plus an annual operating charge for a fixed term, for a renewable franchise. Franchisees would buy a 'turn-key' system with a tightly controlled retail format providing shop fitting and layout, staff training and a stock control system, even help with site identification. The Body Shop International, of course, would also make a margin on the products it sold to the franchisees. Franchisees receive regular visits from company representatives who provide assistance with display, sales promotion and training. Information packs, newsletters, videos and free promotional material are made available and franchisees return a monthly report on their sales. This enables the company to monitor both trading results and the local sales performance of individual products. The company closely monitors the use of The Body Shop's trademark in all franchisees' literature, advertising and other uses.

Visit the website on: www.thebodyshop.com

© loooby – istockphoto.com

Operating plans

The most important part of your business plan is a broad, 'high level' operating plan that identifies major linkages and critical paths. Below that you may have many more detailed action plans about things that are still important, but not to those who will read your business plan. The operations plan should produce a series of milestones – operating objectives that are measurable – and time deadlines for meeting them. Behind these will go a lot of detailed planning (and hard work) that do not show themselves in the business plan. We have split our operating plan into two parts: pre-launch – the things that need to be in place before you launch the business – and operations – the things you need to get right on a day-to-day basis.

Each major activity in the lists you will develop can be broken down into more detail, showing linkages and critical paths. The activities can then be ordered, with critical and high-risk ones scheduled as early as possible. Gantt charts are an excellent way of showing these linkages. Figure 10.1 (overleaf) is a highly simplified Gantt chart based upon the pre-launch key activities checklist for a retailer (Table 10.2), assuming the store location is already decided upon.

- Against each activity a block of time is drawn that represents the estimated length of time it will take to complete the task.
- The red arrows show the linkages between these activities.
- The black arrows indicate the critical path along which each activity must be complete before the next begins.

The critical path is the longest path through the diagram and is the shortest possible time to complete the task – in this case opening the store. Unless the time taken for tasks can be shortened, this will take 68 days. If any task along the critical path line overruns then the opening will be delayed. As you can see from the chart, the last two weeks of August and the beginning of September are congested periods of activity when staff are joining, stocking shelves and undertaking training prior to the store opening.

At the moment there is no slack built into these schedules. An added sophistication would be to build in fastest and slowest completion times and then check the effect on the critical path time. It is very easy to fit dates into the format. You can go on to assign responsibilities and costs for the various tasks, and then identify the risks that might delay completion of any activity. If this all seems a daunting task, there are computer programs that can help you with this sort of project planning.

You might produce a number of operating and action plans for different levels of your business. When it comes to what to include in the business plan, you need to identify your readers and provide a 'high level' plan showing key activities with your critical success factors in the operations plan. Break your 'high level' plans into pre-launch and operational activities. A simplified Gantt chart for these key activities will illustrate clearly what needs to be done and when. You can write a brief line-by-line commentary if needed. These key activities become your operational objectives – milestones in the development of your business. In our example, one milestone would be to open the first store on 9 September.

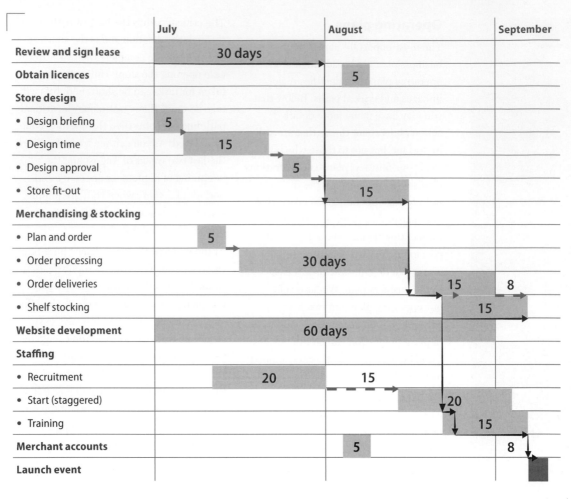

	July		August		September
Review and sign lease	30 days				
Obtain licences			5		
Store design					
• Design briefing	5				
• Design time		15			
• Design approval		5			
• Store fit-out			15		
Merchandising & stocking					
• Plan and order	5				
• Order processing		30 days			
• Order deliveries				15	8
• Shelf stocking				15	
Website development	60 days				
Staffing					
• Recruitment		20	15		
• Start (staggered)				20	
• Training				15	
Merchant accounts			5		8
Launch event					

F10.1 Gantt chart for opening a store

Summary

- You need to identify the key activities to be undertaken to ensure the success of your venture. Some will need to be completed pre-launch, some will be key operational activities that derive from your business model and its core value proposition.

- Your critical success factors are those key activities that you must get right to ensure the successful launch of your business.

- You need to identify the resource and operational implications of these key activities and develop detailed action plans as to how you will deal with them.

- A 'high level' operating plan provides details of the key pre-launch and operational activities and highlights the critical success factors. These key activities and their completion dates become your operational objectives.

- Key activities can be shown in a Gantt chart that shows linkages between activities and identifies the critical path. The critical path is the longest path through the chart and is the shortest possible time to complete the task.

- Partnerships, strategic alliances and joint ventures can be very important for new ventures, particularly in the context of innovation and market penetration. They can enhance your business model without requiring additional capital outlay by:

- simplifying operations;
- leveraging your knowledge and capabilities;
- spreading your risk.

- Franchising can be an effective way of rolling out a business model quickly by leveraging the capabilities and capital of franchisees.

Exercise 10.1

Building partnerships

1 List the areas of activity where some form of partnership is possible (partnership, strategic alliance and joint venture).

2 Alongside these areas:
- List the form(s) such a partnership might take.
- List the advantages and disadvantages of partnership.
- List any organizations or people that you might consider partnering with.

3 Decide whether you wish to investigate partnering with them and list the actions you need to undertake to make the final decision and possibly establish these partnerships.

4 Decide whether franchising is a possible format you wish to explore and list the actions you need to undertake to make the final decision. Establish the time scale for these actions.

Exercise 10.2

Identifying key activities and critical success factors

1 List the key activities that you need to undertake to ensure the success of your venture:
- pre-launch;
- ongoing, key operating activities.

2 List the resource and operational implications of these key activities.

3 Prepare Gantt charts for these activities and identify the critical paths, highlighting any bottlenecks and noting the implications.

4 List the risks that might cause the completion of critical path activities to be delayed.

5 Identify which of these key activities are your critical success factors.

6 Assign responsibilities and estimate costs.

7 Prepare a 'high level' operations pln.

Visit www.palgrave.com/companion/burns-new-venture-creation for chapter quizzes to test your knowledge and other resources.

PART 5

RISK AND STRATEGIC OPTIONS

11 Dealing with risk

www.palgrave.com/companion/
burns-new-venture-creation

The New Venture Creation Framework

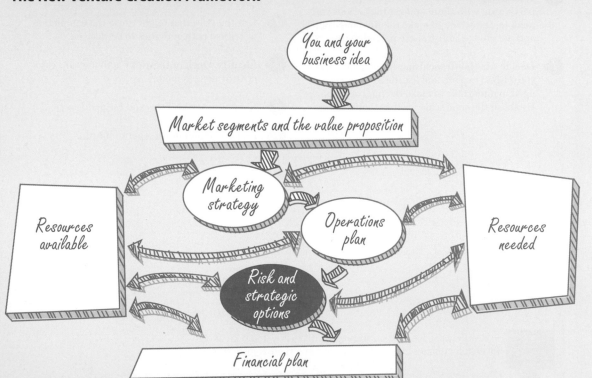

11
DEALING
WITH
RISK

Contents

Learning outcomes

When you have read this chapter and undertaken the related exercises you will be able to:
- Identify the key risks facing your business and the implications for how these can be managed
- Understand how generic strategies for reducing risk might be applied to your business (partnering, networking and the development of strategic options)
- Understand how the financial and legal structure you adopt might reduce risk
- Understand the importance of breakeven and the importance of keeping margins high and fixed costs low
- Identify the critical success factors for your business
- Identify strategic options for dealing with risks

Identifying risks

You cannot start a business without taking risks. By launching your business you are inherently making a judgement – explicitly or implicitly – that you can overcome any risks that you face. And whilst entrepreneurs accept risk-taking, they do not like it and will strive to avoid and minimize it. But have you really identified the risks that you face? How will you know if or when they materialize? And have you contingency plans to deal with them should they materialize? Anybody reading your business plan will expect that you have considered all these questions. Risk often goes hand in hand with return. The higher the returns your business offers the higher the risks that it is likely to face. So, just as financiers evaluate your financial projections (and the likelihood of achieving them), they also evaluate the risks that you face and your ability to deal with them.

Risk is inherent in business. Whilst it cannot be avoided, it can be managed – or, more accurately, identified and even quantified so that it can be managed down to acceptable levels. This might involve putting in place appropriate controls, or at least monitoring early warning of potential problems materializing. If risks can be avoided then less time is spent 'fire-fighting' when they materialize.

You start by trying to identify the key risks that you face. Of course you cannot hope to predict all eventualities but the more you try to anticipate them, the more you are able to generate both plans to deal with these risks and strategic options about the changes in direction that might result. Risk can take a number of forms. The risks associated with a particular course of action or achieving particular objectives might be identified, and also the corporate risks an organization faces. These risks may come from:

- **External incidents** (such as flood, fire and pandemic illness etc.) – These can be difficult to predict and the probability of occurrence might be low. However, the possible impact might be so great – for example, loss of life –that you need contingency plans to deal with them. Some of these risks will be generic to an industry, for example, the reaction of competitors. You should have identified these risks as part of your market/ industry analysis (Exercise 4.3).

- **Internal incidents** (such as the loss of sources of supply, malfunction of a major machine and product contamination etc.) – These can be many

and varied, depending on the operations of your business. You should have identified these risks as part of your identification of key activities (Exercise 10.2).

One approach that can be useful in identifying these risks is scenario planning (Chapter 4). Based on the threats the organization faces, you can explore scenarios about the results of these threats materializing. Table 11.1 gives you a checklist of possible risks that a start-up might face. It is not exclusive and in no particular order of priority. You should look back over the key activities checklists in the previous chapter to find any risks that are specific to your business idea. However, no matter how thorough your analysis, you can never expect to identify every possible risk. As has been said, the only two certain things in life are death and taxes (and one or two multinationals have been working to reduce the latter).

- Pre-launch delays – are any of the pre-launch key activities likely to cause delays?
- Competitors – what are they doing?
- Competitive advantage – is it being eroded?
- Market – how is it changing?
- Customer value proposition – is it being delivered?
- Product/service quality – is it adequate?
- Customer service – are they satisfied?
- Cash flow – is it adequate?
- Sales – are you meeting targets?
- Profits – are you meeting targets?
- Operations – are key activities under control?
- Productivity – is it meeting targets?

- Administration – are processes and procedures working well?
- Brand identity – is it being established?
- IP – is it secure?
- Technology – how are changes affecting you?
- Investment – do you need more?
- Stocks/inventory – are they adequate or too much?
- Merchandising – is it under control?
- Debtors/receivable – are they under control?
- Interest rates – how will changes affect you?
- Exchange rates – how will changes affect you?
- Management – are the team managing well?

T11.1 **Risks checklist**

STOCKBYTE

Identifying the risk is only the start of the process because not all risks are the same. Also important is the probability of the risk materializing. If the probability is very low is there any point in preparing contingency plans? The answer may be 'yes' – if the impact on your business is likely to be large. And then there is the question of how the risks can be reduced or avoided and what you need to do to monitor these risks. Effective risk management is therefore a five-stage process:

1. Identifying the risks (internal or external).

2. Evaluating the probability of the risk materializing.

3. Evaluating the impact if that risk materializes.

4. Deciding how the risk might be mitigated (reduced or avoided).

5. Deciding what early warning signs might be monitored to identify that the risk is materializing.

Assessing risks

Risk management is about prioritization, which will be decided from stages 2 and 3 in the risk-assessment process. Ideally the risks with the highest probability of occurrence and the greatest loss to the organization are handled first and those with the lowest probability of occurrence and the smallest loss are dealt with last. However, superimposed on this is the issue of whether the risks are controllable or not, and whether they can be mitigated in some way. Figure 11.1 shows a useful way of classifying risks along these three dimensions. Any risks that have a major impact on the organization are undesirable, but those which are very likely to happen pose the greatest danger (quadrant D). By way of contrast, risks with a low impact and a low likelihood of occurrence (quadrant A) pose the least risk. The third dimension is controllability. Some risks may be under your control or influence, others might be completely out of your control.

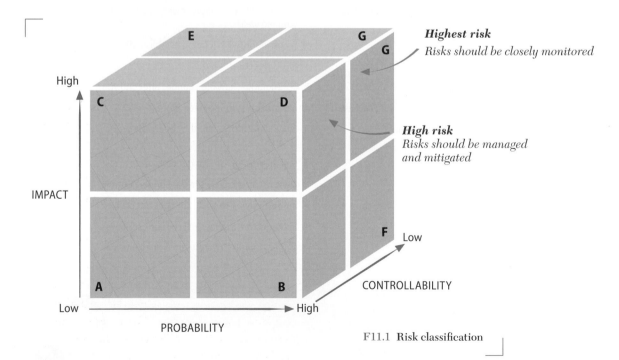

Highest risk
Risks should be closely monitored

High risk
Risks should be managed and mitigated

F11.1 **Risk classification**

Generally, the less you control or influence the risk, the greater the danger it poses. In this way the risk matrix resembles a Rubik's cube, with the greatest danger being in the cube with the highest impact, highest likelihood and least controllability (quadrant C). These risks cannot be mitigated but must be closely monitored. The risks that are very likely to happen and have a major impact on the organization but can be controlled (quadrant D) will be the focus of managerial action to mitigate them.

It is often very difficult to quantify the probability of a risk materializing beyond a simple low (1), medium (2) or high (3). The monetary impact of the risk materializing might be just as difficult to establish beyond a similar low (1), medium (2) or high (3). The composite **risk factor** is defined as the probability of occurrence multiplied by the impact of the risk event. Using the simple classifications above, the highest composite risk factor is therefore 9 (3×3) and the lowest is 1 (1×1). This 1 to 9 scale can then be reclassified as low (1–3), medium (4–6) and high (7–9). This is called a **risk index**. The higher the index number the greater the impact and the probability of the risk happening. These are the really dangerous risks. The question is, how might you control or mitigate them?

Mitigating risks

Once you have your risk index, you can decide what to do about the risks you face. You have four options:

1. **Attempt to eliminate the risk** – You might withdraw completely from the area of activity that generates the risk – an unlikely course of action initially for an entrepreneurial business. However, you need to at least continue to monitor these risks because at some point in the future you might change this decision.

2. **Attempt to reduce the risk** – You might increase internal controls, training or supervision depending on the nature of the risk. Alternatively, you might select strategic alternatives that are less risky. Many of these strategies might involve transferring or sharing the risk with others, for example by partnering.

3. **Transfer the risk** – There are many useful techniques that can be used to transfer both internal and external risks (e.g. insurance, foreign exchange or interest rate hedging). For example, companies constantly 'insure' against currency fluctuations – a risk they neither control nor influence – by buying forward in the currency market. As we saw in the last chapter, partnering in all its forms (e.g. sub-contracting, outsourcing, franchising etc.) is an extremely effective way of transferring risk. For example, when developing a new product, you might find ways of spreading the risk by working with strategic partners or forming strategic alliances. This will also diminish the resources needed to exploit the opportunity but it will almost certainly reduce the return that you achieve.

4. **Accept the risk** – You might simply accept all the risks in quadrant D. If you accept the risk completely, all you can attempt to do is plan to manage the risk and put in place early-warning indicators of it materializing, although this might be uneconomic if the impact on the organization is small. Many industries have inherent risks that need to be accepted if you decide to operate in that sector.

The riskiest situation in the risk cube is the one with a high likelihood of occurrence with a high impact in circumstances where you have little control (quadrant G). In this situation you might consider any of options 1 to 3, but even if you end up accepting the risk it is vital that you monitor it and then take corrective action if it materializes. Quadrant G probably represents the situation you might face with competitors if your business proves successful – and you really need to have some plans and strategic options to deal with this (option 2).

Monitoring risks

All organizations have to accept some residual risk associated with their operations. However, you will need to monitor those risks with the highest risk index numbers, particularly those that are least controllable. As we saw in Chapter 2, entrepreneurs are good at gathering information by networking with customers, suppliers and other professionals. And as we saw in Chapter 6, if you develop deep relationships with your stakeholders then you will receive knowledge and information from them. This can give you foreknowledge of risks materializing. You just need to be as aware of risks as you are of opportunities, and to ensure that you monitor them in a systematic way.

For those risks with the highest risk index numbers you need to identify parameters or events that indicate an increased likelihood of the risk materializing – called **key risk indicators**. These need to be monitored on a regular basis so you can then take remedial action. To be effective, key risk indicators must be easy to monitor as part of your regular activity, highlighting when corrective action is needed and providing guidance on what action is needed. Cash flow is an obvious simple example of a key risk indicator. The risk is bankruptcy – you need cash to pay your bills – and cash flow measures your ability to do this. Most start-ups need to monitor their cash flow on a regular and frequent basis. We deal with this in Chapter 15.

If the reaction of competitors is a major risk to your business you need to develop a risk indicator that will measure this, and put in place processes to ensure that it is monitored. For example, supermarkets regularly and routinely monitor the prices competitors charge for a typical basket of products. Without doing this they risk becoming uncompetitive and losing customers to rivals.

Generic strategies for managing risk

There are some generic strategies for managing risk. We have covered three important ones already:

* **Partnering** – in all its different forms, so as to spread the risk of any venture.

Lyn Lee, founder Awfully Chocolate BBC News Business 8 November 2010

We expanded very slowly and very carefully because in our other jobs we had some experience studying other industries, like the dot.com industry, which seemed to just sort of appear ... and then it just exploded... We basically put into it what we could afford and we were prepared that if it didn't work out we weren't going to be on the streets.

Affordable loss

Sarasvathy's (2001) paper on 'effectuation' (Academic Insight, Chapter 2) was later expanded in a book by Read et al. (2011). In this, they observed that entrepreneurs actually tended to go to market as quickly and cheaply as possible and assess market demand from that – an approach labelled 'affordable loss' but closely linked to the concept of lean start-up outlined in Chapter 3 (Ries, 2011). They set an 'affordable loss', evaluating opportunities based upon whether that loss is acceptable, rather than trying to evaluate the attractiveness of the predictable up-side. They decide what they are willing to lose rather than what they expect to make and therefore do not have to worry about the accuracy of predictions. Affordable loss can be calculated with some certainty, depending on your situation.

The challenge then is to leverage up your affordable loss through knowledge and partnerships and, only finally, through external finance to find a start-up strategy that is achievable. These partnerships can be with suppliers, who provide something you need, customers who may be interested in something you have to offer, or simply a friend who wishes to join you in the start-up. Ideally you need to find partners whose core competences and capabilities complement your own and then build on them. However, more importantly, they must self-select themselves as partners, which means the partnership may alter the venture in some ways. It is far better to have enthusiastic, voluntary partners who help drive the start-up than partners who have been 'sold' the relationship and are passive. Partners need to be dedicated and committed to the start-up.

Sarasvathy, S.D. (2001) 'Causation and Effectuation: Toward a Theoretical Shift from Economic Inevitability to Entrepreneurial Contingency', *Academy of Management Review*, 26(2).

Read, S., Sarasvathy, S., Dew, N., Wiltbank, R., and Ohlsson, A.V. (2011) *Effectual Entrepreneurship*, London: Routledge.

Ries, E. (2011), *The Lean Startup: How Today's Entrepreneurs Use Continuous Innovation to Create Radically Successful Businesses*, New York: Crown Publishing.

- **Networking** – with partners, so as to gain information and knowledge about risks. This gives you information about your key risks, how they might be mitigated and what you might select as your key risk indicators. Both networking and partnering are based on the strong personal relationships you are able to develop with stakeholders.

- **Strategic options** – Create as many as possible. This is contingency planning. One of the keys to dealing with risk is flexibility. The more flexible you are, with strategic options if things do not go as planned, the lower the impact.

There are also some generic strategies that apply to how you finance and structure your businesses:

- **Affordable loss and lean start-up** – The concept of affordable loss was introduced in the Academic Insight on 'effectuation' in Chapter 2. It is linked to the concept of 'lean start-up', presented as an Academic Insight in Chapter 3. The idea is to decide what loss is acceptable to you should the business fail (Exercise 2.3). This defines the maximum extent of your loss from the very beginning and helps shape the start-up in terms of its risk/return profile. It is a two-step

process: first, set your acceptable level of risk (affordable loss), then push to maximize the return this will make, as shown in Figure 11.2.

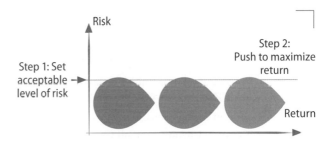

F11.2 **Setting risk and maximizing return**

Using lean start-up you can gain the maximum information about viability by small-scale market entry. As you gain more information, you might set higher levels of affordable loss. Lean start-up allows you to assess the viability of the business model you developed in Chapter 3. This is part of your 'commercialization risk' – the unique risk associated with developing a new product and insuring customer acceptance. You can also help to minimize your commercialization risk through the knowledge and information you gain by networking and partnering.

Richard Branson and Virgin (2)

Mitigating risk

Richard Branson is probably the best known entrepreneur in Britain. Now in his sixties, he started his business life as an 18-year-old schoolboy when he launched *Student* magazine, selling advertising space from a phone booth. His views on risk are interesting. In many ways he has been expert at minimizing his personal exposure. He launched *Student* by writing to well-known personalities and celebrities – pop and film stars and politicians – and persuaded them to contribute articles or agree to interviews. He persuaded a designer to work for no fee, negotiated a printing contract for 50,000 copies and got Peter Blake, the designer of The Beatles' *Sgt. Pepper* album cover, to draw the cover picture of a student. His first Virgin record shop was 'given' to him rent-free.

Branson's Virgin Group is made up of more than 20 separate umbrella companies, operating over 370 separate businesses. If any one were to fail it would not affect the others. Branson shares ownership with various partners. Virgin contributes the brand and Richard Branson's PR profile, whilst the partner provides the capital input – in some ways like a franchise operation – and often the operational expertise. However, Branson is not afraid to commit his own (or borrowed) money when needed, for example when Virgin Atlantic was re-privatized. Nevertheless, whilst he may tolerate risk and accepts that it goes with being entrepreneurial, he continues to try to mitigate it throughout his business empire.

- **Borrowing and bootstrapping** – One way of maximizing the return is by using other people's money as well as your own. So long as the return you are able to make on this investment exceeds the rate of interest you are paying then borrowing is a good option. However, when the reverse happens, you have to foot the bill and find the difference. And if the business should fail, it may be that you will have to repay the borrowing from your own personal funds. We shall deal with this in Chapter 14. It all comes back to the relationship between risk and return (or profit). If you want to minimize your risk, you will have to minimize your borrowings and this may affect your financial return.

  The reality is that the lower your external funding – including borrowing – requirement, the easier it is to start up and the less you might lose if the idea does not work. The funding you need is determined partly by the assets you need to start up (Chapter 10) and partly by your 'affordable loss'. There has got to be a way of bridging any gap. However, if you can minimize your commitment of resources for as long as possible you also minimize your funding requirement. This has implications for how you approach decision-making, but you also need to realize that you do not need to own a resource to be able to use and control it. You may be able to borrow or rent the resource (Chapter 14), or partner with others who provide it (Chapter 10). If you do not own a resource, you are in a better position to commit and de-commit quickly, giving you greater flexibility and reducing the risks you face. In the USA, minimizing the resources or assets that you own but still use and control is called 'bootstrapping'. To bootstrap you need to tap into as wide a network of contacts as possible.

- **Compartmentalizing risk** – Finally, many entrepreneurs compartmentalize their business risks by setting each operation up as a separate legal entity. Should one fail, it will not endanger another. Serial entrepreneurs do this as a matter of course, partly because they probably intend to sell off each business at some point in the future. But, less obviously, other businesses such as the Virgin Group operate as holding companies that own (or partly own) numerous subsidiaries.

One thing is certain in **business**; you and everyone around you will make mistakes. When you are pushing the **boundaries** this is inevitable – but it's important to recognise this. We need to look for new ways to shape up to the competition. So we trust **people** to learn from mistakes; blame and recriminations are pointless. A person who makes no **mistakes**, makes nothing.

Structuring your costs

As we saw in Chapter 5, high contribution margins (sale price minus variable cost) offer greater pricing discretion, which gives you the opportunity to price in different market segments differentially, thus maximizing sales volume. At the same time, low fixed costs mean lower risk of loss, should sales reduce. Both give you greater flexibility.

A combination of high margin and low fixed costs mean that you will have a low breakeven point. Breakeven is a very important concept. It is the point where a business stops making a loss and starts making a profit. It is an important measure of the financial risk your venture faces. The higher the breakeven point, the more sales you have to make to start making a profit and therefore the higher the risk you face. The lower the breakeven point, the less risk you face. Indeed, if the breakeven point cannot, reasonably, be expected to be achieved then the venture is probably not viable. Breakeven (expressed in £ turnover) depends on the fixed costs you face and the profit margins you are able to command:

$$\text{Breakeven point} = \frac{\text{Fixed costs}}{\text{Contribution margin}}$$

You will calculate your breakeven point once all your revenues and costs are determined, in Chapter 15. However, this simple formula emphasizes the two most important principles in any new venture that allow you to keep your financial risks as low as possible at start-up:

1. **Keep contribution margins high** – High margins decrease your breakeven point and lower your risk. As we have observed, high margins generally can only be achieved through strong differential advantage, and they allow you also to cut prices for different market segments.

2. **Keep fixed costs low** – The lower your fixed or overhead costs the lower your breakeven point and the lower your risk. However, high margins are usually associated with high fixed costs.

Since depreciation of fixed assets is likely to be a major element in your fixed costs, this re-emphasizes the need to keep the investment in assets as low as possible and, as we have observed, one way of doing this is by bootstrapping. **Operating gearing** is defined as the proportion of total costs represented by fixed operating or overhead costs. It should be kept as low as possible for a start-up.

Another major element of fixed costs is interest payments. High borrowings – perhaps to finance your investments – mean high interest costs, which are fixed and over which you have little control. In these circumstances interest payments could easily become a quadrant G risk in Figure 11.1. If turnover goes down, interest payments stay the same. Indeed, sometimes interest rates, and therefore interest payments, can go up when turnover, and therefore profit, goes down. This is the classic situation that is created when interest rates go up in order to decrease overall demand in the economy. The small firm faces a squeeze with higher costs and lower turnover. High financing costs are called high **financial gearing** or **leverage**. As already observed, borrowings should be kept as low as possible for a start-up.

Businesses with high operating or financial gearing (or both) need to make certain they achieve their sales targets. They have very little day-to-day influence over their fixed costs so their business imperative is to attract sufficient volume of customers – and that is about marketing and sales. A combination of high fixed costs and low margins is usually a recipe for disaster in a start-up.

Even if you keep your fixed costs low at start-up, they are bound to increase as your business grows. As they increase, your breakeven point will drift up and what is really important about the breakeven point is its position relation to turnover – how much your turnover must drop before you arrive at your breakeven point, measured by the margin of safety:

$$\text{Margin of safety} = \frac{\text{Turnover} - \text{Breakeven}}{\text{Turnover}}$$

The margin of safety (%) measures how far, proportionately, the business is above the breakeven point. It tells you the percentage reduction in sales that will bring you down to your breakeven point. The higher the margin of safety the better, because the firm is safer in terms of maintaining its profitability should sales suddenly decline. This reflects a number of factors: level of sales, contribution margin and fixed costs. It is therefore a simple but powerful piece of information that can be used to control a business as it grows. If the margin of safety can be maintained (or increased) as a business grows, despite the increase in fixed costs, it shows that the financial risks of the business are under control.

You will be expected to show your breakeven point and margin of safety in your business plan and you will calculate both in Chapter 15. You also need to demonstrate that the likelihood of achieving that margin of safety, through your marketing strategies, is high.

Thinkstock

Measuring breakeven point

The breakeven point is the point where a business stops making a loss and starts making a profit – where sales revenues are equal to the total costs. Some costs, often called overhead costs, are fixed costs – they do not change with the volume of activity or sales – for example, property lease/rental costs or fixed wages and salaries. These fixed costs are represented by the dotted horizontal line AB in Figure 11.3. Producing the product or delivering the service will mean incurring additional variable costs – costs that vary with volume such as materials and direct, piece-work labour costs. Every time an additional unit is produced and sold, an additional cost is incurred. Line AC therefore represents the total cost of producing the product or delivering the service – the fixed cost plus the variable cost. Over large volumes, this line may curve downwards as the effects of economies of scale are felt. Line LM represents the revenue generated by sales – sales volume multiplied by unit price, often called turnover. At volume X all costs are covered by revenue. This is the breakeven point. If your target sales volume is Y, this will generate the profit represented by the distance between lines LM and AC (total sales – total costs).

The breakeven point, expressed in £ turnover, can be easily calculated without a diagram using the formula:

$$\text{Breakeven point} = \frac{\text{Fixed costs}}{\text{Contribution margin}}$$

Contribution per unit is the difference between the sales price and the *variable* cost of each unit you sell. Total contribution is the difference between turnover and your *total variable* costs. Contribution margin = contribution *per unit* ÷ sales price *or total* contribution ÷ turnover, usually expressed as a percentage. Where you are selling a range of products/services with different margins the calculation using total sales and variable costs is easier to apply.

For example (assuming target sales of 1000 units per week):

Sales price per unit	£10
Variable cost per unit	£6
Contribution per unit	£4
Contribution margin	0.40 or 40%
Turnover (per week)	£10,000
Total variable costs	£6,000
Total contribution	£4,000
Contribution margin	0.40 or 40%

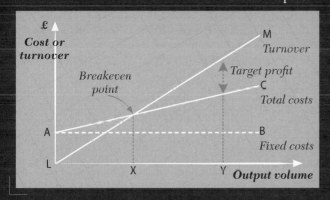

F11.3 **Breakeven point**

Once above the breakeven point, each £1 of sales contributes £0.40 (40%) to profits. If you start with a profit rather than a sales target you can use the breakeven point to work out the level of sales you need to achieve this. Dividing your profit target by your contribution margin tells you how much above the breakeven point you need to be.

For example, if your target profit is £4,000 per week (rather than £2,000 as above) then your sales target would have to be:

$$\frac{£4,000}{0.40} = \frac{£10,000 \text{ } above}{breakeven} = \frac{£15,000}{(1500 \text{ units})}$$

You can check this:

Sales	=	£15,000
Total contribution @ 40%	=	£6,000
Total fixed costs	=	£2,000
Profit	=	£4,000

If your fixed costs are £2,000 per week, your total profit will be £2,000 (£4,000 – £2,000).

$$\text{Breakeven point} = \frac{£2,000}{0.40} = \frac{£5,000 \text{ per week}}{\text{(or 500 units @ £10 each)}}$$

You can check this calculation:

Breakeven point	500 units @ £10	=	£5,000
Total variable costs	500 units @ £6	=	£3,000
Total contribution		=	£2,000
Total fixed costs		=	£2,000
Profit			nil

🧳 *Case insight*

Mitigating risk

In the early 1990s Robbie Cowling started JobServe in his spare time from his bedroom by finding out what contract work was available locally and sending the list to subscribers. It was the world's first 'Jobs by Email' service delivering a handful of jobs to just over a dozen email addresses. This was followed within the first year by the world's first recruitment website which, very quickly, had some 3000 subscribers. At this point Alan's job as an IT consultant with the Ministry of Defence was relegated to four days a week – he was nothing if not cautious. Soon the business started spilling out of the bedroom. This was the point at which he decided to dedicate himself to it full-time. He decided that he needed to move to a bigger house, which he also used as an office. Only one year later did he decide that the business had

grown sufficiently to warrant taking the risk of moving to a dedicated office of its own.

JobServe currently operates in 17 industry sectors and advertises jobs from all over the world. It employs more than 80 staff working from its purpose-built headquarters in Tiptree, Essex, as well as offices in Colchester, Hixon and Swindon in the UK and Sydney in Australia. Jobserve advertises more than 2.5 million jobs a year and 'Jobs by Email' is now sent immediately when requested, more than 800,000 emails a day. JobServe's website receives more than 10,000,000 hits a month from more than 70,000 unique visitors. And Robbie Cowling is a millionaire – at least on paper.

Up-to-date information on Jobserve can be found on their website: www.jobserve.co.uk

⬛ *Case insight*

Gordon Ramsay

Business models and risk

Gordon Ramsay is a famous TV chef with hit shows in the UK and USA such as *Hell's Kitchen*, *MasterChef*, *Kitchen Nightmares* and *Hotel Hell*. But that did not stop his business, Gordon Ramsay Holdings, nearly failing in 2010/11 because he adopted the wrong business model with the wrong business partner. Most celebrity chefs license a partner such as a restaurant chain to use their name. They lend their name, create menus, hire key staff and undertake some promotion. In return the chef receives a fee plus a percentage of turnover. However Ramsay set up and operated all the restaurants around the world himself and paid rent to the restaurant chain – potentially more lucrative but also more risky. This meant that his capital costs, and therefore borrowing, were very high and, when the recession of 2008 hit, his fixed interest costs could not be met by his operating profits. What is more, often Ramsay committed to spend time at these restaurants – time that he did not have because of his TV appearances.

The result was a loss of £4.1 million in 2011, which meant that the company breached its loan agreements. Ramsay also fell out spectacularly with his father-in-law, Chris Hutcheson, who used to run the firm, accusing him publicly of siphoning off £1.4 million of company funds to support a secret family. After an acrimonious court battle, Ramsay bought Hutcheson's 30% stake in the firm, costing the company some £5 million. Ramsay had then to inject £2.5 million of his own money into the company to prevent it from going into bankruptcy.

Ramsay found a new partner, Stuart Gillies, who took 10% of the company. Many of the restaurants around the world were closed and the debt was repaid. The business model was also changed to one that is more conventional and lower risk. The company no longer puts up capital. It takes a fee for Ramsay's name and between 6% and 8% of turnover. Ramsay takes no salary and his media earnings, which exceed £15 million a year, go through a separate company. Ramsay spends most of his time working on TV and books to create the brand that pulls customers into his restaurants. As a result of these changes, profits of Gordon Ramsay Holdings Ltd have started growing again.

Source: Adapted from 'Hell's Kitchen, MasterChef, Kitchen Nightmares and Hotel Hell', *The Sunday Times Magazine*, 14 July 2013.

Decision-making

As we observed in Chapter 2, one characteristic associated with the way entrepreneurs make decisions is their incremental approach. This makes sense in an uncertain world. Each step in the decision-making process gains them more knowledge and delay can increase flexibility, thus reducing risk.

The breakeven point is also a useful technique in helping you make business decisions about expenditure. It can tell you how much additional sales you need to generate to pay for, and hence justify, a fixed cost expenditure. It will not make the decision for you but it does provide you with valuable information to help you make a judgement.

$$\text{Extra sales needed} = \frac{\text{Increase in fixed costs}}{\text{Contribution margin}}$$

So for example, if you are considering an increase in advertising expenditure of £10,000 and your contribution margin is 40%, the extra sales needed to justify the expenditure are:

$$\frac{£10,000}{0.40} = £25,000$$

Breakeven analysis is a simple but powerful technique. This simple principle can be applied to all sorts of decisions that involve increasing fixed costs, including hiring the extra employee as you grow. The consequence of increasing your costs is that you have to pay for this by increasing your sales. If your employees are salaried this is an increase in your fixed costs and the fewer employees you have, the more relevant this calculation. The only way you can avoid this is by paying them on results through commission or piece work, or by offering them a share in ownership of the business.

The breakeven point is invaluable information that must go into your business plan. It also helps you to monitor risk as the business grows and provides information on which to base business decisions, including pricing. It is important to understand the cost structure of your business and to calculate its breakeven point.

Made.com

Business models and risk

Made.com is an online furniture store. It was set up by Ning Li, a serial entrepreneur with experience of selling furniture in France, where he imported furniture from China. Made.com works directly with designers to custom-make exclusive products for customers. Putting the furniture retail market online has helped revolutionize what he calls a 'dusty industry' where retailers were reluctant to take risks with new designs and designers. The internet changed that, allowing experimentation with minimal risk and improving the speed of response to changing trends.

If a new **designer** comes to see us with a new **amazing** table that looks risky, we say 'Why not?' because the only risk that we have is taking the photo. We put it online, if it doesn't sell, we pull it off. And if it sells, then **everybody wins** ... The internet allows us to launch products **much faster** than traditional business ... Speed is king ... The speed of designing new products and also **renewing** your catalogue is key... to keep people's **interest**... keep them coming back to the website.

BBC News Business
3 November 2011

Dealing with risk

231

Made.com

Made.com founders from left to right: Chloe Macintosh (Creative Director), Ning Li (CEO), Julien Callede (COO)

Smak Parlour

Business models and risk

Abby Kessler and Katie Lubieski met at Drexel University while studying design and merchandising. They moved to New York to work in the garment industry but soon returned to Philadelphia to design and sell edgy t-shirts to some 20 stores around the city. In 2005 they opened a fashion boutique in the Old City district of Philadelphia selling affordable clothing and jewellery targeted at trend-conscious women. It was successful and they thought about expansion, but the high costs and risks put them off until they heard about 'fashion trucks' in Los Angeles. These are simply box trucks that have been turned into mobile shops, and follow a trend in mobile vending which was started in the USA by gourmet-food-trucks.

The cost of the truck is $20,000–30,000 and it costs about $70,000 to make the truck into a shop (including air-conditioning, fit-out, changing room, skylight and stocks), depending on what you want. But the overhead costs are then very low. You do not have to apply for leases or utilities, only the vehicle

Abby Kessler and Katie Lubieski

running costs (insurance, fuel etc.) and parking permits (anything from free to $1,000 per day, depending on location). And you can take the shop to the young customers the company targets, advertising its daily location to a loyal customer base on social media sites. You can also visit fairs, festivals and conventions.

Mia Holley

Risk, critical success factors and strategic options

In the last chapter you identified and analyzed your key pre-launch and operational activities (Exercise 10.2). You can now apply the risk management framework from this chapter to those activities. Your critical success factors should be the key activities falling into quadrant D and G in Figure 11.1 – high risk and high impact. If they are controllable, you need to prepare an action plan – decide what actions are required and who is responsible for undertaking them, and establish time-lines for their completion, as outlined in the previous chapter. However, you also need to prepare some strategic options – the actions you need to take if these critical factors do not go according to plan. This is particularly the case if you have highlighted any critical success factors over which you have little or no control, for example with competitive reaction. Thinking through 'worst-possible' cases in advance of them happening allows you to prepare contingency plans rather than trying to react after the event (see scenario planning in Chapter 4).

So far we have only applied this framework to the down-side risks facing your business launch. It can also be applied to your growth strategies, developed in Chapter 8, and the up-side 'risks' they face. However, in this case by 'risk' we mean 'chance of success'. In other words, you would be seeking to identify those strategies with the highest impact and the highest chance of success, over which you have greatest control (quadrant D again). What are the critical success factors for achieving your growth options developed in Exercise 8.1, who is responsible for undertaking them and what are the time-lines? You can even use the Gantt chart technique to help you plan this. And what are the strategic options you face if things do not go according to your plans?

Your success will depend on your ability to mitigate and manage both the commercialization and more general business risks you face – both pre- and post-launch. The key risks you face need to be highlighted in the business plan. How you deal with them will lead to the development of your critical success factors, underpinned by detailed action plans, and strategic options. Both critical success factors and strategic options need to also be highlighted in your plan. This framework can equally be applied to your growth options. Successfully dealing with critical success factors are key milestones for a business. They are things to be celebrated when they have been achieved.

Clippy

Mitigating risk at start-up

Calypso Rose graduated from a technical theatre course at a drama school and got a job in television production. It was while she was working in this job that she made the first see-through bag with pockets to display her collection of Polaroid photographs. She never intended to start a business, but so many people asked where they could buy something similar that she started thinking about the possibility. When her parents offered to lend her £2000 to make the first 250 bags she decided to take the plunge, aged just 22, and Clippy was born.

Calypso decided to work from home to keep her overheads and breakeven low. Her mother, Clare, also helped with the business, so she did not have to hire any employees. She found a UK manufacturer through Kelly's online directory, deciding that this was better than going to China to find a supplier. The UK manufacturer could turn around orders more quickly and, once she established a track record, would offer normal trade terms for payment, thereby helping her cash flow and reducing her risk.

Initial sales were mainly to family and friends – many of the people who had asked where they could buy the first bag. The official launch of Clippykit (now called Clippy) was at Olympia's Spirit of Christmas Fair in 2004. She established a website, customized a large bag with a sign saying 'stop me and buy one' and took a small market stall on the Portobello Road in London to see if her business idea would work. She had done everything she could to minimize her risks and now she wanted to see if the bag would sell. She sold all 250 bags in the first month. Working from home and only using the initial £2000, she managed to build a turnover of £180,000 in the first year. At the age of 22 she was voted London Young Business Person of the Year.

Calypso was worried from the start that the idea could be easily copied – after all it was just a plastic bag with pockets for photographs – and that a bigger company with more resources could roll out an imitation product more effectively than her. So her idea was to push sales as quickly as possible and also to establish a fashion brand. A major breakthrough came when the fashionable Notting Hill boutique, Coco Ribbon, decided to sell her bags. Things got even better when celebrities such as Helena Bonham Carter, Jools Holland and Jamie Oliver started carrying Clippy bags. The bags have even been used as a 'goody bag' at the Brit Awards and the Orange Prize.

It also became clear early on that the concept behind the bags was flexible and could be applied to other products like make up bags, lamp shades, wallets and umbrellas. Another development was that the products themselves could be personalized and Calypso started offering kits to help people do that.

Calypso has been very adept at promoting the product herself. For example, in 2009, working with an enterprise organization called Make Your Mark, 650 girls in London took part in a competition to personalize a Clippy bag with an issue that was relevant to them.

The range of Clippy products has grown. With a turnover of over £500,000 in 2010, Calypso employs two full-time and one part-time staff. The bags are sold through conventional wholesale and retail markets – through about 250 independent boutiques. They are sold as fashion items and promotional products, often customized for the promotion event. However, about one-quarter of sales come from the website which shows how the products can be used, hosts competitions and has a Calypso blog. You can also sign up for a regular newsletter.

Questions:

1. From the information given, map out as much as you can of the business model for Clippy using the New Venture Creation Framework. What are the key elements of competitive advantage in this value proposition?

2. List the things Calypso did to mitigate her risks. What were the down-sides to this?

3. What are her growth options? How would you change her business model, going forward?

Clippykit

Calypso Rose

Visit the Clippy website on:
www.clippykitlondon.co.uk

Summary

- Risk management involves five things:
  1. Identifying the risks (internal or external).
  2. Evaluating the probability of the risk materializing.
  3. Evaluating the impact if that risk materializes.
  4. Deciding how the risk might be mitigated (reduced or avoided).
  5. Deciding what early warning signs need to be monitored to identify that the risk is materializing.

- Risks come from internal and external incidents. You need to identify the highest risks you face and put in place the appropriate procedures to monitor the associated key risk indicators.

- You can analyze risk by the probability of it occurring and the impact it will have, and develop a risk index. You can then decide on the degree of control you have over it.

- There are four ways of dealing with risk:
  1. Attempt to eliminate it.
  2. Attempt to reduce it.
  3. Transfer or share it.
  4. Accept it.

- There are a number of generic strategies to reduce risk. Partnering with others can be used to spread your risk. Your network of professional contacts can be used to bring you knowledge and information, including early warning of risk materializing. You can develop strategic options about what to do if the risks do materialize – the more, the better.

- Your financial structure also affects your risk. Decide on your 'affordable loss' and keep external funding to a minimum by bootstrapping. It may be possible to compartmentalize risk by setting up different parts of the business as separate legal entities.

- The breakeven point measures the risk the business faces. It is the benchmark above which the business starts to make a profit.

- Any increase in costs (e.g. an extra employee or an increase in advertising) has to be paid for by an increase in sales. You can use breakeven analysis to calculate the increase you need.

- A new venture needs to keep its contribution margin as high as possible and its fixed costs as low as possible.

- Critical success factors are the key activities that are crucial to the success of your venture. Strategic options are the contingency plans you have in place should things go wrong.

- The key business risks you face need to be highlighted in the business plan. How you deal with them will lead to the development of your critical success factors, underpinned by detailed action plans, and strategic options. Both critical success factors and strategic options need to be highlighted in your plan.

- The risk management framework can equally be applied to analyzing up-side risk and your growth options.

Exercise 11.1

Reviewing generic strategies to reduce risk

1 Review your pricing decisions from Exercise 5.2 in the light of this chapter. Amend the exercise, as appropriate.

2 Review Exercise 2.3. Write down your 'affordable loss' both in financial terms (financial capital put into the business plus guarantees) and in social terms (e.g. reputation etc.).

3 List the physical and human assets that will be needed to set up the business. Alongside each, estimate the cost/value and whether they can be:
- bootstrapped;
- sourced from partners (review Exercise 10.1);
- leased/rented;
- purchased.

4 From this, estimate the minimum and maximum pre-launch cash investment needed by you. Reflect whether this can be phased in any way. Compare your final figure to your 'affordable loss'. Reflect on this and consider whether it is acceptable.

Exercise 11.2

Risks – critical success factors and strategic options

1 Review Exercise 10.2 and assign a risk index to each key operation. Identify your highest-risk key activities. Decide on which are controllable and which are not.

2 Review the Gantt charts and action plans prepared as part of Exercise 10.2 to see whether they need amending in the light of your risk analysis.

3 Prepare a consolidated list of all the critical success factors you have listed from past exercises (4.3.4, 5.4.2). Ensure that responsibilities have been assigned to guarantee these actions are undertaken successfully.

4 Identify milestones that will establish when the critical success factors are achieved.

5 Develop strategic options that demonstrate the actions you need to take should the risks materialize and your plans to deal with them are not successful.

6 Identify any early-warning signs that need to be monitored and define related key risk indicators.

7 Amend your 'high-level' operations plan to reflect the above, as appropriate.

Exercise 11.3

Growth – critical success factors and strategic options

1 Review Exercises 8.1 and 8.2. Assign an 'impact/probability' index to each growth option. Identify your highest 'impact/probability' key activities. Decide on which are controllable and which are not.

2 Develop Gantt charts and action plans for the options you want to pursue – the ones with the highest 'impact/probability' index.

3 Prepare a consolidated list of all the critical success factors you have listed from previous exercises (8.1.5, 8.2.4 and 8.3.4). Ensure that responsibilities have been assigned to guarantee these actions are undertaken successfully.

4 Identify milestones that will establish when the critical success factors are achieved.

5 Develop strategic options that identify the actions you need to take to exploit these options and the actions you need to take should the options fail to materialize.

6 Amend your 'high-level' operations plan to reflect the above, as appropriate.

Visit www.palgrave.com/companion/burns-new-venture-creation for chapter quizzes to test your knowledge and other resources.

PART 6
RESOURCES

www.palgrave.com/companion/
burns-new-venture-creation

The New Venture Creation Framework

You and your business idea

Market segments and the value proposition

Marketing strategy

Operations plan

Resources available

Resources needed

Risk and strategic options

Financial plan

12
BUILDING
YOUR
TEAM

Contents

Learning outcomes

When you have read this chapter and undertaken the related exercises you will be able to:

- Identify the challenges facing a new venture as it grows and how they might be overcome
- Assess the skills needed for your business and how these might be met
- Understand the different ways of employing people and how to go about recruiting them
- Draw up a job description and person specification
- Understand the benefits of using different sorts of professional advisors
- Understand the factors that determine the selection of an effective team and identify your preferred Belbin team roles
- Creatively address how your business should be structured given its size, the tasks to be undertaken and the environment in which it operates, and how this might change as it grows
- Critically analyze the balance between managerial control and autonomy, and understand how to manage staff that need greater autonomy
- Describe the culture you want in your new venture and understand the managerial tools available to construct it
- Understand how to create an entrepreneurial business by constructing an entrepreneurial architecture

People, people, people

Every business is primarily about people – as customers, suppliers and as employees. Many start-ups do not employ anybody initially, but the only way you will grow is by recruiting appropriate staff, including managers, to deliver your product/service to more customers. Selecting, developing and managing staff will become a key activity for you – something many entrepreneurs have a problem with. With more than one founder, the issue of working with the other partners, so as to become an effective management team, can be just as challenging.

As your business grows you will face challenges and problems that mean you need to adapt and change. You will need to metamorphosize into an entrepreneurial leader. There are a number of models that seek to describe the challenges that you will face as the business grows. They emphasize the need to put in place an effective management team. You will need to recruit reliable managers, delegate to them and control and monitor their performance. The organization will have to become more formal, without becoming

> 'People, people, people' is the **mantra**. If you don't have the right staff, fire them quickly. Be **nimble** and act on your **convictions**.
>
> Gururaj Deshpande, serial entrepreneur and founder Sycamore Networks *Financial Times* 21 February 2000

> The **ability** to find and hire the right people can **make or break** your business. It is as plain as that. No matter where you are in the life cycle of your business, bringing in **great talent** should always be a top priority … The right people in the right jobs are instrumental to a company's **success**.
>
> Michael Dell, founder Dell Corporation *Direct from Dell: Strategies that Revolutionized an Industry* (1999, New York: Harper Business)

bureaucratic. You will need more structure. Your role should also change from being tactical – involved in everyday activities – to being more hands-off and strategic. The more rapid your growth, the more difficult this will be. And all of these changes need to be properly managed alongside the day-to-day delivery of customer service. It is little wonder that so few firms grow to any size. Some entrepreneurs even decide not to grow their business because they realize they cannot manage these changes or because they prefer to move on to another start-up.

You can learn from the case insights that you are not alone in facing these challenges, and also how best to cope with them. This chapter will look at building and controlling your team. The next chapter will look at how you might become an entrepreneurial leader as the business grows.

> You **delegate** but you obviously have got to have that **hands-on** approach for a while, and then you **develop people** that will eventually take over from you.
>
> Divine Ndhlukula, founder Securico, Zimbabwe *BBC News Business* 6 July 2012

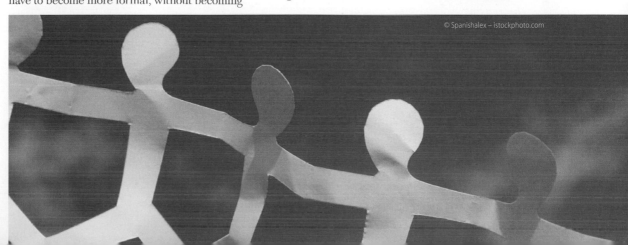

The challenges of growth

The challenges faced by new, growing ventures have been highlighted by a number of growth models. One of the most widely used was developed by Greiner back in 1972. It offers a framework for considering the development of a business, but more particularly the managerial challenges facing the founder. Each phase of growth is followed by a crisis that necessitates a change in the way the founder manages the business. If the crisis cannot be overcome then the business risks failure. The length of time it takes to go through each phase depends on the industry in which the company operates. In fast-growing industries, growth periods are relatively short; in slower-growth industries they tend to be longer. Each evolutionary phase requires a particular management style or emphasis to achieve growth. Greiner's model predicts four crises, shown in Figure 12.1:

1. Leadership – Growth initially comes through creative opportunity-seeking. However, this growth leads to a crisis of leadership as staff, financiers and even customers increasingly fail to understand the focus of the business – where it is going, what it is selling – and resources become spread too thinly to follow through effectively on any single commercial opportunity. Your challenge is to give direction by effective leadership. We return to what this means in the next chapter.

2. Autonomy – Entrepreneurs have a strong internal locus of control, which means that there is a danger they will try to do everything themselves. Not only do they delay recruiting staff, partly because they are careful in managing cash flow, but when they do, they find it difficult to delegate. Your challenge is to develop an effective management team, and delegate to them.

3. Control – There is a danger that delegation becomes an abdication of responsibility and there is a loss of proper control. As we shall see later in this chapter, there is a balance to be achieved between autonomy and control. Your challenge is to coordinate decision-making through appropriate organizational structures and a culture that balances autonomy and control, and encourages collaboration.

4. Bureaucracy – As the business becomes larger, the danger is that it might lose its entrepreneurial drive. The challenge is to facilitate collaboration – making people work together through a sense of mission or purpose rather than by reference to a rule book. Overall you need to develop an organization that balances the need for autonomy and control, avoiding too much bureaucracy.

Greiner, L.E. (1972) 'Evolution and Revolution as Organizations Grow', *Harvard Business Review*, July/August.

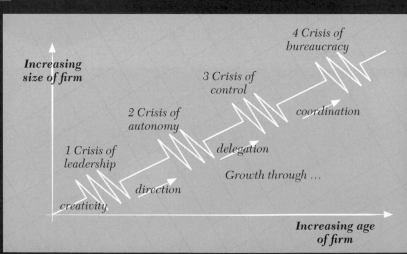

F12.1

Greiner's growth model

Source:
Adapted from Greiner, L.E. (1972) 'Evolution and Revolution as Organizations Grow', *Harvard Business Review*, July/August.

Recruiting people

STOCKBYTE

Recruiting the right new venture team – yourself, other founders, key employees and advisors – is crucial to the success of your business. The bigger the new venture the more important the team. Team members can bring a range of skills, capabilities, knowledge and networks that complement and leverage your own. Industry experience can be vital in a new venture, particularly if the experience comes from a competitor – which is why Yahoo! recruited Marissa Mayers as its President and CEO in 2012. Mayers was one of Google's earliest employees and had been Vice President of Search Products. It might take time to attract everyone you need, and you might even have to launch the business with some key posts not filled. It is important that you recruit the best people, but plug any skill gaps in some way.

You start by developing a **skills profile** for the business and identifying where the gaps exist. You might do this pre-launch and, say, for three years' time. These are operational skills and therefore depend on the nature of your business (Chapter 10). However, you will also need to have coverage of the core functional disciplines of business – sales, marketing, accounting etc. You may also be looking for specific market or industry skills. Depending on the size of your start-up, you may have to be flexible and live with a degree of overlap and indeed cope with some gaps, at least in the short term. It is therefore useful to classify the skills in your profile as 'key', 'important' or 'desirable'. Recruiting appropriate people with key skills, particularly pre-launch, may be a critical success factor (Chapter 11).

You can recruit people to work on a number of different bases:

- **Full/part-time** – Not all people want to work full-time and, for a start-up, each full-time employee can represent a large increase in fixed costs. So, employing part-time staff can be attractive, particularly if they are willing to work shifts and infill to meet customer demand.

- **Regular hours/shift work** – Office workers might expect to work regular 'nine-to-five' hours, but in many industries, such as hospitality, shiftworking is the norm and part-time work is common. The determining factor here is what is required to provide the necessary customer service.

- **Fixed-wage or salary/commission/piece work** – Employing full-time, fixed-wage or salary employees increases the fixed costs of your venture. Whilst this may be necessary to attract the 'right' sort of person – particularly your management team – many types of jobs or even industries have different ways of working. Sales people expect part of their remuneration to come from commission or bonuses based upon meeting their sales targets – the more they sell, the more they earn. Some workers expect to be paid on a piece-work basis – they are paid for the volume they produce.

At some point you will probably be expected to draw up a **job description** for each employee, listing the things they have to do and what they will be held accountable for in this role. This can be problematic in a small, growing business where the nature of the tasks to be undertaken can change from day to day and over time. However, job descriptions can be made flexible, although in some countries employees expect quite detailed and specific job descriptions. For example, the Swedish home furnishing store, IKEA, does not give employees job titles or precise job descriptions, and this created a major problem when it first launched in the USA, where employees are used to clear roles and responsibilities. The resulting high staff turnover rates caused IKEA to change its recruitment processes so as to highlight the company's culture and values. Prospective employees who were not comfortable with this could therefore withdraw during the process.

Based upon the list of duties in the job description, you can then produce a **person specification** that lists the criteria on which to base selection of the person. This is an important document against which you can assess the suitability of a candidate for a post. Table 12.1 gives you a checklist of things that might go into a person specification. You can split these into 'essential' and 'desirable'. In most countries employees expect to be given a **contract of employment** which lays down their terms and conditions of employment. In the UK this must be done within two months. What goes into this contract is laid down by law. There are also a plethora of regulations and laws that regulate how you recruit, employ and dismiss employees.

- Educational attainment
- Experience (e.g. retail sales)
- Knowledge (e.g. marketing)
- Skills/abilities (e.g. team-working)
- Personal attributes (e.g. flexibility)
- Personal characteristics (e.g. friendly)
- Personal circumstances (e.g able to work evenings)

T12.1 **Person specification checklist**

Finding and attracting people

Finding and attracting a new venture team is rarely straightforward. Why should they join a risky start-up, particularly if they have a secure job in an established company? The answer lies in part with your persuasive power but also with the remuneration package you offer them. You may be short of cash to start with, but if you are successful there should be plenty of money to go around later on. So the answer may be to offer incentives such as target-linked bonuses, shares or share options. Most of the really successful start-ups, like Apple, have distributed shares to key managers early in their development.

Sometimes the new venture team will share the ownership of the business between them from the start. The share each has might reflect the cash, intellectual property or simply the time and effort they have put in to get the business off the ground –

called 'sweat equity'. The terms of a shareholders' agreement should specify how this is done, as well as anticipating future issues facing the founders. A shareholders' agreement only applies to those signing it, while the articles of association govern all future shareholders. Typical topics included in such an agreement are shown in Table 12.2.

Whatever the package you put together, you will need to seek out your potential team. Your network of contacts is always a good starting point – family, friends and professional contacts. You may need to advertise (see Chapter 7). However, rather than using the traditional media such as newspapers, an increasingly important mechanism is social media. You can use your Facebook or LinkedIn account to broadcast to friends or contacts that you are setting up a team and what skills, capabilities and knowledge you are seeking. Some companies use Twitter for recruiting. Once you have people interested in joining your team, you need to shortlist those that meet your person specification and then interview them to fully assess their suitability.

Sometimes, no matter what the incentive, you may be unable to find the 'right person' for the role you have identified. In these cases it may be possible to 'buy in' these roles through professional advisors.

- Nature of the business
- Identity, role and title of founders
- Legal form of business
- Distribution of shares between founders
- Consideration paid for shares or ownership share of each founder (for cash or other consideration)
- Intellectual property signed over to company by founders
- Rights to appoint and remove directors
- Dividend policy
- Terms to protect minority shareholders
- Terms regulating the raising of capital (to avoid diluting existing shareholding)
- Conditions affecting founders regarding the valuation and disposal of shares, including buy-back clauses
- Other limitations on directors' and/or shareholders' freedom of action
- Resolution of disputes between shareholders

T12.2 **Typical topics included in a shareholders' agreement**

Professional advisors

Getty

There are likely to be gaps in the professional knowledge and skills of any start-up. Professional advisors can be an invaluable source of this knowledge, skills and advice, as well as providing an additional network of contacts for the founders. They might be persuaded to join a start-up for many reasons. They may simply be friends or family, willing to help because of the relationship with the founders. They might relish the challenge of helping a start-up. Professional advisors can also be hired or, in some cases, paid for by other bodies such as government. The types of professional advisors you might employ include accountants, lawyers and business consultants.

> **Sunday Times 1 February 2009**
> Have great **advisers** and listen to them. You don't have to take their **advice** but it's **valuable** to have other voices.
> *Sara Murray, founder Confused.com*

Accountants – Accountants can help produce your financial plan (Chapter 15). They can then help produce your regular financial statements and assist with analyzing and interpreting them. Often they have access to industry financial norms that you can use to benchmark your performance. Indeed, the whole financial administration of your business can be sub-contracted, including the issuing of sales invoices and collection of cash, the payment of purchase invoices and payroll administration. Accountants also offer tax advice and will handle the filing of information with appropriate bodies. They usually have a network of contacts who can help with finance, from loan to equity capital. Every business needs to succeed financially in order to remain viable, and having reliable accounting information is vital. The more ambitious your aims for your venture, the more likely you are to need good financial advice early on.

> **Bill Gates, founder Microsoft** *Business @ the Speed of Thought (1999, New York: Time Warner)*
> The business side of any company **starts** and **ends** with hard-core analysis of its numbers. Whatever else you do, if you don't understand what's happening in your business **factually** and you're making decisions based on anecdotal or **gut instinct**, you'll eventually pay a big price.

Lawyers/attorneys – Lawyers can help with anything involving the law. They can advise on the legal requirements of establishing the form of business organization you select or the various business licences or permits you might require. They can advise on safeguarding your business idea. They can help you draw up legal contracts – with staff, partners, suppliers or customers. They can be invaluable in drawing up a shareholders' agreement for the founding team. Often, like accountants, they have a network of contacts who can help with finance, from loan to equity capital, and sometimes they offer tax services. However, also like accountants, good lawyers can prove to be expensive, so it is always best to understand how they charge their fees before they start any work.

Business consultants – General business consultants can offer advice on marketing or strategic planning. They can help you draw up your business plan. Often they can provide access to other sources of help and advice, particularly at a local level, including specialist advice on specific industries or topics such as exporting. Local consultants can also provide invaluable access to local networks of other owner-managers and providers of capital. Some consultants might be 'free', paid for by government schemes to help small firms. In the UK this is provided through the Business Link network. In the USA it is provided by the Small Business Administration through its Small Business Development Centers.

Using advisors on a 'pay-as-you-go' basis can offer an attractive way of accessing a range of knowledge, skills and networks that a new venture might not be able to afford to employ on a full-time basis. The relationship with these advisors might be informal or formal – relying on a contract for service. Skills gaps can also be addressed through:

- Your board of directors (Chapter 9)
- Different forms of partnership (Chapter 10);
- Equity investors, such as Business Angels (Chapter 14).

However they are used, new ventures can benefit by surrounding themselves with high-quality advisors to tackle the challenges they face. They add to the credibility of the management team and can persuade providers of finance to invest. The more ambitious your start-up the more important this is.

This range of ways of meeting your need for people and the knowledge, skills and networks that they bring is summarized in Figure 12.2.

Selecting and developing your team

Selecting an effective team will depend upon the skills profile you develop and the individual job descriptions and person specifications. However, personal chemistry between members of the team is also important. For a team to be effective individuals need to have the right mix of a certain

F12.2 Meeting your skills needs

set of personal characteristics. Meredith Belbin identified nine clusters of personal characteristics or attributes which translate into 'team roles', each with positive qualities and allowable weaknesses: three with a 'thinking' orientation – plant, monitor evaluator and specialist; three with a 'people' orientation – coordinator, team-worker and resource investigator; and three with an 'action' orientation – shaper, implementer and completer-finisher. Individuals are unlikely to have more than two or three of these clusters of characteristics, yet all nine need to be present in a team for it to work effectively.

The **best** teams stand out because they are teams, because the individual members have been so truly integrated that the team **functions** with a single spirit. There is a constant flow of mutual **support** among the players, enabling them to feed off strengths and compensate for weaknesses. They depend on one another, trust one another. A manager should **engender** that sense of unity. He should create a **bond** among his players and between him and them that raises **performance** to heights that were unimaginable when they started out as **disparate** individuals.

Alex Ferguson, former Manager
Manchester United Football Club
Managing My Life
(1999, London: Hodder & Stoughton)

Selecting a team: team roles

Developing a successful team depends not just on the range of professional skills it has, but also on the range of personal characteristics – the chemistry of the team. Based upon research into how teams work, Meredith Belbin (1981) identified nine clusters of personal characteristics or attributes which translate into 'team roles'. Most individuals are naturally suited to two or three roles. However, to work effectively a team must comprise elements of all nine roles. If a team lacks certain 'team roles' it tends to exhibit weaknesses in these areas. The roles are:

Thinking orientation

Plant – This is the team's vital spark and chief source of new ideas – creative, imaginative and often unorthodox. However, they can be distant and uncommunicative and sometimes their ideas can seem a little impractical.

Monitor-Evaluator – This is the team's rock – introvert, sober, strategic and discerning. They explore all options and are capable of deep analysis of huge amounts of data. They are rarely wrong. However, they can lack drive and are unlikely to inspire or excite others.

Specialist – This is the team's chief source of technical knowledge or skill – single-minded, self-starting and dedicated. However, they tend to contribute on a narrow front.

People orientation

Coordinator – This is the team's natural chairman – mature, confident and trusting. They clarify goals and promote decision-making. They are calm with strong interpersonal skills. However, they can be perceived as a little manipulative.

Team-worker – This is the team's counsellor or conciliator – mild mannered and social, perceptive and aware of problems or undercurrents, accommodating and a good listener. They promote harmony and are particularly valuable at times of crisis. However, they can be indecisive.

Resource Investigator – This is 'the fixer' – extrovert, amiable, six phones on the go, with a wealth of contacts. They pick other people's brains and explore opportunities. However, they can be a bit undisciplined and can lose interest quickly once initial enthusiasm has passed.

Action orientation

Shaper – This is usually the self-elected task-leader with lots of nervous energy – extrovert, dynamic, outgoing, highly strung, argumentative, pressurizes people into seeking ways around obstacles. They do have a tendency to bully and are not always liked. However, they generate action and thrive under pressure.

Implementer – This is the team's workhorse – disciplined, reliable and conservative. They turn ideas into practical actions and get on with the job logically and loyally. However, they can be inflexible and slow to change.

Completer-Finisher – This is the team's worry-guts, making sure things get finished – sticklers for detail, deadlines and schedules. They have relentless follow-through, picking up any errors or omissions as they go. However, they sometimes just cannot let go and are reluctant to delegate.

Chell (2001) suggested that the 'prototypical entrepreneur' might be a mix of all three orientations – 'thinking', 'people' and 'action': plant (creative, ideas person), shaper (dynamism, full of drive and energy) and resource investigator (enthusiastically explores opportunities). She then suggested that the first team member to recruit should be an implementer (reliable, efficient and able to turn ideas into practical action). The implementer will need a completer-finisher (conscientious, delivers on time), a team-worker (cooperative and unchallenging) and possibly a specialist (with particular knowledge or skills) working under them.

You can download the Belbin Team Roles questionnaire from: www.belbin.com

Belbin, R.M. (1981) *Management Teams – Why They Succeed and Fail*, London: Heinemann Professional Publishing.

Chell, E. (2001) *Entrepreneurship: Globalization, Innovation and Development*, London: Thomson Learning.

The challenge is to select the team and then to build cohesion and motivation. In most cases this involves building consensus towards the goals of the firm, balancing multiple viewpoints and demands. However, too great a reliance on achieving consensus can lead to slow decision-making, so a balance is needed that will strain the interpersonal skills of the leader. In the best entrepreneurial firms leadership seems to work almost by infection. The management team seem to be infected by the philosophies and attitudes of the founder and readily buy into the goals set for the firm, something that is helped if they share in its success.

Successful entrepreneurs build strong relationships with their team. Personal relationships are based upon trust, and trust is the cornerstone of a good team and an effective organizational culture. It is imperative that the management team trust you. This involves having transparent vision and values, being firm but fair, flexible but consistent. It involves being straightforward – doing what you say and meaning what you say: 'walking-the-talk'. It involves being open and spontaneous, honest and direct – being an authentic leader. Whilst always placing the interests of the firm first, it also involves being supportive of individuals and having their wellbeing at heart. Trust takes time to build and needs to be demonstrated with real outcomes, but can be lost very quickly by careless actions and then takes even longer to rebuild.

Gajus – Fotolia.com

Building the organization structure

Informal – Entrepreneurs tend to manage staff through their strong personal relationships, rather than through hierarchy and structure. They prefer informal organization structures and the power of influence rather than rigid rules and job definitions. They often persuade and cajole staff, showing them how to do things on a one-to-one basis, rather than having prescribed tasks. This reflects itself in the culture in the organization. The most typical organization structure seen in a small-scale start-up is the **spider's web**, shown in Figure 12.3. The founder sits at the centre of the web with each new member of staff reporting to them.

This is a very efficient structure that can respond quickly and flexibly to change. The uncertainty and rapid pace of change in a start-up probably means that rigid rules and structures would be out of date quickly. What is more, in a small firm everybody has to be prepared to do other people's jobs

F12.3 **A start-up web organization structure**

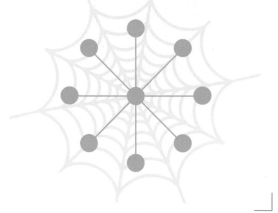

because there is no cover, no slack in the system if, for example, someone goes off sick. The web is perfectly flat and therefore efficient – overheads are reduced. It is responsive – communication times are minimized. It works for up to about 20 staff. Beyond that it becomes increasingly inefficient.

What is more, the spider's web lends itself to meddling by the entrepreneur at the centre, who might be inclined to set up informal reporting lines that bypass managers (Figure 12.4). So, the spider's web will not work for large start-ups or later, as the business grows.

F12.4 **A growing web structure**

- - - - - Informal reporting lines

Hierarchy – The larger an organization the greater the need for a hierarchical structure. It creates order and allows coordination of complex tasks. Hierarchy is the fundamental feature of organizational structure, not only for humans, but for all complex systems. It gives managers confidence that they have the authority to manage and allows coordination, cooperation and specialization. Figure 12.5 shows a simple hierarchical structure with four interactions. This can be contrasted to a self-organizing structure without hierarchy in Figure 12.6, where there are ten interactions between the same number of people. Simple hierarchy offers fewer interactions and relationships to manage. However, whilst this

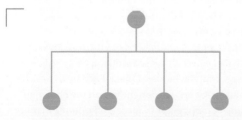

F12.5 Simple hierarchy

may be efficient it says nothing about the quality of the interactions and the hierarchy structure can discourage collaboration and sharing of knowledge.

As an organization grows more structure can be put in place. However, there is no one 'best' structure. Figure 12.7 shows a classic hierarchical structure. Functional groups, such as marketing, production and accounting, might be formed into hierarchical departments, coordinated through central control. This fosters stability and encourages efficient, rule-driven operation. It shows individuals that there is a career path within their department. When a business grows beyond a certain size there is a tendency for it to adopt a divisional structure – representing different product or market groupings. Each division might then have its own departmental structure within it. Divisions might be legally separate companies.

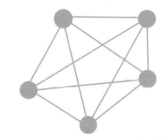

F12.6 **Self-organizing team**

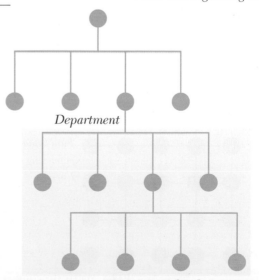

Department

F12.7 **Hierarchical structure**

An issue with any hierarchy is the span of control within it. Some hierarchies have 'tall' structures with more managers, each having a narrower span of control (fewer people reporting to them). Others have 'flat' structures with fewer layers of management, each having a wider span of control (more people reporting to them). The taller the structure and narrower the span of control, the more managers are required. The tendency over recent years has been to delayer – to flatten structures and increase managers' span of control. Technology, in particular the internet, has made this easier. Some Japanese manufacturing companies have only four layers of management; top, plant, departmental and section management. You need to decide on the structure of your start-up and that, primarily, will depend on the number of people you want to employ.

Matrix – A business that has multiple products, functions or geographic locations still needs to coordinate activities across all these dimensions. The organizational structure used to aid this is the matrix structure, shown in Figure 12.8. People have multiple reporting lines – to their functional manager (e.g. accounting) and their geographic or product manager. This was popular among large organizations in the 1960s and 1970s but has become far less common as the excessive complexity and slow responsiveness to change became apparent. Nevertheless, Starbucks still uses a matrix structure, combining functional and product-based divisions, with employees reporting to two managers.

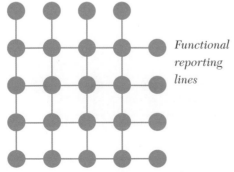

Geographic/product reporting lines

Functional reporting lines

F12.8 **Matrix structure**

Team-working – The matrix blueprint is also the basis for bringing together informal self-organizing project teams (Figure 12.6) from different departments, divisions or geographic parts of an organization. It is used extensively in businesses that seek to encourage creativity and innovation, particularly in technology-based firms such as Apple and Google. They bring together different functional disciplines, foster communication and interaction and can be highly flexible. Teams are also used to allow informal coordination within the formal structures, for example, within multinational companies that need to maintain functional consistency between geographic locations. One company that makes extensive use of project-based team structures with a minimum of top-down direction is Gore, the manufacturer of the famous hi-tech Gore-Tex fabric. Employees (called Associates) apply to or are asked by other team members to join particular teams. They elect team leaders, decide upon their own goals and manage themselves.

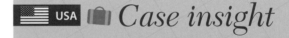

USA *Case insight*

Google

Team-working

Google operates in a fast-moving commercial environment that values innovation and swift action. It has a flat, decentralized organizational structure with lean hierarchies and is highly democratic and tightly interconnected. Each manager has about twenty people reporting to them. It also has an informal culture with low job specialization, emphasizing principles rather than rules and horizontal communication. Staff are allowed 20% of their time to work on new projects. All of the staff involved in product development work in small teams of three or four people. Larger teams get broken down into smaller sub-teams, each working on specific aspects of the bigger project. Each team has a leader that rotates depending on the changing project requirements. Most staff operate in more than one team.

Controlling people

The more staff you employ the greater the need for formalizing the control you have over them. Most organizational control systems are aimed at minimizing risk and uncertainty and promoting efficiency and effectiveness. The degree of control you exert on the people in your business should reflect not only your own philosophy, but also the core value proposition on which your business is based. If yours is a low-cost/price business model then you may need to be highly efficient and controls may need to be tight. By definition, a highly efficient organization has no slack. Everything is tightly controlled, every penny accounted for, all jobs are defined and individuals made to conform. This environment leads to high degrees of efficiency.

However, the degree of control you exert also depends on two other factors: task complexity and the environment in which the business operates. The simpler and more repetitive the task, the easier it is to impose control and the less the need for initiative. Similarly, the more stable the environment, the less the need for initiative. But rigid control stifles initiative and inhibits entrepreneurship and therefore the more complex the task, the greater the need for autonomy. Similarly, the more change in the environment, the greater the need for autonomy. This is shown in Figure 12.9.

Quadrant 1 – A machine bureaucracy is one with hierarchical structures and tight controls. It is most appropriate where the organization is tackling simple tasks with extensive standardization, in stable environments, and/or where security is important and where plans and programmes need to be followed carefully. Well-developed information systems reporting on the production/processing activity need to exist for it to be effective. Power is centralized. It is more concerned with production than marketing and is good at producing high volumes and achieving efficiency in production and distribution. It is appropriate for the continuous and line production typologies outlined in Chapter 10.

Quadrant 2 – As the environment becomes more changeable, standardization becomes less viable and responsibility for coping with unexpected changes needs to be pushed down the hierarchy. Staff are usually given more autonomy, although within guidelines. The structure needs to be responsive to change – although hierarchical, it is relatively flat with few middle-management positions. A matrix sub-structure (teams) can be used to tackle unexpected projects. Culture is important because the workforce needs to be motivated to make frequent changes to their work practices. It is appropriate for the jobbing and batch production typologies outlined in Chapter 10.

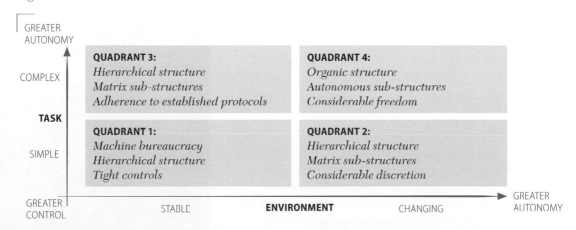

F12.9 **Structure, change and task complexity**

Quadrant 3 – Complex tasks performed in stable environments mean that it becomes worthwhile to develop standard skills to tackle the complexities. The matrix can be an effective sub-structure within a hierarchical organization. The matrix team can work on their complex tasks within set protocols – as they do, for example, in a surgical operation. In a changing environment the matrix team must have a higher degree of autonomy because established protocols may be inappropriate to the changing circumstances, even for the simple tasks they face. It is appropriate for the jobbing and batch production typologies outlined in Chapter 10.

Quadrant 4 – In a changing environment where there is high task complexity an innovative, flexible, decentralized structure is needed, often involving structures within structures. Authority for decision-making needs to be delegated and team-working is likely to be the norm with matrix-type structures somehow built into the organization. Staff autonomy becomes far greater. Clear job definitions should never lead to a narrowing of responsibilities so that people ignore the new tasks that emerge. This is often called an 'organic structure' – one with a highly flexible, ever changing structure with limited hierarchy; one which places greater emphasis on personal relationships and interactions than on structures; one in which power is decentralized and authority is linked to expertise, with few bureaucratic rules or standard procedures. In many ways, far more important than the formal organization structure for a firm of this sort is the culture that tells people what needs to be done and motivates them to do it – a truly entrepreneurial firm. It is appropriate for project production typologies outlined in Chapter 10.

Whilst these principles may seem straightforward, their application in practice can be difficult, particularly in the context of a growing business. As with most areas of management, there are no set rules and their application involves judgement. However, the less stable and predictable the environment you operate in and the more complex the tasks you face, the greater the autonomy you should give your staff and the more important is organizational culture, rather than structure, in giving them direction.

Balancing the degree of control with the need for autonomy in a start-up facing a changing, uncertain environment ultimately boils down to finding the appropriate 'balance' for different members of staff. However, entrepreneurial firms generally need looser control (or staff with greater autonomy) with tighter accountability for meeting targets and objectives. As you grow, you can then afford to establish operating divisions or subsidiaries with different structures, different degrees of control and different cultures.

Autonomy and motivation

Dan Pink (2011) highlighted autonomy as a major motivational influence on individuals undertaking cognitive (compared to mechanical) tasks involving complexity or creativity. He argued that self-direction and autonomy are important motivators if you want people to be innovative, engaged with their tasks and proactive rather than just compliant. Creative people like autonomy. They are also motivated by 'purpose' – a reason for doing something based, not upon monetary remuneration, but upon a wider vision of what the organization can achieve – and 'mastery' – the challenge of completing a complex or creative task

So if autonomy is a motivator, the dilemma is the amount of autonomy to give. Too much, and anarchy or worse might result. Too little, and creativity, initiative and entrepreneurship will be stifled. The answer, provided by Julian Birkinshaw (2003), is 'balance'. He outlined the model used by BP to help guide and control entrepreneurial action: direction, space or slack, boundaries and support. All four need to be in balance. If they are too tight they constrain the business, but if too slack they might result in chaos. This is shown in Figure 12.10.

Academic insight

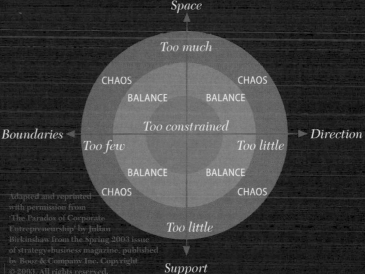

F12.10 Control vs autonomy

Space — Too much — CHAOS — BALANCE — *Too constrained* — CHAOS — BALANCE — *Direction* — *Boundaries* — *Too few* — *Too little* — BALANCE — BALANCE — CHAOS — CHAOS — *Too little* — *Support*

Direction – This is the company's broad strategy and goals. Managers should have scope to develop the strategy for their own operating unit, in line with the company's general direction, values and mission. Pink agrees, saying creative people need a strong sense of 'purpose' which is not just about making profit. Birkinshaw gives two pieces of advice on getting this balance right:

- Set broad direction and re-evaluate periodically as markets and the environment change.
- Let the company's strategy inform that of the unit and the unit's inform that of the company.

Space or slack – This is to do with the degree of looseness in resource availability – monetary budgets, physical space and supervision of time. In a tightly run, highly efficient organization there is no time or other resources to think, experiment and innovate. Creative organizations require a degree of space or slack to allow experimentation. 3M allow researchers to spend 15% of their time on their own projects. Google allow 20%. However, if employees are given too much space they run the risk of losing focus on the day-to-day detail of the job and it can be wasteful. Birkinshaw's advice is:

- Goal-setting should be carefully managed and clear and specific, but individuals should be given freedom in how the goals are to be achieved.
- Individuals should be allowed to learn from their own mistakes.

Boundaries – These are the legal, regulatory and moral limits within which the company operates. But rigid rules that are not shared beg to be circumvented. Boundaries should come from your values – which are shared by your staff. Not having boundaries courts extreme danger, particularly if breaking them might lead to the failure of the organization. Birkinshaw's advice is:

- Identify critical boundaries that, if crossed, threaten the survival of the organization and control them rigorously.
- Manage other boundaries in a non-invasive way through training, induction, codes of conduct and so on.

Support – This refers to the knowledge transfer systems and training and development programmes you provide to help managers do their job. Systems should encourage knowledge sharing and collaboration. Training and career planning should be top-down. Both should, however, be discretionary. The danger here is that knowledge will not be shared and there will be little collaboration, encouraging managers to go their own way. On the other hand, if there is too much support the manager will be 'spoon-fed' and initiative stifled. Birkinshaw's advice is:

- Put in place enough support systems to help managers and ensure they know where to go for help.
- Systems should encourage collaboration.

Birkinshaw, J. (2003) 'The Paradox of Corporate Entrepreneurship', *Strategy and Business*, 30.

Pink, D. (2011) *Drive: The Surprising Truth About What Motivates Us*, New York: Riverhead.

Creating a culture for your venture

Organizational culture is about the unspoken, prevalent norms, basic beliefs and assumptions about the 'right' way to behave in an organization. It can be more important for a start-up than any formal structure it adopts because it manifests itself in the way people are inclined and likely to behave rather than the way they are supposed to behave. As the founder of your venture, you profoundly influence its culture – either consciously or unconsciously. It is grounded in your basic beliefs and values, and these ought to underpin your mission and vision (Chapter 6). How you go about constructing the culture of your business is based upon three influences: cognitive processes, organizational processes and behaviours. All these influences are represented in Figure 12.11.

Cognitive processes – These are the beliefs, assumptions and attitudes that staff hold in common and take for granted. They are embedded and emanate from the firm's philosophy, values, morality and creed. They generate norms of behaviour – rules or authoritative standards. They are strongly influenced by what the founder of the organization really pays attention to and what they actually do – not just what they say. But the important point is that they take time to frame. They do not happen overnight.

Organizational processes – These can be deliberate or just emerge, evolving organically, perhaps in an unintended way. There are many influences on this:

- Leadership styles – These send signals about appropriate behaviour. How you treat people, react to situations, even allocate your time, sends powerful signals about priorities.

- Organizational structures – Hierarchical organizations can discourage initiative. Functional specialization can create parochial attitudes and send signals about which skills might be valued. Flat, organic structures with broader spans of control and frequent use of teams encourage creativity, innovation and entrepreneurship.

- Controls and rewards – People take notice of which behaviours get rewarded (as well as which get punished) and behave accordingly. If salaries are based mainly on sales bonuses and there is a monthly league table of the best sales people, what does this tell you about the firm, its values and its goals? Criteria used for recruitment, selection, promotion and retirement are all important. Status, praise and public recognition are powerful motivators.

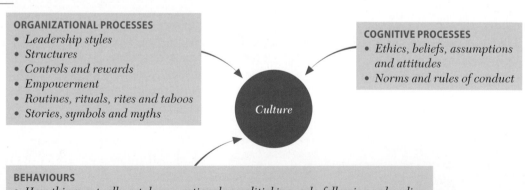

ORGANIZATIONAL PROCESSES
- *Leadership styles*
- *Structures*
- *Controls and rewards*
- *Empowerment*
- *Routines, rituals, rites and taboos*
- *Stories, symbols and myths*

COGNITIVE PROCESSES
- *Ethics, beliefs, assumptions and attitudes*
- *Norms and rules of conduct*

Culture

BEHAVIOURS
- *How things actually get done – rational vs politicking, rule-following vs bending*
- *Vocabulary – job titles, slogans, metaphors, signals, gossip*

F12.11 **Influences on organizational culture**

- Empowerment – The power to make (or not make) decisions sends defining signals. Flat, decentralized structures with delegated decision-making send signals about encouraging local decision-making, although sometimes informal power can lie outside formal hierarchies. The reaction to failure is an important message in this.

- Routines, rituals, rites and taboos – These form the unquestioned fabric of everyday life, and say a lot about the organization. 'Guarded' or 'open' management offices, reserved or unreserved parking spaces, dress codes, normal methods of communication all influence culture.

- Stories and symbols – Who are the heroes, villains and mavericks in the firm? What do staff talk about at lunch? Are there symbols of status that are important such as car or office size? How do staff talk about customers, other key managers and even you? These stories and symbols perpetuate a culture.

Behaviours – This is what actually happens in an organization. It decides whether outcomes are rational, transparent or the result of politicking. It influences whether the organization does actually follow rules, or is about bending them in the appropriate circumstances. Behaviour is also about vocabulary – job titles, slogans, metaphors, signals, even gossip. Language is laden with value judgements that we do not realize most of the time – but they subconsciously influence the culture of the organization. To cement an organizational culture, behaviours must be congruent with the other influences and consistent with your organizational structures and your leadership style.

Even if you do not actively try to create a culture one will emerge anyway. If it is the wrong one you have nobody else to blame. However, having the 'right' culture can help you manage the business and achieve success. So, what culture do you want to create in your business and what are the behaviours you wish to encourage that will reinforce this?

STOCKBYTE

Tony Fernandes and AirAsia (2)

Management style

Tony Fernandes set up AirAsia in 2001. An article in *The Economist* ('Cheap, but Not Nasty', March 2009) made a number of observations about his management style and its effect on the company's culture, saying that 'he came to the industry with no preconceptions but found it rigidly compartmentalized and dysfunctional. He wanted AirAsia to reflect his own unstuffy, open, and cheerful personality. He is rarely seen without a baseball cap, open-neck shirt and jeans, and he is proud that the firm's lack of hierarchy (very unusual in Asia) means anyone can rise to do anyone else's job. AirAsia employs pilots who started out as baggage handlers and stewards; for his part, Mr. Fernandes also practises what he preaches. Every month he spends a day as a baggage handler, every two months as a cabin crew, every three months as a check-in clerk. He has even established a "culture department" to "pass the message and hold parties".'

Tony Fernandes puts the success of AirAsia down to 'culture, focus and discipline'. The company's culture is reflected in his comments on his management style:

> If you sit up in your **ivory tower** and just look at financial reports, you're going to make some **big** mistakes ... Employees come number one, customers come number two. If you have a happy workforce they'll look after your customers anyway ... You can have all the money you want in the **world**, and you can have all the **brilliant ideas** but if you don't have the people, forget it ... I look for people who have drive, who have **ambition**, who are **humble**. I've hired many people at very strange places ... Good leadership is to know when to go and you only **succeed** as a good leader if you've transported someone else in and the company gets **stronger**. Then you've succeeded as leader.

BBC News Business
1 November 2010

Entrepreneurial culture

Establishing an entrepreneurial culture is vital if you want your business to remain entrepreneurial as it grows and avoid becoming bureaucratic. You can describe the organizational culture by collecting words that describe what it is like to work there – the structures, stories, rituals and routines, symbols, controls and the basis of power and authority within it.

Creating a **culture** in which every person in your organization, at every level, **thinks** and **acts** like an owner means that you need to aim to connect individual **performance** with your company's most important objectives ... A company composed of individual owners is less **focused** on hierarchy and who is in a nice office, and more intent on **achieving** their goals.

Michael Dell, founder Dell Corporation Direct from Dell: Strategies that Revolutionized an Industry (1999, New York: Harper Business)

An entrepreneurial culture should reflect the character traits and approaches to management of an entrepreneur. Above all it is about empowering staff to use their initiative to make decisions and seize opportunities. Indeed decision-making will be delegated down, as far as possible, and information will be shared rather than hoarded. It encourages experimentation, creativity and innovation. It understands risk-taking and tolerates failure but encourages and rewards success. It learns from mistakes and tries not to repeat them. The culture is underpinned by strong personal relationships that generate a strong sense of group identity. It should be egalitarian but slightly anti-authoritarian – always daring to question and to be different. It sees change as the norm, certainly not something to be feared and should have confidence in its future.

The words that might describe an entrepreneurial culture are shown in the cultural web in Figure 12.12.

Entrepreneurial architecture

Entrepreneurial organizations thrive in competitive, changing environments where tasks are complex, and creativity and innovation are important. They are created by constructing an organizational architecture through:

- **Structure** – As shown in Figure 12.9, quadrant 4, it requires an organic structure with autonomous sub-structures allowing staff considerable freedom.
- **Culture** – The words describing an entrepreneurial culture are shown in Figure 12.12.

F12.12 The cultural web of an entrepreneurial organization

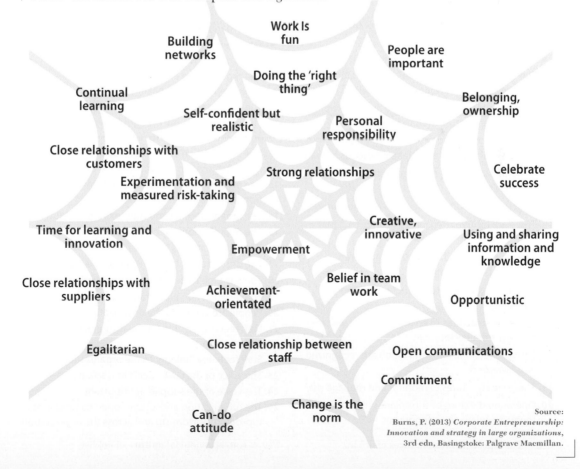

Source:
Burns, P. (2013) *Corporate Entrepreneurship: Innovation and strategy in large organizations*, 3rd edn, Basingstoke: Palgrave Macmillan.

- **Leadership** – The next chapter will highlight how your leadership can create and reinforce this architecture.

Like the marketing mix, to be effective all three elements of architecture must be congruent – each reinforcing the other. Architecture creates value. An entrepreneurial architecture means that the whole business comprises entrepreneurs and it will continue to thrive after you have left. Investors know that is worth paying for.

Many of the structural and cultural characteristics need to be embedded within your organization once you get going and can only be assessed after some time. Table 12.3 provides a checklist of organizational characteristics that would demonstrate that your structure encourages entrepreneurship. Table 12.4 provides a checklist of organizational characteristics that would demonstrate that your culture encourages entrepreneurship. You might apply them three years into your start-up, but they give you an insight into what to aim for.

1. The management team are organized organically
2. The organization is broken down into small sub-structures
3. The organization is **not** hierarchical
4. The organization is **not** bureaucratic
5. The organization structure is flexible
6. Spans of control are broad
7. There is loose organizational control but tight accountability
8. Team-working is encouraged and facilitated
9. The organization participates in strategic alliances/partnerships or joint ventures
10. The organization has developed and participates in a number of professional networks
11. Intrapreneurs and/or new cross-functional venture teams are used to take new ideas forward
12. Structures encourage and facilitate intrapreneurship
13. Structures encourage delegated decision-making
14. There are facilities (resources, rooms, etc.) that encourage creative thinking
15. Crowdsourcing and open innovation are encouraged and facilitated
16. There are structures to facilitate continuous innovation
17. There are structures to encourage and facilitate training and development
18. Entrepreneurship and innovation are recognized and rewarded
19. There are structures to monitor and manage risk
20. Operating divisions or subsidiaries (if you have them) are relatively autonomous

T12.3 **Entrepreneurial structures checklist**

1. The organization encourages entrepreneurial risk-taking
2. The organization is an empowering one
3. The organization sees change as normal
4. The organization encourages staff to build relationships at all levels
5. The organization encourages creativity and innovation
6. The organization encourages continuous innovation
7. The organization is egalitarian
8. The organization is tolerant of mistakes
9. The organization encourages and facilitates delegated decision-making
10. The organization encourages team-working
11. The organization encourages internal information and knowledge sharing
12. The organization encourages building networks of relationships with external people and organizations
13. The organization encourages continual learning from both inside and outside
14. The organization encourages experimentation
15. The organization celebrates success
16. The organization is informal
17. The organization is achievement-orientated
18. There is time for learning and innovation
19. The organization encourages strategizing
20. People are valued in the organization
21. Staff feel responsible for the future of the organization
22. Staff feel they 'belong' to the organization
23. The voice of the customer is important
24. The voice of the supplier is important
25. The organization encourages open communication, top-down, bottom-up and across the organization

T12.4 **Entrepreneurial culture checklist**

Virgin Group (3)

🧳 *Case insight*

Corporate culture and structure

In Chapter 6 we looked at how Richard Branson built the Virgin brand. Virgin describes itself as a 'branded venture capital company' – a big brand made up of lots of small companies. And in Chapter 11 we saw how Branson structured the company so as to mitigate his personal risks.

The Virgin Group is made up of more than 20 separate umbrella companies, operating over 370 separate businesses, employing approximately 50,000 people in 30 countries, with global brand revenue in excess of £11.5 billion. Virgin uses its brand as a capital asset in joint ventures. Virgin contributes the brand and Richard Branson's PR profile, whilst the partner provides the capital input – in some ways like a franchise operation – and often the operational expertise. This structure mirrors a Japanese management structure called *keiretsu*, in which different businesses act as a family under one brand. If there is a theme linking Virgin's reasons for setting up in these diverse sectors, it is simply commercial opportunity. Many have been bought from governments around the world as businesses were privatized (e.g. Virgin Money). Many were set up because of customer dissatisfaction with existing monopolistic suppliers (e.g. Virgin Atlantic) and, more recently, bypassing the supplier to offer products/services direct to customers (e.g. Virgin Direct). Also there has been a rash of businesses based upon the technology, media and telecommunication boom at the turn of the twenty-first century (e.g. Virgin Media).

Branson is the archetypical entrepreneurial leader. Will Whitehorn, Branson's right-hand man since 1996, said of Richard some years ago:

'He doesn't believe that **huge** companies are the **right way** to go. He thinks **small** is beautiful … He's a one-person venture capital company, raising money from selling businesses and **investing** in new ones, and that's the way it will be in the **future**.' (1)

The Virgin structure is complex and difficult to disentangle, involving offshore private companies and the existence of (unidentified) bearer shares. Equity interest in the umbrella organizations is owned by Virgin Group Investments. The Virgin trademark and logos are owned by Virgin Enterprises and these are licensed to companies both inside and outside the Virgin Group. Virgin Management is the management arm of the organization which appoints board members and senior executives, and coordinates activities. Wikipedia states: 'Although Branson retains complete ownership and control of the Virgin brand, the commercial set-up of companies using it is varied and complex. Each of the companies operating under the Virgin brand is a separate entity, with Branson completely owning some and holding minority or majority stakes in others. Occasionally, he simply licenses the brand to a company that has purchased a division from him, such as Virgin Mobile USA, Virgin Mobile Australia, Virgin Radio and Virgin Music (now part of EMI).'

As Branson has observed:

'Virgin is not a big company – it's a **big brand** made up of lots of small companies. Our priorities are the **opposite** of our large competitors … For us our employees matter most. It just seems common sense that if you have a **happy**, well-motivated workforce, you're much more likely to have happy customers. And in due course the resulting profits will make your **shareholders** happy. Convention dictates that big is **beautiful**, but every time one of our **ventures** gets too big we divide it up into **smaller** units … Each time we do this, the people involved haven't had much more work to do, but necessarily they have a greater **incentive** to perform and a **greater** zest for their work.' (2)

'Our companies are part of a **family** rather than a hierarchy ... They are empowered to run their **own** affairs, yet the companies help one another, and solutions to problems often come from within the **Group** somewhere. In a sense we are commonwealth, with shared ideas, **values**, **interests** and **goals**.' (3)

Companies in the Virgin group are diverse and independent. In 1986 Virgin was floated on the stock market but later re-privatized because Richard did not like to be accountable for his actions to institutional shareholders. Companies in the group have different organizational structures, reflecting the different nature of their core businesses. At the centre is Virgin Management Ltd., which provides advisory and managerial support to the group companies. It has offices in London, New York and Sydney, each with sector teams, run by a Managing Partner.

Branson runs the Virgin empire from a large house in London's Holland Park. Although there does not appear to be a traditional head office structure, Virgin employs a large number of professional managers. Branson believes in delegation and is good at it, encouraging managers to be entrepreneurial. He sets direction and then steps back to allow the managers to get on with things, giving them the freedom and initiative to be creative. This willingness to delegate helps develop trust between Branson and his management team. The atmosphere is characterized as being informal and information-driven – one that is bottom-heavy rather than strangled by top-heavy management. Virgin sees itself as having minimal management layers, no bureaucracy, a tiny board and a small headquarters. The working environment is informal, almost casual, but there is a belief in hard work and individual responsibility. Generally, despite the informal structures, performance expectations are high.

Getty Images

Richard Branson

Managers at all levels in Virgin are set goals. Managers at headquarters are set overall goals such as improving brand loyalty or expanding the business. Managers in group companies are set more specific goals associated with their own business. The further down the hierarchy you go the more specific and short-term the goals.

Branson's main skills are said to be networking, finding opportunities and securing the resources necessary for their exploitation. His network of personal influence and contacts is legendary. He hates formal meetings and prefers to make decisions on a face-to-face basis, albeit sometimes over the phone, but always developing and testing his personal relationships. Another of Branson's skills seems to be inspiring staff and bringing out the best in them. He can do this on a very personal basis and still regularly invites groups of employees to his house. Most people who meet him find him extremely likeable – charismatic – with boundless enthusiasm and an inquisitive mind. He can be a good listener but says he never listens to critics. He encourages communication at all levels, using many different media. He seems to have an ability to 'connect' with people and loves challenges, whether related to the business or his own personal life.

'If people are properly and regularly **recognized** for their **initiative**, then the business has to **flourish**. Why? Because it's their business, an extension of their personality. Everyone feels Virgin is theirs to keep and look after. And it runs deeper. I am a firm believer in **listening** to your staff at all times. The moment you stop doing this, you are in **danger** of losing your best people.' (3)

Employees are encouraged to come up with new ideas and development capital is available. Once a new venture reaches a certain size it is launched as an independent company within the Virgin Group and the intrapreneur takes an equity stake. Branson's personal approach is to listen to all ideas and offer feedback.

'Many of our businesses run **innovation** schemes where employees can submit new business ideas to be considered by the strategic **leaders**. We also facilitate peer-to-peer nominations to recognize top **performers** around the four Virgin values of innovation, customer service, **community** and **environment**. One lucky person even gets to spend a week on [my] Necker Island.' (3)

Virgin is inexorably linked to Richard Branson. Now he is over 60, the question is how long will he continue? When he retires what will the future hold for Virgin? Is it just a loose confederation of diverse, independent businesses or is there something else unifying these business that will last beyond Branson? And, when he retires, what will happen to his shareholding?

Re-read the two previous Case Insights about Richard Branson and Virgin on pages 131 and 226.

Questions:

1. How would you describe the structure and culture of the Virgin Group?
2. What are the advantages and disadvantages of the structure?
3. What is the role of head office with the operating subsidiaries? Describe the culture in head office.
4. How does the structure and culture of Virgin Group reinforce the brand and how does the brand reinforce the structure and culture?
5. How important is Richard Branson to the company? What might happen when he retires?

References
1. *The Guardian*, 30 April 2002.
2. Branson, R. (1998) *Losing my Virginity*, London: Virgin.
3. www.hrmagazine.co.uk, 13 July 2010.

Summary

- Any business is primarily about people. You need to develop a skills profile for your business – the skills, knowledge and networks that are needed to launch and operate your business. You meet your skills needs through people – founder(s), employees, partners, investors, professional advisors, and the board of directors.

- Using professional advisors can be an attractive way of accessing a range of knowledge, skills and networks. Surrounding yourself with high-quality advisors can help tackle the challenges of growth and add to the credibility of your management team.

- Using your skills profile, you can draw up job descriptions for key roles and, based on these, person specifications that profile the skills, knowledge and attributes of those who might be able to undertake these jobs.

- Picking an effective management team is also about assembling a mix of different personalities than can work together as a team. Belbin identified nine sets of characteristics that are needed: three with a 'thinking' orientation – plant, monitor-evaluator and specialist; three with a 'people' orientation – coordinator, team-worker and resource investigator; and three with an 'action' orientation – shaper, implementer and completer-finisher.

- Structures create order but there is no single 'best' structure. This depends on task complexity and environmental turbulence.

- As shown in Figure 12.9, the less stable and predictable the environment you operate in and the more complex the tasks you face, the greater the autonomy you should give your staff. The appropriate structure is 'organic' – one that is highly flexible, ever changing, with limited hierarchy, one which places greater emphasis on personal relationships and interactions than on structures, one in which power is decentralized and authority is linked to expertise, with few bureaucratic rules or standard procedures. In this structure culture is very important in providing direction.

- Culture is an organization's basic beliefs and assumptions – what it is about, how its members should behave and how it defines itself. It is based upon its values and beliefs and these are normally taken from the founder.

- Culture can be created through behaviours and organizational and cognitive processes.

- As it grows a business will face predictable challenges. The implications of Greiner's growth model is that, in order to retain its entrepreneurial edge, an organization needs to retain its creativity but with clear direction. It needs delegated but coordinated decision-making with effective collaboration. It needs to avoid potential crises of effective leadership, balancing the need for staff autonomy and control and avoiding at all cost too much bureaucracy. This means putting in place an appropriate organizational architecture.

- An entrepreneurial architecture is based upon an entrepreneurial culture (Figure 12.12) set in an organic structure (Figure 12.9), created and reinforced by effective leadership.

Exercise 12.1

New venture skills profile

Using the format opposite:

1 List the skills, knowledge and competences required for your business, pre-launch, and the job roles these translate into. Make sure all skills etc. are covered by these roles.

2 Classify roles as 'key', 'important' or 'desirable'.

3 Classify roles as 'full/part-time' and 'regular/shift work' and note any special remuneration arrangements.

4 Identify the roles the founder(s) will take and identify the resulting role gaps.

Skills, knowledge and competences	Role		Key/ important/ desirable	Full/ part-time	Regular/ shift work	Remuneration

5 Identify which roles or skill gaps might come from professional advisors, partners, the board of directors and/or providers of finance.

6 For the remaining role gaps, prepare a brief job description and person specification.

7 If any of these role gaps are critical to your success amend Exercise 11.2, as appropriate.

8 Repeat the process for three years' time.

Exercise 12.2
Finding professional advisors

1 Based on the above exercise, list the areas where you will need professional help and advice.

2 Review Exercise 9.2 and amend as appropriate.

3 Draw up an Action Plan to show how you will go about hiring professional advisors to meet these needs.

Exercise 12.3
Recruiting staff

1 Decide on remuneration levels (including bonuses and incentives) for all posts, including those occupied by founders.

2 If your new business is a limited company, decide which members of the new venture team will become shareholders. Draft the main features of a shareholders' agreement. Remember that you will need to ask the advice of a lawyer about this before anything is signed.

3 List the staff's goals, performance measures and targets.

4 Draft job advertisements for job gaps and decide how these will be advertised.

 Visit www.palgrave.com/companion/burns-new-venture-creation for chapter quizzes to test your knowledge and other resources.

Exercise 12.4
Team roles

1 Complete the Belbin team roles test yourself.

2 Get your existing new venture team to complete the test.

3 List the implications of this for you and the rest of the team.

Exercise 12.5
Building the organization structure

1 Identify where in Figure 12.9 your venture falls (environment vs task complexity).

2 Draw up the organization chart for your business. Identify which are the key roles for your management team.

3 Jot down words that describe the degree of control you wish to establish over people in your business. List the implications for management.

Exercise 12.6
Building the organization culture

1 Building on your answer to the previous question, jot down words that describe the culture you would like to establish in your business.

2 List the actions (behaviours, organizational and cognitive processes) you need to undertake or establish to achieve this culture.

3 Review Exercise 6.1 and ensure that these values are consistent with the culture you wish to establish.

13
LEADING
YOUR
TEAM

Contents

Learning outcomes

When you have read this chapter and undertaken the related exercises you will be able to:
- Describe the difference between management and leadership
- Explain what the job of leader involves
- Critically analyze the theories of leadership that have been proposed and their contribution to an understanding of how to lead an entrepreneurial organization
- Understand and explain how leadership style can be tailored to different circumstances, and evaluate your preferred leadership style
- Understand how conflict can be handled and evaluate how you handle it
- Understand how to build an organizational architecture – leadership, structure, culture and strategies – that creates an entrepreneurial organization

Leadership and management

Leading and managing people is a challenge that requires some distinctive skills and capabilities. Leadership and management are different and distinct terms, although the skills and competences associated with each are complementary. Management is concerned with handling complexity in organizational processes and the execution of work. It is linked to the authority given to managers within a hierarchy. Back in the nineteenth century Max Fayol defined the five functions of management as planning, organizing, commanding, coordinating and controlling. Today, these sound very much like the skills needed to lead a communist-style command economy. Fayol's work outlined how these functions required certain skills which could be taught and developed systematically in people. Management is therefore about detail and logic. It is about efficiency and effectiveness.

Leadership on the other hand is concerned with setting direction, communicating and motivating. It is about broad principles and emotion and less detail. If management is the head, leadership is the heart of an organization. It is therefore quite possible for an organization to be over-managed but under-led, or vice versa. An organization needs both good leadership and good management. In a start-up good leadership is essential while effective management quickly becomes increasingly important to get things done. But good leadership is situation-specific. Some leaders are good in one situation but not in others. Leaders can have roller-coaster careers as they exhibit successful leadership characteristics at certain discrete times, in certain circumstances, with particular people, but these characteristics do not work when things change. They fail to adapt. Winston Churchill was widely acknowledged as a great war-time leader but a poor peace-time leader. Therefore entrepreneurs might be good leaders at start-up but poor leaders as the business grows – unless they adapt and change their leadership style.

*Business is like a relay race and I am very, very good at the **first** leg and I am very, very good at the **last** leg, and I'm really not the best person to do the **second** and **third** legs … At that point I start to lose focus and so that's when you need to recognise what your **strengths** and **weaknesses** are and then you come back in to sell the business. It's not that you disengage completely during the second and third legs, but you certainly pass the responsibility over to somebody who is more **capable** than you.*

Management Today 18 July 2008 www.managementtoday.co.uk Management Mykindaplace.com and Brightstone Ventures

Shaa Wasmund, founder Mykindaplace

The one certain characteristic that separates leaders from other people is the obvious one that they have willing followers. Why is this? What is it about them that persuades others to follow them? The characteristics and personality traits of good leaders tell us a limited amount about good leadership. Leadership is not about who you are. It is more about what you do with who you are and how you form relationships with your followers. It is also group-, task- and situation- or context-specific. And, as we see later in this chapter, leadership style can be crafted to meet these changing circumstances. However, whilst it is too simplistic just to say that leaders have certain enduring character traits, some individuals can and do seem to emerge as leaders across a variety of situations and tasks. And this gives us some indications of the leadership characteristics and *behaviours* needed to lead an entrepreneurial organization. What is more, we are beginning to better understand the importance of a leader's personal cognitive abilities, motives, social skills, expertise and problem-solving skills. What emerges is a complex interaction of many factors that underlines that effective leadership is an art rather than a science – and it is very dependent upon the context. Whilst we can isolate the main factors that influence it and point to good practice in particular contexts, there is no magic formula.

Defining the role of leader

Our traditional view of leaders is that they are special people – often charismatic 'heroes' like Churchill – who set direction, make key decisions and motivate staff, frequently prevailing against the odds at times of crisis. They have vision – something most entrepreneurs have aplenty. They are strategic thinkers and are effective communicators whilst still being able to monitor and control performance. Above all, they create the appropriate culture within the organization to reflect their priorities. Indeed leadership is more about guiding vision, culture and identity than it is about decision-making. If there were ever a job description for a leader, therefore, it would probably include five elements:

Having a vision for the organization – This gives people a clear focus on the direction of the organization, the values it stands for and the key issues and concerns it faces in achieving its goals. Visions are underpinned by the values of the organization and the values are reflected in the culture of the organization. You created your vision based upon your values as part of the exercises in Chapter 6.

Being able to develop strategy – It is one thing to know where you want to go, it is quite another to know how to get there. The heart of leadership is about being able to chart a course for future development that steers the organization towards

> *Warren Bennis and Burt Nanus, Leaders; The Strategies for Taking Charge (1985, New York: Harper & Row)*
>
> If there is a **spark** of genius in the leadership function at all, it must lie in the transcending ability, a kind of **magic**, to assemble ... out of a variety of images, signals, forecasts and alternatives ... a clearly articulated **vision of the future** that is simple, clearly understood, clearly desirable, and energizing.

💼 *Case insight*

Gary Redman and Now Recruitment

Changing your leadership style

Now Recruitment, founded in 1991, is an industry-award-winning global recruitment agency with offices across the UK and international offices in Australia and the United Arab Emirates. It is 90% owned by Gary Redman, who readily admits that his management style has had to change dramatically to accommodate the growth. The company stalled when turnover reached £6 million and staff turnover shot through the roof. Gary brought in a management consultant:

> 'He told me that the **biggest** problem in the business was me. He explained that staff were saying they were not **clear** where the business was going, they didn't know what I **wanted** and they didn't get a chance to voice their **opinions** ... The way I operated was to shout at people ... I thought you got results out of people by putting them **under pressure**. It was a ruthless kind of culture where if you **performed** well you were in, and if you didn't perform well you were out.'

Sunday Times
8 August 2004

Gary went on a management development course which taught him how to delegate responsibility rather than try to control everything himself. Changing his style of leadership worked. Staff retention improved and the business started to grow again.

the leader's vision. This is what strategy is about – linking various actions and tactics in a consistent way that forms a coherent plan. Your business plan gives you the strategy for how you will achieve your vision for this business. There is a wonderful Chinese proverb:

> *Tactics without strategy is*
> *the noise before defeat.*

It underlines, not only the need for a consistent, coherent strategy to ensure success, but also that without it miscellaneous tactics will just cause 'noise' or arguments among your followers about what to do and why they should be doing it.

Being able to communicate effectively, particularly the vision – There is no point in having a vision for the organization unless you can communicate it effectively and it inspires and motivates staff. Staff need to understand how the vision will be achieved, and believe that they can achieve it, particularly in an uncertain world. They need to understand where the organization is going and the strategies that are being adopted to take it there.

Academic insight

Seven principles for communicating a vision

1. Keep it simple – **Keep the message focused and jargon-free.**

2. Use metaphors, analogies and examples – **Engage the imagination.**

3. Use many different forums – **The same message should come from as many different directions as possible.**

4. Repeat the message – **The same message should be repeated again, and again, and again.**

5. Lead by example – **Walk-the-talk.**

6. Address small inconsistencies – **Small changes can have big effects if their symbolism is important to staff.**

7. Listen and be listened to – **Work hard to listen, it pays dividends.**

Adapted from Kotter, J.P. (1996) *Leading Change*, Boston, MA: Harvard Business School Press.

Roger Ashford-Fotolia.com

Creating an appropriate culture in the organization – As we saw in the last chapter, the culture of an organization is the cement that binds it together. It influences how people think and how they act. Creating an appropriate culture for an entrepreneurial organization is probably the single most important thing a leader has to do – but it is not an easy task.

Managing and monitoring performance – Leaders still have to manage. You need to be a good leader and a good manager. This may be a routine task, but in an entrepreneurial organization there are special challenges such as dealing with rapid change, the balance between freedom and control and managing risk – all of which we have covered in previous chapters.

Personal attributes of leaders

A key mind-shift for a leader is to become a **strategic thinker**. They move away from operational detail to a broad, strategic, organizational perspective – an ability to rise above day-to-day crises and see the bigger picture. It involves taking a longer-term, holistic view of the organization. Strategy sets a framework within which short-term actions can be judged. Leaders understand where they have come from – knowledge of the past – and how it affects the current situation, where they are going to and how to get there. They are also engaged in perpetually 'scanning' the environment, both for opportunities and risks. They therefore become **strategic learners**. This learning may involve looking at the big picture, trying to find patterns over time and looking for complex interactions so as to understand the underlying causes. The exercises accompanying the chapters in this book have helped you develop these attributes. The discovery skills needed to find your original business idea are essentially a process of 'scanning' (Chapter 3). You need to learn to use them as your business grows and develops.

Based on this information, leaders can then envision a new and desirable future and reframe this new future in the context of the organization – **strategic intent**. During the process they engage in synthesis as well as analysis. However, leadership is about persuading people to follow you. As we shall see in the next section, there are a number of ways you can do this. However, they all require **emotional intelligence**:

- An understanding of yourself, your strengths and weaknesses.
- An appreciation of different circumstances – both people and the environment or context in which they find themselves.
- An ability to adapt your behaviour to meet these different circumstances.
- An ability to relate to people and communicate with them.

A key skill for this whole process is honest reflection, and that requires time. It also means that you need to check that your perception of yourself or of different circumstances corresponds with that of others. Is it real? This involves a degree of mature judgement that is not easily taught, but develops over time and can be much enhanced by having a supportive network of people around you with whom you are able to talk.

Smarta

Shaa Wasmund

I believe in as flat a management structure as possible … in leading without title … I never put any emphasis on my title. I most certainly try to lead by example and I'm very much a big believer in making my mistakes public so that other people feel confident and comfortable to be able to air their own mistakes.

Shaa Wasmund, founder, MyKindaPlace.com and Brightstone Ventures Management Today 18 July 2008 www.managementtoday.co.uk

Trust and respect underpin the relationship that a leader needs to establish with those they wish to lead. Followers need to want the new future and buy into the strategies that will make it happen. But they also need to trust that the leader can and will deliver it, and it is easier to trust someone who has high moral characteristics or ethical values. These are the leaders who really command our respect and loyalty. They generate more commitment from staff. But ethics are not an 'add-on'. It is not easy to adopt personal attributes that do not represent the person you really are. Eventually your guard will slip and your followers will see through the image you portray. To sustain your leadership, you need to be 'authentic' – you need to believe in and act out these ethical underpinnings. Trust and respect come not just from words but also from actions – 'walking-the-talk'.

Authentic leaders

Reflecting on interviews with 125 of today's top leaders, George and Sims (2007) talk about 'authentic leadership' coming from those individuals who follow their real values and beliefs – their internal compass. Authentic leaders build a support team of people with whom they have a close relationship (spouses, family members, mentors etc.) and they have a network of professional contacts to provide counsel and guidance. These are people with whom they can reflect honestly on the issues they face.

Authentic leaders also have strong values and beliefs that they practise at work and at home – 'pursuing purpose with passion'. They have ethical foundations and boundaries and lead with their hearts as well as their heads. They establish enduring relations with staff because they listen to them and demonstrate that they care. George and Sims argue that, in this way, authentic leaders not only inspire those around them but also empower people to lead. But they only do this by always being true to their own principles, values and beliefs. They are authentic. And that cannot be faked.

Academic insight

Brubaker (2005) gives us an insight into what your staff might consider ethical foundations. When asked in a survey what values they looked for in ethical leaders, respondents listed nine major attributes:

1. Truth and honesty
2. Integrity and alignment of words and actions
3. The keeping of promises
4. Loyalty to the organization and the people in it
5. Fairness between staff
6. Concern and respect for others
7. Law abiding
8. Pursuit of excellence
9. Personal accountability, taking responsibility, admitting mistakes and sharing success.

In an earlier work George (2003) outlined the skills and personal attributes needed by authentic leaders. They have high levels of emotional intelligence incorporating:

- Self-awareness – the ability to understand yourself and your emotions;
- Self-management – control, integrity, initiative and conscientiousness;
- Social awareness – empathy, sensing other people's emotions;
- Social skills – communication, collaboration and, above all, relationship-building.

Brubaker, D.L. (2005) 'The Power of Vision', in D.L. Brubaker and L.D. Coble (eds) The Hidden Leader, Thousand Oaks, CA: Corwin Press.

George, B. (2003) Authentic Leadership: Rediscovering the Secrets to Creating Lasting Value, San Francisco: Jossey-Bass.

George, B. with Sims, P.E. (2007) True North: Discover your Authentic Leadership, San Francisco: Jossey-Bass.

Leadership style and contingency theory

Leadership style is a complex thing. It is dependent upon the interactions and interconnections between the leader, the task, the group being led and the situation or context. The appropriate style to adopt depends upon how these factors interact. This is called situational or contingency theory. Three broad styles of leadership have been popularized:

Authoritarian – This style focuses decision-making powers in the leader. It is most appropriate in times of crisis but usually fails to win 'hearts and minds'.

Democratic – This style favours group decision-making and consensus-building. It is more appropriate in circumstances other than crisis.

Laissez-faire – This style allows a high degree of freedom for followers. However, a leader adopting this style is often perceived as weak.

As shown in Figure 13.1, each style involves different degrees of freedom or control for the employees. In reality there are many permutations of these three extremes and contingency theory states that the leader should adapt their style to suit different situations or contexts.

INCREASING CONTROL – DECREASING FREEDOM

F13.1 Leadership styles and control

Contingency theory emphasizes that there is no one 'best' way of managing or leading. It depends on the interaction of all the factors in Figure 13.2 – leader, group, task and situation or context. A leader may personally prefer an informal, non-directional style, but faced with an inexperienced apprentice working a dangerous lathe they might be forgiven for reverting to a fairly formal, directive style with heavy supervision. In that situation the change in style is appropriate. Try the same style with a

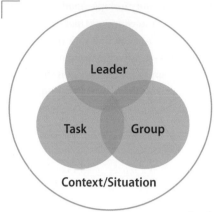

F13.2 Leadership style

group of senior creative marketing consultants and there would be problems. Many different styles may be effective, with different tasks, different groups and in different contexts. Remember there is no evidence of any single leadership style characterizing successful businesses. What is more, the ability of leaders to change and adapt their styles may vary enormously.

Nevertheless, by picking off the individual elements of these four factors we can understand what style is best suited to different circumstances.

Leader and task

Leaders have to work through others to complete tasks. The degree of concern for the people they are leading, compared to the task in hand, will, in part, determine the style they adopt. The leadership grid shown in Figure 13.3 shows style as dependent upon the leader's concern for task compared to the concern for people. Entrepreneurs are usually more concerned with completing the task but, as the firm grows, you must become more concerned with people if the tasks are to be accomplished. Task leadership may be appropriate in certain situations, for example emergencies. However, concern for people must surface at some point if effective, trusting relationships are to develop. Low concern for both people and task is hardly leadership at all. High concern for people – the country club style – is rare in business but can be appropriate in community groups, small charities or social clubs where good relationships and high morale might be the dominant objectives. You can find your preferred style on this grid by answering the leadership questionnaire at the end of this chapter and mapping your results on the scoring grid. The questionnaire is also available on the website accompanying this book.

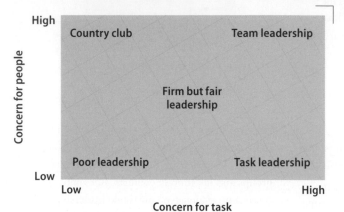

F13.3 Leader and task

Adapted from Blake, R. and Mouton, J. (1978) *The New Managerial Grid*, London: Gulf.

Leader and group

Leaders are likely to adopt different styles with different groups approaching the same task. Leadership style also depends on the relationship of the leader with the group they are leading. Figure 13.4 shows this in relation to the leader's degree of authority and the group's autonomy in decision-making. If a leader has high authority but the group has low autonomy, they will tend to adopt an autocratic style, simply instructing people what to do. If they have low authority (for example because of past failure) they will tend to adopt a paternalistic style, cajoling the group into doing things, picking off individuals and offering grace and favour in exchange for performance. If the leader has low authority and the group has high autonomy, then they will tend to adopt a participative style, involving the whole group in decision-making and moving forward with consensus. If the leader has high authority then they will seek opinions but make the decision themselves using a consultative style.

Leader and context/situation

The weight the leader should put on these different influences depends on the situation or context. However, obtaining an objective view of any context is always problematic as we view life through our own, biased lens. As already observed, a leader's judgement about context might be faulty. What is more, they might be tempted to 'construct' social contexts that legitimate their intended actions, rather than viewing them objectively. And most leaders have a preferred style that they are predisposed to use.

Entrepreneurial firms face an environment that is uncertain, ambiguous and constantly changing, which can often lead to conflict as they try to get people to do different things or things differently. The Thomas–Kilmann Conflict Modes instrument gives us an insight into how conflict might be handled. Whilst each style has its advantages in certain situations, compromise, or better still collaboration, is generally thought to be the best way for a team to work.

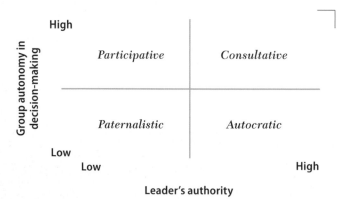

F13.4 Leader and group

Dealing with conflict

Often in business you find yourself at odds with others who hold seemingly incompatible views. For a leader to be effective they need to understand how they handle these conflict situations and be able to modify their behaviour to obtain the best results from others. Based on research by Kenneth Thomas and Ralph Kilmann, the Thomas–Kilmann Conflict Modes Instrument shows how a person's behaviour can be classified under two dimensions:

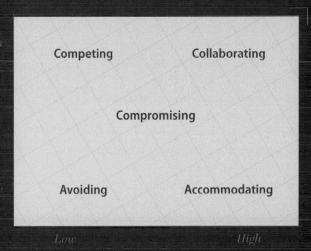

F13.5 Thomas–Kilmann Conflict Modes

- Assertiveness – the extent to which individuals attempt to satisfy their own needs.
- Cooperativeness – the extent to which they attempt to satisfy the needs of others.

These two dimensions lead the authors to identify five behavioural classifications which the questionnaire can identify in individuals:

1. **Competing** is assertive and uncooperative. Individuals are concerned for themselves and pursue their own agenda forcefully, using power, rank or ability to argue in order to win the conflict. This can be seen as bullying with less forceful individuals or, when others use the same mode, it can lead to heated, possibly unresolved, arguments.

2. **Accommodating** is unassertive and cooperative, the opposite of competing. Individuals want to see the concerns of others satisfied. They might do so as an act of 'selfless generosity' or just because they are 'obeying orders', either way they run the risk of not making their own views heard.

3. **Avoiding** is both unassertive and uncooperative. It may involve side-stepping an issue or withdrawing from the conflict altogether. In this mode any conflict may not be even addressed.

4. **Collaborating** is both assertive and cooperative, the opposite of avoiding. Issues get addressed but individuals are willing to work with others to resolve the conflict, perhaps finding alternatives that meet everybody's concerns. This is the most constructive approach to conflict for a group as a whole.

5. **Compromising** is the 'in between' route, the diplomatic, expedient solution to conflict which partially satisfies everyone. It may involve making concessions.

Each style of handling conflict has its advantages and disadvantages and can be effective in certain situations. However, management teams or boards of directors, if they are to get the most from each member over a longer period of time, work best when all members adopt the collaborating or compromising modes. A team made up of just competitors would find it difficult to get on and, indeed, to survive. A team made up of just accommodators would lack assertiveness and drive.

The Thomas–Kilmann Conflict Modes Instrument is available on: www.kilmanndiagnostics.com/catalog/thomas-kilmann-conflict-mode-instrument.

Entrepreneurial leadership

The academic literature provides many leadership paradigms – transactional, transformational, visionary and dispersed leadership are but a few (see Academic Insight). Each is appropriate to different situations. Context is everything in leadership and the entrepreneurial context of leadership is one characterized by uncertainty, rapid change and risk-taking. So what are the attributes, skills and behaviours of entrepreneurial leaders – leaders of growing entrepreneurial businesses?

> The notion of the **leader** as a **heroic** decision maker is untenable. Leaders must be recast as social-systems **architects** who enable **innovation** ... Leaders will no longer be seen as grand **visionaries**, all-wise decision makers, and ironfisted disciplinarians. Instead they will need to become social architects, constitution writers, and **entrepreneurs of meaning**. In this new world, the leader's job is to create an environment where every employee has the chance to **collaborate**, **innovate**, and **excel**.
>
> Gary Hamel, 'Moon Shots for Management', *Harvard Business Review*, February 2009.

Leadership paradigms

Academics have developed a number of paradigms that describe different leadership styles.

Transactional leadership – This style of leadership is about setting goals, putting in place systems and controls to achieve them and rewarding individuals when they meet the goals. It is about efficiency and incremental change, reinforcing rather than challenging organizational learning. It is associated with closed cultures, rigid systems, formal procedures and bureaucratic organization structures. Bass (1985, 1998) contrasts this with transformational leadership.

Transformational leadership – This is more emotional and is about inspiration, excitement and intellectual stimulation. It is a style best suited to highly turbulent and uncertain environments where crises, anxiety and high risk are prevalent (Vera and Crossan, 2004) – which tends to describe the entrepreneurial context. Not surprisingly, this style of leadership is associated with open cultures, organic structures, adaptable systems, and flexible procedures. Transformational leaders are often seen as being charismatic, inspirational, intellectually stimulating and individually considerate (Avolio et al., 1999), and as having empathy and self-confidence (Egri and Herman, 2000). They inspire and motivate people with a vision, create excitement with their enthusiasm and get people to question the tried-and-tested ways of doing things and 'reframe' the future (Bass and Avolio, 1990).

Visionary leadership – Sashkin (1996) characterized this style as providing a clear vision which focuses people on goals that are part of that vision and on key issues and concerns. The visionary leader has good interpersonal and communication skills. They get everyone to understand the focus for the business and to work together towards common goals. They act consistently over time to develop trust and they care and respect others, making them self-confident, whilst having an inner self-confidence themselves. Finally, they provide creative opportunities that others can buy into and 'own' – empowering opportunities that involve people in making the right things their own priorities. (Sashkin's Leader Behaviour Questionnaire is a 360-degree assessment instrument that measures visionary leadership behaviours, characteristics and contextual effects. It needs to be filled out by 3–6 colleagues and is available on www.hrdpress.com/visionary-leader-questionnaire-set-5-pack-VLQS.)

Entrepreneurial leaders are subtly different from these leadership paradigms. They are both visionary and transformational but, importantly, they should set out to build and embed leadership into the organization – and this is more than just dispersed leadership. To become an entrepreneurial leader you need to transform not only yourself but also your organization. You need to build an organization that is fundamentally entrepreneurial, one that embodies your character traits or DNA, as well as your approach to management. You need to build a business that is both visionary and transformational. You do this by building structures and a culture (outlined in the previous chapter) and developing strategies that combine with your leadership style to create an organizational architecture that is entrepreneurial. And instead of concentrating just on acquiring the individual attributes of leadership, you should take an architectural approach – build these leadership attributes into the organization and spread them throughout it.

Academic insight

Dispersed leadership – This style draws on models of dispersed or distributed leadership which focus on leadership across all levels and in different forms (Bradford and Cohen, 1998; Chaleff, 1995; Mintzberg, 2009). It emphasizes the importance of 'emotional intelligence' in the leader and their ability to listen, empathize and communicate with those they lead (Goleman, 1996) – social skills essential to building effective relationships. As already mentioned, it emphasizes 'authenticity' (George, 2003; George and Sims, 2007) – leaders being true to their own beliefs (having an ethical underpinning) so that trust and respect can be built. The literature also emphasizes leaders as 'servants' of their workforce, acknowledging that self-interest is part of any relationship (Greenleaf, 1970) as well as 'educators' that develop organizational learning (Heifetz, 1994).

Avolio, B.J., Bass, B.M. and Jung, D.I. (1999) 'Re-examining the Components of Transformational and Transactional Leadership using the Multifactor Leadership Questionnaire', Journal of Occupational and Organisational Psychology, 72.

Bass, R.M. (1985) Leadership and Performance Beyond Expectations, New York: Free Press.

Bass, B.M. (1998) Transformational Leadership: Industry, Military and Educational Impact, Mahwah, NJ: Lawrence Erlbaum Associates.

Bass, D.M and Avolio, B.J. (1999) 'The Implications of Transactional and Transformational Leadership for Individual, Team and Organizational Development', Research in Organizational Change and Development, 4.

Bradford, D.L. and Cohen, A.R. (1998) Power Up: Transforming Organizations Through Shared Leadership, New York: John Wiley & Sons.

Chaleff, I. (1995) The Courageous Follower: Standing Up, To and For Our Leaders, San Francisco: Bennet- Koehler.

Egri, C.P. and Herman, S. (2000) 'Leadership in the North American Environmental Sector: Values, Leadership Styles and Contexts of Environmental Leaders and their Organizations', Academy of Management Journal, 43.

George, B. (2003) Authentic Leadership: Rediscovering the Secrets to Creating Lasting Value, San Francisco: Jossey-Bass.

George, B. with Sims, P.E. (2007) True North: Discover your Authentic Leadership, San Francisco: Jossey- Bass.

Goleman, D. (1996) Emotional Intelligence: Why It Can Matter More Than IQ, London: Bloomsbury.

Greenleaf, R.F. (1970) The Servant as Leader, Mahwah, NJ: Paulist.

Heifetz, R.A. (1994) Leadership Without Easy Answers, Cambridge, MA: Harvard University Press.

Mintzberg, H. (2009) Managing, London: FT Prentice Hall.

Sashkin, M. (1996) Becoming a Visionary Leader, Amherst, MA: HRD Press.

Vera, D. and Crossan, M. (2004) 'Strategic Leadership and Organizational Learning', Academy of Management Review, 29(2).

LEADERS' CHARACTERISTICS
STRATEGIC LEADERS
- *Strategic thinkers*
- *Reflectors*
- *Strategic learners*

AUTHENTIC LEADERS
- *Emotional intelligence*
- *Self-awareness*
- *Self-management*

*Contingency/
Situational
theory*

*Entrepreneurial
leadership*

LEADERSHIP PARADIGMS
- *Transactional leadership*
- *Transformational leadership*
- *Visionary leadership*
- *Dispersed leadership*

F13.6 **The entrepreneurial leader**

However, even an entrepreneurial leader needs to remain flexible and modify their style to suit changing circumstances. In this way the entrepreneurial leader may modify their leadership style as an organization cycles through periods of rapid change (transformational leadership) followed by consolidation (transactional leadership). This combination of influences is shown in Figure 13.5.

This chapter has underlined the need for the leader of an entrepreneurial organization to be a good strategic thinker and learner – and all that entails from vision to execution. It has emphasized the need for you to have strong emotional intelligence – good interpersonal and team-working skills, alongside good conflict resolution skills – but, more than anything, you need strong influencing skills to manage through your informal structures and culture. These skills are all focused towards taking the organization with you by consensus and agreement rather than by dictate. And if you succeed you will make your business self-sustainingly entrepreneurial, increasing its ability to thrive in a changing, competitive environment and boosting its value, should you decide to sell it on.

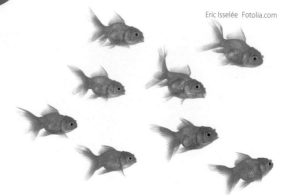

Eric Isselée Fotolia.com

Table 13.1 summarizes the attributes, skills and behaviours that an entrepreneurial leader should have. However, you will always need to 'fine-tune' your approach to suit specific audiences, undertaking particular tasks in different contexts. These skills can be developed and improved over time and some can be shared with the rest of your management team, who might be more at ease leading certain groups in certain situations. However, the main aim of the entrepreneurial leader is always to build an entrepreneurial architecture for their organization so that it can operate effectively on its own, without them. There is an ancient Chinese proverb that still rings true:

Apple The Real Leadership Lessons of Steve Jobs, Walter Isaacson, HBR April 2012

Making an **enduring** company is far **harder** and far more important than making a great **product**.

Steve Jobs, founder Apple

The wicked leader is he who the people despise. The good leader is the one who the people revere. But the great leader is he who the people say 'we did it ourselves'.

1. **Visionary** – the essential bedrock of leadership. The vision should give clear direction and be underpinned with values. It should, however, be grounded in reality.

2. **Good communicator/motivator** – the vision should be shared by all the staff in the organization and motivate them to achieve it. Motivation should be underpinned by loyalty to both the leader and the organization.

3. **Strategic thinker and learner** – the vision should be supplemented with an understanding of how to achieve it and what the strategic options for direction might be.

4. **Emotionally intelligent with strong interpersonal skills** – able to listen, to influence rather than direct, to resolve conflict and to manage 'with a light touch'. They should 'walk the talk'; model the behaviour they expect from others.

5. **Relationship builder** – able to build a cohesive, open and trusting management team. This comes about by acting consistently over time based upon a dominant set of values so as to generate trust (firm but fair) and is underpinned by care and respect for staff.

6. **Team player** – willing to share information and delegate to the team. This is based upon an understanding of how teams work.

7. **Builder of confidence** – encouraging organizational self-confidence and self-efficacy in the face of uncertainty and risk-taking. They should inspire others to share their visions and dreams.

8. **Builder of an open organization that shares information** – fostering the sharing of knowledge, information and ideas, and the willingness to question the status quo and to experiment and take measured risks.

9. **Clarifier of ambiguity and uncertainty** – so as to give a clear focus on the key issues and concerns facing the organization in the face of rapid change. This focus should be effectively communicated.

10. **Builder of empowering opportunities** – so that staff make 'the right thing' for the organization their own enthusiastic priority. In other words, spreading entrepreneurship and leadership throughout the organization.

T13.1 Attributes, skills and behaviours of entrepreneurial leaders

Source: Burns, P. (2013) *Corporate Entrepreneurship: Innovation and Strategy in Large Organizations*, Basingstoke: Palgrave Macmillan.

Entrepreneurial architecture

Leadership styles, organizational cultures and structures are linked – one reinforcing the other. As already observed, to be effective all three elements of architecture must be congruent – each reinforcing the other. And, as we saw with leadership styles on their own, certain combinations are appropriate for different tasks, different groups of people and different situations or environments.

In his book, *Gods of Management* (1995, London: Souvenir Press), Charles Handy popularized four leadership typologies – based upon Greek mythology – and the cultures and structures for which they are most appropriate. These are summarized in Table 13.2. Zeus is characterized as the charismatic and visionary entrepreneur, managing through interpersonal relationships and sitting in the middle of the spider's web. This contrasts with Apollo's traditional hierarchical bureaucracy and its rules and regulations. Athena is the team-working leader in a matrix organization, continually solving problems or addressing new tasks. Finally there is Dionysus, the partner rather than the leader in an organic organization that supports people's independence without threatening it.

Leadership style	Organizational culture	Organizational structure
Zeus The patriarch of all gods. Charismatic/visionary leader: visionary, independent, instinctive, persuasive, builder of relationships, power and networks; excited by the challenge of uncertainty.	**Club culture** Individuals are independent but responsible, trusted (not controlled) to make the right decisions, understanding the consequences of wrong decisions. Power relationships influence behaviour.	**Spider's web structures** Built upon relationships with the leader in the middle. Managers are professionals, free to follow instincts. They are also leaders.
Apollo The god of rules and order. Leader by appointment: authoritarian, logical, sequential, analytical, scientific, with everything in its place. Enjoys repetition.	**Role culture** Individuals are assigned tasks and organized and controlled through rules, regulations, job descriptions and direct supervision. People are cogs in the wheel, predictable, inflexible, and unresponsive to change.	**Traditional hierarchical bureaucracies** Strong management control. Managers are administrators.
Athena The warrior goddess and problem-solver of craftsmen and pioneering sea captain. Leader by expertise and experience: credible, convincing, focused, but unadventurous.	**Task culture** The problem is the task. Individuals are judged on how well they undertake the task/problem. Talent, creativity, initiative and intuition are all valued.	**Matrix structures** Project-based team-work. Managers define and solve problems by assigning staff and resources. They are valued for their expertise and experience. Teams form and reform to undertake different tasks/problems.
Dionysus The god of wine and song, individual and independent. Partner rather than leader. Professionally competent.	**Culture of individualism and independence** The organization is the servant of the individual. No boss. Individual talent is valued. Decision-making by consent and consensus.	**Organic structures** Supporting structures with loose coordination of independent individuals with talent. No boss.

T13.2 **A summary of Handy's Gods of Management**

Of course no organization is exclusively dedicated to one god, they balance the gods. The task of leadership is getting that balance right. Handy sees this as influenced by four factors:

- **Size** – The larger the group of people (or organizations) that need to work together, the more likely Apollo is to rule. Small groups or teams prefer Athena.

- **Work patterns** – Where work is repetitive and routine, Apollo rules. Where work is continually changing, Zeus and Dionysus rule but if it is undertaken in groups, Athena rules.

- **Life cycle** – If the life cycle is short and new product development is important, Athena rules. If the life cycle is long Apollo re-exerts his influence.

- **People** – Professionals, the young and better educated people prefer Dionysus. Countries with conformist cultures are more comfortable with Apollo, whereas countries that value individualism prefer Zeus or Dionysus.

Handy's typologies illustrate how combinations of different cultures and structures support or result from different leaders. The entrepreneurial leader we have described is definitely not Apollo, but is a mix of Zeus, Athena and Dionysus and their related cultures and structures. This is not surprising since, whilst wanting to retain a strong entrepreneurial focus (Zeus), we have emphasized small group-working (Athena), speed of competitive response (Athena) and continuous change (Zeus and Dionysus). And that is before we consider the people you might lead. It all goes to underline the statement at the beginning of this chapter that effective leadership is an art rather than a science and, whilst we can isolate the main factors that influence it and point to good practice in particular contexts, there is no magic formula.

Finally, many of the leadership characteristics we have discussed need to be embedded within your management team once you get going. Table 13.3 provides a checklist of organizational characteristics that would demonstrate the practice of entrepreneurial leadership. You might not apply them until three years into your start-up, but they give you an insight into what to aim for.

1. There is a clear vision for the organization
2. The management team model the vision and values of the organization – they 'walk-the-talk'
3. The vision for the organization is clearly communicated
4. There are clear values underpinning everything the organization does
5. There is a clear strategy for achieving the vision
6. The vision is realistic and achievable but stretching
7. There is an understanding of the opportunities and threats that the organization faces
8. The organization has strategic options for the future
9. The management team work as a team
10. The management team are accessible and approachable
11. The management team listen
12. The management team influence rather than direct; they manage with a 'light touch'
13. The management team are good at reconciling conflict
14. The management team are good at clarifying uncertainties going forward, focusing effort on important things
15. The management team are reflective and self-aware
16. The management team have good relationships with staff
17. The management team show care and respect for staff
18. The management team are trustworthy
19. The management team are consistent in their behaviour with staff
20. The management team think and act strategically
21. Team-working is encouraged in the organization
22. Cross-functional team-working is commonplace in the organization
23. Information and knowledge is shared in the organization
24. The management team empower people to deal with problems and opportunities
25. Decision-making is delegated

T13.3 Entrepreneurial leadership checklist

Steve Jobs and Apple (2)

Entrepreneurial leadership

We looked at the story of Steve Jobs and Apple in Chapter 1. This case will look more critically at his approach to leadership. Jobs was the epitome of an entrepreneurial leader who revolutionized three industries – computing, music sales and cinema animations. And his was the story of a Silicon Valley hero. By the time he died in 2011, Apple had become the second most valuable company in the world, measured by market capitalization, with a cash mountain of some $80 billion.

However, many of Jobs' personal character traits did not endear him to others in business. He was a perfectionist who was highly secretive and had, at the very least, what might be described as a hard-driving management style. In 1993 *Fortune* magazine placed him on the list of America's Toughest Bosses for his time at NeXT, quoting cofounder Daniel Lewin as saying: 'The highs were unbelievable … but the lows were unimaginable' (18 October 1993). Fourteen years later it called him 'one of Silicon Valley's leading egomaniacs' (19 March 2007). He was notorious for micromanaging things from the design of new products to the chips they used. In his obituary, the *Daily Telegraph* (6 October 2011) claimed he was 'almost pathologically controlling' when it came to dealing with news reporters and the press, actively trying to stifle any reports that might seem critical of him or Apple. It went on to reveal some elements of his dark side:

'He oozed arrogance, was vicious about business rivals, and in contrast to, say, Bill Gates, refused to have any truck with notions of corporate responsibility. He habitually parked his car in the disabled slot at Apple headquarters and one of the first acts on returning to the company in 1997 was to terminate all of its corporate philanthropy programs … He ruled Apple with a combination of foul-mouthed tantrums and charm, withering scorn and flattery … and those in his regular orbit found he could flip with no warning from one category to the other … Yet members of Jobs' inner circle, many of whom came with him from NeXT, found working for him an exhilarating experience. To keep them on the board, Jobs eliminated most cash bonuses from executive compensation and started handing out stock options instead.'

The *Sunday Times* (30 October 2011) was just as scathing about his personality, giving examples of his bad-tempered, often rude, tantrums with staff and suppliers. He had a propensity for tears and the article cited the example of him throwing a tantrum and crying when he was assigned No. 2 on the Apple payroll and Wozniak was assigned No. 1. Jobs insisted on being 'number zero'. It cited examples of him often claiming the ideas of other Apple employees as his own and described him

Steve Jobs

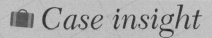

as 'selfish, rude, aggressive, lachrymose, unpredictable … a good candidate for the boss from hell'. It described Apple as 'a cultish, paranoid, joyless organization where public humiliations were a regular occurrence and cut-throat competition among the ranks was encouraged' (*Sunday Times*, 29 January 2012). And yet it also observed that Jobs could inspire incredible loyalty, albeit in the people he had helped to make rich.

Jobs' personal life was equally murky. Before starting up Apple, he famously paid his partner Steve Wozniak only $300 for a job he was paid $5000 for by Atari, when the agreement with Wozniak was for a 50:50 split. At a point in his life where he was already wealthy, he denied paternity of a daughter, leaving the mother on welfare, even swearing an affidavit that he was not the father because, in effect, he was 'sterile and infertile'. He eventually acknowledged paternity. Jobs went on to marry Laurene Powell and have three more children, living in an unassuming family home in Palo Alto, on San Francisco Bay.

Writing after Jobs' death, Adam Lashinsky (2012) gives us a rare insight into the effects this must have had In generating an organizational culture at Apple. As he says: 'you're expected to check your ego at the door' because there really is only room for one – that of Jobs, who he says exhibits 'narcissism, whimsy and disregard for the feelings of others'. Jobs emerges as a short-tempered, authoritarian dictator ruthlessly pushing, even bullying, staff to complete assigned tasks. On a (slightly) more positive note Jobs is described as 'a visionary risk taker with a burning desire to change the world … charismatic leader willing to do whatever it takes to win and who couldn't give a fig about being liked'.

Central to Apple's culture is product excellence – a cult of product – where employees do not want to let the company down by being the weakest link. And if they do, they can become collateral damage because of the aggressive, competitive environment. It is work-orientated and definitely not play-orientated – long hours, missed holidays and tight deadlines were expected and encouraged. However, Lashinsky admits that 'by and large, Apple is a collaborative and cooperative environment, devoid of overt politicking … but it isn't usually nice, and it's almost never relaxed'. In his view unquestioning collaboration and cooperation were necessary to ensure instructions were communicated and followed in this command-and-control structure. He believes that employee happiness was never a top priority

Leading your team

281

Getty Images

for Steve Jobs. But on the other hand, employees derived pride from Apple's products and in working for Jobs' vision. Jobs appeared omnipresent, or at least visible, around the campus, despite the fact that very few people had access to his office suite.

Secrecy, mistrust and paranoia seem to underpin the Apple culture. According to Lashinsky:

> 'Apple is secretive … Far from being empowered, its people operate within narrow bands of responsibility … employees are expected to follow orders, not offer opinions … Apple's CEO was a micromanager … and to an amazingly low level … Apple isn't even a nice place to work … Jobs' brutality in dealing with subordinates legitimized a frighteningly harsh, bullying, and demanding culture … a culture of fear and intimidation found roots.'

Apple's organization structure encouraged secrecy – it did not have organization charts, although Lashinsky's attempt to draw one showed Jobs in the middle of a spider's web. He describes Apple's organization as 'unconventional', with 15 Senior Vice Presidents and Vice Presidents reporting directly to Jobs 'at the centre'. Staff were frequently organized around small project teams with teams isolated from each other and operating under strict secrecy rules – 'siloes within siloes'. Staff only knew about the elements of new product development that they needed to know about. The fact there were no conventional organization charts limited the number of people employees knew outside their immediate environment – a cell-like structure.

Just like all entrepreneurs, Jobs' personality was integral to his leadership style. And he built an organization structure and culture to match his leadership style. However, it was almost the direct opposite of most successful high-tech businesses in Silicon Valley – Lashinsky frequently contrasted Apple with Google. And, at the time of his death, many commentators observed that this organization was so based upon one man, that they questioned how long it would prosper without him.

Nevertheless, Jobs had many admirers and he certainly achieved enormous things in his life. Walter Isaacson (2012) believes that you should not 'fixate too much on the rough edges of his personality'. He said of Jobs that:

> 'He acted as if the normal rules didn't apply to him, and the passion, intensity, and extreme emotionalism he brought to everyday life were things he also poured into the products he made. His petulance and impatience were part and parcel of his perfectionism'.

Isaacson said there were 14 keys to his success:

1. **Focus** – Jobs was always able to focus and spend time on what he considered important, often to the frustration of others trying to get him to consider other things. As he explained to the 1997 meeting of the Apple Worldwide Developers Association: 'Focusing is about saying no … and the result of that focus is going to be some really great products where the total is much greater than the sum of the parts.'

2. **Simplify** – Jobs admired simplicity and simplicity of use was a key design feature of all Apple's products: 'It takes a lot of hard work to make something simple, to truly understand the underlying challenges and come up with elegant solutions.'

3. **Take responsibility end-to-end** – In his quest for simplicity, Jobs took end-to-end responsibility for the user experience, integrating hardware, software and peripherals – part of his controlling nature and drive for perfection.

4. **When behind leapfrog** – Rather than copying competitors, Jobs would always try to create something better and different.

5. **Push for perfection** – Jobs was a perfectionist and would delay production until he thought the product was 100% right.

6. **Put products before profits** – Because he was a perfectionist he also wanted his products to be the best, whatever the price. He believed that if the product was great, profits would follow.

7. **Don't be a slave to focus groups** – Because Apple's products were so innovative, Jobs never trusted focus groups and market research, preferring his own instincts: 'Customers don't know what they want until we show them.'

8. **Bend reality** – Jobs' famous 'reality distortion field' persuaded people that his vision of the future would prevail. Some called it bullying and lying, others called it effective communication of strategic intent.

9. **Impute** – Jobs used the design of products and even its packaging to 'impute' signals to customers, signals that underpinned the brand identity.

10. **Tolerate only 'A' players** – Jobs' passion for perfection extended to employees and, perhaps, explains his rudeness to people who did not perform as he expected.

11. **Engage face-to-face** – Jobs was a believer in face-to-face meetings. His executive team met once a week, without an agenda, to 'kick around ideas'.

12. **Know both the big picture and the detail** – Jobs had both vision and a grasp of detail, or at least the detail he thought important.

13. **Combine humanities and sciences** – Jobs was able to connect ideas from different disciplines to create features in his products that customers valued (a creativity 'discovery skill').

14. **Stay hungry, stay foolish** – Jobs never wanted to lose the drive he had in his youth and always wanted Apple to keep the culture of a start-up.

So was Steve Jobs a great entrepreneurial leader? He certainly was a great entrepreneur. And under his leadership Apple certainly was extremely successful. But has he created an organization that is entrepreneurial and that can succeed and prosper without him? Only time will tell.

Questions:

1. *Review your answers to the case questions in Chapter 2. What elements of the entrepreneurial DNA do you spot in Jobs? What are the positive and negative aspects of these character traits?*

2. *How important is it for the culture and structure of an organization to reflect the character traits of its leader?*

3. *Was Jobs a great entrepreneurial leader? Explain and justify.*

4. *Do you have to be a likeable character to be a great entrepreneurial leader? Explain and justify.*

Lashinsky, A. (2012) *Inside Apple: The Secrets Behind the Past and Future Success of Steve Jobs's Iconic Brand*, London: John Murray.

Isaacson, W. (2012) 'The Real Leadership Lessons of Steve Jobs', *Harvard Business Review*, April.

Summary

- Management and leadership are different and distinct terms, although the skills and competences associated with each are complementary. Management is concerned with handling complexity in organizational processes and the execution of work. It is about detail and logic, efficiency and effectiveness. Leadership, on the other hand, is concerned with setting direction, communicating and motivating. It is about broad principles and emotion. It is particularly concerned with change.

- The ability to influence and build relationships requires certain characteristics in leaders – emotional intelligence, self-awareness and self-management. Leaders also need to be able to be strategic thinkers and learners and be able to reflect.

- Contingency theory tells us that the leadership style appropriate for one situation may be inappropriate for another. The appropriate leadership style depends on the leader, the group, the task and situation or context facing the leader.

- The entrepreneurial context of leadership is one characterized by uncertainty, rapid change and risk-taking. There are various other leadership paradigms that inform us about leadership in this context – transactional leadership, transformational leadership, visionary leadership and dispersed leadership.

- The attributes, skills and behaviours needed for effective leadership of an entrepreneurial organization are summarized in Table 13.1. In line with contingency theory, however, these may need to be 'fine-tuned' for specific contexts.

- Leadership styles, organizational cultures and structures are linked. If any one is inappropriate for the other two then the organization will not function as well as it should. The task of the entrepreneurial leader is to construct an organizational architecture that is consistent and where one reinforces the other.

Exercise 13.1

Your leadership

The aim of this exercise is to get you to focus on *your* leadership skills and how they might be developed as the business grows.

1 Complete the Leadership Style questionnaire below. It evaluates your 'people vs task' orientation. For each of the following statements, tick the 'Yes' box if you tend to agree or the 'No' box if you disagree. Try to relate the answers to your actual recent behaviour as a manager. There are no right and wrong answers. When you have completed the test, score yourself with the answers on the next page. What does this tell you about your leadership style?

	Yes	No
1. I encourage overtime work	○	○
2. I allow staff complete freedom in their work	○	○
3. I encourage the use of standard procedures	○	○
4. I allow staff to use their own judgement in solving problems	○	○
5. I stress being better than other firms	○	○
6. I urge staff to greater effort	○	○
7. I try out my ideas with others in the firm	○	○
8. I let my staff work in the way they think best	○	○
9. I keep work moving at a rapid pace	○	○
10. I turn staff loose on a job and let them get on with it	○	○
11. I settle conflicts when they happen	○	○
12. I get swamped by detail	○	○
13. I always represent the 'firm view' at meetings with outsiders	○	○
14. I am reluctant to allow staff freedom of action	○	○
15. I decide what should be done and who should do it	○	○
16. I push for improved quality	○	○
17. I let some staff have authority I could keep	○	○
18. Things usually turn out as I predict	○	○
19. I allow staff a high degree of initiative	○	○
20. I assign staff to particular tasks	○	○
21. I am willing to make changes	○	○
22. I ask staff to work harder	○	○
23. I trust staff to exercise good judgement	○	○
24. I schedule the work to be done	○	○
25. I refuse to explain my actions	○	○
26. I persuade others that my ideas are to their advantage	○	○
27. I permit the staff to set their own pace for change	○	○
28. I urge staff to beat previous targets	○	○
29. I act without consulting staff	○	○
30. I ask staff to follow standard rules and procedures	○	○

Adapted from Pfeiffer, J. and Jones, J. (eds) (1974), *A Handbook of Structured Experiences from Human Relations Training*, vol. 1 (rev.), San Diego, CA: University Associates.

2 Complete a Thomas–Kilmann Conflict Modes Instrument (www.kilmann.com/conflict.html). What does this tell you about your style of dealing with conflict?

Exercise 13.2

Review the results of your Belbin test in Exercise 12.4.

Exercise 13.3

With the results of these tests in mind, evaluate your ability to lead an entrepreneurial organization against the ten attributes, skills and behaviours listed in Table 13.1.

Exercise 13.4

Review the results of Exercises 12.5 and 12.6 and change, as appropriate, to reflect your leadership style.

Exercise 13.5

List the implications of these exercises for your current leadership skills. Think about what you need to do to develop them further.

Leadership Style Questionnaire: Scoring

To obtain your leadership orientation rating, score 1 point for the appropriate response under each heading, then total your scores. If your response is inappropriate you do not score. As a guide, a score of 5 or less is low and 12 or more is high.

Concern for PEOPLE score (maximum score 15)

'Yes' for questions 2, 4, 8, 10, 17, 19, 21, 23, 27.   'No' for questions 6, 13, 14, 25, 29, 30.

Concern for TASK score (maximum score 15)

'Yes' for questions 1, 3, 5, 7, 9, 11, 15, 16, 18, 20, 22, 24, 26, 28.

'No' for question 12.

Next plot your position on the Leadership Grid below.

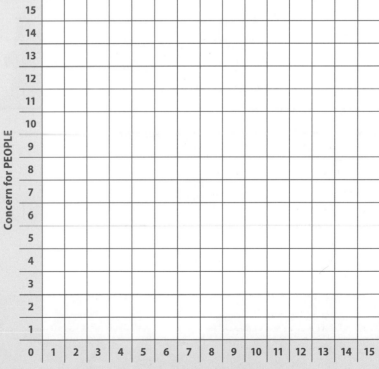

Visit www.palgrave.com/companion/burns-new-venture-creation for chapter quizzes to test your knowledge and other resources.

14
OBTAINING
FINANCE

Contents

Academic insights 📑

Case insights 💼

Learning outcomes

When you have read this chapter and undertaken the related exercises you will be able to:

- Understand the principles of prudent financing
- Describe the sources of finance available to small firms and evaluate which are appropriate for different needs
- Understand how banks assess lending to start-ups and small firms and how they monitor the performance
- Understand how business angels and venture capitalists assess investments in start-ups and small firms, and how they might work with the founder
- Make a preliminary assessment of the finance needed for your business
- Understand how the equity investment in a start-up can be realized

Selecting the right sort of finance

Many new ventures require finance to get started. The more fixed assets you need, the higher your stock-holding and the longer debtors take to pay, the greater your need for finance. And whilst a cash flow forecast will tell you how much you require and for how long (we deal with this in the next chapter), it will not tell you what sort of finance you require.

The first thing to realize is that not all money is the same. Different sorts of money ought to be used for different purposes and not all types of money are available to all new ventures. In fact many entrepreneurs, particularly at start-up, try to avoid using money at all by borrowing or using other people's assets wherever possible – 'bootstrapping'. They also use their personal credit cards, often repaying and recycling balances month-by-month. Where this fails, they might borrow money from friends or relatives. Friends and relatives can be flexible, perhaps agreeing to lend at a low or zero interest rate and without any guarantees because they know and trust you. They might even help with running the firm and bring valuable experience with them.

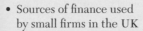

John Elliott, founder Ebac Sunday Times 10 March 2013

To succeed in business you should never chase money. If you achieve success money will chase you. If you get too attached to the money you never reinvest. You have to treat the money in the business like it's not yours.

Duration of finance	Source of finance	Use of finance

Long- and medium-term	• Equity
	  • Personal, family and friends' investment
	  • Angel finance
	  • Venture finance
	• Long- and medium-term loans
	  • Personal, family and friends
	  • Bank
	• Lease and hire purchase
	• Crowdfunding (equity or loan)
		• Fixed assets: land, buildings, machinery, plant, equipment, vehicles, furniture etc.
		• Permanent working capital: stock, debtors (net creditors)

Short-term	• Bank overdraft
	• Short-term loans
	  • Personal, family and friends
	  • Bank
		• Seasonal fluctuations in working capital: stock, debtors (net creditors)

T14.1 Matching sources and uses of finance

However, rather than relying on informal agreements, most advisors would recommend that more formal loan agreements are drawn up so as to avoid misunderstandings and arguments later. Inevitably, however, most firms will need to obtain some form of external finance at some point in their life.

Table 14.1 summarizes the major forms of finance and how they *ought* to be used – in theory. The principle is that the term-duration of the source of finance should be matched to the term-duration of the use to which it is put. Fixed or permanent assets, including the permanent element of working capital (stock and debtors, net of creditors) should be financed by long- or medium-term sources of finance and only fluctuations in working capital should be financed by short-term finance, such as an overdraft.

For a limited company the money that you put into the venture can take two forms – equity or loans. Equity takes the form of share capital. Over time the shareholders' equity grows with profitable trading. But if the venture fails then the shareholder risks losing everything, including the share capital they have put into the venture. For profitable, fast-growing businesses with a good management team there may be the opportunity to attract further equity investment from crowdfunding, business angels or venture capital organizations. These are covered in more detail later in this chapter.

Loans can come from many sources, but most firms will have to turn to the banks for finance at some point. Loans are serviced by regular interest payments and the capital will, ultimately, have to be repaid, depending on the duration: short-term (under one year), medium-term (up to five years) or long-term (over five years). Interest may vary with base rate or be fixed for the term of the loan. Agreeing to a fixed rate may involve a certain amount of crystal-ball gazing, but it does ensure that a small firm knows what its financing costs will be for some time to come.

As we shall see in the next section, bankers are likely to look for the security of assets to act as collateral against any loan and, if they cannot get this, they may ask you for personal guarantees. Personal guarantees can come from you or family or friends. Many countries have government loan schemes that offer lower rates of interest to small firms and/or guarantee provisions to replace or supplement personal guarantees. Some countries have credit mutual schemes for small firms that offer similar advantages.

There are two other ways of financing the purchase of fixed assets:

- **Lease** –allows the firm to use the asset without owning it by making regular lease payments.
- **Hire purchase** –allows the firm to purchase the asset over a period of time, again, by making regular payments with the asset acting as security in the event of default.

The main practical difference between the two methods is their tax treatment. Interest rates on lease and hire purchase schemes may be higher than on loans, but for a firm with little security to offer a banker they might be the only way to secure finance.

> Tim Ewington, co-founder Shortlist Media Daily Telegraph 5 July 2013
>
> We did look at **securing** [a conventional loan] but we quickly ended up where we are – invoice **discounting** … A lot of friends run **small** businesses, and banks are not being **generous** to say the least. They're very careful – which is why they prefer to offer **invoice discounting**, because it's **safe** for them

Once you start trading other sources of finance become available. Most suppliers of goods and services offer trade credit terms (e.g. payment in 30 days), although they might insist on taking credit references and might also undertake a credit check. They will also place credit limits on accounts. Start-ups may have to establish a payment history to be offered credit and only gradually will the credit limit be extended. Trade credit is an important source of finance for most established firms – and it is free. It is also worth mentioning **factoring** and **invoice discounting** which is, again, only available once you establish a trading history. These are ways of obtaining finance against the invoices you issue (typically 75–80% of the value). You pay interest on the cash advanced, until the invoice is paid. It

Government loans, grants and other support schemes vary from country to country. They also change regularly.

For details of the Enterprise Finance Guarantee scheme in the UK go to: www.gov.uk/understanding-the-enterprise-finance-guarantee

For details of schemes in the USA go to: www.sba.gov (click on 'Loans & Grants')

To access an interactive tool that tells you what grants, loans and other support might be available for your business in the UK go to: www.gov.uk/business-finance-support-finder

and in the USA go to: www.sba.gov/loans-and-grants

can be expensive and there are many restrictions but it can be a lifeline to undercapitalized, rapidly growing businesses. Your bank will put you in touch with organizations offering these facilities.

Finally, it goes without question that if there are grants or 'soft loans' available then they should be considered. Grants are 'free money', although they can involve bureaucracy and take time to come through. They vary enormously between countries and even regions, changing frequently to reflect national and regional priorities. There are often special schemes for start-ups, particularly social enterprises and often for younger people.

Most new ventures will struggle to find finance appropriate for their needs. It is rarely easy. The flowchart in Figure 14.1 (overleaf) attempts to guide you through the process of deciding what form of finance is most appropriate and available to you. In practice, you are most likely to use two or more sources of finance. For example, some resources could be bootstrapped, leaving a smaller shortfall to be covered by grants and/or outside equity in some form. Of course, actually persuading somebody to offer you the equity or loan finance will be more difficult.

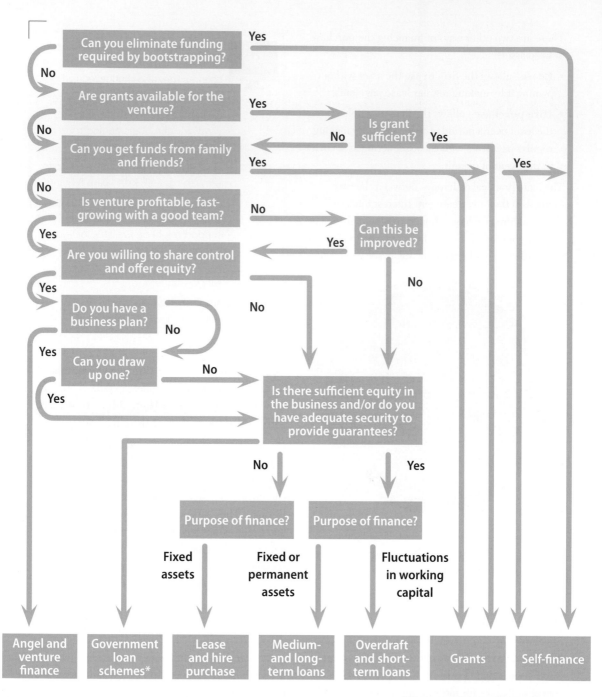

F14.1 Selecting the appropriate sort of finance for a new venture

*These vary from country to country

💼 *Case insight*

Softcat

Factoring

Peter Kelly never finished his degree, instead he travelled the world before returning to the UK. He worked for Rank Xerox in Sales and Training for 7 years before starting Software Catalogue, a mail-order software business, in 1993. This became Softcat Limited and is now based in Marlow, UK. Peter is still Chairman. Softcat employs more than 200 people and has a turnover in excess of £100 million. It has become a leading supplier of software licensing, hardware, security solutions and related IT services to companies.

Success brought unexpected problems early in Softcat's life. Initially, Peter drew up a business plan, put in of £35,000 of his own money and found two external investors, each willing to put in a further £10,000. The mail-order software market was virtually untapped at the time and it was the firm's success that caused the problem. Within a year it had run out of cash and had reached the end of its ever-increasing overdraft limit as debtors/receivables were increasing at an alarming rate. The firm was overtrading – trading beyond its financial resources. Peter's response was to factor his debts – relying on the one asset in his balance sheet for security. It might have been more expensive than overdraft finance, but it helped the company to survive, grow and become the success it is today.

Up-to-date information on Softcat can be found on their website: www.softcat.com

Obtaining finance

💼 *Case insight*

Hotel Chocolat

Raising funds from customers

Hotel Chocolat is a luxury chocolate maker and retailer set up in the 1990s by Angus Thirlwell and Peter Harris. Over the years it developed a loyal customer base that opened up interesting funding opportunities for the business later in its life. In 2010 it raised £3.7 million by offering 100,000 members of its 'tasting club' three-year, £2000 or £4000 bonds, with the interest paid in bi-monthly deliveries of a chocolate tasting box.

The bonds fell due for repayment in 2013 and the company re-offered them to their customers on similar terms. 97% signed up for another three years.

> This was prompted by our customers asking how they could get more **involved** with the company. We found a way of inviting them to **invest** in our development plans in exchange for a return paid in chocolate. And we have been **bowled over** by their response. We are now in a **strong** position to grow the business further using funds provided **directly** from our customers.

Angus Thirlwell The Independent 14 July 2010

Find out more about the company on: www.hotelchocolat.com

Sources of finance used by small firms in the UK

Based upon a random sample of 160 UK start-ups (less than two years old) interviewed in 2008, Fraser (2009) found 85% used internal finance. Of these, 91% used personal savings, 13% loans or gifts from family or friends, 4% home mortgages and 4% personal credit cards. (The total is more than 100% because some businesses used more than one source.) Only 13% of start-ups used external finance, of which 94% used bank loans and 7% used grants or subsidies.

The same study looked at a random sample of 2500 established small firms (under 250 employees) and found that they all used some sort of external finance. It found 54% still used credit cards, 43% used overdrafts, 37% (free) trade credit, 21% asset finance (lease and/or hire purchase), 16% term loans, 9% loans from family or friends but only 3% used equity (which mainly came from the owner or family or friends) and 2% used factoring, invoice discounting or stock finance. (Again, the total is more than 100% because businesses used more than one source.)

Two interesting points emerge. Firstly, the continuing but increasing use of credit card finance, where balances might be paid off and recycled month-to-month. Secondly, the low use of equity finance, particularly from external sources. Indeed only 1.7% of the firms used business angels and fewer than 1% used venture capitalists.

Fraser, S (2009) 'How Have SME Finances Been Affected by the Credit Crisis?', BERR/ESRC Seminar, March.

Lingo 24

The funding dilemma

Lingo 24 is an Edinburgh-based online translation business started by Christian Arno in 2002 while still at university. Today it has a turnover of over £7 million and more than 200 staff. Surprisingly this growth has been entirely self-funded. However, in order to finance a new automated translation platform, in 2013 Christian was considering selling an equity stake in the business. But he would have preferred to find a bank loan and was reluctant to give away equity to venture capitalists, so he hired corporate finance advisors to help him select the right option.

> I've been **nervous** and kept costs low at every turn to avoid the needs for **funds**. But now it's a pace thing. We need to move ahead quickly … If a bank could give us a **£3 million** loan, I'd love it – but they'll never do that with a business like ours because of the type of **assets** we have. We only have our debtor book and that won't facilitate that level of **borrowing** … Someone I know had a very bad experience with outside investors. You hear horror stories of people losing control and losing the **value** they've built up. But with the level of **ambition** we have and the dynamic of the marketplace at the moment, we need those **funds**.

Daily Telegraph 5 July 2013

UK

Bank loans and overdrafts

Banks are the main source of loan finance to small firms. And so long as the return you make on the total assets in the business (see Chapter 15) exceeds the current rate of interest, then you benefit by getting an extra return on the bank's money. However, if your return drops below the rate of interest then the loan will drain money out of the firm.

> The banks are very supportive but they either **lend** you twice what you need, or **half** what you need.
>
> *John Elliott, founder Ebac Sunday Times 10 March 2013*

imageSource

Banks can be reluctant to lend to small firms, and new ventures in particular, because they view them as risky propositions. And it is worth understanding why this is the case. Banks lend a sum of money in return for agreed interest payments and the repayment of the sum borrowed. They do not share in the profits of the business and, if a firm fails, they stand to lose their capital. That bad debt is expensive to recoup. For example, if banks make a 4% margin on a loan (the difference between the rate they can borrow at and the rate they can lend at), then every £100 lost as a bad debt will need a further £2500 to be lent for the sum to be recovered (£2500 × 4% = £100). Put another way, the bank has to make a further 25 loans to cover this one bad debt. Not surprisingly, therefore, banks are risk averse and will do all they can to avoid a bad debt. Since they are all too aware of the failure statistics for business start-ups, entrepreneurs have an uphill task convincing banks of the viability of their project and obtaining a loan or even an overdraft facility.

Entrepreneurs seem naturally drawn to overdraft finance – surveys show it to be the major source of finance for small firms. After all it is flexible, once agreed you can dip into it when you need it and you will only pay interest when you use it. However, it is repayable immediately should the bank demand it and it can be expensive if you are in permanent overdraft as the rate of interest charged is usually higher than on term loans. Term loans (short-, medium- or long-) are loans for a fixed period of time. They are usually not repayable on bank demand (but do check terms). The capital repayments are fixed and known in advance. The interest rate can vary or be fixed and is usually lower than for an overdraft.

Banks expect higher rates of return from loans that they perceive to be higher risk. New ventures are therefore likely to face higher rates of interest than larger businesses with an established track record. They are also likely to face a demand for collateral against the loan. Collateral is the additional security demanded in case there is a default on a loan. It can take many forms and is normally specified by some form of charge or guarantee in the legal loan agreement. Collateral might come from business assets but if these are insufficient then the entrepreneur (or their family or friends) may well be asked to provide personal collateral or guarantees for the loan. This can mean that the separation between your finances and those of your limited liability company is little more than theoretical.

In valuing business collateral the bank assumes that the assets will be sold on a second-hand market and this typically leads to far lower values being put on assets than you might expect. Table 14.2 gives a guide to what to expect. Given these asset security values, it is clear that the full cost of new fixed assets will never filter down to the collateral base of your business – an incentive to use lease or hire purchase.

Asset	% value that can be borrowed	
Freehold land and buildings	70	
Long leasehold	60	
Specialist plant and machinery	5–10	100% can be obtained through leasing
Non-specialist plant and machinery	30	100% can be obtained through leasing
Debtors	30–50	Depends on age of debts and 'quality'
Stock	25	Depends on age of stock and 'quality'. In the event of business failure, raw materials will be worth more than work-in-progress or finished goods stocks.

T14.2 **Asset security values**

What banks look for

Banks are in business to make as much money as possible with the least risk. Bank managers are employees, they work in a highly regulated environment, and they have very limited discretion. Lending decisions are heavily influenced by bank lending policies and procedures. Some banks use computer-based credit scoring systems to produce lending recommendations for managers. Lending decisions can reflect general economic conditions and the balance of the bank's lending portfolio as much as the lending proposition itself. One bank can turn down an applicant that another will accept.

For a bank, the starting point for agreeing to any loan is its **purpose.** Is this consistent with bank policy? Is it legal? Is it in the best interest of the business? Next, the bank needs to assess whether the **amount** is appropriate. Have all associated costs for the project been included? Has the borrower put money in themselves? Is there a contingency? It also wants to ensure that interest is paid and the loan capital repaid on the due date. So is cash flow adequate? Finally, the bank will

want to assess whether the **repayment** terms are realistic. To make this judgement the bank will want to understand the fundamentals of the business – whether it is viable – and will ask for financial information. In short, the bank will normally ask for a business plan.

Within the business plan, banks are particularly keen to scrutinize the **cash flow forecast** because it shows whether interest payments can be made and what 'slack' there might be. They expect interest to be paid first and that may mean delaying capital expenditure and reducing or delaying personal drawings. They are also keen to look at the **breakeven point** and the margin of safety (Chapter 11) which tell them about the operating risk of the business in terms of the overheads it faces and the margin it is able to command. These are vital pieces of information in judging a loan to a start-up. Banks may also look at the projected future **gearing** ratios (particularly

> Initially when I was first starting the business and approaching the big five banks for a corporate bank account, it was quite challenging. Their response to me becoming a consultant for improving financial services was to pat me on the head like a dog, saying 'there, there, little girl'.
>
> Elizabeth Gooch, founder EG Solutions Venture online 12 April 2007 (www.venturemagazine.co.uk)

for larger-scale start-ups), to see whether the business might become over-borrowed. These financial measures are explained in Chapter 15. Banks are also keen to see good financial controls are in place since this should lead to strong cash flow.

However, banks understand that most small firms are dominated by the owner-manager and usually seek to establish a good understanding of the person they lend to. They are interested in your **personal character**. Honesty and integrity are difficult to judge, but most bankers still think lending is a very personal thing and making a judgement on your character is vital. Your business track record and personal credit history are important. They will also make a judgement about your **personal ability**. How likely are you to turn this business plan into a successful business? Do you have a good management team behind you? Banks usually judge your personal character and ability by looking at your credit history, education and training, relevant business experience and proven track record. Unfortunately, with all these personal judgements, one person's objectivity might just be another's prejudice.

◢ *Academic insight*

Agency theory and information asymmetry

Agency theory is relevant when there is an arms-length relationship between a principal (such as a bank or an equity investor) and an agent (such as a small firm). It seeks to identify the mechanisms and costs that the principal has to put in place to ensure that the agent conforms to some legal agreement – such as a loan agreement. Information asymmetry is where these two parties do not have the same information on which to base their decisions.

Agency theory is relevant to how providers of finance approach new ventures. By definition, a new venture has no track record, and the provider of finance has little information on which to base their financing decision. What they have may not be reliable or relevant to this specific financing decision. This is when asymmetric information favours the entrepreneur who should have more or better information than the provider of finance. This means that the provider of finance must incur extra costs in obtaining and checking the information they need in order to make, and then monitor, their decision. Many of these costs are fixed, whatever the size of the deal or the return made by the small firm. The conclusion is that providers of finance are naturally reluctant to

lend or invest in start-ups or smaller ventures. This is less of a problem with larger firms because they have a track record and there is so much more public information about them, with many independent analysts reviewing this information for investment purposes.

Agency theory suggests that the natural response of a bank to these problems is to charge higher rates of interest, to impose conditions in the loan agreement (e.g. on use of funds or the provision of information) and/ or to ask for business or personal collateral. Where sufficient collateral can be made available, the bank may feel that less information is required because the debt is more likely to be recovered in the event of default. Indeed, the bank may also feel that the provision of collateral gives the entrepreneur a

strong incentive to see the business succeed. Agency theory also explains why the bank will want to be kept up to date on the progress of the business.

Similarly, the response of an equity investor is to look for higher rates of return. However, they will also expect the entrepreneur to maintain a controlling interest in the business so that, in the event of failure, they have more to lose than the other investors. This might impose a funding limit. The investor is also likely to want a greater involvement in the business so they can monitor their investment. Because of the fixed costs involved, many larger providers of equity finance will not get involved in small-scale start-ups because the return they can obtain does not cover their costs.

Banking relationship

Even after the loan is granted, banks will continue to monitor the financial performance of the business – using many of the ratios outlined in the next chapter. They expect to see annual audited accounts and sometimes budgets for the next year. What is more, they will also monitor the bank account itself, looking out for irregularities and checking that throughput is in line with expectations. And their expectations will be based upon your cash flow forecasts.

Despite increasing centralization and the declining importance of local banking, you still need to have a good working relationship with your local bank manager. A close relationship has the potential to provide them with the information they need about your firm and thus avoid the problem of information asymmetry. Like any relationship, this must be based on two elements: trust, that both parties will honour the terms of the loan, and respect, that both parties are good at what they do. It is a personal thing that is developed by keeping in regular contact. The bank must ultimately trust and respect you, not just the business. That means visits and the provision of information. Bankers like to make regular visits. They like to feel they know the business and the individuals in it. However, bankers, more than anything, do not like surprises. Some of the things that start to make them worry that all is not well in a firm include:

- *Frequent excesses on the bank account beyond the agreed overdraft facility*: This makes the bank start to think cash flow is not being properly controlled.

- *Development of hard-core borrowing on an overdraft facility*: This makes the bank believe that a term loan would be more appropriate.

- *Lack of financial information*: If the accounts and other information do not arrive regularly, they worry about the firm's ability to produce control information and, in extremis, can become suspicious that all is not well.

- *Your unavailability*: If you are never available for a meeting or even a telephone conversation, the bank will start to believe something is wrong. Most people do not want to give bad news and avoidance is one way of not having to.

- *Inability to meet forecasts*: The bank will eventually start to question the credibility of your forecasts and your ability and understanding of the market.

- *Continuing losses, declining margins and rapidly diminishing or even increasing turnover*: At the end of the day the bank is really only interested in your ability to service its loan.

- *Overreliance on too few customers or suppliers*: The loss of just one customer or supplier can create a disproportionate problem for small firms.

© shironosov Istockphoto.com

Crowdfunding and peer-to-peer lending

The recession that started in 2008 saw bank lending contract as banks tried to recapitalize and consolidate their balance sheets. The first victims of this were those 'riskier' loans to start-ups and small businesses. However, the growth of the internet has spawned the development of a new form of funding called crowdfunding, and peer-to-peer (P2P) lending which connects borrowers directly with potential private lenders. The connection is made through internet platforms which act as a sort of eBay for lenders and borrowers. Registered lenders can browse through lending opportunities posted by prospective borrowers and decide whether they wish to lend.

P2P lending offers advantages to both lenders and borrowers. Lenders generally earn far more than they would if they put the money in a savings account – an average of over 9%. Borrowers who may not necessarily be approved for a bank loan might find it easier to borrow, albeit at a higher interest rate if their credit rating is low. The intermediary normally has registered lenders and charges the borrower a percentage of the funds raised. This is how they make money. As with bank borrowing, borrowers and lenders will be party to a legal loan agreement which, among other things, will specify interest rates and capital repayment. These are organized by the intermediary. The industry is in its infancy – the first British company, Zopa, was started in 2005 – and is unregulated. However, with confidence in banks falling, many people are predicting P2P lending will grow and could change the way we invest and borrow our money.

Some intermediaries allow you to browse through small-scale projects posted by not-for-profit organizations and donate funds (e.g. Global Giving). There are also platforms that facilitate crowdfunding of loans managed by microcredit organizations in developing countries (e.g. Kiva).

Some intermediary platforms offer equity as well as loan funding opportunities, again charging the business a percentage of the funds raised. Typically each investor purchases only a very small percentage of the company. The first equity deal in the UK using crowdfunding was agreed in 2013, using an intermediary called Crowdcube (see Case Insight). In many ways this is the logical extension of the business angel networks discussed in the next section. However, as we shall see, equity investment is inherently riskier than loans and crowdfunding investors probably have less expertise than business angels in making this sort of investment. What is more, the issue about how and when their investment will be realized in the form of a capital gain remains even more up in the air. All of these issues make this sort of investment very risky, which is why each investor will only ever contribute a small proportion of the funds raised and why the success of this source of finance – for both parties – is yet to be proved. So far, it has only been successful for 'quirkier' businesses with quasi-social objectives where investors might be less interested in risk and return than supporting the objectives of the venture.

Is there discrimination in lending?

PhotoDisc/Getty Images

An issue often raised about finance is that bankers discriminate against certain sections of society in their lending decisions. So is there any evidence of prejudice and discrimination causing financing gaps for groups within society? It is true that women-owned businesses tend to attract less outside funding than male-owned businesses. Studies have repeatedly found that women-owned businesses start with significantly less financial capital (typically only one-third) than men-owned start-ups (Carter and Rosa, 1998; Coleman, 2000; Hisrich and Brush, 1984). Women are also more likely to rely on personal savings, however limited, and are rarely given access to venture funding (Green et al., 2000; Marlow and Patton, 2003). The question of whether there is active discrimination against women in the provision of finance or the existence of a supply-side finance gap therefore needs to be addressed. However, firstly, research in the UK and USA has reported no differences in bank loan rejection rates by gender (in the UK: Fraser, 2006; in the USA: Treichel and Scott, 2006). It has also failed to unearth evidence of a supply-side finance gap for women (in the UK: Fraser, 2006; in the USA: Levenson and Willard, 2000). These studies could not find evidence of actual discrimination by financial institutions – which suggests that other demand-side factors were at play. Although not conclusive, other researchers broadly concur.

Turning to ethnic minority businesses, in the USA Cavalluzzo and Wolken (2005) found striking differences between ethnic groups in terms of denial of credit. In the UK, there appears to be no difference between ethnic and white businesses in their dependence on bank finance, although this is significantly less for Black African and Black Caribbean business (Bank of England, 1999). Specialist banks have grown up to cater for the needs of different ethnic groups; for example, specialist Islamic banks which allow Muslim businesses to bank according to their principles and faith. There is also evidence of a strong preference for informal sources of finance (Ram et. al., 2002). This study found the reliance on informal finance was most significant in South Asian-owned businesses. These informal sources are usually accessed from a wide network of family, friends and others within the ethnic community, thus combining social with financial capital. Many of these sources are not available to white entrepreneurs.

Although, as with female entrepreneurs, there is a strong feeling of prejudice from traditional banks, the Bank of England (op. cit.) could find no evidence of this in the UK, citing sectoral concentration, failure rates and lack of business planning for rejection rates. A large-scale study of ethnic minority businesses and their access to finance broadly supported this (Ram et al., op. cit.) noting, however, that the issue was 'complex'. It did find evidence of diversity of experience from bank manager to bank manager and between different ethnic minority groups, confirming the existence of particular problems for Africans and Caribbeans. Not surprisingly, it found that best practice was where the bank manager had built up trust with their local minority community through close contact and stable relationships. More recently, Fraser (2009) used econometric analysis on a large-scale survey of UK small business finance to look for evidence of ethnic discrimination (loan denials, interest rates and discouragement). He concluded firstly that there were large differences across ethnic groups – Black and Bangladeshi businesses experiencing poor outcomes compared to White and Indian businesses. For example, from the finance provider's perspective, Black African firms were significantly more likely to miss loan repayments or exceed their agreed overdraft limit. He also noted that many from the ethnic minorities felt they were discriminated against. However, he concluded very firmly that there was no evidence of discrimination. He felt that many in these groups needed to tackle fundamentals like a lack of financial skills and advice and poor levels of financial performance rather than just addressing cultural differences and the effects they might have. In conclusion, academic studies in the UK and USA cannot uncover any systematic discrimination on grounds of ethnicity or gender.

Bank of England (1999) *The Financing of Ethnic Minority Firms in the UK: A Special Report*, London: Bank of England.

Carter, S. and Rosa, P. (1998) 'The Financing of Male and Female Owned Businesses', *Entrepreneurship and Regional Development*, 8.

Cavalluzzo, K. and Wolken, J. (2005) 'Small Business Loan Turndowns, Personal Wealth, and Discrimination', *Journal of Business*, 78.

Coleman, S. (2000) 'Access to Capital and Terms of Credit: A Comparison of Men and Women-owned Small Businesses', *Journal of Small Business Management*, 38(3).

Fraser, S. (2006) *Finance for Small and Medium-sized Enterprises: A Report on the 2004 UK Survey of SME Finances*, Warwick Business School, Centre for Small and Medium-sized Enterprises, Coventry.

Fraser, S. (2009) 'Is there Ethnic Discrimination in the UK Market for Small Business Credit?', *International Small Business Journal*, 27(5).

Green, P., Brush, C., Hart, M., and Saparito, P. (2009) 'Exploration of the Venture Capital Industry: Is Gender an Issue?', *Frontiers of Entrepreneurial Research Series*, Wellesley, MA: Babson College.

Hisrich, R. and Brush, C.G. (1984) 'The Woman Entrepreneur: Management Skills and Business Problems', *Journal of Small Business Management*, 22(1).

Levenson, A.R. and Willard, K.L. (2000) 'Do Firms Get the Financing They Want? Measuring Credit Rationing Experienced by Small Businesses in the USA', *Small Business Economics*, 14(2).

Macmillan, H. (1931) *Report of the Committee on Finance and Industry*, Cmd 3897, London: HMSO.

Marlow, S. and Patton, D. (2003) 'The Financing of Small Business – Female Experiences', in M. Davies and S. Fielden (eds), *International Handbook of Women and Small Business Entrepreneurship*, Cheltenham: Edward Elgar.

Ram, M., Smallbone, D. and Deakins, D. (2002) *Ethnic Minority Business in the UK: Access to Finance and Business Support*, London: British Bankers' Association.

Treichel, M.Z. and Scott, J.A. (2006) 'Women-owned Business and Access to Bank Credit: Evidence from Three Surveys since 1987', *Venture Capital: An International Journal of Entrepreneurial Finance*, 8(1).

Obtaining finance

InSpiral Visionary Products

Crowdfunding

Dominik Schnell and Bella Willink founded InSpiral Visionary Products in 2010. Starting life in a vegan café near Camden Market in London, the company sells organic products, including crisps made from dried kale that originally sold for £3.49 a packet. In 2013 InSpiral became the first company to raise equity rather than loan finance from crowdfunding. Using Crowdcube, the company raised £250,000 from 120 investors, handing over 10% of their equity – valuing the company at £2.5 million. Crowdcube charged InSpiral a fee of 5% of the money raised. Crowdcube has 30,000 registered investors and has raised over £5.5 million since it was launched in 2011.

InSpiral has used the money raised to redesign its packaging and to sell its products online through Graze.com and through other retail outlets. It also now produces own-label products for a number of major high street stores. Increasing production allowed it to spread its overheads and bring down its sales prices significantly. For example, the price of kale crisps came down to £2.19 per pack, and that opened up more retail opportunities.

InSpiral

Angel and venture finance

For a company with real growth potential, there may also be the opportunity to get private individuals (called **business angels**) or a venture capital institution to invest equity in the business. Equity funding is not available to sole traders or partnerships. Equity investment involves giving up a percentage of the ownership of the business, and potentially some of the control, in exchange for cash. That means giving up some of the future wealth the business will create. Investors are paid dividends, which are only paid at the discretion of the company. Whilst the capital invested can be sold on in the form of shares, it is unlikely to be repaid by the business unless it ceases to trade, and only then if other creditors are paid in full. It is therefore long-term risk finance.

Both angel and venture financiers might expect dividends but, more importantly, they hope to see the value of their shares increase if the firm does well. They will probably expect to realize their investment at some time in the future (normally 5–10 years) by selling on their shares in the business. Often an angel investment helps take the investee business to a point at which it is attractive for a venture capital firm.

Business angels invest smaller amounts of money than venture capital institutions (£10,000–£1 million) and operate in less formal ways. They are usually 'high net worth individuals', often with a successful entrepreneurial background themselves. They are looking to back start-up and early-stage ventures. The typical UK angel makes only one or two investments a year. Many have preferences about sectors or stages of investment based on their personal knowledge. Many also expect to exercise some degree of directorial control over the business. Most prefer local investments, in companies within, say, 100 miles from where they live or work. Most also prefer to stay anonymous.

Since angels are mainly locally based, angel networks can now be found from Cambridge in England to Mumbai in India. These networks circulate business plans among the angels ahead of a physical pitch or presentation to the angels. If any angels are interested in investing, then a period of investigation and negotiation will take place before funds are committed. Often a fee is charged to the business seeking the investment and some networks take a stake in the company if a deal is successfully negotiated. Some of the networks can also provide help in raising finance from other sources and in preparing a business plan for an additional fee.

In the UK many business angels belong to the British Business Angel Association. It has a code of conduct for its members and a directory of members is available on its website. Local business angels can also be contacted through the local Business Link or Enterprise Agency, who also have their own Local Investment Network Company (LINC) that seeks to match small firms seeking funds with potential investors. Investors receive a monthly bulletin of opportunities available, submitted to LINC as business plans from small firms seeking finance. LINC Scotland is the national association for business angels in Scotland. In the USA, angel groups are also locally based. Your local Chamber of Commerce or Small Business Development Center should be able to put you in touch with your local group.

Venture capital institutions typically invest larger amounts than business angels (typically over £2 million). They mainly invest in established businesses (often buying out angel investments), **management buy-outs** (the management of a firm buying it) and **management buy-ins** (external managers buying a firm and normally replacing the management), but they can invest in larger start-ups. Neither business angels nor venture capitalists want to take control of the business away from the entrepreneur, and therefore usually limit their investment to less than 50% of the share capital. However, because venture capitalists invest larger amounts, they often put together funding deals that involve ordinary shares, preference shares (non-voting, with dividends at a fixed percentage of face value but with preference over ordinary shareholders in the event of liquidation) and loan finance. In the past, some of the management buy-out and buy-in deals they have structured have been notable for their high leverage or gearing. The British Venture Capital Association produces a free Directory of Members, which gives a full list of venture capital institutions and their investment criteria.

Case insight

Purplle.com

Early stage finance

Manish Taneja and Rahul Dash left professional jobs to set up Purplle.com, a website selling beauty and grooming products, in Mumbai in 2012. One year later, based in a tiny office and warehouse in the north of the city, they employ 25 people:

'We realized that beauty and grooming was at an inflexion point in India and we knew that it would take off.'

Initially they used their own savings to set up the business and establish the website but they then approached family and friends for loans and equity as well as using trade credit to finance the products they sell. Once the business model proved successful, they decided they needed more equity and approached a group of 15 business angels in Mumbai to whom they pitched their business model. They were successful and the investors brought not only capital but also website expertise and a network of contacts. Time will tell if the business succeeds.

Questions:

1. Softcat used factoring to raise finance, Hotel Chocolat customer bonds, InSpiral crowdsourcing and Purplle business angels. Under what circumstances might you use these different forms of finance?

2. Are any appropriate for your business? If so, why and at what stage?

India

You can see the range of products offered by Purplle on: purplle.com

What investors look for

Whilst business angels and venture capital institutions may look at the same range of criteria as a banker, their perspective is very different because, unlike the banker, they are sharing in the risk of the business. If it fails, they stand to lose everything. Consequently they are interested in both **return** and **risk**. In particular, they are interested in the return they will make on their investment rather than the security they can obtain from the entrepreneur. The return on one investment must compensate for the loss on another. They will also want to be assured that they can sell on their investment at some time in the future and realize their profit – called the **exit route** in the UK or **liquidity event** in the USA. Assessing these things, inevitably, will take longer than arranging a bank loan.

Return and risk – Most investors are interested more in the capital gain on the sale of their investment than the dividends they might receive. Typically they will be looking for an annual return on their investment of 30–60%, depending on the perceived risk. Start-ups will usually be at the top end of that spectrum, but the final deal always requires negotiation. So for example, an investment of £100,000 might be expected to yield £400,000–£800,000 in 5 years' time – a multiple of four to eight times the original investment. And, whilst some may achieve this return, others will not and the investor will be lucky to exit with their money intact. The business plan for a start-up is very important to an investor – they do not take

Will King, founder King of Shaves RealBusiness interview 1 July 2009

If your business is **demanding** of capital you've got to have a very **clear** business plan … because people will only lend you **money** to make money. They'll want a three times **return** on their investment within a three- to four-year window.

guarantees and there is no track record to rely on. They will be particularly interested to see an identified and accessible market with strong growth potential. If yours is a technology-based start-up, the technology must be market-ready. Investors also pay far greater attention to the quality of management – your experience and that of your management team. This is the only track record they have. And they expect this experience and expertise to be reflected in the quality of the business plan. When looking at the financial projections they will apply the full range of performance criteria, profitability and risk ratios outlined in Chapter 15. They will also pay great attention to your detailed assessment of the business risks and how they might be overcome.

Exit route (liquidity event) – Most business angels will want to realize their investment within a time frame of 5 years. Venture capitalists may take a longer-term view, perhaps up to 10 years. For a start-up that may be a problem because there may not be an established market for their shares within this time frame. So who might buy the shares? One option could be that you will want to **buy back** the shares and regain 100% control of your business. A **management buy-out** or **buy-in** might be another option. Angels might sell on their shares to venture capitalists. Another option for both angels and venture capitalists is to sell on their share in the business (and perhaps the founder's share) to another company, often in the same industry, by way of a **trade sale**. They might also seek to obtain a **stock market floatation** – a listing on a stock

Ajith Jayawickrema, business angel Sunday Times 2 June 2013

I **want** to know whether it will be **attractive** to buyers. The only way someone like me can **make money** is if someone will **buy** me out.

market – so that they can sell their shares to other institutional investors or the public. Called an initial public offering, or IPO, this can be expensive (a trade sale is far cheaper) and means that the business will have to comply with a whole range of regulations and disclosure requirements designed to make trading in their shares fairer. It also means that the firm needs a track record of solid profitability and good growth potential. There are two 'junior' markets in the UK that ultimately lead to a full listing on the Stock Exchange Main Market. These are the OFEX and the Alternative Investment Market (AIM) and offer limited trading. However, many entrepreneurs (like Richard Branson) do not like the public accountability and loss of control implied by 'going public' on the Stock Market.

Both angels and venture capitalists will undertake a thorough investigation of both the founder(s) and the business. They will want to be represented as a non-executive director on the board. This is their response to the issues raised through agency theory and information asymmetry, mentioned earlier. Business angels, particularly, may also expect a more 'hands-on', day-to-day involvement in the business. As with

Ajith Jayawickrema, business angel Sunday Times 2 June 2013

I always back the jockeys because they can ride any horse. That's fundamental. I think 'If things get difficult, will they still be there?'

bank managers, it is important to develop a close personal relationship. Ultimately they invest in people rather than businesses and, since they face more risk than the banker, they need to be convinced that the entrepreneur and the management team can make the business plan actually happen. Trust and respect are important. Since they only make money if the firm succeeds, they are highly committed to helping the growing firm through the inevitable problems it will face. They can be an invaluable sounding board for sharing both problems and ideas. Many have useful business experience, sometimes in the same business sector, and they can provide a strategic overview that helps you see through the day-to-day problems of business. They may also bring with them a wealth of business contacts. In short, used properly they can be a valuable asset to the firm. As we saw, when Kirsty Henshaw (Case Insight on page 208) entered the Dragons' Den she was seeking the experience and knowledge of the Dragons as much as their finance.

PhotoDisc Getty Images

Mears Group

The funding ladder

Mears Group started life as a small, private building contractor in 1988. It is now a leading UK PLC. In 1992 Mears was awarded its first multidisciplinary maintenance and repairs contract from a local authority. Since then it has grown to become the leading social housing repairs and maintenance provider in the UK. In 1996, with a turnover of £12 million and 83 employees, its Chairman and Chief Executive Bob Holt floated the company on AIM, raising £950,000 with a market capitalization of £3.6 million. Over the following years it grew, partly through organic growth and partly through acquisition, moving into the domiciliary care market. In 2008 it moved to the Main Market of the London Stock Exchange, with a turnover of £420 million and more than 8000 employees. In 2009 Mears Group won the PLC Award for New Company of the Year on the London Stock Exchange Main Market. Mears is listed on the FTSE4Good Index in recognition of its Community and Social Responsibility activity.

Up-to-date information on Mears Group can be found on their website: www. mearsgroup.co.uk

The funding ladder

For any start-up, deciding what assets are needed, when to acquire them and how this is to be financed are important strategic decisions where independent professional advice can be valuable. Generally, you are best advised to minimize the resources you need at each stage of the business. Remember you do not necessarily have to own an asset to use it. You can bootstrap or partner with others (see Chapter 10). Although it is inevitable if you want to maximize the potential of your business, once you start to use external funds you start to limit your flexibility and lose control. Deciding on the form of this funding is therefore every bit as important a decision as anything else that goes into the business plan.

Most firms use a range of finance to suit their differing needs and circumstances. The advantages and disadvantages of these different methods of financing your business are summarized in Table 14.3. Getting started on the funding ladder can be difficult, particularly in a depressed trading environment. Many sources may not appear to be open to you as a start-up. Getting that first tranche of funding requires you to persuade financiers that you can make your business dream come true. They need to believe in you. You need to have credibility and to gain their trust and respect. However, a good business idea will always eventually find backing, particularly if you have a good business plan to explain it. And a good plan will help give you credibility and so gain their trust and respect.

> You have to **hang** on to that initial money like it is gold. Look after every pound because it will allow you to get your idea **right** and prove it. Nobody will give you money until you can prove your idea is a **winner** … There's lots of money out there but only for proven **concepts**.
>
> John Elliott, founder Coffee Nation *Sunday Times* 23 May 2004

Getty

Source	Advantages	Disadvantages
Equity Personal, family and friends' Investment	• Good, secure long-term finance • No interest or capital repayment • Can be used to lever further loan finance	• Dividends may be expected • Selling shares to outsiders dilutes your stake in the business and may lead to loss of control • Outsiders providing equity may want to interfere in the business
Equity Angel finance	• Good, secure long-term finance • Can be used to lever further loan finance • Small amounts of equity available • Investment based on business plan rather than security • Investment usually made for 5 to 10 years • Often offers hands-on expertise	• Only really available to businesses with growth prospects • A significant proportion of the profits and capital growth of the business will go to the angels • Dividends may be expected • Angels will want to sell on their stake in the business at some point in the future to realize their profit • Hands-on expertise may be seen as interference in the business
Equity Venture finance	• Good, secure long-term finance • Larger amounts of equity available – often used as second-stage finance rather than at start-up • Investment based on business plan rather than security • Investment usually made for 5 to 10 years • Can offer longer-term strategic advice • Not normally involved in day-to-day running of business • Should be able to arrange loans to go with equity investment, if required • No interest or capital repayments, unless loans are part of the package	• Only really available to businesses with very significant growth prospects and with a view to stock market floatation • A significant proportion of the profits and capital growth of the business will go to the investor • Dividends may be expected • Investors will want to sell on their stake in the business at some point in the future to realize their profit, usually through a stock market floatation • Will require very detailed information about the company • Takes time to arrange
Equity Crowdfunding	• Good, secure long-term finance • Can be used to lever further loan finance • Small amounts of equity available • Investment based on business plan rather than security	• Investors will need to see an exit route (liquidity event) – how they can dispose of their equity investment • Dividends may be expected • Crowdfunding website will expect a fee based on funds raised
Term loans Personal, family and friends	• Security unlikely to be required • Loans may be 'informal' – capital repaid as and when cash flow improves • Interest payments may not be required or may be deferred	• Interest payments may be required • Can strain relationships if repayments are not made as expected • If business fails, family and friends may suffer • Family and friends may interfere in the business
Term loans Bank and crowdfunding	• Term of loan is fixed – usually not repayable on bank demand (but do check terms) • Capital repayments fixed and known in advance • Interest rate can vary or be fixed and is usually lower than for an overdraft	• Usually secured against business or personal assets • Can be refused because of lack of security • Requires good cash flow to pay interest and meet capital repayments • Crowdfunding website will expect a fee based on funds raised
Lease and hire purchase	• Guarantees not required – security is on assets purchased	• Expensive compared to rates of interest charged on loans • Requires adequate cash flow to meet regular payments
Bank overdraft	• Flexible – once agreed, available on demand • Can be cheap if you dip into and out of it – you only pay interest when you use it • Good solution to short-term financing needs	• Repayable on bank demand • Interest rate is variable • Can be expensive if you are in permanent overdraft as the rate of interest charged is usually higher than on term loans • Usually secured against business assets and can be refused because of lack of security • Personal guarantee may then be required

T14.3 Advantages and disadvantages of different sources of finance

Is there a financing gap for small firms?

If you ask any business person during a recession whether there is a shortage of finance for business they would answer 'yes, of course', and look at you as if you had only just landed on the planet. And of course, since 2008, the statistics support the view that bank lending is down as the banks consolidate their balance sheets. And yet the paradox is that, during the same period, large companies have been sitting on increasingly large cash mountains. They do not need to borrow, but refuse to invest. Could it be that the problem is lack of consumer demand rather than lack of supply of finance that is to blame?

Banks are the major source of external finance for small firms. Before the 2008 recession, one survey covering the early part of this century showed that, on average, 89% of UK loan applications were successful (Fraser, 2005). In the USA it was 72% (Cavalluzzo and Wolken, 2005). However, evidence in the UK shows that, while bank funding certainly reduced after the 2008 recession, as did the proportion of small firms using it, loan acceptance rates remained high – dropping from 92.6% in 2004 to 83.7% in 2008 (Fraser, 2009). Put another way, only 16% of applicants are turned down. What has happened is that small firms have been 'discouraged' from applying in the first place, and if you add those in you get to about one in four (25%) small firms not accessing finance from a bank.

Notwithstanding the recession that started in 2008, the question remains as to whether there is a long-term financing gap for small firms – defined as an unwillingness on the part of financiers to supply finance on terms that owner-managers need. Owner-managers who are unsuccessful in obtaining finance will always say there is. Survey after survey of owner-managers will reveal this to be a major 'barrier to growth'. Almost inevitably, lack of appropriately priced finance will be cited as a major constraint, particularly for fast-growing and newer firms.

However, this proves nothing – perception is one thing and reality another. Even if accurate, the lack of appropriately priced finance for certain projects may actually indicate that the market is working perfectly well. However, just because the owner-manager might want finance – on specific terms – does not necessarily mean that it should be provided – either for the good of the owner-manager, the financier or the economy as a whole.

Economists would criticize the use of the word 'gap' and prefer to use the term 'market failure' or 'credit rationing', because there may be a 'gap' even in a perfect market: an owner-manager may be unwilling to pay higher rates of interest or investors may judge a project to be too risky. 'Gaps' can easily arise, largely as a result of information asymmetry, the fixed costs of providing small amounts of capital, in terms of assessing the project and monitoring the investment, and the requirement of bankers for small firms or owner-managers to provide collateral. Also there is the inherent reluctance of the owner-manager to share equity in their business. The question is, however, whether there is evidence that the gap actually exists.

The fact is that numerous surveys in the UK have been unable objectively to establish that a 'gap' exists in any systematic way. In the early 1990s a survey of small, albeit mainly innovative, growing firms (Aston Business School, 1991) into growth constraints concluded that 'small firms in Great Britain apparently face few difficulties in raising finance for their innovation and investment proposals'. Most authors of that period agreed. For example, Cosh and Hughes (1994) concluded that it was 'difficult to argue that there were financial constraints on business formations as a whole in the 1980s or that there is a more pervasive market failure for small firms in the availability of funds at least in quantitative terms'. Similarly, in his review of the literature, Storey (1998)

Academic insight

concluded that 'the major empirical studies of the UK small business sector do not suggest the existence either of market failure or credit rationing on a major scale'. He added that 'although there are instances where small firms are unable to obtain finance in the quantities and at the price they would like, the financial institutions in the provision of both loan and equity capital have increased their involvement with the small firm sector over the last ten years'. Reviewing the evidence over a decade later, Storey and Greene (2010) came to broadly the same conclusion: 'for much of the period from the early 1990s until recent times, small businesses in the UK were able to draw upon an increasingly diverse source of funds. However, the 2008 recession abruptly halted the trend, to the extent that perhaps one in four UK small businesses were unable to access the funding they required.' The recession has certainly changed the financing environment – for businesses of any size.

Aston Business School (1991) *Constraints on Growth of Small Firms*, Department of Trade and Industry, London: HMSO.

Cavalluzzo, K. and Wolken, J. (2005) 'Small Business Loan Turndowns, Personal Wealth, and Discrimination', *Journal of Business*, 78.

Cosh, A. and Hughes, A. (1994) 'Size, Financial Structure and Profitability: UK Companies in the 1980s', in A. Hughes and D.J. Storey (eds), *Finance and the Small Firm*, London: Routledge.

Fraser, S. (2005) *Finance for Small and Medium-sized Enterprises*, London: Bank of England.

Fraser, S. (2009) *How Have SME Finances Been Affected by the Credit Crisis?* London: BERR/ESRC Seminar.

Storey, D.J. (1998) *Understanding the Small Business Sector*, London: International Thompson Business Press.

Storey, D.J. and Greene, F.J. (2010), *Small Business and Entrepreneurship*, Harlow: Pearson.

Harvesting your investment

Progressing up the funding ladder presents opportunities for a founder to harvest all or part of their investment in the form of capital gains as they sell off all or part of the equity in the business. You may realize that you are better at starting up than running a business and want to sell on the business as soon as it is successful – so you can go on to set up another. And harvesting your investment can happen earlier than you might expect. Research by Nesta (National Endowment for Science, Technology and the Arts) showed the average life cycle of a technology start-up from its first-round funding to exit was only six years in 2008 – and this had actually increased by 18 months since 2005. But not all entrepreneurs want to leave the business quickly. Increasing numbers want to take money out when the firm gets its second or third round of equity funding, only exiting some years later. They want to share in the success of the firm as it grows without taking capital out, and thus endangering its growth, by relinquishing some ownership and even control.

Moonpig

Harvesting your investment

In 2011 Nick Jenkins sold Moonpig, the personalized greeting card business he had started twelve years earlier, for £120 million to the French online photo album business Photobox. He started the business with £160,000 of his own money, but had attracted other private investors including a neighbour and two friends of friends who had experience of greeting cards. When he sold the business he still owned 34% himself:

'When you have investors they want an exit. Floating the business did not make sense. It just wasn't big enough.'

Nick had prepared well in advance for the sell-off. He had employed an experienced managing director four years earlier and had gradually handed over the reins to him.

Nick's father was a director at the engineering and building firm Alfred McAlpine. He studied Russian at Birmingham University before working in Russia at the time the Soviet Union collapsed. It was working there that he made the money to start up Moonpig, but he came up with the idea whilst doing a MBA at Cranfield. While on the course he worked on five business ideas: growing exotic mushrooms, running company gyms, running internet incubators, teaching English to Japanese businessmen online and the one he eventually decided upon, Moonpig. Moonpig allows you to select a greeting card and write a personalized message on it, all online. The physical card is delivered to you or another recipient within 24 hours:

'I used to buy cards, Tipp-Ex out the caption and write my own – I just thought if I could use the internet to do that, I could make a better product.'

It also proved to be a unique product, with no competition so no price pressure and high barriers to market entry once established. When he sold the company it claimed 90% of the British online card market and made profits of £11 million on a turnover of £32 million with just 100 employees. But starting a business that sold personalized physical cards seemed quite a risk in 1999, when most competitors thought e-cards would be what customers wanted. Nick's MBA taught him the important things needed to lead a business.

Sunday Times 31 July 2011

My job is just to keep the business on track, the **right people** doing the **right jobs**, and the strategy sound ... It's a fun environment. I'm a firm **believer** that the culture of a company comes from the **top**. You can have an HR department saying 'we have a collaborative **culture**', but if the guy at the top is a total arse, it's not going to happen ... I'm a firm believer in creating enough **spare time** to get a bit bored to think up new things. If you're fire **fighting** you don't do that.

Questions:

1. Why would a larger company want to purchase a smaller one in the same industry?
2. Why might they be willing to pay a premium to purchase it?
3. If you were to sell on your business, after how many years would this be and what would you need to do to prepare for it?

Nick Jenkins

If your business has grown to the point where it has a stock market quotation then there is a ready market for your shares. However, if you sell up completely or relinquish operational control the share price is likely to drop. If you have not reached this point and want to sell up, then the most attractive option is probably to find a trade buyer – a competitor that understands the industry. They are likely to place a higher value on the business than others because they can see ways of 'adding value' through the purchase, perhaps by synergy. This is particularly the case with technology start-ups, where the smaller business offers innovation and the bigger company offers resources to take the innovation to a mass, global market much more quickly than the smaller business might be able to. In many cases the big company might be willing to pay cash, so you can walk away from the firm on the day of sale, although they are likely to place restrictions on you setting up in competition to them within a certain time frame. If you have other equity investors like business angels or venture capitalists it is probable that they will have to agree to the sale. Indeed, they are likely to be able to help with it. Of course the business must be able to demonstrate success, usually in the form of a good financial track record and it must be able to function effectively without you. That means it must have good control systems and a good management team.

Another option may be a management buy-out or buy-in. For buy-outs, it depends on the intentions of your managers. Management buy-ins are more difficult to identify but some accountants keep confidential registers of managers searching for firms to buy into.

Finding a buyer, valuing the business and negotiating its sale are a daunting series of tasks that really should not be undertaken without professional advice and help. Many larger firms of accountants can help find buyers, just as they can help find companies to purchase, and they can act as a confidential 'front' in the search process. They are also likely to take a more objective view on company valuation than the entrepreneur (a topic we address in the next chapter) and are essential in sorting out the detail of the deal, including the inevitable warranties and indemnities that will be requested by the purchaser. Finally there is the important consideration of taxation, where planning can considerably increase the money actually pocketed by the entrepreneur.

Case insight

Vivid Imaginations

Harvesting your investment

Vivid Imaginations specializes in producing toys related to TV or cinema series by purchasing the franchise rights. Its offerings have included products like Crayola, Moshi Monsters, Harry Potter, Disney Princess, Toy Story, Shrek, Roary the Racing Car, High School Musical and Monsters vs Aliens and many others. It was originally set up by Nick Austin and Alan Bennie in the 1960s with £250,000 obtained by pooling their severance pay from their old jobs and re-mortgaging their houses. They also convinced friends to provide them with a loan of £380,000. After some time a bank offered a rolling overdraft for the same amount.

By 1998 Vivid had become one of the fastest growing private companies in the UK and Austin and Bennie decided to realize their investment and sell off the business to Jordan Group, an American venture capital company for £27 million – a deal that generated almost £10 million each for them. This included an agreement for the pair to stay with the company for the next five years. But when the time to go arrived, they could not bring themselves to leave the business they had set up. Instead, with the help of Phoenix Equity Partners, a British venture capital firm, they staged a management buy-out, buying back the company for £62 million, sharing ownership with employees and retaining 4% each for themselves. Vivid Imaginations remains Britain's biggest independent toy company.

Visit the website on: www.vividimaginations.co.uk

Summary

- Before using external sources of finance you should minimize your use of assets (bootlegging resources), partner with others, use your own money, and borrow money from family and friends.

- Deciding on the nature and source of finance for a start-up is an important strategic decision. To be prudent you should match the term duration of the source of finance with the use to which it is put. Fixed or permanent assets should be financed with equity, medium- and long-term bank finance or lease/hire purchase. Working capital can be financed by short-term loans and factoring, with fluctuations financed by overdraft.

- Table 14.3 summarizes the advantages and disadvantages of different sources of finance.

- Banks are very risk averse. They do not share in the success of the business but stand to lose all their capital if the business fails, and therefore they will do all they can to avoid a bad debt. Small firms present a riskier lending proposition than larger firms.

- Banks are likely to seek personal or business collateral for a loan which will offer them security in the event of default. Since the asset base of a start-up is unlikely to be able to provide this, bankers often ask for personal collateral or guarantees.

- Bankers look at a range of financial indicators in arriving at their lending decisions but they are particularly interested in the cash flow forecast because this shows the ability of the firm to make its interest payments and repay capital.

- It is important that you establish a good working relationship with your banker. This is based upon mutual trust and respect.

- Internet-based crowdfunding has emerged in recent years as a way of matching lenders and investors with small firms in need of finance. It is too early to evaluate its success, but 'quirkier' businesses, often with a social aim, have found it a useful mechanism.

- Equity finance can be obtained from family, friends, business angels and venture capitalists. Equity investors share in the success or failure of the business, consequently they can be expected to scrutinize your business plan very closely.

- Angels and venture capitalists expect an annualized return of 30–50%, normally as a capital gain. They also normally expect to realize their investment within five years. They will expect a seat on the board of directors and many angels will expect a closer involvement in the management of the business.

- Angels and venture capitalists might realize their investment through a trade sale, management buy-out or buy-in or stock market floatation. These are also opportunities for the founder to realize all or part of their investment.

- Despite the recession which began in 2008 and surveys that suggest the supply of finance is a major constraint on growth, it has been impossible to objectively establish that there is a long-term, systematic financing gap for small firms.

Exercise 14.1

Identifying the assets you need

1 Review Exercise 11.1.3 and, below, list the assets you need to launch the business.

2 List the cost of the assets and decide which must be purchased and which might be rented, leased or bootlegged.

3 Repeat the process for the assets you need for your second and third year of operations.

Asset	Cost	Buy/lease/rent/bootleg

Exercise 14.2

Financing

1 Review the results of Exercise 2.3 and decide how much financial capital you are willing to invest.

2 How might the difference between this and the total cost of the assets you need in years one to three (from Exercise 14.1) be best financed:

- Are there alternatives to bank or equity finance that might be attractive? If so, prepare an action list of what you need to find out and how to do so to decide whether or not to use them.
- Do you want to give away equity in your business? If so, how much might you need and where might it come from? List the pros and cons of this. Investigate sources of equity investment in your region.
- Consider the range of bank finance available and decide which is the most appropriate for you, matching term duration with asset type.

We shall return to these exercises after the next chapter.

Visit www.palgrave.com/companion/burns-new-venture-creation for chapter quizzes to test your knowledge and other resources.

PART 7
FINANCIAL PLAN

VIDEO

www.palgrave.com/companion/
burns-new-venture-creation

The New Venture Creation Framework

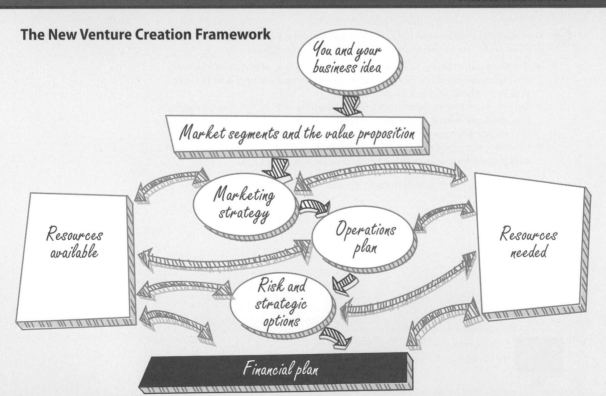

15
FINANCIAL FORECASTS

Contents

Learning outcomes

When you have read this chapter and undertaken the related exercises you will be able to:
- Understand the relevance and importance of different measures of financial performance
- Develop the financial forecasts for your new venture – income statement, cash flow statement and balance sheet
- Evaluate these forecasts of financial performance
- Understand how companies are valued
- Understand how financial information can be used to monitor and control performance

Financial objectives

For a new venture to survive and grow it needs to be financially viable. This can mean a number of different things. For it to be attractive to an equity investor – and the founder – it needs to be profitable and efficient. For it to survive it needs to be sufficiently liquid to enable it to pay its bills. For it to be attractive to a banker offering to lend money it needs to be low risk – and risk is equally relevant to the founder and equity investor. To assess these things involves looking at a range of different concepts and measures.

> *Daily Telegraph 6 February 2009*
>
> Keep your costs to a **minimum**. If you can work from **home** and do your own PR in the beginning this will give you the **cash** to develop the **product**.
>
> *Calypso Rose, founder Clippy*

- Profitability – Profit is the difference between your sales/turnover and your costs. The higher the profits of a commercial business the better. However, profit is not the same as cash. You may not have received payment for your sales nor indeed paid your costs. You can therefore be profitable, but illiquid – or vice versa. The two things are different. Profit measures how *all* the assets of the business have increased through your trading activities (sales – costs), not just cash. It is true that eventually the profit should turn into cash, but meanwhile bills and wages have to be paid and, if you do not have the cash to pay them, you may go out of business. Profitability is shown in the income statement of a business.

- Efficiency – Efficiency measures how profitably a business is using its assets. It is a measure of the *quality* of the profit you generate using these assets. Since those assets are paid for by the investors – including you – then it will be a significant influence on whether you can obtain finance. If the return you make (profit : assets) is less than the going rate of interest, you are better off putting your money in the bank. Assets are shown in the balance sheet of a business. It should be obvious that to be efficient you need to be as profitable as possible by using the minimum of assets. There are a number of measures of efficiency that we shall deal with later using a technique called ratio analysis. Notice, however, that, since cash is also an asset, there is a tension between being highly efficient and highly liquid.

- Liquidity – Liquidity measures a firm's ability to meet routine, short-term financial obligations. The most liquid of all assets is cash, and the cash flow statement shows your estimate of how quickly it will come into and go out of the business. Cash flow is the life blood of a business – it pays the bills and the wages. Without adequate cash flow the firm might go out of business. The cash flow statement shows how quickly cash from your sales comes in and when you make the expenditures associated with your costs and capital investments, such as buildings or plant and machinery. It also shows cash inputs from loan or share capital. There are other measures of liquidity that we shall deal with later.

- Risk – There are two sorts of risk measurement in the financial statements. Operating risk is measured by comparing the level of operating fixed costs (costs that cannot be altered easily, such as the cost of a lease on premises) to your

profitability. This is usually measured by the breakeven point (Chapter 11). Financing risk is the level of your interest payments (which you cannot affect) compared to your profitability. It is also measured by the amount of borrowing you have compared to your total assets. This is called gearing (UK) or leverage (USA). You have little discretion over these two sorts of fixed costs. The higher your operating or financing fixed costs, the higher your risk.

The financial objectives of a commercial business will usually involve being highly profitable and efficient, whilst maintaining adequate liquidity and minimizing operating and financial risk. The challenge is quantifying these things and then achieving them. For a social enterprise with social objectives, profitability and efficiency may be constraints rather than things to be maximized.

The measurement of these things in the business plan involves drawing up financial forecasts for at least a three-year period – five years for larger projects where significant commercialization risks, which are particular to this project, have not been resolved. These forecasts include:

- income statements (including breakeven projections);
- cash flow statements;
- balance sheets.

How your business actually performs is measured by your historical financial statements, usually produced annually. These are used as a basis for taxing the business. Companies in the UK must submit them to Companies House, where they are publicly available. Most businesses, however, will produce monthly income statements and monitor their cash flow on an even more regular basis.

Forecasting sales/turnover

Financial forecasts can either start by forecasting sales/turnover, the costs needed to generate this level of sales and the resulting profits (this is the most usual approach), or by calculating the costs needed to set up the business and then working back to the level of sales needed to generate a target profit level. Either way, a number of iterations – altering price, volumes and/or costs – will probably be necessary before a satisfactory profit target is calculated. Monthly sales forecasts will be needed for the first year – perhaps for longer where these significant commercialization risks remain unresolved.

Realistic, achievable sales forecasts are the starting point for the rest of the financial forecasts so it is important that they are more than just aspirations.

However, as we saw in Chapter 3, the more radical the product/service innovation and/or market innovation you are introducing in your new venture, the more difficult it will be to forecast sales. As we observed, market research is unlikely to yield an insight into demand for this kind of new product/ service or market because customers do not understand it. Often the only sure way of knowing whether the idea will make a lucrative business is to try it out – launch the business but minimize your risks. That means calculating the minimum costs needed to set up the business and then working back to the level of sales needed to generate a target profit level. After that it is about taking the leap of faith that Henry Ford and Steve Jobs did, but if you need financial backers you will need a persuasive argument and very attractive profit targets.

NinaMalyna Fotolia.com

For more incremental innovations in products/services or markets your sales forecasts need to be justified by demonstrating that:

1. **There is sufficient market demand** – You might be able to do this by market research that demonstrates a market need that is, as yet, unmet. This can take many forms but must be underpinned by a convincing understanding of customers, competitors and differential advantage. The advantages and disadvantages of field and desk-based market research are shown in Table 15.1. For example, you might be able to demonstrate from desk research that there are relatively few competitors within a certain geographic area compared to market demand, you might be able to establish the total size of the market (TAM and SAM) and should certainly be able to show market growth (Chapter 4). Alternatively, if you can identify potential customers you might decide to contact them directly to establish whether they might be willing to at least try your product or service. And if you want to open a new shop in a certain area, you might decide to measure footfall in that area yourself by field research. Another approach is to demonstrate that your share of a particular market – and this needs careful definition – is so small that you are highly likely to achieve it (your SAM compared to the TAM). Whilst you will not be able to *prove* there is sufficient market demand, you should be able to establish that there *probably* is.

2. **Targets are achievable, within the operating and cost parameters of the business** – Your forecasts need to be internally consistent. There is no point in convincingly forecasting sufficient demand if you have not built in sufficient costs to meet the sales you forecast. It is important to establish the assumptions upon which your sales forecasts are based. That means clearly stating selling prices and volumes and ensuring that the volumes predicted are consistent with costs. Some costs are fixed costs that need to be incurred to set up the business but will not change significantly if your sales forecast is inaccurate – they do not change with the volume of activity or sales – for example, property lease/rental costs or fixed salaries (Chapter 11). These forecasts need to be based upon a reasonable estimate. Some costs are variable costs that vary with sales volumes – for example, materials or piece-work labour costs. Every time an additional unit is produced and sold, an additional cost is incurred. These costs vary with your sales forecast, and can be calculated based upon a percentage of sales.

Investors will typically pay great attention to the assumptions underpinning the financial forecasts of a new venture and, if they feel they are unrealistic, the credibility of the entire plan may be severely dented. They will often apply a range of pragmatic, common-sense tests. For example, predicted sales for a retail business could be divided by the selling space taken up. This can often be compared to industry norms. Alternatively, forecast sales per day might be calculated and divided by the expected average spend per customer to arrive at a figure for buyers per day, which can then be compared to footfall and buyer conversion rates. In a bar or restaurant you might look at the number of covers and the average spend per cover to see whether sales estimates are realistic. However you show it, investors will certainly want to know the volumes and price assumptions that underpin these estimates.

	Field research	Desk research
Advantages	• Reflects your needs • You control quality • Up-to-date	• Cheap • Quick • Good for background information
Disadvantages	• Expensive • Takes time • Can tell competitors what you are up to	• Not specific to your business • Can be incomplete, inaccurate • Can be out-of-date

T15.1 Market research: advantages and disadvantages of field vs desk research

Xtreme SnoBoards

Building the financial forecast – sales/turnover

Xtreme SnoBoards is a company set up by two young snowboarding enthusiasts to manufacture a specialist snowboard that they have perfected after two years of development. The boards have been tested and used by professionals in competition and proved to be particularly responsive. So responsive, in fact, that a number of retailers have contacted the company to enquire about placing orders. There are three variations on the board, designed for different conditions. The pair have researched their market and lined up two national retail chains and one overseas distributor who have placed advance orders for the board. The initial sales estimates for the boards in the first year are shown opposite. These figures represent total numbers of boards. 60% of these sales will go through the two major retailers and the overseas distributor. The sales estimates are highly seasonal with sales mainly in the winter months.

Getty

The founders intend to establish their small manufacturing facility in September and start manufacturing in October. These boards will be sent out to shops as demonstration models but, by agreement, they will not be invoiced as sales until January. The founders expect to have produced some 400 boards by then. These will be counted as starting stock in January and the sales invoices will be issued in the same month. They estimate that their maximum production capability in any month is 320 boards, and this will be reached by March. This means that they will be unable to meet the initial sales estimates for March. Consequently they have revised their sales forecasts. Unlike sales, production levels have to be kept constant, although production is lower in August and December because of holidays. Forecast total production is therefore 3780 boards (3380 + 400), revised forecast sales is 3140 boards, leaving 640 (3780 − 3140) boards in stock at the end of the first year.

Initial sales forecast	Units	Production Start stocks	+prodn	− sales	End stocks
Jan	400	400*	180	400	180
Feb	400	180	240	400	20
March	440	20	320	340**	0
April	280	0	320	280	40
May	100	40	320	100	260
June	100	260	320	100	480
July	80	480	320	80	720
Aug	80	720	160	80	800
Sept	200	800	320	200	920
Oct	360	920	320	360	880
Nov	360	880	320	360	840
Dec	440	840	240	440	640
Total	3240		3380	3140	

*pre-January production
**unable to meet sales estimate

The revised sales forecast, including income as well as numbers of boards, can now be drawn up. The sales price of £135 (trade price) is net of delivery costs and represents the average of the three boards because the best guess at the moment is that the boards will sell in equal proportions.

Revised sales forecast	Units	Value (£000) @ £135
Jan	400	54.0
Feb	400	54.0
March	340	45.9
April	280	37.8
May	100	13.5
June	100	13.5
July	80	10.8
Aug	80	10.8
Sept	200	27.0
Oct	360	48.6
Nov	360	48.6
Dec	440	59.4
Total	3140	423.9

Xtreme SnoBoards
is a fictitious company

Forecast income statement

Once you have estimates of your sales and costs, you can prepare your forecast of profits – called a forecast or pro-forma income statement. This is simply a case of slotting the estimates into an accepted format for an income statement, such as the one in Exercise 15.1. The amount of detail you give is a matter of judgement, but the larger the start-up the greater the detail that will be expected.

Financial statements generally highlight the gross profit of a business. The operating costs (such as selling, marketing, administrative costs etc.) are deducted from this to arrive at the operating profit

and financing costs (interest) are deducted from this to arrive at net profit (before taxes and dividends).

Gross profit = Turnover – Cost of goods sold

Operating profit = Gross profit – Operating costs

Net profit = Operating profit – Interest

The cost of goods sold is exactly what the words imply. However, these costs can comprise both variable and fixed costs. For a shop these costs represent the cost of the items sold – which indeed is a variable cost. For a service business, such as a consultancy, most costs (principally salaries) will be fixed and very few costs will be variable. For

Xtreme Sno Boards

Building the financial forecast – income statement and breakeven

The founders need a range of machinery to produce their boards. They estimate that the total cost of this machinery will be £55,680 and that it will last some 8 years before needing replacement. Depreciation is therefore calculated at £6,960 per year (£8,700 in the first period of 15 months). They have also found a suitable unit that can be used as a factory. The annual lease cost for this is £11,520, including rates (£960 per month or £14,400 for the first 15 months).

The founders intend to employ two factory workers from October. They will be paid a fixed monthly wage – a total of £3,000 per month. An extra member of staff will be taken on in March, when production gets up to its maximum level. They will be paid £1,300 per month. The founders will also work in the factory and intend to pay themselves a fixed monthly wage – £2,000 per month each – in the first year, starting in January. The estimated wages bill during the first 15 months (October to December) is therefore £106,000.

The founders undertook a detailed costing exercise that showed that the average material costs for each board was £32 and the average variable factory overhead was £5 per board (consumables, electricity etc.). Total variable costs are therefore £37 per board.

The average cost of producing a board is shown below (based on 3780 units):

Variable costs:		
Direct materials		£32.00
Direct factory costs		£5.00
Fixed costs:		
Direct labour	£106,000	
Factory overhead – depreciation	£8,700	
– factory lease	£14,400	
	£129,100 ÷ 3780 =	£34.15
Total average cost of producing each board		£71.15

The founders therefore estimate that they should make an average profit of £63.85 (47.3%) on each board, before other running costs.

a manufacturing business, as well as the cost of the raw materials, there will also be labour costs involved in adding value to the goods. If workers are paid by the volume they produce – called piece work – then this is a variable cost. However, most employees now expect to be paid a regular weekly wage – which is fixed. The cost of sales will also represent other fixed factory overheads such as the depreciation cost of machinery and equipment used in the process. Cost of sales for a manufacturing business therefore might comprise material costs (variable), labour costs (variable and/or fixed) and factory overheads (fixed). To work out the cost of goods sold (and the value of the goods you hold in stock) you need to know the cost of each manufactured good. That means undertaking a costing exercise so that the fixed costs can be spread over the volume of goods *produced* – not necessarily the same as goods sold. This is the basis for what is called 'cost+ pricing' (see Chapter 5). If a manufacturing business fails to sell everything it produces, the cost of the excess is reflected in the valuation of the unsold stock/inventory. To summarize, the cost of sales is a variable cost for a shop, probably fixed for a service business and comprising both variable and fixed for a manufacturing business.

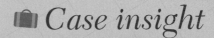 *Case insight*

They intend to spend £10,000 on promotional material in October. After that, they estimate that their marketing and other general costs will be £3,000 per month (£45,000 in the first 15 months) and professional fees, paid at the end of the year, will be £3,000. These are all fixed costs. The founders work out their breakeven point for this first 15-month period of trading by adding these to the fixed production costs and dividing by the contribution margin:

Contribution (Sales price – Variable costs) = £135 – £37 = £98 per unit
Contribution margin = £98 ÷ £135 = 0.726 or 72.6%

Fixed production costs (15 months)	= £129,100
Other fixed costs (15 months)	= £58,000
Total fixed costs (15 months)	£187,100
Breakeven point = £187,100 ÷ 0.726	= £257,713
Margin of safety = (£423,900 – £257,713) ÷ £423,900 × 100 =	39.2%

The founders are very pleased that they have such a high contribution margin and, combined with keeping their fixed costs low, such a low breakeven point compared to their forecast sales. They feel that this high margin of safety in their first year, combined with a high level of advance orders for their snowboards, means that they are really on to a winning business idea.

They go on to estimate their income for the 15-month period on sales of 3140 units:

Sales	3140 × £135	=	£423,900
Cost of sales	3140 × £71.15	=	£223,422
Gross profit			£200,478 (47.3%)
Marketing and general costs	£55,000		
Professional fees	£3,000	=	£ 58,000
Operating profit			£142,478 (33.6%)

Forecast cash flow statement

Profits are important but they are not the same as cash and your survival might depend upon an accurate forecast of cash flow – how quickly the cash from your sales comes in and when you make the expenditures associated with your costs and capital investments. A new venture might spend cash on premises, equipment, stock/inventory and so on before the first customer even walks through the door. The first sale might even be on credit and it can take time before debts are collected. During this time the business will have a negative cash flow. It can be difficult to survive this Death Valley curve, shown in Figure 15.1. Without external finance, the company would be unable to pay its creditors. The length and depth of the valley depends on how quickly you pay out and collect cash. Its depth determines how much you need

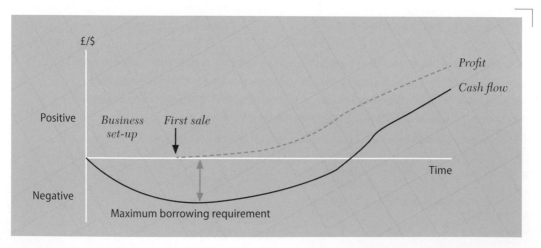

F15.1 **Death Valley curve**

Corbis

to borrow and its length determines how long you will need to borrow for. It can vary from industry to industry and be affected by the economic cycle. And the faster your growth the deeper and longer it is likely to be. Indeed, if sales increase beyond your projections, your cash flow is likely to worsen and Death Valley will lengthen. So, be warned – many firms do not survive long enough to come through Death Valley.

You need to plot Death Valley's course and plan how to navigate it – and that means preparing a cash flow forecast. Only this will tell you how much finance you might need to launch your business. What is more, by altering the assumptions on which your cash flow model is based, you can see the effects on Death Valley. A good model should allow you to understand how you might reduce the depth and length of Death Valley.

A cash flow forecast lists the expected cash receipts and payments for the business in the period they are expected to come in or go out. It can be prepared on a daily, weekly or, more normally, a monthly basis.

$$\text{Cash flow} = \text{Total cash receipts} - \text{Total cash payments, in any period}$$

In Death Valley you have run out of cash – your cash reserves are negative – and you will need to borrow. The cash you have in any period is calculated by adding (or, if negative, subtracting) the period cash flow to the cash balance brought forward from the last period. You can see Death Valley clearly in the cash flow projections for Xtreme SnoBoards If you forecast a negative cash balance then you will need to seek external finance or agree on an overdraft in order to pay your bills. The consequences of being unable to pay those bills might be bankruptcy, despite the fact you are profitable.

Xtreme SnoBoards

Building the financial forecast – cash flow statement

The founders are convinced that their snowboards present a highly attractive opportunity but they need to know how the opportunity can be financed, so they decide to prepare an initial cash flow forecast. Their estimates are based on the following assumptions:

1. Sales receipts are lagged by 2 months.

2. Purchases for materials and other direct factory costs (£37 per unit) can be matched directly to production, which means at maximum production of 320 units purchases are £11,840 (320 × £37). Payments are lagged by 2 months, but payments related to the pre-January production of 400 units must be paid for in December (400 × £37 = £14,800).

3. Wages are paid monthly.

4. The £10,000 promotion expenditure will be paid in November. Other marketing and general costs are spread equally over the period.

5. Professional fees are paid in December.

6. Machinery purchased in September for £55,680 will be paid for in November.

7. Lease costs and rates are paid annually, in advance in October (£11,520).

| £000 | Receipts | | Payments | | | | | Net | | |
	Sales	Materials	Wages	Marketing	Prof. fees	Machinery	Lease	Cash flow	Cash B/F	Cash C/F
Oct			3.00	3.00			11.52	−17.52	0.00	−17.52
Nov			3.00	13.00		55.68		−71.68	−17.52	−89.20
Dec		14.80	3.00	3.00				−20.80	−89.20	−110.00
Jan			7.00	3.00				−10.00	−110.00	−120.00
Feb			7.00	3.00				−10.00	−120.00	−130.00
March	54.00	6.66	8.30	3.00				+36.04	−130.00	−93.96
April	54.00	8.88	8.30	3.00				+33.82	−93.96	−60.14
May	45.90	11.84	8.30	3.00				+22.76	−60.14	−37.38
June	37.80	11.84	8.30	3.00				+14.66	−37.38	−22.72
July	13.50	11.84	8.30	3.00				−9.64	−22.72	−32.36
Aug	13.50	11.84	8.30	3.00				−9.64	−32.36	42.00
Sept	10.80	11.84	8.30	3.00				−12.34	−42.00	−54.34
Oct	10.80	5.92	8.30	3.00			11.52	−17.94	−54.34	−72.28
Nov	27.00	11.84	8.30	3.00				+3.86	−72.28	−68.42
Dec	48.60	11.84	8.30	3.00	3.00			+22.46	−68.42	−45.96
Total	315.90	119.14	106.00	55.00	3.00	55.68	23.04	−45.96		

When the founders review this, they see that, despite the profitability of the company, there is a cash deficit in every month, with a maximum of £130,000 in February. The overall deficit for the year is £45,960. They also observe that the deficit is reducing by the end of the year, just as the prime time for sales (and cash receipts from sales) is approaching, and speculate that the deficit might be corrected in the following year. Because they do not want to share ownership of such a profitable business, they decide to put in £42,000 of their own capital – £30,000 in share capital and £12,000 by way of a two-year interest-free loan. They decide to seek bank finance – probably overdraft – for the balance of their funding. The revised cash flow forecast is shown below. The maximum overdraft requirement is £88,000 in February but thereafter the requirement reduces rapidly. Nevertheless, the founders are aware that this is just a forecast and things can go wrong, so they decide to ask the bank for an overdraft facility of £120,000.

Revised cash flow forecast

£000	Net cash flow	Capital	Cash B/F	Cash C/F
Oct	−17.52	42.00	0.00	−24.48
Nov	−71.68		+24.48	−47.20
Dec	−20.80		−47.20	−68.00
Jan	−10.00		−68.00	−78.00
Feb	−10.00		−78.00	−88.00
March	+36.04		−88.00	−51.96
April	+33.82		−51.96	−18.14
May	+22.76		−18.14	4.62
June	+14.66		4.62	19.28
July	−9.64		19.28	9.64
Aug	−9.64		9.64	0.00
Sept	−12.34		0.00	−12.34
Oct	−17.94		−12.34	−30.28
Nov	+3.86		−30.28	−26.42
Dec	+22.46		−26.42	3.96
Total				

Forecast balance sheet

The balance sheet is a snapshot at a point of time that shows two things:

- The assets the business has – cash, debtors/ receivables (amounts you owed from sales), stock/ inventory (raw materials, work-in-progress and finished goods stocks) and fixed assets (things the business means to keep over a number of years such as equipment, machinery, vehicles, premises etc.).

- Where the funds for these assets came from – overdraft, loans, creditors/payables (amounts you owe to suppliers of goods and services), share capital invested in the business and the accumulated profits of the business. (Remember, profit measures how *all* the assets of the business have increased through trading activities.)

There are two sides to the balance sheet and they must always balance. If you drew up a balance sheet when you invest £10,000 capital in a new venture it would show two things: Cash £10,000 and Share capital £10,000. If you went on to purchase assets with the £10,000 of cash, those assets would be listed together with their purchase price, and the other side of the balance sheet would remain the same, showing where the funds of £10,000 for these assets came from. If you can secure more funds or credit, this would be shown in the balance sheet as a liability, with the assets purchased on the other side of the balance sheet as assets. For example, stock/inventory purchased on credit for £5,000 would be shown on one side of the balance sheet as a creditor/payable, with the stock/inventory on the other side as an asset. Once the business starts trading and making a profit by charging a higher price for a product/service than the cost of production, the assets of the business will start to grow.

Assets	£10,000	Creditors/payables	£5,000
Stock/inventory	£5,000	Share capital	£10,000
	£15, 000		£15,000

Stock/inventory will be bought and sold as part of normal trading and therefore shown in the cash

flow statement and, eventually, the income statement. However, when a company purchases fixed assets – assets that it uses to create value but will last for a number of years – it has to find a way of allocating the cost of these assets to the income statement. Whereas the cash cost of the fixed asset is recognized in the cash flow statement when the cash is spent, the cost of the asset needs to be allocated, over its life, to the income statement. Depreciation is a way of showing this in the profit statement. It is not a cash expenditure and is therefore a major difference between profit and cash flow.

The simplest method of calculating depreciation is called 'straight-line' which writes off the asset in equal amounts over its life. For example, if the asset cost £10,000 and has a working life of 5 years, at which time it can be sold off for £2,000, the annual depreciation would be:

$$\frac{\text{Initial cost} - \text{final residual value}}{\text{Life of fixed asset}}$$

$$= \frac{£10,000 - 2,000}{5} = £1,600 \text{ per annum}$$

The value of the asset would go down by £1,600 each year. At the end of year one it would have a value of £8,400, year two £6,800 and so on, until year five when it would be £2,000. Depreciation does not represent any cash expenditure – that takes place when the asset is purchased.

A pro-forma balance sheet is shown in Exercise 15.4. As well as listing the assets owned and liabilities owed by the company, a balance sheet highlights the total investment by the shareholders, called shareholders' funds – share capital plus accumulated profit. On the other side of the balance sheet this represents the net assets the shareholders own – total assets minus total liabilities.

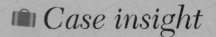 *Case insight*

Xtreme SnoBoards

Building the financial forecast – balance sheet

The founders are now in a position to draw up a balance sheet for Xtreme SnoBoards after the first 15 months of trading. They realize that they have assets that comprise machinery, stock of snowboards, money they are owed for sales (called debtors or receivables) and lease costs they have paid in advance (called prepayments). They also realize they owe money for the purchase of materials (called creditors or payables) and an overdraft.

Machinery	Cost – depreciation	=	£55,680 – £8,700	= £46,980
Stock/inventory	No. of boards × average cost	=	640 × £71.15	= £45,538
Debtors/receivables	Nov + Dec sales	=	£48,600 + £59,400	= £108,000
Prepayments	9 months' lease costs	=	£960 × 9	= £8,640
Total assets				£209,158
Creditors/payables	Nov + Dec purchases	=	(320 + 240 boards) × £37	= £20,720
Overdraft	from cash flow forecast			£3,960
Shareholders' funds:				
Founders' loan capital			£12,000	
Founders' share capital			£30,000	
Profit for the year			£142,478	£184,478
Capital and liabilities				£209,158

Ratio analysis

The performance of a business can be analyzed using a technique called ratio analysis. Investors want to maximize the return they get on their investment. If they invest £100 and receive £10, they get a 10% return which they can then compare to other investment opportunities. Owners (shareholders), who own all the assets of the firm, want to maximize the return they receive on their investment. The critical performance ratio, that investors expect to be kept as high as possible, is return to shareholders:

$$\text{Return to shareholders} = \frac{\text{Net profit}}{\text{Shareholders' funds}} \quad \text{(expressed as \%)}$$

To maximize this, operating profit should be as high as possible, interest should be as low as possible and shareholders' funds should also be as low as possible. And here lies the dilemma. One way of keeping shareholders' funds low is to borrow (shareholders' funds = total assets – liabilities), but this increases interest payments and reduces net profit. So the question is, how much to borrow? The answer is that it pays to borrow as much as you can, as long as you can obtain a return on the loan funds that exceeds the interest rate.

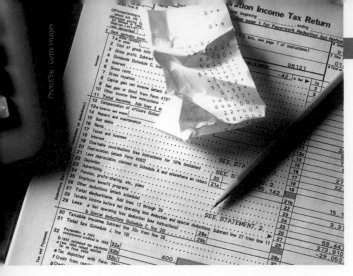

For example, the founder puts £5,000 into the business and then obtains a bank loan of £5,000 with an interest rate of 10%. If the return on this investment is 25% then they will make an extra 15% on the bank loan – a total of £750 (£5,000 × 15%). This goes directly to the founder, on top of the £1,250 (£5,000 × 25%) from their own investment, giving them a total of £2,000, equal to a return to the shareholders of 40% (£2,000 ÷ £5,000 × 100). The down-side of this is that the financial risk of the business increases with the higher level of borrowing. The business is obliged to pay interest of £500 whatever profit it makes and, if it were only able to make a 5% return on the £10,000, then all the money would go to pay interest (£10,000 × 5% = £500), leaving nothing for the shareholders, despite the fact that they had invested £5,000. The appropriate level of borrowing is the classic risk/return trade-off decision – it is a question of judgement. Bankers have some benchmark ratios to inform their lending decisions, as we shall see later in this section.

As far as the business is concerned, the critical performance ratio is the return on total assets. This measures the operating performance of the business (stripping out the effects of borrowing) and must be kept as high as possible:

$$\text{Return on total assets} = \frac{\text{Operating profit}}{\text{Shareholders' funds} + \text{loan capital}}$$
(expressed as %)

where $\text{Shareholders' funds} + \text{loan capital} = \text{total assets} - \text{current liabilities}$

However, be aware that founders take a salary, which is deducted when calculating the operating income, and therefore the ratio (and return to shareholders) can be distorted if salaries are unrealistically low or high.

In seeking to be as efficient as possible a company will look to do two things: maximize its operating profit and minimize its total assets, minus current liabilities. Ratio analysis can help with an understanding of this by looking separately at profit management and asset management.

Profit management

Profits normally increase as turnover increases. Therefore, looking at profit in isolation tells you nothing about the operating efficiency of a business. You need to assess the profit as a proportion of sales/turnover.

The operating profit margin measures overall profitability compared to sales/turnover. It reflects the price you are able to charge, compared to the costs you face. The ratio should be as high as possible.

$$\text{Operating profit margin} = \frac{\text{Operating profit}}{\text{Sales/Turnover}}$$
(expressed as %)

The gross profit margin reflects how well the direct costs of the product/service – the cost of goods sold – are controlled. It should be as high as possible.

$$\text{Gross profit margin} = \frac{\text{Gross profit}}{\text{Sales/Turnover}}$$
(expressed as %)

Gross profit margin is different from the contribution margin – which reflects your control of variable costs. Companies often break this ratio down further by looking at ratios of key direct costs such as materials or labour, compared to turnover/sales.

Asset management

Assets also normally increase as sales increase. Therefore, looking at asset levels in isolation tells you nothing about the operating efficiency of a business. The key ratios below measure the efficiency of asset usage compared to sales/turnover.

They are all expressed as numbers and should be as high as possible:

$$\text{Total asset turnover} = \frac{\text{Sales/Turnover}}{\text{Total assets}}$$

$$\text{Debtor/receivables turnover} = \frac{\text{Sales/Turnover}}{\text{Debtors (receivables)}}$$

$$\text{Stock/inventory turnover} = \frac{\text{Sales/Turnover}}{\text{Stock (inventory)}}$$

Liquidity

There are also a number of ratios that measure the liquidity of a business. The first two are of particular interest to anyone offering credit as they measure the firm's ability to repay the debt. They are all expressed as numbers:

$$\text{Current ratio} = \frac{\text{Current assets}}{\text{Current liability}}$$

This is expected to be greater than 1, indicating that current assets exceed current liabilities.

$$\text{Quick ratio} = \frac{\text{Current assets excluding stock/inventory}}{\text{Current liabilities}}$$

This is expected to be near to 1, perhaps as low as 0.8.

The level of borrowing is called gearing or leverage. Ratios that measure this are of particular interest to bankers. High gearing or leverage is risky.

$$\text{Gearing/leverage} = \frac{\text{All loans + overdraft}}{\text{Shareholders' funds}}$$
(expressed as %)

Bankers like this ratio to be under 100%, indicating that shareholders have put in more money than the banks. Frequently for growing firms this is not the case. Above 400% is considered very high risk – the business is likely to fail. However, some management buy-outs have had gearing levels even above this. Often bankers will also look at the proportion of all the loans that are short-term (due within one year). They are also interested in the security of their interest payments.

$$\text{Interest cover} = \frac{\text{Operating profit}}{\text{Interest}}$$
(expressed as a number)

This measures how many times interest is covered by profit. The higher, the better.

Evaluating performance

Ratios allow you to evaluate performance. They are useful because they measure one number against another – they therefore allow for growth. So, for example, debtors/receivables are bound to increase as the business grows and sales increase, but what is important is not the absolute value of debtors/receivables but rather its relationship to sales, measured by debtor turnover. Similarly, there is no way of knowing whether a £2 million profit in one company is better than a £1 million profit in another unless you know how much was invested in each to achieve it.

To obtain a high return to the shareholder, a firm needs effective profit management and efficient asset management. Put crudely, margins need to be as high as possible and assets should be kept as low as possible. Systematic calculation of these ratios can give you clues about how profit might be increased and where assets might be reduced. Of course to do this you need some benchmarks. One fundamental benchmark is the rate of interest. The return on total assets should never fall below this, otherwise you are better off closing the company and putting the money in the bank. All the other measures are a question of judgement, but you can assess them against:

- Forecasts – Ratios can be calculated both on forecast and actual financial information. Comparing actual to forecast financial performance is part of effective financial control.

- Trends over time – Ratios do change over time and trends can give both good and bad news.

- Industry norms – Industry-based ratios, often based on published financial statements, are produced by a number of organizations (e.g. in the UK, Centre for Interfirm Comparison and ICC Business Ratios). These are important benchmarks against which to judge the realism of projections. If your margins are higher than industry norms, how can you justify this? Founders and investors use these norms and ratios to validate a set of financial projections.

Building the financial forecast – evaluating performance

The founders can now evaluate the performance of Xtreme SnoBoards in its first 15 months of trading using ratio analysis.

$$\text{Return on total assets} = \frac{\text{Net profit}}{\text{Shareholders' funds}} = \frac{£142,478}{£184,478} = 77.2\%$$

$$\text{Operating profit margin} = \frac{\text{Operating profit}}{\text{Turnover}} = \frac{£142,478}{£423,900} = 33.6\%$$

$$\text{Gross profit margin} = \frac{\text{Gross profit}}{\text{Turnover}} = \frac{£200,478}{£423,900} = 47.3\%$$

$$\text{Contribution margin} = \frac{\text{Contribution per unit}}{\text{Sales price per unit}} = \frac{£98}{£135} = 72.6\%$$

$$\text{Margin of safety} = \frac{\text{Turnover} - \text{Breakeven point}}{\text{Turnover}} = \frac{£423,900 - £257,576}{£423,900} = 39.2\%$$

$$\text{Total asset turnover} = \frac{\text{Turnover}}{\text{Total assets}} = \frac{£423,900}{£209,158} = 2.0$$

$$\text{Debtor/receivables turnover} = \frac{\text{Turnover}}{\text{Debtors (receivables)}} = \frac{£423,900}{£108,000} = 3.9$$

$$\text{Stock/inventory turnover} = \frac{\text{Turnover}}{\text{Stock (inventory)}} = \frac{£423,900}{£45,538} = 9.3$$

Although the founders do not have any industry norms and there are no trends to observe in the first period of trading, they feel that this is an exceptional level of performance by any standards, reflecting a high profit margin and strict cost control. However, they are aware that they have accepted a lower salary than they wish (estimated as an additional £20,000) and provided an interest-free loan for the company (estimated as an interest cost of £2,000). They calculate that, if these costs had been charged, the return on total assets would be reduced to 65% and the operating profit margin to 29% – still very good. The debtors' turnover reflects the 2 months' credit terms they require from shops, and the high stock turnover reflects both the high value added, reflected in the board price, and the minimal stocking policy they are trying to adhere to.

The high margin of safety leads them to believe that this is a relatively low-risk venture. The pair do intend to pay themselves more in the second year of trading. However, a quick calculation shows them that they could double their salaries and still make over 50% return on total assets at this level of profitability. This gives them confidence that, if all goes according to plan, they should look forward to expanding the business in its second year.

$$\text{Current ratio} = \frac{\text{Current assets}}{\text{Current liabilities}} = \frac{£162,178}{£24,680} = 6.6$$

$$\text{Quick ratio} = \frac{\text{Current assets, excl. stock}}{\text{Current liabilities}} = \frac{£116,640}{£24,680} = 4.7$$

Despite the early need for cash, the business looks highly liquid by the end of the first period because of the high value of debtors compared to creditors, again reflecting the high value added in the board price. The pair are, however, very aware that earlier in the year, when the actual overdraft was far higher, these ratios would have been much lower.

$$\text{Gearing} = \frac{\text{All loans} + \text{overdraft}}{\text{Shareholders' funds}} = \frac{£15,960}{£184,478} = 8.7\%$$

Not only is this gearing level low, the outstanding interest-free loan is from the founders and not from an external borrower. This encourages them to think that, not only might the company repay their loan early next year, it should be in a very strong position to borrow money to expand. The founders conclude that these financial forecsts look very encouraging. However, being inherently cautious, they are aware that they are just forecasts and the pair will have to work hard to turn them into reality.

Valuing your business

Valuing an established business can be difficult. Valuing a start-up is even more so because of the uncertainties involved and the lack of any track record on which to evaluate forecasts of future income. However, if you are seeking equity investment then the investor will try to judge the value of the business before making you an offer for a proportion of it. It is therefore worthwhile trying to value the business yourself before going to an outside investor. This allows you to judge how much equity you might need to give away to raise a given investment.

So, for example, if they offer you £50,000 for a 20% stake, they are valuing the business at £250,000 (£50,000 ÷ 0.2). If you judge that the amount of equity being demanded by an investor for a given investment to be too high, you are, in effect, putting a higher value on the business than them. (If you thought £50,000 was worth only 10%, you value the business at £500,000.) In this case you might be able to adjust your financial model to reduce the amount of equity investment you need, or to find some way of persuading them to improve the valuation they place on the company. For example, information asymmetry might result in investors being unaware of some information you have, and therefore placing a lower value on the business.

There are two widely-used ways of valuing a business:

1. Market value of assets – Businesses that are asset-rich, such as farms or freehold retail premises, are often valued in this way. Tangible assets such as debtors/receivables, stocks/inventory, equipment, fixtures and fittings and particularly property are valued at their market rate. For certain kinds of businesses this might give a higher value than the second approach, but for any business the asset value provides a minimum valuation.

2. Multiple of profits – Many firms, particularly those with few tangible assets, are valued on the basis of some multiple of net profit. For example, if an appropriate multiple of profits were 5, a

company making £100,000 per year would be valued at £500,000. If the multiple were 20, its value would be £2 million. If you look in the financial press (e.g. *Financial Times*), every public company has its price–earnings or PE ratio quoted. This is the multiple of net profits (from the previous year) that the current share price represents.

Companies can also be valued using a mix of both methods. Where there are tangible assets, such as property, these might be valued at market rates with an additional element of 'goodwill' based upon a multiple of profits.

Whilst the PE ratio in the financial press is based on actual reported profits, start-ups only have forecast profits to work on. This is not an issue in principle because buyers of stocks and shares are interested in the future profits of the business and only use actual profits as a proxy measure. However, one factor that influences the size of the multiple is the 'quality' of earnings. The longer the firm's track record of profitable trading, the higher the multiple is likely to be. So start-ups, with no track record, tend to command a lower multiple than established firms. Other factors can increase the size of the multiple because they make the forecast of profit more credible, for example the experience of the management team or the existence of substantial pre-launch orders. Different industry sectors tend to have different multiples that reflect the risks that are perceived to exist in that sector. The lower the perceived risk, the higher the multiple. So, the higher the risks an investor perceives your venture as facing, the lower the multiple they will apply. However, despite the risks they face, start-ups involved in disruptive innovations or new technologies can sometimes command a very high multiple if it is believed that they may achieve substantial first-mover advantage by creating a whole new industry (for example, Facebook or Twitter). It has to be said that these valuations often prove to be unfounded.

The key question, then, is what multiple of profits to use? There is no straightforward answer to this. It is all a matter of judgement. Just like the price of any product or service, it requires a willing buyer and a willing seller – and a company can be 'marketed' in the same way as any product or service. However, for a start-up:

• Risks are high.

• There is no track record.

• If the buyer wishes to sell their shares, there is no established market to sell them on (unlike for a public company).

These factors mean that multiples in single figures are currently quite normal for a start-up. However, if your venture is involved in disruptive innovation the multiple could be very much higher. Once established, with a proven track record, the multiple will improve. And if you decide to sell the business, the multiple can be very high if a larger company perceives it as strategically important for some reason. For example, when Avis bought Zipcar in 2013 it paid $500 million – 34 times net profits of $14.6 million (see Case Insight in Chapter 3).

External factors that you cannot control are also important in company valuations. The recession of 2008 saw private company valuations plunge as forecasts of economic activity were cut back. As economies emerge out of recession, valuations should improve. Another factor is the rate of interest. High interest rates usually mean lower multiples and therefore lower valuations, since an investment in a company is competing against that market rate of interest. Interest rates are very low at the time of writing so future increases will mean that valuations should decrease. Nevertheless, the net effect is likely to be that company valuations will improve in the future. Accountants experienced in raising equity funding for start-ups can provide advice on the 'going rate' for multiples in particular sectors.

One way of dealing with the problem of early valuation – particularly for fast, high-growth businesses – is to delay valuation but set out the details of how it will be determined at some point in the future. The initial investor then receives equity based on a discount of that future valuation. This is particularly effective when equity funding is to be sought in tranches and valuation is easier at these later stages. For example, a new venture receives equity funding of £100,000 on the understanding that the valuation will be based on a 50% discount on the next investor's valuation when £200,000 is needed in one year's time. If this valuation turns out to be £2 million and the investor receives 10% of the equity, then the original investor will also receive 10%, reflecting the 50% discount.

Xtreme SnoBoards

Building the financial forecast – valuing the business

The founders were very pleased with the performance of Xtreme SnoBoards in its first 15 months of trading, having evaluated it using ratio analysis. Although they were not thinking of selling the business so early, they were curious about how much it might be worth if they achieved their targets.

Starting with basics, they would have put £42,000 of their own money into Xtreme and built a company with some £184,000 of capital or net assets (although almost £50,000 of this would be represented by machinery that may or may not have this market value). Against this, they would have liked a higher salary and did not take interest on the loan to the business. This would have reduced profit and assets by some £22,000. Still, if they could realize or sell the assets for £184,000 that would make the venture worthwhile.

However, they had learned that a thriving business is normally valued as a multiple of its profits, and with net profits of some £142,000 (or £120,000 after their additional salary and interest) they tried to find out what that multiple might be. The problem was that nobody would give them a firm indication. On the one hand they were told that the business probably had great future potential, but on the other hand it had no track record and the stock market was generally depressed because of a recession. The multiples they were given ranged from 12 to 3, although most advisors thought that at this stage the multiple was probably in single digits. This wide range valued the company at anything between £426,000 and £1.7 million (or £360,000 and £1.4 million after their additional salary and interest) – quite a lot more than the net assets.

The founders were astounded. Taking the net asset value and the lowest multiple of income the company would be worth something between £184,000 and £426,000 (£162,000 and £360,000 taking the additional salary and interest into account). Not bad for a £42,000 investment and a lot of hard work over 15 months. Whichever way they looked at it, if the forecast was achieved, the business would be highly successful, and that made them even more determined than ever.

Questions:

1. *Work through all the financial projections of Xtreme SnoBoards, making sure you understand how they were constructed and where the information came from.*
2. *Do you think the assumptions on which they are based are realistic? If not, assess the effect of any changes you would make.*
3. *Do you agree with the founders about the projected performance of the company? Is their valuation of the company realistic?*
4. *Going forward, do these projections alert you to any potential issues facing the company?*

Corbis

Monitoring performance

Having prepared forecasts of income, cash flow and a balance sheet, you might be forgiven for thinking that the job is done. Unfortunately, actually achieving these target forecasts will involve even more hard work. These forecasts can be used to monitor your performance and help control the business. They provide a framework against which the performance of the firm can be judged. By comparing actual financial results to the forecast on a timely basis you can 'manage by exception', only intervening when performance deviates from your forecasts. This can free up time to concentrate on strategy or dealing with real business problems.

Computer-based accounting systems provide the financial information you need to monitor your performance, normally on a monthly basis. However, sometimes they can provide so much financial information that you become 'numbers-blind' – unable to see the important pieces of information because of the detail provided. In fact, most firms can be controlled by monitoring just six pieces of information that tell you different, but vital, information on the performance of the business. These are called financial drivers. They are like the instruments on a car dashboard. They tell you different things about the engine of the business. Different pieces of information are important at different times and in different circumstances. On a road with a speed restriction you watch your speedometer. When changing gear at speed you watch your rev counter. When low on petrol your eye never strays from the fuel gauge.

> Mark Mason, serial entrepreneur and business angel *Sunday Times* 2 June 2013
>
> My own businesses have always been very tightly controlled. I was able to sell my (first) business because the books were very clean, we had grown steadily, we never lost money and I knew where all the figures were month by month, if not day by day.

The financial drivers tell you all you need to know about driving the business. They can be reproduced on a single piece of paper and provide the headline information on how the business is doing. If they disclose a problem, more information will be needed to accurately diagnose the cause and decide on the appropriate corrective action. There are six financial drivers:

- Cash – It is vital for monitoring your liquidity – your cash flow and cash balance. Early in the life of a business, as you negotiate Death Valley, you will probably need to monitor this on a weekly basis. But if you are really short of cash you may have to monitor it on a daily basis.

- Sales/turnover – This tells you about the volume of work going through the business. It drives all the other financial results. Early in the life of a business you will probably need to monitor this on a weekly, possibly even a daily, basis. If you are ahead of your forecasts, do you have the resources to meet the increased demand? If you are behind your forecasts, are there sufficient sales in the pipeline, or do you have to cut back on expenditure?

- Profit margins – These tell you whether your costs are in line with your sales. Your target margins will only be achieved if the sales volume targets are met, at the appropriate prices, and costs are under control. The operating profit margin, gross margin and contribution margin each give you different information. They probably only need to be monitored monthly.

- Margin of safety – This tells you about the operating risk of the business. A deteriorating margin of safety should sound warning bells. It means you are approaching breakeven point. That could mean sales volumes are going down, contribution margins are not being maintained (prices are being discounted, or variable costs are increasing) or fixed costs are out of control. If the deteriorating margin of safety is due to falling sales, then you might try to reduce fixed costs – particularly the ones that you have some discretionary control over. This is therefore a powerful piece of information and should be monitored monthly.

- Productivity – For most firms the single largest and most important expense they face is their wage costs. It therefore needs to be controlled carefully. Wages are best measured in relation to the productivity that they generate and for many firms this is most easily measured by the simple percentage of wages to sales. Often there are industry norms to compare this to. For example, in the UK licensed trade, wages of bar staff should be about 20% of sales. If higher, the bar is over-staffed, if lower, it is under-staffed – a crude but simple and effective measure that needs to be checked at least monthly. Of course, to achieve this benchmark staff need to work shifts, being brought in at peak periods.
- Debtor/receivables and/or stock/inventory turnover – Similarly most firms will have one important current asset on their balance sheet that represents over 50% of their total assets. For a service business this will probably be debtors/receivables, for a retail business stock/inventory and for a manufacturing business it is likely to be both. You can use debtors/receivables and stock/inventory turnover ratios to monitor this investment, again on a monthly basis.

Controlling performance

Forecasting is not just for start-ups. You should continue to prepare financial forecasts as the firm grows because they help you control the business. Forecasts for an established firm are called budgets. They can be prepared at the department as well as company level, consistent with how you structure the business (Chapter 12). You can use budgets to help you delegate responsibility to your management team and then monitor their performance, consistent with your leadership style (Chapter 13). The budgeting process can then be used as a process for communicating and coordinating the activities of your management team. It can become a systematic tool for establishing standards of performance, providing motivation and assessing the results your managers achieve.

Morgan Motor

An essential element in this process of making managers accountable is that each knows exactly what they are held responsible for, and each does indeed control this aspect of the firm's operations. Responsibility cannot be assigned without authority. A clear management structure is a fundamental necessity alongside this. The principle is to make every manager responsible for the costs and revenues they control, even if they, in turn, delegate responsibility down the line.

Of course, if managers are going to be held responsible for the costs and revenues they control, they are going to want to be involved in the budgeting process. This is consistent with a dispersed leadership style where you want to involve them in developing strategies for the business. Indeed, as the business grows, they should come to know more about the area they are responsible for than you. So, involving managers in setting their own budgets means that they should remain realistic. If budgets are to motivate staff generally, they have to 'buy into' them and believe that they are realistic and achievable. Once they accept the standards of performance against which they are to be judged, they will normally try hard to achieve them. Imposing budgets from above normally causes resentment and leads to a lack of commitment.

Having effective monitoring and control processes in place for your venture will help you manage it. They will help you delegate and control. They will help you achieve your targets. And they add value to your business.

Summary

- For a new venture to survive and grow it needs to be financially viable. This means it needs to be profitable and efficient, sufficiently liquid to pay its bills, whilst minimizing the risk that it faces.

- Profit is measured by sales/turnover minus total costs. It is represented by the growth in all the assets owned by a company.

- Profit is not the same as cash flow. You can be profitable but illiquid, without cash to pay your bills. If you cannot pay your bills you risk going bankrupt. A new venture therefore needs to plan and monitor cash flow carefully as it moves through 'Death Valley'.

- The balance sheet is a snapshot at a point of time that shows the assets the business has and where the funds for these assets came from.

- The business plan can provide information on these things by including forecast income statements (including breakeven projections) and balance sheets for three years (five years for larger projects). Your cash flow forecast will indicate the funding you need to launch the business.

- Monthly sales forecasts should be provided for at least the first year (longer where there are substantial commercialization risks) and the detailed assumptions on which your sales and costs are based should be listed.

- Ratio analysis allows you to assess your financial performance. It can be based both on forecast and actual financial information. Ratios can be compared to industry norms or used to assess trends over time.

- Companies can be valued on the basis of their assets or a multiple of earnings or net profits (or both). There is, however, no set formula for judging what that multiple should be.

- Rather than valuing a start-up business straight away, another approach, particularly suitable for fast, high-growth businesses, is to delay valuation but set out the details of how it will be determined at some time in the future. The initial investor then receives equity based on a discount of that future valuation.

- Actual performance is normally compared to forecasted performance – called budgets. As the business grows, the preparation and monitoring of budgets on a decentralized basis can encourage delegation and help control the performance of managers.

- Financial drivers are headline measures of the financial performance of a business: cash, sales, profit margins, margin of safety, productivity and debtor/receivables and/or stock/inventory control. They are quick and easy to calculate and monitor.

Exercise 15.1

Forecast income statement

1 Estimate the sales volume and value in each month of your first year. Check that there is sufficient demand and that your targets are achievable, within the operating and cost parameters of the business. Jot down the assumptions on which this is based.

Forecast income statement

TURNOVER

Cost of sales

Materials

Wages

Factory overheads

GROSS PROFIT   A

Operating expenses

Selling & marketing costs

Distribution costs

Administrative & general costs

Other costs

Depreciation   B

OPERATING INCOME   A – B

Other income

Interest income

Less: Interest expense   C

NET INCOME   A – B – C

2 Review Exercise 14.1. For any fixed assets you need to purchase, estimate their useful life and calculate the annual depreciation charge. This goes to the income statement as a cost and reduces the value of the assets in the balance sheet.

3 Using the pro forma above, draw up a forecast income statement for your first year of operation.

4 Repeat the process for your second and third years.

Exercise 15.2

Estimating your breakeven

1 Using the figures from the previous exercise and the pro forma below, re-analyze your costs into variable and fixed.

2 Calculate your contribution margin (B ÷ A).

3 Calculate your breakeven point, before [C ÷ (B ÷ A)] and after interest [(C + D) ÷ (B ÷ A)]

4 Calculate your margin of safety after interest (A – [(C + D) ÷ (B ÷ A)] ÷ A).

5 Repeat the process for your second and third years.

TURNOVER		A
Variable costs		
Materials		
................(other)		
................(other)		
CONTRIBUTION		B
Fixed costs		
Selling & marketing costs		
Administrative & general costs		
Depreciation		
................(other)		
................(other)		C
OPERATING INCOME		B – C
Other income		
Interest income		
Less: Interest expense		D
NET INCOME		B – C – D

Exercise 15.3

Forecast cash flow statement

1 Using the pro forma opposite, draw up a forecast cash flow statement for your first year of operation based upon the information you have used for Exercises 14.1 and 15.1.

2 Decide on the salary or drawings you will take out. Update the forecast to reflect this.

Forecast cash flow statement

Month	1	2	3	4	5	6	7	8	9	10	11	12	Total
Cash receipts													
Sales													
Capital introduced													
Total receipts													

Cash payments													
Materials													
Wages													
Sales & marketing													
Admin. & general													
Asset purchases													
Drawings													
.... (other)													
.... (other)													
Total payments													

Net cash flow													
Cash B/F													
Cash C/F													

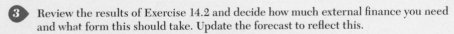

3 Review the results of Exercise 14.2 and decide how much external finance you need and what form this should take. Update the forecast to reflect this.

Exercise 15.4

Forecast balance sheet

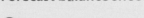 *1* Using the pro forma overleaf, draw up a forecast balance sheet at the end of your first year by listing your assets and liabilities:

- Remember to insert the capital you will introduce yourself and any loan or equity finance you need to raise.
- The fixed assets cost should be reduced by the depreciation charge (Exercise 15.1.2).
- The 'profit for current year' figure should be your 'net income' (Exercise 15.1.1).
- The 'cash' or 'overdraft' figure should be your final 'cash c/f' (Exercise 15.3.1).

2 Repeat the process for your second and third years.

Forecast balance sheet

Fixed assets:

Cost

Less: Depreciation   A

Current assets:

Stock

Debtors

Cash

Total   B

Less: Creditors due within one year:

Overdraft

Trade creditors

Other liabilities

Total   C

Net current assets   B − C

NET ASSETS   A + B − C

Less: Long-term loans   D

                                         A + B − C − D

Capital and reserves:

Share capital

Profit brought forward

Profit for current year

Exercise 15.5

Evaluating your forecast performance

1 Using the checklist opposite, calculate your forecast performance ratios, based upon Exercises 15.1, 15.2 and 15.4.

Performance	Year 1	Year 2	Year 3
Return to shareholders $\dfrac{\text{Net profit}}{\text{Shareholders' funds}}$ (total assets − total liabilities)			
Return on total assets $\dfrac{\text{Operating profit}}{\text{Shareholders' funds + loan capital}}$ (total assets − current liabilities)			
Profitability			
Operating profit margin $\dfrac{\text{Operating profit}}{\text{Sales/turnover}}$			
Gross profit margin $\dfrac{\text{Gross profit}}{\text{Sales/turnover}}$			
Contribution margin $\dfrac{\text{Contribution}}{\text{Sales/turnover}}$			
Asset management			
Total asset turnover $\dfrac{\text{Sales/turnover}}{\text{Total assets}}$			
Debtor/receivables turnover $\dfrac{\text{Sales/turnover}}{\text{Debtors/receivables}}$			
Stock/inventory turnover $\dfrac{\text{Sales/turnover}}{\text{Stock/inventory}}$			
Liquidity			
Current ratio $\dfrac{\text{Current assets}}{\text{Current liability}}$			
Quick ratio $\dfrac{\text{Current assets, excluding stock/inventory}}{\text{Current liabilities}}$			
Risk			
Gearing/leverage $\dfrac{\text{All loans + overdraft}}{\text{Shareholders' funds}}$			
Interest cover $\dfrac{\text{Operating profit}}{\text{Interest}}$			
Margin of safety $\dfrac{\text{Sales/turnover − breakeven point}}{\text{Sales/turnover}}$			

2 Write a brief evaluation of your performance based on these ratios.

Exercise 15.6

Review of your objectives and milestones

1 Have these results met the objectives you set yourself in Exercise 2.2? If not, list the things you need to do or amend your objectives.

2 Update Exercise 11.3.4 to create a list of milestones (achievements) for your business plan.

Exercise 15.7

Financial controls

List the things you need to put in place to ensure good financial control.

Visit www.palgrave.com/companion/burns-new-venture-creation for chapter quizzes to test your knowledge and other resources.

16
THE
BUSINESS
PLAN

Contents

Learning outcomes

When you have read this chapter and undertaken the related exercises you will be able to:

- Explain the purpose, structure and content of a business plan
- Draw up a business plan for your new venture
- Recognize the information needs of bankers and equity investors
- Be able to present the plan effectively

Purpose of a business plan

The business plan framework exercises at the end of each chapter should provide you with all the information you need to write a formal business plan. The business plan is a formal written document often used for external purposes, such as obtaining finance. It is the result of your business planning process. The plan should set out what your venture seeks to achieve and how it will achieve it. There are no set rules that can be used to create a 'perfect' business plan. However, remember that the written plan is a formal business document that needs to be succinct, professional and well-presented. Whilst the next section sets out a general pro-forma plan, each plan is particular to its business and will be different from others. Sections might be expanded or contracted and it may well be appropriate to omit or add complete sections to suit different circumstances. Each business is unique.

The complexity and length of the plan will vary with the scale of the start-up. What is more, this may vary with the purpose for which the plan was written. If it is simply for you, to help you organize the venture systematically, then it might be brief and functional, almost an 'aide-memoire' or summary plan, running to 10 pages or less. In these circumstances the discipline of using the New Venture Creation Framework to develop a plan is probably of more value than the written plan. However, the written plan can still provide an invaluable set of milestones against which progress can be checked. And if assumptions and circumstances change, then you may have to start altering your plans. A business plan should be sufficiently detailed to give you direction but should never be so rigid as to blind you to new opportunities or threats.

If the plan is intended for external use, for example to help you raise finance, then it will need to be thorough, better presented and, inevitably, longer.

> What is the right plan? It's the one that helps you identify what you need to ensure success. It's the one that rallies your employees around a few common goals – and motivates them to achieve them. It's the one that involves your customers' goals and suppliers' goals and brings them all together in a unified focus.
>
> Michael Dell: Direct from Dell: Strategies that Revolutionized an Industry (1999, New York: Harper Business)

After all, it is a document that should be 'selling' your venture to a financier, supplier or business partner. A full business plan of this sort will typically run to about 20 pages, with financial projections and other details going into the appendices. If it is intended to help you raise finance, the more money you are trying to raise, the more thorough it will need to be. Indeed, if you are trying to raise equity finance it will need to be extremely thorough and well-presented. Although you might keep to approximately the same length of plan, the appendices could easily run to 30 pages and be placed in a separate document. Having said that, keep the plan as succinct as possible. Do not pad it out unnecessarily.

As we shall see later in this chapter, bankers are interested in slightly different things from equity investors. Most equity investors prefer to see a business plan (or at least the executive summary) before they meet the entrepreneur behind it. Some plans for large-scale start-ups can take the form of professionally produced brochures. However, there is always a fine balance between including sufficient detail in the plan to convince the reader that you know what you are talking about, but not so much that they lose interest. Indeed, too much focus on the operations may convince equity investors that you are product- rather than market-focused – and that will definitely turn them off.

Structure and content of a business plan

The structure and content of a full business plan intended for external use is shown in Table 16.1. This is a general pro forma and, as already stated, it may be appropriate to omit or add complete sections to suit different circumstances. The contents of each section may also need to be adapted to suit your venture. For example, location is a vital part of a business plan for a retail start-up, web functionality for an internet start-up. Your plan should read like a professional business report – succinct and to the point, and full of vital information. It must be convincing. A guide to content follows. The indicative page extent (in brackets) is based upon a typical 20-page plan – anything more should go into the appendices.

- Cover
- Table of contents
- Executive summary
- Business details
- Industry and market analysis
- Customers and value proposition
- Marketing strategy
- Operations plan
- Management team and company structure
- Resources
- Financing
- Financial projections
- Risks and strategic options
- Key milestones
- Appendices

T16.1 **Business plan structure**

Cover

The cover should include the business name and contact details. You should consider whether the plan needs to be marked 'confidential'.

Table of contents

This is a list of sections and sub-sections, with page numbers.

Executive summary (1–2 pages)

If you are seeking external finance, this is probably the most important section of the plan. Many equity investors will only read the full plan if they find the summary attractive. It should only be written after the full plan is complete, and then it should be written with the reader and purpose of the plan in mind. If it is to be used to attract funding, it should state what is requested from the lender or investor and how they will benefit by providing the funds.

It must be a summary of the plan – not an introduction. It should highlight the nature of your product/service, target customers, value proposition and competitive advantage. It should appeal to the reader by highlighting the distinctive capabilities and potential of the business, including the financial return. If the plan is written to attract an equity investor it should state what deal you are offering; for example, '20% of the business in exchange for £100,000'.

Above all, the executive summary must be focused and succinct – no more than one or two pages long.

Business details (1–2 pages)

This section covers basic information such as business name, address, legal form and ownership. It should include:

- A description of your product/service;
- Your mission and vision statement;
- Your aims and objectives.

If this is an existing business, you should include a brief business history.

Industry and market analysis (2–3 pages)

This section provides background information on your industry sector and the market segments within it. It should take the form of a narrative informed by academic models such as a SLEPT analysis and Porter's Five Forces. You should review your competitors and their strengths and weaknesses. The more you know about an industry and market, and the competitors you face, the more confidence your readers will have in your ability to compete within it. This section should include:

- Industry size, growth, structure (macro and micro/local level).
- Industry and market trends (macro and micro/local level).
- Market segments and reasons for target market(s) selection.
- Buyer behaviour across segments.
- Competitor analysis (strengths and weaknesses).
- For an existing business – market share.

In most industries there are some key success factors that industry players have to have mastered in order to compete. These need to be highlighted but judgement is required about what is important for your particular venture.

Customers and value proposition (2–3 pages)

This is the section where you outline your target market segment(s) and the value proposition(s) for your product/service. It is essential that your 'unique selling proposition(s)' are clearly and simply articulated. In doing this you should highlight your differential advantage over competitors. The more points of difference and the stronger and more sustainable these differences, the better.

This is where you also set out your sales targets. If you have firm orders for the product or service, be sure to mention this.

Marketing strategy (3–4 pages)

This section provides the details about how you propose to achieve those sales targets – not only the details of your marketing mix but also the details of your sales tactics (how the product or service will actually be sold). As well as the launch strategy, this should also highlight the growth potential through market and product development, your competitive reaction and strategy for establishing your brand. It should include:

- Price, promotions, distribution etc.
- Launch strategy.
- Sales tactics.
- Brand development.
- Competitive reaction.
- Product and market development.
- Growth potential.

Investors are always particularly interested in pricing strategy because this is a prime determinant of the profitability of the business.

Operations plan (2–3 pages)

This section outlines how your business will be run and how your product/service will be produced. What goes into the operations plan varies depending on the nature of the venture. However, what is important is that the key activities for your venture are highlighted. The operations plan must convince the reader that you understand the operation of the business – how to do whatever needs to be done to deliver your product/service. So, issues of business control, if critical to the business, need to be covered. Also, the prospect of scalability – should the business prove to be even more successful than planned – can be addressed in this section. What are your strategic options?

The content of this section is difficult to predict but might include:

- Key operating activities (e.g. manufacturing processes, business model etc.);
- Partnerships;
- Business controls;
- IP issues;
- Scalability.

Management team and company structure (1–3 pages)

This section outlines all the people involved in the venture – details of their background and experience – as well as the organizational structure you are adopting. A new venture team with an established track record in the industry or with relevant experience will certainly add credibility to any start-up. Remember that investors ultimately invest in people, not products. An experienced board of directors can achieve the same result. Brief CVs can go in the appendices. For larger start-ups, an organization chart can go in this section. This section should include:

- Key people, their functions and background;
- Business organization or structure;
- Directors, advisors and other key partners;
- Skills gaps and plans for filling them.

Resources (1–2 pages)

This section describes the firm's facilities, equipment and staff requirements. It should include:

- Premises and facilities;
- Machinery and equipment;
- Staff.

Financing (1–2 pages)

This section highlights the finance you need to launch your business. External funders will expect you to contribute some capital. Lenders will be interested in the risks they face and the security they can obtain. Equity investors will be interested

in the overall return they might make and how this might be realized. This section should include:

- Founders' contribution;
- Loan and/or equity finance requirements;
- Gearing/leverage;
- Time scale and exit routes for equity investors.

Financial projections (1-page summary, plus appendices)

Typically financial projections for three years are expected by funders, with a monthly cash flow forecast for the first year. A very small-scale start-up might only provide financial projections for the first year. Five-year forecasts might be expected for larger projects where significant commercialization risks have not been resolved. You should provide a one-page financial summary and place the detailed projections in the appendices.

Financial details going into your appendices should be as long as it takes to provide all the information required. These should include:

- Income projections;
- Cash flow projections;
- Balance sheet projections;
- Key ratios;
- The assumptions on which your financial projections are based, particularly the basis for your sales projections.

© loooby – istockphoto.com

Risks and strategic options (1 page)

This section should identify the key risks you face and explain how they will be monitored and mitigated. You need to identify your critical success factors and the strategic options you face should these key risks materialize. Strategic options are valuable because circumstances can, and do, change. They give you flexibility in a changing environment. This section should include:

- Identified risks;
- Risk monitoring and mitigation;
- Critical success factors;
- Strategic options.

Key milestones (1 page)

These milestones, often incorporating critical success factors, highlight the progress needed to launch and grow the business. They might include prototype completion, formalization of partnerships, obtaining finance, securing of key customers etc. This section gives an overview of the sequence and timing of important events.

Appendices

Any information that is vital, but might impede the flow of the plan, should go into the appendix. One key piece of information is the assumptions upon which the financial projections are based, in particular the sales projections. These need to be made explicit and you can expect an investor to scrutinize them closely. This section might include:

- Detailed financial projections;
- Financial assumptions – start-up costs, basis for sales projections, fixed/variable costs, profit margins;
- Background information (CVs) on key people;
- Location information (maps, layouts etc.);
- Operations information (Gantt charts etc.)
- Details of market research;
- Details of IP protection;
- Website screenshots;
- For an existing business – historic financial statements, brochures etc.

If used for external purposes, the business plan must convince the reader that you understand the industry, market and business you want to establish. It must convince them of the viability of the business – that you have a good product/service and value proposition, and that you know how to combat the competition. It must enhance your creditability and make them trust your judgement. They need to believe that you can turn your business idea into reality. So, when you have written the plan, get friends or relatives to read it and give you honest feedback.

> Luke Johnson, serial entrepreneur and business angel Sunday Times 2 June 2013
>
> I see some (business plans) where the CV is so vague as to be useless. Give me dates, give me details. Be honest about things that have gone wrong. Talk about the setbacks and mistakes and explain how you fixed them.

Five practical tips on preparing your business plan

1. Keep the plan as short and simple as possible. Do not pad it out. The plan should be sufficiently long to cover the project adequately but short enough to maintain interest. To do this you need to be able to prioritize and focus on the important things for your business. If you over-complicate your plan you risk losing that focus and the interest of the reader.

2. Keep it as realistic as possible. Are sales targets, costs, milestone deadlines and so on realistic? If your claims are unrealistic you will never gain the trust of lenders and investors. It is better to under-estimate and over-deliver than vice versa.

3. Make it clear, specific and unambiguous. Are market segments clearly identified? Are objectives concrete and measurable? Are targets and deadlines clear? Lack of clarity is often taken to indicate a lack of knowledge or willingness to be committed.

4. Check your spelling, grammar, punctuation and, most important of all, financial accuracy. Errors will damage your credibility and, if noticed at a presentation, can put you off your stride. Computers have grammar and spelling checks – use them. Using a spreadsheet package for your cash flow forecast can ensure arithmetic accuracy.

5. If you are not confident about putting the financial projections together yourself, seek professional advice, but be sure you understand how they were arrived at.

Using your plan to obtain finance

Your initial cash flow forecasts show you how much finance you need and Chapter 14 should have helped you decide on the appropriate type of external finance. External funders will expect you to have contributed some capital yourself. They will expect to see a business plan and, whilst both lenders and investors might look at the same elements of information from the plan, each places a different weight upon these elements. However, the reality is that both banks and equity investors ultimately invest in individuals, not in businesses or plans. The plan is just one way, albeit a very important one, of communicating with them.

 The UK government provides further information on writing a business plan, examples for different sectors and a free pro forma download on: www.gov.uk/write-business-plan

The USA the Small Business Administration provides information about how to write a business plan on: www.sba.gov

It must therefore reinforce the perceptions the banker or investor has of you and your venture team.

Before letting anybody see your business plan you need to consider whether they should be asked to sign a non-disclosure agreement, which binds the reader to confidentiality. If you are then invited to meet with the lender or investor, you need to be clear whether you are expected to present your plan or simply discuss it. If you are asked to present the plan, you need to know how long you have and then prepare a professional presentation. However, first it is worth recalling what banks and investors are looking for.

Banks

Banks are in the business of lending money; in that respect they are just like any other supplier of a commodity – and there are many banks you can approach. The thing to remember about banks is that they are not in the risk business. They are looking to obtain a certain rate of interest over a specified period of time and to see their capital repaid. They do not share in the extra profits a firm might make, so they do not expect to lose money if there are problems. What is more, the manager stands to lose a lot if he lends to a business that subsequently fails. The plan therefore needs to demonstrate how the interest on the loan can be paid, even in the worst possible set of circumstances, and how the capital can be repaid on the due date. In this respect the cash flow forecast is something that the bank manager will be particularly interested in. Where a long-term loan for product development or capital expenditure

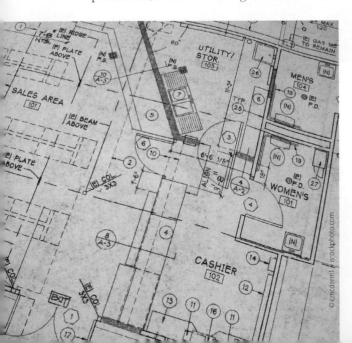

is being sought and there is little prospect of loan repayment in the short term, the plan must emphasize the cash-generating capacity of the business and take a perspective longer than one year. In addition, banks are also particularly interested in the breakeven and gearing ratios. In an ideal world, they would like both of these to be as low as possible.

Bank managers represent a set of values and practices that are alien to many entrepreneurs. They are employees, not independent professionals, and lend only within very strict, centrally dictated, guidelines. They often talk 'a different language' and are subject to numerous rules and regulations that an entrepreneur would probably find very tedious. Since they trade in money, they often cannot make decisions on their own without getting approval from 'up the line'. In these circumstances the business plan is an essential weapon in helping them get authorization for a loan. Any manager will only be able to lend within the bank's own policies, at acceptable levels of risk and with adequate security to cover the loan. However, each of these

three constraints requires the exercise of judgement and can therefore be influenced, not only through the style and content of the business plan but also the credibility and track record of the founder and their team.

Bank managers are trained to examine business plans critically. So expect to be questioned. They will ask about the assumptions that it is based on. They will ask about risks. They will always ask questions about some of the claims in the plan, so you must be able to back them up. Avoid any tendency to generalize in order to disguise a weakness in your knowledge. Your plan should seek to identify and then reassure the bank manager about the risks the business faces. They tend to dislike plans that they see as over-ambitious since they do not share in the success and see this as an unnecessary risk.

However good the business plan, bankers are still likely to ask for a personal guarantee After all, if they don't ask, they certainly won't get it. And it does make any loan more secure from their

perspective. But be prepared to haggle and shop around. This is just a sales negotiation like any other and the banker is trying to 'sell' you a loan, albeit at a certain price and with certain conditions.

Equity investors

Prospective equity investors will normally expect to see a business plan before meeting you. And, whilst most entrepreneurs will submit business plans to more than one investor for consideration, most investors are inundated with business plans seeking finance. Fewer than 1 in 20 will ever lead to a face-to-face meeting. To a large extent, therefore, the decision whether to proceed beyond an initial reading of the plan will depend crucially on its quality. The business plan is the first, and often the best, chance that an entrepreneur has to impress prospective investors with the quality of their investment proposal. A good executive summary is, therefore, vital – many investors do not read beyond it.

Because of this and the fact that equity investors share in both the risks and returns from the business, business plans tend to be longer. They are more comprehensive, offering greater detail, and are better presented. As we saw in Chapter 14, investors want to know about the return they will make and when they will make it (the exit route). They need to be convinced that the founder and their team are as good as the business idea and they are the right people to trust an investment with. This requires a careful balance between making the proposal sufficiently attractive, on the one hand, while realistically addressing the many risks inherent in the proposal, in particular how rapid growth will be handled. To do this the plan needs to emphasize the strengths of the business, particularly compared to the competition. Behind all plans there are people, and investors, like bank managers, need to be convinced that you and the venture team can deliver what you are promising. It is often said that the single most important element in the investment decision is the credibility and quality of the firm's management.

The most difficult aspect of any deal is deciding on the split of equity between the various partners. The simple answer is that there is no set of rules and the final result will depend on the attractiveness of the proposal and the negotiating skills of the individuals concerned. Investors will not normally want control of the business (over 50% of the shareholding) as this might affect your motivation, but they will want a sufficiently large say to influence important decisions. Key managers on your team might also want a share in the business, so you need to think through the final shareholding you will be left with. You will not want to surrender control, so you need to consider how much equity you want, not just at this point, but also when the equity investor seeks to sell their shares. Who can they sell them to?

You need to find out how the investor operates. Some investors prefer a 'hands-on' approach to managing their investment whereby they have a non-executive director on the board, visit the firm monthly and keep in regular phone contact. Business angels can bring considerable experience and a network of contacts to the business, so do your homework on the background of your angel. Other, mainly institutional, investors have a more 'hands-off' approach, preferring not to interfere once they have invested, perhaps meeting once a year to review the progress of the business.

I see business plans so complicated that you need to set aside a week to read them but it's the ability to identify a simple solution that continues to set apart the best entrepreneurs.

Duncan Bannatyne, serial entrepreneur and Dragon *Sunday Telegraph 30 July 2009*

STOCKBYTE

As explained in Chapter 14, business angels and venture capitalists expect an annualized return of 30–50%, usually as a capital gain. They also normally expect to realize their investment within five years, so work out in advance what you think their share of the business will then be worth and the return they will make. They will expect a seat on the board of directors and many angels will expect a close involvement in the management of the business. You need to find out how your investor wants to realize their investment – dividend or capital gain. You should not be afraid to ask about the time scale they have for realizing their investment. They may also have views about who they might sell their stake to. This may be an opportunity for you to increase your stake in the business by buying out the investor, as happened with Mark Constantine and Lush (Case Insight, Chapter 6). Alternatively, it may be an opportunity for you to dilute your share of the business or exit completely by encouraging a merger with, or a buy-out by, another company.

> Jeff Weiner, CEO LinkedIn Sunday Times 14 July 2013
>
> Managing a hyper-growth company is like putting a rocket into space: if you are off by inches at launch, you will be off by miles in orbit.

Finally, whereas a bank loan will probably take weeks to arrange, an equity investment will take months. It will involve numerous meetings, interviews and presentations. The investors, or their accountants, will undertake their own investigations into the business (called due diligence) and the production of the legal documentation will involve lengthy, detailed work. You will need professional advice.

Presenting your case for finance

At some point you might be asked to 'present' your business plan to financiers. Part of the reason for this will be to support and elaborate on details contained in the business plan but part of it will be to allow the potential backer to form judgements about you, and possibly your venture team. They will be looking for motivation, enthusiasm and integrity but, most of all, the managerial ability to make the plan actually happen.

'Presentations' can take a number of forms. A bank might just expect an informal meeting to discuss the business plan, perhaps coming back to discuss issues that might arise. Investors are likely to require a number of meetings. The first meeting might involve a 15–20-minute formal presentation of the plan, using PowerPoint or Prezi, followed by questions which could easily go on for twice as long. If this is successful you will be invited back for a second meeting to sort out details about an investment.

The first thing to do is to follow instructions. If you are asked to make a 15-minute presentation, keep it to 15 minutes – and that means about 10 slides. Make sure a computer and projector are available. If they are not, you need to make your own arrangements

> Martyn Dawes, founder Coffee Nation Sunday Times 23 May 2004
>
> They're backing you. You've got to convince your investors that you won't give up. You've got to create a vision for the backers.

– a large tablet computer can be useful if there is only one investor because it breaks down the 'us and them' feel of using a projector. Remember that what you really want is to engage in a discussion – to start forming a relationship – and you need to work to break down barriers. It is always good to bring in samples or examples of the product, service website etc., so that the audience can see and/or touch it. You need to grab their attention.

Slides should be clear and uncluttered, focusing on the main points of the topic and inviting the audience to engage and ask questions because the topic interests them. Remember to 'brand' every slide with your business name. Highlights to be covered on individual slides include:

- Why you are there – the financing you are seeking and the deal you are offering. Remember that in doing this you are placing a value on the business. You will inevitably be asked what you intend to spend the money on.

- The product/service offering and the value proposition to customers. You need to explain and/or demonstrate your product or service, the problem customers currently have and how this will solve it for them.

- Target market and opportunity. You need to be able to describe the prospective customers (better still, name names) and explain how you will get to them. If you already have orders for the product or service this will add enormously to your credibility.

- The competition (they will expect you to name names), your competitive advantage and how you will react to competitors when they respond. If you have any IP, this is the point to highlight it.

- Marketing strategy. This is where you can sketch out how you will achieve your sales targets over the planning period. They will be interested in your sales processes and your distribution channels. Primary market research information can add to the credibility of your plans.

- Your management team, including board of directors. What is important is your background and experience. If you have skill gaps, explain how they will be filled.

- Financial highlights – not financial details – sales and profit, when profitability is achieved, capital investment, cash flow implications and breakeven. They will ask about the details, in particular how your sales projections and costs were arrived at, so you might want to prepare some additional slides to go back to. Remember, they will be thinking about what their share of this will be and how it might convert into business valuation.

If you have or are looking to find prospective partners then this will need to be highlighted in the presentation. If there are particular issues of control related to your industry, these may also need to be covered, albeit briefly.

The presentation is an opportunity to demonstrate your personal qualities and start to develop a relationship. First impressions are important, but an in-depth knowledge of the key areas in the business plan will go a long way towards generating the confidence that is needed. There are ways of enhancing a presentation. It is important to rehearse it thoroughly. Always stress the market and the firm's competitive advantage, rather than the product's features. Stress the competences of the management team. In terms of style, it is important to demonstrate the product and, in Western culture, to make frequent eye-to-eye contact. You should manage the presentation with respect to any co-presenters. Finally, never try to weasel your way out of questions to which you do not know the answers. The best advice is to say you do not know but will get back with the answer in a few days.

An experienced investor once admitted that, whilst discussions with the entrepreneur might centre on the business plan, the final decision whether or not to invest was really the result of 'gut feel' – a personal 'chemistry' between them and the entrepreneur. At the end of the day, that chemistry must lay the foundation for a long-term relationship based, as always, on trust and respect.

Beyond the business plan: strategy development in established firms

This book has given you a framework for developing strategy in a systematic way and encouraged you to underpin this with a formal, written business plan. But do successful entrepreneurs approach strategy development in this way?

Many entrepreneurs seem to develop strategy instinctively and intuitively – often they call it 'gut feel'. For them strategies evolve on a step-by-step basis. If one step works then the next is taken. At the same time they will keep as many options open as possible, because they realize that the outcome of any action is very uncertain. It was Mintzberg (1978) who first coined the phrase 'emergent' strategy development to describe this where: 'the strategy-making process is characterized by reactive solutions to existing problems … The adaptive organization makes its decisions in incremental, serial steps.' He contrasted this with the more systematic approach which he called 'deliberate'.

However, in a study of growing firms, McCarthy and Leavy (2000) showed that strategy development was *both* deliberate and emergent; changing from emergent to deliberate as the firm went through recurrent crises followed by periods of consolidation (Greiner's model, Chapter 12). These crises force the entrepreneur to change their preconceptions and 'unlearn' bad habits or routines ahead of learning new ones (Cope, 2005). Therefore, rather than having only

F16.1 **Strategy formulation cycle**

Growth

Emergent strategy formulation

Emergent strategy formulation

Crisis

Consolidation

Deliberate strategy formulation

one style of strategy development, entrepreneurs would seem to adopt both, depending on circumstances. In this way the well-documented process of growth to crisis to consolidation parallels a process of emergent to deliberate and back to emergent strategy formulation, shown in Figure 16.1.

There is nothing wrong with strategy that is emergent, incremental and adaptive. Indeed it is an approach that resonates with complexity theory, which attempts to describe how to navigate complex, unpredictable systems that are affected by multiple independent actions – a good description for today's turbulent, interconnected global market place. Burns (2013) observes that successful entrepreneurs 'have a strong vision and this helps them build a strategic intent for the organization that allows them to reconcile where they are with where they want to be, even when the path to achieve this vision is not clear. They continually strategize and that means that strategy will often be seen as emergent. However, there are always strategic options that they have thought through and developed. Decision-making is then incremental, based upon opportunistic circumstances at the time.'

So, whilst you may not always want to write a formal business plan you will still need to strategize – to think about the future, analyze your options and develop strategies. The strategic frameworks developed in this book will help you do that by giving your thoughts structure and focus. And the New Venture Creation

Academic insight

Framework can easily be adapted to apply to a changing environment or new product/service launches. The use of these strategic frameworks is important, particularly when engaged in distributed strategizing. If you are trying to replicate strategizing across an organization, a set of commonly-known and understood techniques and processes can help – not least because they generate a common language and mechanism for communication. They help you to make the right decisions consistently. Strategic frameworks replicate good practice. They ought to be logical and common-sense. They are not in the nature of a scientific discovery. They are, to quote a colleague, 'a glimpse of the blindingly obvious' – something you knew all along but were never quite able to express in that simple way. As John Kay (1998) explains:

'An organizational framework can never be right, or wrong, only helpful or unhelpful. A good organizational framework is minimalist – it is as simple as is consistent with illuminating the issues under discussion – and is memorable ... The organizational framework provides the link from judgment through experience to learning. A valid framework is one which focuses sharply on what the skilled manager, at least instinctively, already knows. He is constantly alive to strengths, weaknesses, opportunities, threats which confront him ... A successful framework formalizes and extends their existing knowledge. For the less practised, an effective framework is one which organizes and develops what would otherwise be disjointed experience.'

The important thing is to keep strategizing, formally or informally.

Burns, P. (2013) *Corporate Entrepreneurship: Innovation and Strategy in Large Organizations*, Basingstoke: Palgrave Macmillan.

Cope, J. (2005) 'Toward a Dynamic Learning Perspective of Entrepreneurship', *Entrepreneurship Theory and Practice*, 29(4).

Kay, J. (1998) *Foundations of Corporate Success*, Oxford: Oxford University Press.

McCarthy, B. and Leavy, B. (2000) 'Strategy Formation in Irish SMEs: A Phase Model of Process', *British Academy of Management Annual Conference*, Edinburgh

Mintzberg, H. (1978) 'Patterns in Strategy Formation', *Management Science*.

Summary

- A business plan describes what your new venture seeks to achieve and how it will do this. It can be used for internal purposes, as a management 'aide-memoire', or for external purposes, particularly to raise finance.

- Plans for external purposes are generally longer and more formal than those for internal use. The larger the start-up and the more finance being sought the longer and more detailed the plan is likely to be. Plans for equity investors are likely to be the longest and best presented.

- Although there is no set format, a typical structure of a typical business plan for external use is set out in Table 16.1.

- A business plan presented to a bank needs to demonstrate how interest on the loan can be paid and the capital repaid on the due date, with minimum risk. Particular attention, therefore, needs to be paid to the cash flow forecast. To obtain a loan you need to gain the trust of the bank manager and develop their respect in your business ability. Personal credibility is vital.

- A business plan developed for an equity investor needs to demonstrate that a business opportunity exists that can earn a high return – typically 30–50% per annum – that can be realized in a five-year time frame. It also needs to convince the reader that the management team is capable of exploiting the opportunity. Investors place great reliance on the managerial credibility of the founder and their team.

- A business plan presentation needs to be just as good as the plan itself – focusing on the highlights of the plan and well-executed. You are trying to interest and engage with the audience and invite them to enter into a discussion about your venture. You want to gain their trust and respect.

Exercise 16.1

Writing your business plan

Decide who you are writing your business plan for and write it, using the format in Table 16.1, reproduced as a pro forma on the website accompanying this book.

The business plan framework exercises at the end of each chapter should provide you with all the information you need. But remember that the written plan is a formal business document that needs to be succinct and professional.

Business plan section	Relevant exercises
• Business details	6.2; 6.4; 9.2
• Industry and market analysis	4.1; 4.2; 4.3; 5.3; 5.4
• Customers and value proposition	5.1; 5.2; 6.1; 6.3
• Marketing strategy	5.1; 5.2; 5.4; 7.1; 7.2; 7.3; 7.4; 8.1; 8.2; 8.3
• Operations plan	9.1; 10.1; 10.2; 11.2; 11.3
• Management team and company structure	9.2; 12.1; 12.2; 12.3; 12.5; 15.7
• Resources	12.1; 12.2; 12.3; 14.1
• Financing	14.2; 15.3
• Financial projections	15.1; 15.2; 15.3; 15.4; 15.5
• Risks and strategic options	11.2; 11.3
• Milestones	15.6

Exercise 16.2

Presenting your business plan

Prepare a 10-minute presentation of your business plan using no more than 8 slides.

Exercise 16.3

Pitching your business plan

An 'elevator pitch' is a brief presentation of your business idea to a financier, so-called because of the short time you might be confined in an elevator with them. It must be extremely succinct, summing up your value proposition, the problem it solves for customers and why it will beat competitors, the returns it will make and the deal that is on offer to the financier. That is all you have time for! If you need support there is only time for one slide.

Using the executive summary in your business plan, prepare a 2-minute 'elevator pitch' for your business proposal.

Full references are given in all Academic Insights. These are listed in the Author Index on page 361. You might also find the following useful as further reading.

Entrepreneurship and start-up

Aulet, B. (2013) *Disciplined Entrepreneurship: 24 Steps to a Successful Start-up*, New York: John Wiley & Sons.

Barringer, B.R. and Ireland, R.D. (2012) *Entrepreneurship: Successfully Launching New Ventures*, Harlow: Pearson.

Blank, S. and Dorf, B. (2012) *The Startup Owner's Manual: The Step-by-step Guide for Building a Great Company*, Pescadero, CA: Ranch.

Blundel, R. and Lockett, N. (2011) *Exploring Entrepreneurship: Practices and Perspectives*, Oxford: Oxford University Press.

Burns, P. (2011) *Entrepreneurship and Small Business: Start-up, Growth and Maturity*, 3rd edn, Basingstoke: Palgrave Macmillan.

Kuratko, D.F. (2013) *Entrepreneurship: Theory, Process, Practice*, 9th edn, Mason: South-Western Cengage Learning

Read, S., Sarasvathy, S., Dew, N., Wiltbank, R. and Ohlsson, A.V. (2011) *Effectual Entrepreneurship*, London: Routledge.

Ries, E. (2011) *The Lean Startup: How Today's Entrepreneurs Use Continuous Innovation to Create Radically Successful Businesses*, New York: Crown Publishing.

Related topics

Corporate entrepreneurship and intrapreneurship
Burns, P. (2013) *Corporate Entrepreneurship: Innovation and Strategy in Large Organizations*, 3rd edn, Basingstoke: Palgrave Macmillan.

Corporate strategy
Grant, R.M. (2012) *Contemporary Strategic Analysis*, 8th edn, New York: John Wiley & Sons.

Grant, R.M. and Jordan J. (2012) *Foundations of Strategy*, New York: John Wiley & Sons.

Kay, J. (1998) *Foundations of Corporate Success*, Oxford: Oxford University Press.

Mintzberg, H. (1994) *The Rise and Fall of Strategic Planning*, New York: Free Press.

Mintzberg, H., Ahlstrand, B. and Lampel, J. (1998) *Strategy Safari*, New York: Free Press.

Osterwalder, A. and Pigneur, Y. (2010) *Business Model Generation: A Handbook for Visionaries, Game Changers and Challengers*, Hoboken, NJ: John Wiley & Sons.

Creativity and innovation

Boyd, D. and Goldenberg, J. (2013) *Inside the Box: A Proven System of Creativity for Breakthrough Results*, London: Profile Books.

Drucker, P.F. (1985) *Innovation and Entrepreneurship: Practice and Principles*, London: Heinemann.

Johnson, S. (2010) *Where Good Ideas Come From: The Natural History of Innovation*, London: Allen Lane.

Tidd, J. and Bassant, J. (2013) *Managing Innovation: Integrating Technological, Market and Organisational Change*, 5th edn, New York: John Wiley & Sons.

Social entrepreneurship

Gunn, R. and Durkin, C. (2010) *Social Entrepreneurship: A Skills Approach*, Bristol: Policy Press.

Keohane, G.L. (2013) *Social Entrepreneurship for the 21st Century: Innovation Across the Non-profit, Private and Public Sectors*, Maidenhead: McGraw-Hill.

Riddley-Duff, R. and Bull, M. (2011) *Understanding Social Entrepreneurship: Theory and Practice*, London: Sage.

Yanus, M. (2010) *Building Social Business: The New Kind of Capitalism that Serves Humanity's Most Pressing Needs*, New York: Public Affairs.

AUTHOR INDEX

3i European Enterprise
Centre 156–157

A

Abell, D.F. 172
Aggarwal, R. 205
Anderson, E. and Weitz, B. 210
Aston Business School 306–307
Avolio, B.J., Bass, B.M. and
Jung, D.I. 274–275

B

Bank of England 299
Bass, B.M. 274–275
Bass, B.M. and Avolio, B.J. 274–275
Belbin, R.M. 247 248
BERR 6
Birkinshaw, J. 252–253
Birley, S. and Westhead, P. 156–157
Boston Consulting Group 156–157
Boyd, D. and Goldenberg, J. 04
Bradford, D.L. and
Cohen, A.R. 274–275
Brubaker, D.L. 270
Burns, P. 66, 156–157, 257–277, 354
Business Green 126
Buzzell, R.D. and Gale, B.T. 156–157
Buzzell, R.D., Heany, D.F. and
Schoeffer, S. 156–157

C

Caird, S. 32
Carroll, A.B. and Shabana, K.M. 126
Carter, S. and Rosa, P. 299
Cavalluzzo, K. and Wolken, J. 299,
306–307
Chaleff, I. 275
Chaston, I. 47, 66
Chell, E. 247–248
Chen, P.C., Greene, P.G. and
Crick, A. 27
Coleman, S. 299
Cope, J. 354
Cosh, A. and Hughes, A. 306–307
Coviello, N.E. and Munro, H.J. 205

D

Delmar, F. 27
Department of Business, Enterprise and
Regulatory Reform 210
Drucker, P. 52
Dunkelberg, W.G., Cooper, A.C.,
Woo, C. and Dennis, W.J. 156–157
Dyer, J.H., Gregersen, H.D. and
Christensen, C.M. 54–55

E

Egri, C.P. and Herman, S. 274–275
European Commission 6

F

Fraser, S. 292, 299, 306–307

G

GE Capital 6
George, B. 270, 275
George, B. with Sims, P.E. 270,
274–275
Goleman, D. 274–275
Grant, R.M. 172
Green, P., Brush, C., Hart, M. and
Saparito, P. 299
Greenleaf, R.F. 274–275
Greiner, L.E. 242

H

Hamel, G. and Prahalad, C.K. 117,
156–157
Handy, C. 277
Harrison, J. and Taylor, B. 157–158
Heifetz, R.A. 274–275
Hisrich, R. and Brush, C.C. 299
Hofstede, G. 29
Hofstede, G. and Bond, M.H. 29

J

Johnson, J.E. 58, 205

K

Kay, J. 355
Kim, W.C. and Mauborgne, R. 47
Kotler, P., Kartajaya, H. and
Setiawan, I. 120–121
Kotter, J.P. 268
Kurucz, E., Colbert, B. and
Wheeler, D. 126

L

Levenson, A.R. and Willard, K.L. 299
Levy, H. and Sarnat, M. 172
Lewis, J.D. 210
Litvak, I.A. 205
Lorange, P. and Roos, J. 210
Luffman, G.A. and Reed, R., Mason,
R.H. and Goudzwaard, M.B. 172

M

Macmillan, H. 299
Macrae, D.J.R. 156–157
Margolis, J.D. and Walsh, J.P. 126, 172
Marlow, S. and Patton, D. 299
Mason, R.H. and
Goudzwaard, M.B. 172
McCarthy, B. and Leavy, B. 354
Michel, A. and Shaked, I. 172
Mintzberg, H. 274–275, 354

N

Nohria, N. and Joyce, W. 156–157

O

Oakley, P. 205
Ohmae, K. 117, 210
Orlitzky, M., Schmidt, F.L. and
Rynes, S.L. 172
Osterwalder, A. and Pigneur, Y. 15
Oviatt, B.M. and McDougall, P.P. 205

P

Palich, L.E., Cardinal, L.B. and
Miller, C.C. 172
Park, C. 172
Peters, T.J. and Waterman, R. 172
Piercy, N.F. 120–121
Pink, D. 252–253
Porter, M. 78, 93, 156–157
Porter, M.E. and Kramer, M.R. 126

R

Ram, M., Smallbone, D. and
Deakins, D. 299
Ray, G.H. and
Hutchinson, P.J. 156–157
Read, S., Sarasvathy, S.,
Dew, N., Wiltbank, R. and
Ohlsson, A.V. 11, 225
Ries, E. 66, 225

S

Sarasvathy, S.D. 34–35, 225
Sashkin, M. 274–275
Scott, J. 207
Siegel, R., Siegel, E. and
MacMillan, I.C. 156–157
Solem, O. and
Steiner, M.P.
156–157
Storey, D.J. 306–307
Storey, D.J. and
Greene, F.J.
306–307
Storey, D.J., Watson, R. and
Wynarczyk, P. 156–157
Stormer, R., Kline, T. and
Goldberg, S. 32
Strangler, D. 6

T

Treacy, M. and Wiersema, F. 93,
156–157
Treichel, M.Z. and Scott, J.A. 299

V

Vargo, S.L. and Lusch, R.F. 90
Ven de Velde, E., Vermeir, W. and
Corten, F. 126
Vera, D. and Crossan, M. 274–275

W

Wernerfelt, B. and
Montgomery, C.A. 172
Weston, J.F., Smith, K.V. and
Shrieves, R.E. 172
Woo, C.Y., Cooper, A.C.,
Dunkelberg, W.C., Daellenbach, U.
and Dennis, W.J. 156–157
Wynarczyk, P., Watson, R., Storey, D.J.,
Short, H. and
Keasey, K.
156–157

Y

Yelle, L.E. 156–157

QUOTES INDEX